D0517067

Teaching and the Adolescent Brain

NORTON BOOKS IN EDUCATION

Teaching and the Adolescent Brain

JEB SCHENCK

W.W. NORTON & COMPANY
NEW YORK • LONDON

Copyright © 2011 by Jeb Schenck

All rights reserved
Printed in the United States of America
First Edition

For information about permission to reproduce selections from this book, write to
Permissions, W. W. Norton & Company, Inc., 500 Fifth Avenue, New York, NY 10110

For information about special discounts for bulk purchases, please contact W. W. Norton
Special Sales at specialsales@wwnorton.com or 800-233-4830

Manufacturing by Hamilton Printing
Book design by Gilda Hannah
Production manager: Leeann Graham

Library of Congress Cataloging-in-Publication Data

Schenck, Jeb, 1950–
    Teaching and the adolescent brain : an educator's guide / Jeb Schenck.
      p. cm.—(Norton books in education)
    Includes bibliographical references and index.
    ISBN 978-0-393-70621-5 (pbk.)
1. Learning, Psychology of. 2. Learning--Physiological aspects. 3. Teenagers—Education.
4. Brain. I. Title.
    LB1060.S353 2011
    370.15'23—dc22   2010052119

ISBN: 978-0-393-70621-5 (pbk.)

W. W. Norton & Company, Inc., 500 Fifth Avenue, New York, N.Y. 10110
                    www.wwnorton.com
W. W. Norton & Company Ltd., Castle House, 75/76 Wells Street, London W1T 3QT

1 2 3 4 5 6 7 8 9 0

For

Gail, who continues to amaze and inspire me,

and

Jess, for her vision and tenacity.

CONTENTS

ACKNOWLEDGMENTS

I am indebted to many, and without them the task of writing the book would have been difficult in the extreme. This project would simply not have been possible without my wife Gail's unfailing support (along with her critical comments) and the ideas of my daughter, Jessica Cruickshank. Their patience borders on the extraordinary. I am also especially thankful for the suggestions and guidance of Deborah Malmud, my editor, as she helped me mold a mass of information into something usable, and to Vani Kannan, who helped move the project along in so many ways.

This broad undertaking also requires the kind assistance and support from many others, including Robert Cruickshank, Linda Wyss, Bob Greenleaf, Tracey Tokuhoma-Espinosa, Kurt Fischer, Zackery Stein, Kimberly Carraway, Mary Helen Immordino-Yang, Laura Ann Petitto, Marty Kozba, Hilary Welborn, the University of Wyoming Outreach Staff, Chris Price, Pamela Qualter, James Flynn, Theo Dawson, Steve Radibaugh, Eric Kay, Dustin Hunt, Michael Schmidt, Robert Sylwester, Robert Stickgold, Marc Schwartz, Kirtsy Tallick, Joshua Lord, Elizabeth Clementson, Michael Geer, Kathleen Geer, Kelly Williams, Dave Huff, Mike Connell, Catherine Crumpler, Cody McClean, Robert Kelso, Carol Dowdy, Deb Brown, Megan Kruashaar, Carol Dowdy, and last, but not least, the COE Library staff at the University of Wyoming.

Doubtless there are others, too, that my notorious memory is overlooking, and to them I offer my sincere thanks and apologies.

Finally, I wish to thank all my students, both in high school and graduate school, who provide many keen insights that help all of us to go forward.

Teaching and the Adolescent Brain

Introduction

Gail lay in bed, her shaved head wreathed in bandages after the brain surgery. A tumor-like mass was discovered only weeks earlier in her cerebellum in the back of her brain, and the prognosis was grim. I was grateful she was alive and hopeful that she still had the use of her limbs. After some days had passed it was clear that she could move both arms. We had no idea what to expect because we knew nothing about the brain, other than a little about tumors. And people with those usually didn't have good outcomes. Most died. We had been told almost nothing, except that whatever she would regain in terms of ability to move would occur in the first 2 years after surgery, and after that we should not expect anything.

My wife wanted to regain her ability to feed herself, something that we both expected she would be able to do, even if slowly. When I placed the spoon in her right hand, her movements were grotesquely clumsy and only vaguely oriented in the right direction to bring food to mouth. With the spoon clamped in her hand like a 3-year-old, she would try to maneuver the wildly waving hand to her mouth, missing badly, sometimes hitting her check, other times missing her mouth and face entirely. She would dissolve into a puddle of tears, feeling discouraged and helpless. This began our joint education about the brain, learning what the doctors thought they knew and what we didn't know at the time. All of it would change.

One of the first lessons we both learned about the brain was how it directed movement, or didn't seem to in Gail's case. She would make valiant efforts to try to feed herself with her right arm, and I would be coaching, cajoling, and cheerleading her efforts using all the motivational techniques I had learned as a football coach.

It was an utter disaster. The harder she tried, the more exaggerated her arm movements were and the worse the result. Then she would finally back off in near exhaustion before meekly trying one more time. In this final attempt her movements were much smoother and less wild; as weeks passed, each try was much more successful. Less stress, more success. With less forced effort she had less amplified, exaggerated arm movements.

Eighteen years later, the shuffled walk and cane were gone. Gail could still not walk more than a few hundred meters before tiring out, and sudden stress still caused frustrating memory lapses. Then one day, Gail called, with excitement in her voice and a beaming smile on her face. "Look!" She made a tiny hop straight up. "And I can do this, too!" She made a short, trotting run for about 10 feet. We learned that sometimes the brain can still grow and heal, and not to limit others because of what we think they can't do. *Our lack of vision should not be their limitation.*

I slowly realized that my vision of what learning was, or could be, had directed what I did in the classroom. From the very first, as a classroom teacher I wanted to do a better job reaching the students. After my wife's brain surgery, my voyage of discovery with the brain and mind continued by considering what students still appeared to remember learning after a class was long over, or their long-term memory. Long-term memory is effectively at the end of the food chain of learning. Everything that happened before it seemed to have varying degrees of influence on what a student retained. What would affect memory the most? In trying to understand that, I slowly had to back up through many convoluted processes, discovering that there wasn't a single most important process, but many, leading me to learn about each in turn, and, as I researched further I found that, similar to an onion, there were yet more layers of knowledge to peel back. Sometimes a layer revealed a new insight that came from the most unexpected place. The first unexpected turn was my wife's brain surgery, but the second happened on the opposite side of the world 6 years later. I had never given it a thought that the brain does its business through an extraordinary number of chemical reactions. That the chemistry of the brain might be important became evident when I was high on the slopes of Mt. Everest in the thin, oxygen-deprived air. It took me 5 minutes to generate an answer to a routine task that I had performed thousands of times before. The atoms and molecules are the stuff of the brain and they are being manipulated moment by moment; somehow, thoughts, memories, and the functions of the mind are created from infinite combinations. A third unexpected event confirmed for me that, when working with the brain, seeming dissimilar events could provide connections about how learning works. While I produced a documentary on the wildflowers of Yellowstone National Park, I realized that a pattern in the visual information played a key role in one's ability to identify a flower. For example, water hemlock, a poisonous plant, has leaves that are quite different from cow's parsnip, an edible plant, but the flowers look nearly the same. The number of items that cluttered around the leaves in the background of a photograph made it easier or more difficult to identify the flower. That connected right back to the classroom. How many things could a student's brain handle before it overloaded? Those three disparate events—my wife's brain injury, my climb on Everest, and my work with wildflowers—set me on a journey to understand what was happening in the student brain. For students, the classroom is a place of discovery where I guide them, using what I know about the mind and brain, but the classroom is also a place of discovery for me as I learn from my students.

Why Do We Need a Brain?

It may seem obvious why we need a brain, but it would be a lot less obvious if we went far back into time. What might it have been used for back hundreds of millions of years ago? Our brains have changed over millions of years. But in spite of all the complex changes and new tasks our brains can perform, the brain's fundamental use appears to have remained the same. The brain is used for taking action. From an evolutionary viewpoint, having a brain gives you a survival advantage, and if the body that houses the brain gets to survive, the multitude of genes that help make the brain also survive and may get to be passed on to the next generation. How might that work? Take movement, for example. If you can move to avoid a predator, or move to secure some food better than a competitor, you're more likely to survive. Having a brain to stimulate or direct the movement would definitely be an advantage. Some hypotheses suggest that the need for movement helped to select organisms that had genes that were beneficial to making brains.

Let's drop back in time to just 8,000 or 10,000 years ago and consider our more immediate ancestors who lived a hunter-gatherer existence. Suppose you had a bunch of genes that helped to develop a brain that was responsive to even slight stimulation, like a small movement in the brush or the rustling of some leaves. You'd probably be a bit edgy, and your eyes would dart about, seeking what might be lurking in the shadows. And you'd probably respond fairly fast to those movements, your body tensed, on high alert; otherwise a lion might be having you for lunch, or a nearby warring tribe might be taking off with your mates and children. Having Attention-Deficit/Hyperactivity Disorder would be an advantage in those circumstances. You'd live longer, possibly long enough to pass your genes along. The brain confers survival advantages. But it's less obvious today in most industrialized countries. However, in other areas of the world, your "smarts" still keep you alive. Today, a well-functioning brain is more helpful than a poorly functioning one in most situations.

We are now very dependent on our brains. By comparison, we can see lives led by those with damaged or defective brains and their continuous struggles. Using other parts of the body, the brain constantly monitors the external physical environment as well as its internal biological environment. The brain makes millions of tiny adjustments to help keep the body within just a small range of variations so the whole body functions properly. And to make sure we keep the body healthy we have a system called memory, for storing crucial information such as what that growl in the bushes meant, in order to reduce the number of harmful mistakes.

The collecting, sorting, and retrieving of information is learning. In short, we have brains to learn and improve our prospects of staying alive and healthy.

With the brain and learning, there is rarely a direct cause and effect. Understanding the brain doesn't provide a quick fix because in the classroom, or even in nontraditional classes, teaching and learning problems are the results of how the brain works in very complex environments. Because of that complexity we will explore how we can appropriately apply strategies to problems based upon *general* properties of the brain's processing. For example, there will be strategies that focus on the properties of emotion or attention, and others on memory. Often there will be a mix of suggestions, such as methods of studying for tests, derived from different research areas of cognitive neuroscience, cognition, and education. However, the problems and strategies we will explore may not be affected by just one type of processing in the mind. For example, both emotion and attention affect memory. When we address one problem, we invariably work with other processes, too, because the brain is connected to many different systems, and, like a pebble dropped into a pond, its effects ripple out in all directions. As a result, suggestions that will be presented here are not absolutes, or silver bullets that will fix problems, but are tactics that have been found helpful in a particular area of processing. As neuroeducation studies the mind and brain processes in real, dynamic environments, we will understand more, and if we use that information wisely we will become better at our profession. An understanding of brain systems can inform public educational policy.

When any instructional strategies are being selected, *what guides teaching and learning?* Even though our understanding of learning continues to grow, most of those charged with providing instruction at every level (local, state, and national) have no well-considered theory of teaching or learning to provide genuine guidance. The concept that educators must help their adolescent students develop better problem-solving skills rather than encouraging students to memorize rapidly outdated facts is well known. However, I see little evidence that many classroom educators or administrators are receiving much, if any, graduate training that helps them to develop and organize their thoughts on a theory of teaching and learning or in understanding how it takes place in the brain. Having a theory of learning is assumed rather than consciously developed. Consequently, in respect to how the student's mind/brain systems actually learn, administrators are left relatively ill equipped to guide their staff. There is no rudder on the boat. Ask an administrator, teacher, or politician how the brain learns; at this time, few really have any idea. Then ask if their administrative practices of their theory of teaching and learning is in alignment with how the brain learns. The challenge here is that educators and administrators haven't gotten the first part, so they cannot know whether they have an evidence-based theory of learning to guide their policies. Having a theory of learning without understanding how the brain works is like having a theory on day and night without any knowledge of the earth's rotation. More often than not, in a given school there is not a coherent, articulated theory of teaching or learning being used to guide the actual teaching. However, in some private schools that I have visited, it is not the same. More frequently, a few of these schools have some unifying concept of how learning takes place. By increasing our understanding of how the brain and mind processes work, we might start building the rudder we so badly need. One place we can start is in adolescence, since it lasts a considerable portion of a student's educational life.

The Adolescent—A Time of Change, a Time of Promise

In this journey about the brain and learning, I focus on the adolescent because adolescence occupies most of a student's educational life, starting somewhere around 9 to 10 years of age, and lasting to approximately the mid-twenties. That encompasses a span of roughly 15 years. Vast changes occur in the brain and body during this period, and the array of instructional strategies a student will be exposed to is considerable. By concentrating on this critical period of students' lives, we have the potential to positively affect them for the remainder of their lives.

The Journey Begins

Our encounters with the mind, brain, and education start early on. For many of us it began in kindergarten or first grade as we tried to remember the letters of the alphabet, or our very first spelling words. Somewhere in school we realized that remembering had something to do with what was going on in our head. After all, the mind harbored our thoughts, dreams, and frustrations. As we grew we became more aware that we have a mind and our life experiences were shaped by what we believed was happening.

Our beliefs on how learning occurs also affect government policies, not just in the United States but all around the world. Whatever we think learning is will influence what schools we choose, what we do or don't do at home, what environmental and cultural experiences we may provide our children, and how we train staff. Any misunderstandings about learning can potentially handicap not only our students but also, in some cases, whole countries. The bedrock of all learning ultimately lies within the brain. As Dr. John Ratey of Harvard Medical School has observed, "Everything counts."

The brain receives a constant stream of information from the body that houses it as well as from the world surrounding the body, all of which impact learning. Sometimes the effect is direct, and we can quickly see a result in our classroom or teaching situation, such as the speed that we present information and whether or not the students are overwhelmed. *More often, the effect on the brain and learning is indirect,* and the results show up in various ways. When it all works together properly, the brain can produce an intricate dance that is beautiful to see; when the brain doesn't work smoothly, the resulting missteps are painful to witness.

In reflecting on this journey you are about to take, you will find that this book is very much an exercise in metacognition, our awareness of how we learn. Although the focus is on how the adolescent thinks and learns, it is also, almost by default, about how we as educators think about the adolescent. Our attitudes, our philosophy, how we think: all of it affects our work with students. We'll learn not only about how the adolescent mind/brain systems work but also about how our adult minds interact with their younger minds in terms of our expectations, problems, and stresses we face while teaching. The interaction between adolescents and teachers in the creation of learning is an ongoing journey of continued surprises and discovery.

Our journey will be a fascinating one because we will explore many real issues that educators face on a daily basis, and what we can do about them based on neuroeducation, which is created from the combined fields of cognitive neuroscience, cognitive psychology, and education. As with any exploration, there will be some surprises, with the unexpected and unexplained, along with some "A-has," and comforting reassurances of why some practices work so well. We will gain new teaching ideas and strategies derived from the combined efforts of three fields. With this journey we should also gain some insights that can provide direction to our students, parents, fellow educators, and policy makers. It is the journey that we learn from; it is not a destination where we arrive already knowing it all. Each of us has a personal journey with the brain and learning that began years ago although we didn't realize it at the time. We travel on this journey for the rest of our lives, so let us continue to learn and grow, to understand even more from the experiences we will encounter.

CHAPTER ONE

An Introduction to Neuroeducation

The brain is not a static thing;
a learning brain is a growing brain.
—Jeb Schenck

The Adolescent Brain Is Important

I would that there were no age between 10 and 23,
for there's nothing in between but getting wenches with child
—William Shakespeare, *The Winter's Tale*, Act III

After nearly 400 years, Shakespeare's description of adolescence as being between 10 and 23 years of age is remarkably accurate. The period between childhood and adulthood is a time when the body and brain undergo great changes. Puberty triggers the beginning of many physiological changes and those can start well before the teenage years. Nearly 50% of girls worldwide have their first hints of pubescence by the age of 8, and puberty is occurring at steadily earlier ages than in previous centuries (Dahl, 2004). Adolescents' brains also rapidly change until early adulthood, which, in terms of brain growth, is somewhere in the mid-twenties. At that point, adult social roles and responsibilities are handled. Judging by both biological changes in the body and the contemporary social measures of when adolescents attain full adult responsibilities, the period of adolescence spans roughly 12 to 24 years of age, or from about sixth or seventh grade through the end of college (Dahl, 2004).

For educators, this means that their students are in a period of adolescence for approximately half of all the time students are being formally educated. Educators must try to teach a brain that is largely adolescent, being neither a child's nor an adult's. The adolescent brain is influenced by a period of swift changes. Fortunately, a considerable amount of new research from several fields that focus on the brain's thinking and learning can provide insights into what educators can do to improve their teaching skills for the adolescent.

Everything that an adolescent does involves his or her brain. When educators are teaching and working with adolescents they are trying to engage and communicate with young, growing minds, and adolescents are trying to engage with adult minds as well. In most cases both the student and teacher are unaware that they are engaged in a partnership until efforts go awry, prompting the question "Why can't he understand?" It can be asked of either the student or the teacher. Something wasn't working as they thought it should, and that "something" was the way that their two minds interacted. With the brain so intricately involved with learning, the more educators know and understand about how the brain works the better they can design their instruction, communication, and assessments. Attaining such knowledge and skills can lead to improved teaching and to greater student performance.

Two major problems about adolescent learning continue to face educators as illustrated by the question "Why can't he understand?" The first problem is, "Why do students process and learn the way they do?" Why did one student get it while another student right beside her remained confused? To address why adolescent students learn in particular ways, educators and researchers must look at what's going on inside students' heads. Despite what it sometimes looks like when a student's eyes are glazed over, there *is* a lot going on. In the first portion of each chapter I investigate some of the educationally relevant processes involved in the brain's learning, how it works, and what affects it. These major cognitive processes are particularly affected in the adolescent, and in turn those processes affect their learning.

The second major problem embedded in the question "Why can't he understand?" is, "What can educators do about the student's learning?" As teachers, paraprofessionals, and administrators, we can significantly affect the adolescent brain's processing, and, if done properly we can facilitate students' learning. In the latter portion of each chapter, I will address how educators can implement changes in realistic ways. Much is implied when I suggest that we are going to facilitate a student's performance and apply the principles of how the brain learns in a practical manner. Students are breathing, moving, and thinking beings, not widgets to be worked on in a factory, into whose heads we pour some knowledge. Adolescents need to be engaged fully as humans; they have feelings, desires, hopes, and needs, not just bodies that happen to have brains.

Educators teach the whole person, which suggests that I will be taking a different perspective on teaching the adolescent. As I explore the workings of the adolescent brain I will make teaching suggestions that are well grounded in research from the cognitive neurosciences and cognitive psychology, and in the realistic context of what educators face in the context of their classrooms. The overall approach to solving these two problems—how the adolescent brain learns and what educators can do about it—will be the use of a new viewpoint. I will regard the problems from the perspective of the brain's involvement, breaking away from the traditional philosophical approach where the brain was not considered. This new viewpoint combines what researchers have learned from cognitive neuroscience, cognitive psychology, and education. The fresh approach is called neuroeducation.

Neuroeducation

Neuroeducation is an emerging field that tries to solve educational problems, both large and small, by combining and sharing the resources of three fields—cognitive psychology, cognitive neuroscience, and education—thus creating a comprehensive approach to understanding learning and what educators can do about improving their students' learning. Neuroeducation considers how the brain can process information, how those processes affect thinking, and how cognition affects learning. Neuroeducational research postulates how educators can appropriately incorporate the knowledge and skills into classroom practices, as well as inform educational policies. To achieve these goals of combining and sharing information, the relationships between the three fields must also be different. No longer are scientists working in isolation, oblivious to each other and unaware of educators' needs. Cognitive psychologists, cognitive neuroscientists, and educators have joined together to focus on the problems of thinking and learning in order to do a better job of helping our students. This joint effort also involves a reciprocal flow of information from the three groups.

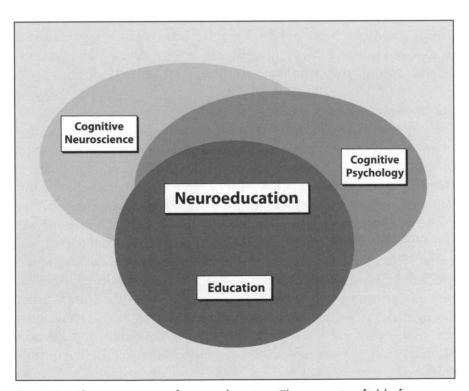

Fig. 1.1. The emergence of neuroeducation. The emerging field of neuroeducation results from the overlap of common interest in three fields, cognitive psychology, cognitive neuroscience, and education.

Birth of a New Field

The brain is fascinating for many people, because its workings are shrouded in mystery; it is a part of us, yet it seems elusive. We cannot feel what it does, unlike with other parts of the body, such as the stomach or muscles, because the brain lacks sensory neurons. It does most of its work beyond our awareness. Somehow it allows us to solve problems while simultaneously perplexing us with quirky little things like "The name is on the tip of my tongue, and I can't get it out." When students started taking tests they experienced the nagging feeling, "I knew it just a moment ago, now I can't think of it!" And as many have reached middle age, different mind and brain issues developed: "Dang! Where did I put my keys!! I just had them less than a minute ago." If it is about the brain, it is about all of us, and the world we live in, moment by moment. Educators wanted to know more about the brain because many have realized that the brain (and the mind that it creates) is the essence of who our students are. Interest in these widespread problems then evolved into research.

Research on the brain and mind started to come into its own during the 1980s and 1990s with a boost from cognitive science, which describes how thinking occurs, and the development of cognitive neuroscience, which describes the biology behind thinking and learning, while education's focus had been on what can be done to affect both thinking and learning. Thoughts about applying this new knowledge to learning and education soon followed. The overlapping interest in thinking and learning by cognitive psychology, cognitive neuroscience, and education had become apparent to researchers and educators. A short description of their shared interests will illustrate their common ground on thinking and learning.

Cognitive Psychology

Cognitive psychology is a vast field, essentially focusing on how we think and learn. Some of its areas of common interest to education include how learning and thinking is affected by how we perceive information, solve problems, and define intelligence; how the different forms of memory work; and how attention and motivation affect thinking. Cognitive psychology also considers the role of emotions, impulse control, and decision making, and how language and speech are part of systems of communication, including reading, dyslexia, writing, and math among many others. All of these are crucial to adolescent performance. As information is processed in the adolescent brain, there are many complex processes that affect each other in often poorly understood ways. Even so, these processes are very important to teaching and learning. Should there be a deficit in any one, an adolescent may have problems, especially in school. A collapse, or even a partial failure of one of these processes can be devastating to an adolescent's ability to function in school. For example, errors in processing may result in dyslexia, while other processing errors may emerge as poor impulse control, and both reading skills and impulse control are important to a student's academic success. Educational efforts to help our students prepare for life depend on proper functioning of a multitude of cognitive processes. However, the problems educators encounter can only be partially addressed by cognitive psychology; it provides only a few pieces to the puzzle of learning. Other pieces have to come from another source such as cognitive neuroscience.

Cognitive Neuroscience

Cognitive neuroscience bridges neuroscience and cognitive psychology by understanding the biology of the brain to discover how thinking and learning take place—thus, filling in more pieces of the puzzle of learning. Advances in technology are allowing researchers to map, observe, and better understand processes in the adolescent brain in increasingly finer detail in order to see their function, including such processes as movement control, memory formation, emotional control, and attention, all of which are scattered throughout the brain. Cognition, or thought, is the result of the brain's biological processes.

How well someone's brain functions is influenced by his or her genetic makeup. Genes are the programs for building the brain's structure and for creating the materials that carry out cell functions. The biology of the brain is also affected by the external environment, which includes both the body that houses the brain and the physical world. This means that family life and culture all influence the brain. Both internal and external influences on the brain will be explored throughout the book.

Cognitive neuroscience also considers the brain's biological processes at the cellular level, particularly how cells take information and make changes in relationships with other cells, creating computations that give rise to the mind (Pinker, 1997). The mind is the expression of all the brain's processes. In other words, when we are working with the brain, the mind is simultaneously being affected. The brain is not the mind, but it is the brain's processing of information or computations that creates what researchers call the mind. The boundaries of the mind and brain are not known; in acknowledgment of the inability to make clear distinctions between the two, it is often referred to collectively as the "mind/brain." If a teacher has changed a student's brain, he or she has changed the mind as well. What educators are trying to do is more precisely direct their efforts to affect the brain's processing of information and thus make changes in the mind.

Therein lays one of the great mysteries. How does a 3-pound mass of cells use a multitude of processes, which can be influenced by the external world of education, to create what is called the mind? As I noted earlier, some answers to the question of what the mind/brain system is are being teased out by researchers in both cognitive neuroscience and cognitive psychology, but even with the combined efforts of both fields, parts of the mind/brain puzzle are still missing. Education can also provide insights into the mind. No single discipline has a monopoly on the answers to the riddle of how the mind is created and how it works. It appears that each discipline has a piece of the puzzle and in order to put it together, the respective parts from each discipline are needed. Education can make its own contributions to the mind/brain puzzle.

Education

Education is of equal importance because its focus is also on the common ground of thinking and learning, but it is located in the real-world context of daily instructional practices. When neuroscientists are asked how some discovery applies to education, they typically don't know, and rarely does a finding have a direct impact. However, the neuroeducation approach is a vehicle to learn and better understand what those discoveries might mean. The findings of cognitive neuroscience provide more explanations and directions for research for the cognitive psychologists, whose work often directly impacts education. But how are education and the work of teachers as important as the work of these scientific researchers? It is the engineer who designs the car, the mechanic who keeps it working, and the commuter that drives it. Without feedback from drivers and tweaking by the mechanics in the field, the engineer would miss critical information as to how well his design works, and he wouldn't know what other important ideas to consider in his new designs. Educators are the only ones who have crucial information about how well researchers' theories actually work. People are biological beings who develop and learn, and there are many unanswered questions about how they do both of these. Researchers can't fully address these fundamental questions about the mind/brain systems with clinical studies alone; they need the practical knowledge of educators in the field to see what actually happens and what they may have overlooked. To reach the goals of better teaching in order to produce greater learning requires a reciprocal relationship between educators and the research community (Fischer et al., 2007). It is a symbiotic relationship between educators and the research community. Each benefits from the other. To more precisely focus on critical educational problems, educators help to provide the direction researchers need about the nature of those problems, and the researchers and educators jointly develop the changes to make. That is new in the field of mind/brain research, and it is hugely important. Feedback from those educators in the field informs the researchers about areas that work but also alerts them to problems that need to be examined but had not been considered before. The symbiotic fruits of neuroeducation can then be used to inform educators and even policy makers in designing better teaching practices.

Early Struggles in the Application of Neuroeducation

The symbiotic relationships in neuroeducation are slowly evolving. During the 1980s and 1990s, a few dozen individuals scattered across the world in the fields of education, cognitive psychology, and neurosciences had noticed problems of mutual interest in learning. The neurosciences were undergoing rapid changes as technology allowed a burst of new discoveries that helped to usher in the field of cognitive neurosciences, which studies how thinking occurs in the brain. A few pieces of early research from the neurosciences about differences in the right and left hemispheres of the brain sparked interest in some educators. But the educators' lack of full comprehension of the findings resulted in popular myths about being right- or left-brained. Thus, the first neuromyth was born. A neuromyth is a statement about the brain that is false but is widely accepted as being true. In this case the neuromyth of being right- or left-brained was soon followed by popular self-help books, with some at the very dawn of cognitive neuroscience suggesting how to improve artistic skills (Edwards, 1979). Educators and the public alike eagerly gobbled up the latest discovery announced on the evening news. Educators wanted solutions, something that would fix their problems. Change was happening, but it wasn't clear whether it would turn out to be a genuine revolution or just a fad that would dim with time (Fischer & Immordino-Yang, 2008).

Neuroeducation is an emerging field, and because of that several terms are sometimes used to convey roughly similar topics, but no single name for the field has been accepted by all. Sometimes it is called mind/brain education (MBE), educational neuroscience, and, in the popular press, it can be loosely referred to as brain-based learning. There is a distinction, however, from brain-based learning. Neuroeducation, MBE, and educational neuroscience are developing solid footings in the research community. Brain-based learning, as advocated by many educators, is certainly more accessible to the public; however, it has a tendency to use more pop neuroscience and pop psychology that are not considered scientifically rigorous. Many of the popular books on brain-based learning make inappropriate linkages between the brain sciences and education. It is not surprising because few people have a background in more than one field, and neuroeducation encompasses three huge fields, which, when combined, are discussed in over 300-plus journals (Alkire & Westgermna-Alkire, 2006). However, what is remarkable is the fact that people from each field independently realized the mind/brain issues that connected them, and neuroeducation emerged.

A New Approach to Understanding and Learning

Teams for Complex Problems

When one faces a problem of bewildering complexity, having several people look at the problem can often be a better way to solve it. The brain is the most highly complex system ever studied. For years, the most effective approach in science to solve most problems was to reduce it down and isolate what was going on, then change a single part and see how that affected the overall problem. A complex system had to be broken down into simpler parts where cause and effect could be observed. However, when it comes to the brain, that simplistic approach rarely works. There is cause and effect, but there are too many variables in dynamic relationships for us to always use the standard approach. One problem of the reductionist approach is making errors of oversimplification, which researchers learned from the right-brain/left-brain neuromyth. Another common example occurs within genetics, which was alluded to earlier; it is a common misconception that a single gene is responsible for some trait, such as with speech. A gene, such as *Foxp2*, doesn't cause speech, it *influences* the ability to speak. There are no single genes for speech, intelligence, math skills, Alzheimer's disease, and so on. Sometimes hundreds of genes may be involved. The brain's complexity makes it difficult to appropriately simplify and directly apply what we know about the brain to education. Part of the complexity derives from the brain's extraordinarily dynamic ability to process information and continuously change. But this plasticity permits learning. If the brain couldn't change, students couldn't learn. But these very same dynamic qualities make it ineffective to use a reductionist method and break the problem into simpler steps. That very complexity often requires teams of experts from multiple disciplines to bring their powers of understanding to bear on a single problem. Neuroeducation routinely needs that team approach to sort out questions about thinking and learning.

Many problems related to the mind/brain system are too complex for individual researchers. We've begun to realize that the mind/brain functions in a dynamic system that is interacting with the environment at the same time. This creates an enormous amount of variability and complexity, which researchers can address by pooling their skills and knowledge from a variety of arenas. For example, Kurt Fischer examined brain growth related to skill development and assessment design. Laura-Ann Pettito and Maryanne Wolf worked out speech and reading problems by studying language processing in the brain. Michael Posner's findings demonstrated how we pay attention to things. In Japan, Hideaki Koizumi developed a new method of scanning the brain that allows a research subject to move around rather than to lie motionless inside a huge noisy machine. Mary Helen Immordino-Yang has explored the brain's plasticity, or its ability to adapt to changes. There are many others, of course, and their work and relevance to education will be introduced in turn. From the educational perspective, these visionary researchers have looked beyond the classic stimulus-and-reponse learning. Biology, they feel, plays a key but largely unrecognized role in learning.

Education Acquiring a Biological Foundation

The second advance in the development of a new approach to learning was the realization by educators that the process of learning was taking place in the mind/ brain system and that they knew very little about it. The scientific method had been in use by educators to study teaching and learning practices for some time, but that didn't include actual fields of science, such as biology of the brain as a foundation. Indeed, during the era of behaviorism and the stimulus-response style of investigations, the brain was ignored by educators and most psychologists. This left too many questions unanswered and prompted some educators to start looking toward the biological sciences for answers. However, figuring out how it is that the brain can handle all the processes and learn is a monumental challenge, more difficult than the rocket science of sending a spacecraft to the moon. Although rocket science is hard, and science has figured out how to get to the moon and back, most details of how the brain works remain beyond the reach of science. Even so, the public frequently wants simple answers to complicated problems. As they will attest, veteran educators know that they are expected by students' parents to understand how learning works, to be able to answer why their children are having difficulties with reading or doing algebra. In trying to understand thinking and learning, neuroeducation uses a more scientific approach than education alone by the incorporation of cognitive neuroscience, genetics, cognitive psychology, and new methods of analysis that use dynamic systems theory, more popularly called chaos-complexity. In turn, these multipronged efforts allow us to reconsider why some educational practices work and why others fail in nearly the same circumstances. The result is a shift in how educators understand and practice teaching and learning, similar to the changes medicine went through 150 years ago in learning how the body works and how to treat it (Fischer & Daley, 2007).

It appears to those in neuroeducation research that the field of education, like medicine before it, is shifting to a new foundation based in the biological sciences, using more brain research and less social theory. In the 1800s doctors passed on collective wisdom and experience to each other. The practice of medicine at the time did not have a significant basis in the biological sciences. Like medicine over a century ago, education is now developing a biological foundation for learning as demonstrated by more graduate education courses on the mind and brain. However, as of this writing, this approach to learning doesn't appear to have trickled down yet to regular teacher preparation programs. A comparison of how both medicine and education currently approach problems will illustrate the differences.

Imagine taking a friend to the doctor for stomach pain. His pain is the obvious problem, the outward symptom. The doctor uses a variety of assessments to make a diagnosis, giving her the best idea of what is *causing* the problem. To determine the cause, she asks questions. What did he eat? How long ago? What allergies does he have? Did he have an argument that day? What medicine is he taking? She also takes some objective measures: height, weight, temperature, blood pressure, and age. Using still more assessment methods she carefully probes and prods, trying to rule out other potential causes. She uses a *variety* of assessments to determine what might be causing the pain, trying to find and address the source in order to reduce or eliminate the symptoms. Pain is the brain's expression of a biological problem, but education has only rarely considered that learning is also the result of biology.

Now suppose a teacher sends out a report card for a high school student. The student's grade for English is dismal. Unfortunately, grades tell us virtually nothing because it is a vague measurement that does not spell out the student's strengths or weaknesses, or take into account all the applicable environmental influences. If a doctor used the same quality of measures, the student might be described as a bit sick, which of course would not be helpful because it tells us almost nothing. A teacher can often see the expression of a problem—in this case, reading—but not the cause, which may be elusive. Reading difficulties result from a biological problem in the brain. The teacher has observed that the young teen is slow, has trouble sounding out words, and hates to read out loud: all three are symptoms but not a cause. Without knowing the cause and how the symptoms result, the teacher can't be certain of the treatment. Most teachers don't have an arsenal of techniques, let alone the advanced training to sort out the problem using brain biology. Educators simply aren't there yet. Neuroeducation hopes to move the practice of education closer by providing information about what is going on in the mind/brain system and what they can do about it.

Trying to figure out the learning process and the best way to teach has been argued almost from the very beginning of written history. It can be claimed that educational methods have had an impact upon the course of Western civilization. What should be taught and when, and how should it be taught? Even Plato in his famous *The Republic* used Socrates in a fictionalized dialogue to address these very concerns more than 2,000 years ago. Those problems have been around so long historians can even trace some of them to the earliest schools for scribes learning cuneiform, one of the first written languages. Learning cuneiform was an arduous process and it took around nine years to master it. A fragment of translated cuneiform revealed one of the very first indications of teaching and learning, but tragically it also reflected the misery of the student learning to read: "And then he caned me" (Wolf, 2008, p. 37).

Can Knowledge of the Brain Make a Real Difference in Educational Practices?

Two Actual Events

A *classroom*

T. S. stormed into class. He was livid. His face was red and he seemed about to burst. Just minutes earlier in his previous class he had a major confrontation with his teacher. The teacher had insisted that he perform a task in a particular way. T. S. argued and refused, wanting to do it in his own way. Fortunately, an all-out physical confrontation was averted by the end-of-class bell. T. S. was still a barely contained explosion that needed only the tiniest spark to set him off. He stormed into his next class, slammed down his books defiantly, and tossed a look about that was an open challenge to everyone, student and teacher alike. The teacher immediately noted the explosive situation and made no comment, but without delay he got all the students redirected into an unplanned activity that would keep them occupied for at least 10 to 15 minutes. The teacher gradually eased up to T. S. from the side and knelt down, making sure he was lower than T. S.'s eyes. T. S. had laid his head down on his books and did not even attempt to do the assignment. The teacher recognized it was not so much a refusal as he was still focused on what happened in the prior class. The teacher softly said, in almost a whisper, "Hey, T., look at me." It was not a challenge or a command, just a tone that indicated a conversational request. No response. The teacher repeated again, "Hey, come on, just look at me. I'm not going to chew you out." A flicker and then a glance. "T., look at my eyes, I want to show you something." T. S. gave a longer glance. At still a near whisper level: "This isn't about the assignment; we can worry about that later. I want to help you feel better; I know you're upset." A pause. "Okay, look at me and watch this." He watched a little longer. The teacher drew in a long slow breath, held it, and slowly blew it out. "Okay, you try it; take in a long, deep breath." Gradually, after three or four token tries T. S. took in a long, slow breath, held it briefly, and exhaled. His bright red face almost visibly drained and normal color was restored. The actual change in his face took place in about 10 to 15 seconds. He was still trying to act grumpy and resistant but he was feeling better and it was plainly visible. He didn't want to lose face as a tough guy and openly acknowledge the change; it took a little effort to suppress a smile. With gradual, nonconfrontational coaching, T. S. was "back" and within 15 minutes was participating with the class. No attention was ever drawn to him; the class was periodically monitored by the teacher while he was working with T. S. When there was a problem the teacher silently redirected the students by pointing and whispering so work could continue with T. S. This teacher used knowledge of the brain's attentional and emotional systems to quickly address a very real student crisis *while* simultaneously continuing to control the class. The result made a lasting impression on both T. S. and other students. That crisis was the beginning of an emotional bond between the student and the teacher. It launched a series of changes in T. S.'s behavior and performance in his classes.

Staff development

We filed in. Another staff development meeting, and we had no idea about the topic, let alone what we would be doing. Doing? There was still a faint glimmer of hope. We were holding out the expectation that we might actually do something. Some administrations are slow to learn; and unfortunately the repeated failures of staff developments had not resulted in any adjustments. The school administration was in an advanced state of fossilization. A number of the staff were mumbling and grousing. They had stacks of papers to grade, lessons that needed to be fine-tuned, and time was short. The training began with a guru. We sat at our tables, listening. After the first 2 hours with a single insignificant activity that required no thought or application, several side conversations started up. Those teachers were no longer attentive. At 3 hours into the training, we were still motionless, sitting, our backsides getting sore, our bladders beginning to scream, and legs going numb. Our brains had long since shut down. Paying attention, even fleetingly, was like enduring torture. A single thought coursed through our collective brains: "When would this pain end?" A number of survivors of similar workshops had pulled out papers to grade. Several laptops popped open, a few games of solitaire were being played, and e-mail messages zipped back and forth. The same lesson, learned earlier, was being reinforced yet again in the faculty minds. It wasn't the one that the administration hoped for, or what the taxpayers had paid for. An understanding of basic principles of how the brain's attentional and emotional systems worked coupled with motivation could have changed the day from the perception of a torturous workshop to an active, productive day, a win-win situation. As it was, both the presenter's and administrator's lack of understanding created an undesirable outcome.

It's All About Learning

If neuroeducation is going to be valuable to educators, it will need to make a difference in both the student's learning *and* the teacher's learning and classroom practice. An educator's business is learning, but *what is learning?* Trying to define learning is something akin to nailing Jell-O to the wall. There is substance, but every time a teacher looks at it, it's changes and slowly morphs. And just when they think they've got something clearly nailed down, the concept of learning squishes sideways and didn't act quite the way they expected. Our concept of learning continues to evolve. Over the years educators have been told all manner of things about what learning is, and just as often many of the definitions have been conflicting. Not very long ago a famous researcher-educator used three different meanings, all in the course of a single presentation. Clearly researchers' and educators' beliefs about learning not only affect how we raise our children, but these beliefs also inspire national policies the country adopts such as No Child Left Behind (NCLB). Neuroeducation, used appropriately, should also inform education policy from the local school district all the way up to the Department of Education. Public education is a political "business" and what educators learn from neuroeducation should potentially influence policies. At the governmental level, legislatures are adopting policies that have little or no foundation in how learning occurs. Learning is not an "on-off" event of now we learn, now we don't. It doesn't start or stop with school; in fact the environment outside of school, including the home, has a significant and continuous impact upon the formal part of education. Learning is a dynamic process.

Learning is considerably more than a change in behavior. With regard to learning, we typically use the standard of "I know it when I see it," which is an ineffective standard to train future teachers and improve the overall process of education. Both educators and the public have attempted to use test scores to measure learning as heavily emphasized in NCLB. That was based in part upon a naïve conception that tests clearly represent whether and to what degree learning has taken place. Learning is more than the mere acquisition of information consisting of knowledge and skills, and it can't be fully represented by a single number from a test. This leads to a significant point: when research on learning is from only one field, such as education, its conclusions are frequently rather circumscribed. Taking limited data and making broad generalizations to teaching practices is generally not a sound approach; the generalization often either won't apply or must be more precisely described. The same principle applies in taking very limited test scores and judging how much learning has taken place: it may lead to inaccurate conclusions. Limited research inhibits what we can take away and apply to teaching. However, when coordinated research that has reached the same conclusions stems from several fields some broader generalizations might be appropriate. This caveat suggests that we be cautious in our claims. It is important to keep our statements in context, in order to make more accurate applications. In that respect, it is necessary to explain what is meant by the term "learning" in this book.

A Description of Learning

For educational purposes, the working definition for learning used in this book is that learning is a series of processes that includes the acquisition of stimuli that are represented in neural connections and that are consolidated while still remaining in dynamic relationships, creating networks of information that are retrievable as memory. Notice I did not mention test scores or single assessments of any kind. Learning is not that simple.

This is a working or temporary definition that we can use, not an absolute or final one. The definition also hints at things that will influence learning. Each of these involves major processes or circuits in the brain:

- *Acquisition of stimuli.* A lot happens here on the road to encoding information into the brain. Most of the stimuli come through interactions with their surrounding environment, often in a social context. Attention is but one aspect of the acquisition. Our brain must pay attention to information, and it has to pay attention long enough to detect some sort of pattern. Attention systems will be involved with learning.
- *Neural connections.* The pattern of information that was detected is compared to (or connected to) information already stored in memory, and connections are established with other processing circuits, all of which help establish meaning. Assembling different types of memory circuits are part of learning.
- *Consolidation.* The neural connections holding the information must become more or less stable. If the information disappears or fades away, we can't use it very well, and we certainly can't recall it or use it to compare with even newer information. For example, our social customs of diet and sleep can affect consolidation of memory. Proper sleep contributes to the stability of memory, while other social customs of adolescent partying or staying up until the wee hours playing video games can interfere with memory consolidation.
- *Dynamic relationships.* This suggests the connections can become stronger or weaker in their interactions with other networks. Some memories become very well established and at a later time are connected to new information or a different network of information. Other connections become weaker and some connections may be lost.
- *Retrievable memory.* For learning, one must have a memory that can be consciously retrieved. Information that is needed must be accessible

on demand. Habits, attitudes, and bias are part of memory, too, and may influence what is retrieved. Certainly there are other issues, including the effects of priming the brain, so it is ready to process certain types of information. Throughout the chapters a number of practical methods will be presented for building retrievable memories that contribute to learning.

Brain Development

In order to understand how the mind works in education, it is also necessary to understand how the brain works. Steven Pinker suggested that the mind is what the brain does and the brain is what produces that mind. We use the brain all the time in teaching and learning, but use doesn't equate to understanding (Brynes & Fox, 1998). Merely knowing where certain processes occur in the brain does not help to explain them. It would be like claiming that a person can understand how the federal government works because he knows where the U.S. Capitol is located. Educators need to know how parts affect each other under different conditions because the context radically impacts performance. An individual's brain development is the most fundamental context as it can affect everything else in education. Therefore, a foundation of education starts with understanding how cognitive skills develop.

The brain grows in cycles, adding new connections and new layers (Marcus, 2004, pp. 143–145; Matousek & Petersen, 1973). These cycles of growth also correspond to changes in our learning skills (see Figure 1.2; Fischer & Daley, 2007). The growth cycles also mean the brain is changing. For example, many educators have heard about how the adolescent's brain has not finished growing. That is just part of a growth cycle. In addition to knowing about the cycles educators will also need to understand how that growth affects their learning and performance in school.

Plasticity and Cycles of Development

One of the most important characteristics of the brain is that it can change; during adolescence we witness many cognitive changes. If the brain couldn't change, no one could learn in order to adapt and survive. Learning physically changes the brain (Gazzaniga, Ivry, & Mangun, 2009; Hofer, Mrsic-Flogel, Bonhoeffer, & Hübener, 2008).

Everyone depends upon the brain's plasticity and adaptability. Some evidence of the plasticity is more easily observed as a baby grows. For example, babies go through a sequence of being able to roll over to propping up on their knees and rocking back and forth, to crawling, to a tottering walk to walking, and finally running. While these occur around certain months of growth, the changes are usually not smooth. A baby may stand up and totter a few steps, but then revert back to crawling for a while before attempting to walk again.

The results of the brain's plasticity are not only visible in babies but in adolescents, too. Take the classic problem of immaturity. I suspect what educators often call immaturity is a reflection of the dynamics of brain growth. A corresponding facet of their behavior and thinking that educators have observed is *when* many adolescent students start vocalizing their classic rebelliousness. A teacher asks them to do a task and they respond by asking, "Why should I?" "This is dumb, ridiculous!" indicating that they don't think the task is worthwhile. For many teachers, that type of response is a button pusher, but it is really a cause for celebration. Perhaps for the first time, they are demonstrating the next level in their developing mind and expressing their own reasons (if a bit inadequately). They are starting to construct arguments with limited logic as opposed to simply grumbling and being more or less compliant, and their desire for some autonomy is becoming known. However, such expression varies with the culture. Certainly educators can reply with ten reasons for each one of the teenagers' newly found objections. They are starting to think at a new level. While classic teenage rebelliousness and being argumentative is something most educators face at some time in Western cultures, it wouldn't happen if the adolescents' brains hadn't grown. Their brains have grown sufficiently to see new relationships, other ways of doing something. The significance is that some students get to this developmental level sooner while others arrive at that

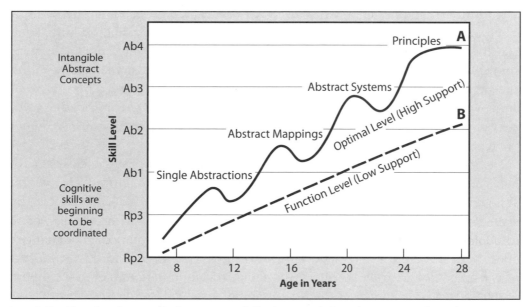

Fig. 1.2. The development of cognitive skills that result from brain growth is shown. While the brain is growing, it may not always be clearly evident by the student's display of cognitive skills. If the student receives ideal educational support, represented by line A, we may observe uneven spurts or cycles of increasing more complex levels of cognitive skills. As each new level is reached, new skills emerge. Increasingly complex levels of abstract thought are represented as Ab1 to Ab 4. Rp for Representations is a lower level of thought representing simple cognitive skills. Highly abstract thought, where principles are derived, may not be obtained even with optimal support. A student who has little or no support in developing their thinking skills is represented by line B. The spurts in cognitive growth are not as evident, and their ability to handle and understand more abstract ideas may be limited by the lack of support.

point much later. Those who demonstrate that they are more capable of higher level thought at the beginning of the year may be arriving developmentally months earlier than their peers. As with a baby's wobbly first steps or a teenager's first real counterargument, mind and brain growth is not a smooth ladderlike progression of moving on from one stage to another. The brain grows and learns in fits and starts, with a series of dynamic cycles as illustrated in Figure 1.2 (Fischer & Bidell, 2006). During these cycles of growth, however, the environment can influence development, as Piaget first observed.

The development of cognitive skills is not driven by the brain alone but also by how both the physical environment and cultures affect the brain. Piaget (1983) described how the organism changes to adapt to the environment; this implied that the same child would behave differently if the circumstances changed, but the explanations were incomplete and could not describe or predict later changes. Also influencing their behavior is the culture surrounding the child and adolescent. Vygotsky (1978) described this as the zone of proximal development. This is evident in observations educators make about student behavior. They see the student acting in three distinct ways: one way when at school, another way when at home, and still a third way when around only friends. In teenagers around the ages of 15 or 16, it is not uncommon to see a number of these students still acting and thinking much like 14-year-olds while others already demonstrate a greater ability to handle more complicated material than their peers. By the end of a school year many of the slower peers will have caught up because their brains have grown a bit more and are now able to process more complex lessons. Kohlberg (1984) noted that there was a set of cognitive skills but they were not all developed equally. Adolescents do not process information as if it were in a single system.

The cognitive development of the brain goes through a series of cycles that are more apparent when a student receives direct support in the form of instruction and guidance from a teacher. The cycles of growth do not occur at precisely the same time for each person, just as children don't reach the same height at the same time. Further, while the overall pattern of the cycles is the same, there is a difference of timing in the cycles within the individual relevant to various types of cognitive skills. Not all skills develop at the same rate. Different areas of the brain are undergoing their growth cycles at different times and at different rates. The result is there is variation in the development of skills for both the level of proficiency that is reached and when those skills develop.

The electroencephalogram, or EEG, is a scan that shows brain-wave patterns. Analyses of EEG brain scans have revealed there are several dynamic growth patterns for different areas of the brain, and these growth cycles, which contribute to Kurt Fischer's dynamic skill theory (1980), can provide useful insights for educators. Such insights can be where a student is developmentally in their thinking and what cognitive skills they are capable of, instead of the seat-of-the pants guesses of where educators think they are. To illustrate this, consider the following example.

Suppose the high school teacher had a classroom full of kids who were not only all the same age, but who also shared the same birthday. What would teachers see? As various lessons were taught some adolescents would be able to do lessons more easily, while others were noticeably further behind in their cognitive skills. Although they are the same age, their brains have not developed at exactly the same rates. Brain development is not uniform from student to student. Many parents noticed this difference years earlier with their children if they took them to a doctor for a yearly check-up. As mothers so often do, they compare notes. When did their baby start crawling, or sit up? They reached these milestones in more or less the same range of months, but not at the same time; they were on a similar but not identical schedule of brain development. And that continues as they grow all the way through adolescence. One of the important problems educators face is they know very little, if anything, about a student's cognitive development. There is no equivalent of a baby guide for adolescents that is reliably researched, and even a baby guide gives only approximations on development. Teachers have been pretty much on their own, passing on bits and pieces of their collective wisdom. Piaget made significant advances in understanding how children develop cognitively through a sequence of recognizable changes with his careful observations, and unquestionably his work has helped in understanding the development of a child's brain. However, cognitive development that accompanies brain growth, researchers and educators are learning, is vastly more intricate and continues longer than we originally thought. Even so, Piaget's efforts provided a springboard to the more detailed view we have today.

Cognitive development is uneven

Back in the classroom with our identically aged students, the teacher discovers another characteristic about the brain's cognitive development of skills. Obviously the skills vary from student to student, but they also *vary within* the student for the same content, sometimes even from day to day. In some subjects a student could handle a task and reason efficiently, but when the student had to switch tasks within a subject, or changed subjects altogether, that same student might really zoom ahead or, in contrast, struggle. She might be able to read easily but can't comprehend fractions. Perhaps she can do math but she socializes poorly: she doesn't know how to play and associate with other young adolescents very well in games. It is common that, *within* a single brain, development is not uniform and cognitive skills do not develop evenly in a steady progression across different types of content.

Notice in Figure 1.2 that the cycles in the optimal support line have steeper portions with spurts of growth where the next higher tier is reached. For educators, there is a very important development characteristic found here. The development is also not smooth for *each* content area but goes through periods of rapid growth, followed by a drop in performance skills as new, more complicated materials and relationships are acquired. It may not be a matter of how well a student paid attention, but a new level of development the student is going through. This is not abnormal: Teachers should expect to see such variations as a student develops, and as education's understanding of dynamic characteristics of development improves, the performances become more predictable. With this knowledge, educators can be more ready for the normal stutters of development. The brain's level of cognitive skills performance is not the same in all tasks, even though many assessments and standards expect them to be. The student brain grows through a series of repeating cycles where different areas of the brain have growth spurts. In the next section we will examine how the brain's cycles of development affect cognitive skills.

The Effect of Support on Cognitive Skills Development

Two patterns of development for cognitive skills emerge, depending on the type of instruction or support provided to the student. With optimal support there is direct teacher involvement with the student perhaps by coaching, guiding, and explaining. The support can be individual help at times or within group instruction as long as there is continual interaction between the teacher and student, and information is being exchanged from teacher to student and from student to teacher. The teacher can adjust the instruction when the student needs assistance.

Support from teachers and coaches makes a difference in performance and whether students are likely to attain higher cognitive skills. In addition, support will affect their pattern of cognitive development. In Figure 1.2, Line A represents the repeating cycles of cognitive growth when there is instructional support and the student's cognitive skills show periods of acceleration. This is particularly noticeable when the learner has optimal support. If the student receives optimal support with direct teacher involvement, then the repeating cycles in Line A reach a considerably higher level of cognitive skills (e.g., learning to speak and write properly works better with continual high-quality guidance) (Wolf, 2007).

Let's look at photography students, for example. When novice high school photography students receive direct support from a teacher they very rapidly learn a variety of skills. With time and guided practice, the photography students' understanding and ability to make good images changes. They are able to view a new image and see a number of potential options that would improve it. As their cognitive skills develop further, their perspectives shift yet again. They view an image and think of what the entire end result should look like. They have learned to take different abstract processes and use them together as a system to improve the images. In order to move students to higher levels of cognitive skills, it will take *time and steady support including direct instruction, making corrections, explaining errors, encouraging when it is needed, and providing students with realistic feedback about their progress.*

As students move on to new and more difficult problems, another set of new skills is required. As they acquire the new skills they will *still drop down to a fundamental level of understanding* for that new skill level (represented by the dip in the cycles of Line A) and then slowly improve in performance as they learn to combine new skills with the older ones in that domain. Again, this works best if they have optimal support. When the optimal support is missing, and there is little or no individual support from teachers or parents, we see a noticeably lower level of development in student skills, represented by Line B in Figure 1.2 (Fischer, Yan, & Stewart, 2003). This lower pattern may be reflected in a student who receives little help, shuns all supportive efforts, does not explore limits, and is essentially abandoned to his own means. For this student, it is sink or swim; for those who swim without support it's more likely to be a thrashing struggle than the smooth strokes accomplished with years of attentive teacher coaching. *Without support, students are less likely to move to higher levels of thought.* If the teacher is not able to provide optimal, close support, then students advance at a much slower pace and gains may be incremental. As students discover new problems that require more than one skill, without close guidance at critical points, many can't figure out what to do. Newer skills must be acquired and combined (Dawson, Fischer, & Stein, 2006). It doesn't matter what a person's age is, a lack of optimal support (Line B) can result in a lower performance. Take basketball, for example (we could just as easily use learning trig functions, or designing science experiments). Players on their own, even pro basketball players, without a coach, will see their performance drop; the best performance is obtained with coaching.

As cognitive development occurs, the brain can handle not only more difficult tasks, but ones that are more multifaceted as well. At the highest levels of cognitive development, which not everyone can achieve, a person can see how different systems work together and also the underlying principles that are common to all the systems. Without support, the student isn't likely to come close to those higher levels of performance.

That there is an uneven cognitive development within a student, and that a student's repeated cycles of increasing cognitive skills are obtained only with support, is not the typical understanding of the process of development. The view of development that many of us, including administrators and politicians, have is that it is uniform. There is an expectation that most students at particular ages should be able to know and do the same things. However, the development and ability to handle new skills in a content area will gradually increase over about 3 to 4 years. This is not uniformly fixed. For some students the time is longer. Different subject areas or domains will have similar patterns of development, but students' cognitive growth is not necessarily in sync with other skills within their own brains, or with other students' skills. The evidence is clear that at any given age, there is not a single ability that emerges across all the domains and skills at the same time (Fischer & Daley, 2007) (see Table 1.1).

Questions of support and unrealistic expectations of uniform development come sharply into focus when considering computer-based learning. This is particularly noticeable when the learner has optimal support. Computers can improve some skills, but currently the level of cognitive challenge is low. Computers cannot (yet) respond and guide in a way to provide all the appropriate feedback that produces the higher performance in complex learning (Mike McConnell, personal commu-

		Table 1.1 TABLE OF COGNITIVE SKILL DEVELOPMENT		
Tiers	**Levels**		**Age of Emergence** (Optimal Support)	**Functional** (Low Support)
Principles	Ab4 = P	Single principles	23–25 years	30–45 years, or never for many domains
Abstractions (intangible, abstract concepts)	Ab3	Several aspects of two abstractions are coordinated	18–20 years	23–40 or never for many domains
	Ab2	Different abstractions are coordinated with each other	14–16 years	17–30 years
	Rp4 = Ab1	Single abstractions. A relation between two systems	10–12 years	12–20 years
Representations	Rp3	A representational system in which several aspects of two concrete representations are coordinated	6–7 years	7–12 years
	Rp2	Two or more concrete representations are coordinated with each other	3.5–4.5 years	4–8 years
	Sm4 = Rp1	A single representation. Single, unassociated, concrete actions or categories	2 years	2–5 years
Action	Sm3	Sequential actions that are coordinated	11–13 months	
	Sm2	Coordinated actions	7–8 months	
	Sm1	Single action	3–4 months	

Functional level estimates are approximate and there is considerable variation. Information is combined from multiple studies (see Fischer 1980; Kitchener, Lynch, Fischer, & Wood, 1993; Fischer & Bidell, 2006) on middle-class American and European children and varies culturally. Adapted with permission from Fischer, Yan, & Stewart (2003).

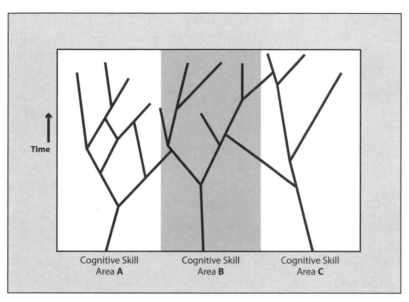

Fig. 1.3. A web-fractal like pattern of cognitive skill development across different cognitive skills emerges with growth. Cognitive skills influence the development of other skills.

nication, 2009). Yet many virtual schools are starting to emerge across the country. While educators might be able to keep more students engaged with some electronic form of learning, it is not known yet how well these students will fare in regard to achieving the higher cognitive skills.

When we view cognitive skills development from three different subjects in a dynamic perspective, a weblike pattern emerges (Fischer & Daley, 2007). The lines of the strands represent different content and cognitive skills within a subject. For some strands development is relatively consistent, but there is some variation within other strands (see Figure 1.3). Additionally, cognitive skills don't develop in complete isolation either; they interact with other domains that make up the other strands. Variability of developing skills occurs not only within subject domains but across other subject domains as well. The context in which skills are used is also important. How a student works on a task will change with the environment in which they find themselves. Being able to execute a basketball play in practice is quite a different context from when someone needs to shoot a basket in an actual game, or a student who is able to solve a math problem in a class where mistakes don't count may not complete the same problem well when taking a final exam. Knowledge may be present, but mastery is not reached where students are able to make connections that were previously beyond their understanding. The strands are linked in multiple ways, creating more support for processing at still higher levels.

For cognitive development to occur, neurons must change their relationships with other neurons. These cells, which do much of the heavy lifting that is learning, make up only about 10% of the brain (Ward, 2006). Each person is born with an estimated excess of 100 billion to 150 billion neurons (Beyerstein, 1999; Ikonomi-dou et al., 2001). During the developmental processes these extra cells that are not used or don't receive enough stimulation are pruned or culled out. There are major periods of pruning throughout the life span. Other developments have a significant impact on learning, too. These include neurons making connections to other neurons (which is called *synaptogenesis*), and when a substance called myelin sheathes the nerve fibers of the brain (which is called *myelination* and helps to keeps signals from fading). These developmental properties and their possible effects on learning were discovered through technological advances in brain imaging. Many imaging studies have helped cognitive neuroscientists to confirm a number of hypotheses from cognitive psychology research. The following section will review a number of major imaging techniques that are frequently used.

How Do We Know the Brain Does That?

The path to discovering just how the anatomy of the brain is related to our functions has been painful and difficult, built on the studies of tens of thousands of tragic injuries people have suffered, often through wartime. The journey of mapping the brain began over 2,000 years ago when Galen, the great Roman physician to the gladiators, made observations about the brain (Ward, 2006). The collected information that we benefit from today has been hard-won. Many people along with their families have paid an unimaginably high price in suffering. Today, the thousands who suffer from traumatic brain injury, resulting from war injuries, sporting mishaps, or automobile accidents, give us a small inkling into what too many others have gone through over thousands of years without any sort of help. Our advances now are less dependent on tragedy. The use of brain imaging allows us to make discoveries in both healthy and damaged brains by mapping processes such as language, memory, and how learning takes place at the cellular level. Because so much information is derived through these, brief descriptions of some of the major imaging methods and their limitations are in order.

Limitations in Gathering Information

Neuroeducational researchers would like to have information about what circuits or individual neurons are doing while a learning event is happening. What goes on in an adolescent's brain processing helps to bring into sharper focus what educators can do to facilitate the processing. For example, brain imaging could provide confirmation of whether a certain type of teaching is "sticking" and can give better diagnostics for trying to determine what the learning problems are.

The teaching environment creates a significant problem in understanding how the brain works. Most real learning situations have some sort of movement going on, while most of the imaging procedures require the person to remain absolutely still, often inside a large machine. This is not very helpful in seeing what the students' brains are doing while in the middle of a real classroom or natural learning situation. To complicate matters, if researchers want to test a specific intervention for a student that involves normal physical activity and observe which circuits are activated, any movement would blur the image. It's similar to taking a time exposure of a flower over several seconds in the wind. The flower is moved slightly all around and the image ends up showing a fuzzy blob instead of the flower. To solve this problem, some of the newest technology may be able to resolve the issue of gathering brain data in learning environments. One type of portable technology, such as near-infrared optical tomography (NIROT) (see page 30), allows movement while gathering data. Other technologies, such as PET or SPECT scans are invasive, which usually means injecting or inhaling a chemical in order for the brain activity to show up. However, other imaging procedures don't require introducing anything into the brain.

The imaging processes also differ in the amount of detail they provide. Some can indicate where the activity is (called *spatial resolution*), while other processes have more detail on exactly when the activity occurred (called *temporal resolution*). There are trade-offs. Images with better spatial resolution have problems showing temporal resolution because an image can take a number of seconds to minutes to be generated. This means the image being seen is the average of a lot of different activities, often more than what we want to study. Other imaging techniques have the opposite problem. The electroencephalograph (EEG), which shows brain waves, can measure activity down to the millisecond, telling when something happened but not precisely where it is happening (i.e., it has poor spatial resolution). All of this means researchers must often infer what is going on because the measurements are indirect. For example, people who have ADHD often have general areas of underactivity in the front of their brains, but precisely which circuits are involved remains unknown. Knowing which circuits are involved might tell what interventions could be helpful. All information must be painstakingly pieced together from many different types of studies including a variety of imaging techniques. There is not a single method of imaging that can tell precisely where a circuit is for each process we are interested in. Teasing out the secrets is done through *indirect measures* of the brain. Imaging is just one of the better-known research tools.

Brain Imaging

The following is a list of some imaging tools. All require years of skilled professional training in order to read the resulting scans properly.

- **Computed tomography** (CT or CAT) generates an advanced form of X-ray, which can identify the larger structures of the brain. If the problem area is smaller than about 4–5 mm (¼ of an inch) there isn't enough resolution to detect it. For example, the surface or cortex of the brain is where many key thinking processes take place, and it is about 4 mm thick. The CT scan can't distinguish the cortex from the underlying tissue but can easily pick up spaces, called ventricles, within the brain.
- An **electroencephalograph** (EEG) records the electrical waves produced by brain activity as a series of continuous wavelike images. The EEG is an

older but well-established tool that is noninvasive. Small, pea-sized electrodes are pasted on the scalp and these pick up faint electrical signals that are amplified anywhere from 125,000 to 250,000 times so they may be seen on a computer screen. The EEG has excellent resolution for when neural events occur, down to the millisecond, but poor spatial resolution, so there is not great certainty about which tissues are involved. This is frequently used in research and increasingly used as a specialized biofeedback called neurofeedback for people with some mental health difficulties such as bipolar depression, ADHD, and Posttraumatic Stress Disorder (PTSD). Some schools use EEGs as part of their intervention for students with ADHD and a few other disorders.

- *Functional magnetic resonance imaging* (fMRI) is a noninvasive procedure that has better resolution than PET or EEG. There is still a delay of about 6–10 seconds from when the neural activity occurred to the changes in the blood (Gazzaniga et al., 2009), which makes it difficult to measure precisely where each portion of thought is being processed. This tool is becoming one of the most common in cognitive neuroscience research.

- *Near-infrared optical topography* (NIROT) is a relatively new and promising scanning tool that may have significant educational implications because it can monitor higher order brain functions as they occur in natural conditions. This noninvasive tool allows the person to be mobile and it can even be used on infants. Near-infrared light is carried by optical fibers and radiated onto the scalp. Light can penetrate about 30 mm (roughly 1 and ¼ inches) into an adult's brain, easily reaching the cortex underneath. Hideaki Koizumi, who has led a group trying to miniaturize the head gear, described the light as similar to the "sun on a cloudy day in winter" (2007, p. 247).

- *Positron emission tomography* (PET) helped to pioneer major advances in our understanding of the brain. PET uses radioactive oxygen (^{15}O) with a very short half-life. The oxygen, carried in the cerebral blood, is taken up by the brain and used to metabolize glucose. Glucose is the food that powers the brain. The more active the brain area is, the more fuel it needs, which is the glucose sugar. In order to use that glucose, oxygen must also be available. The brain areas that are slightly more active show up as brighter areas on the computer monitor. The resolution measured is roughly 5–10 mm^3, a volume about the size of a bean, so the spatial resolution is sufficient to identify specific areas (Gazzaniga et al., 2009). However, PET has poor temporal resolution; you can't tell precisely when the nerve cells were active because it takes minutes to collect data and the whole brain is continuously active. The activity across the whole brain means images must be compared, with one set when the person was actively doing a mental task against baseline images made when the person wasn't engaged in the task. The baseline image is subtracted from the activity image and what is left is the area that is more active. It looks like the rest of the brain isn't active, which to some people can falsely confirm the neuromyth that we use only 10% of the brain. A PET scan shows the brain is active everywhere.

- **_Transcranial magnetic stimulation_** (TMS) is a noninvasive technique that produces a strong, localized magnetic field that temporarily disrupts the neuron signaling in an area roughly 1 cm^3, or about the volume of a large green pea. By temporarily "knocking out" portions of some neural circuits for a few seconds it is possible to learn more about the roles specific circuits play. Therapeutic uses for TMS are also beginning to emerge.

Overview of Chapters

Teaching and the Adolescent Brain is about more than just learning processes; it takes in the sweep of interlocked processes that affect learning and, ultimately, student performance. The remaining chapters will explore the different processes that influence the adolescents' performance and what we might be able to do to improve them. Since developmental changes in the brain continue beyond adolescence, the suggested interventions described here can potentially have an impact throughout our lives. In each chapter, I present research-based teaching recommendations.

Chapter 2 will explore the underlying anatomy and key parts of the brain, the function of neurons, how neurons change when creating memories, and how all of these affect learning. We'll see that different areas of the brain have specific functions that relate to and influence other areas of the brain and what is retained in memory. How exercise and diet affect the brain is also explored, along with discussion of major neuromyths.

Chapter 3 will examine the complexities of pattern detection and attention, and how the brain's ability to process the information affects student performance. One of the first tasks of the brain is to direct attention. In following one of the core educational problems of what educators can do, a series of tested interventions and insights about capturing and maintaining attention in adolescents will be presented. By addressing overall attention problems that students generally have in the classroom, we can also simultaneously and successfully address how to teach students who have ADHD. We'll examine what the ADHD brain seems to be doing and why stimulation is actually helpful to them and the other students because virtually every classroom has students who have ADHD. In the regulation of attention, a dynamic interplay with emotional processes of the brain is also encountered, which is the topic of Chapter 4.

Chapter 4 explores how emotional processing can redirect what the student pays attention to, something particularly noticeable during adolescence. The brain's ability to make emotional evaluations about new information will be explored. The brain's evaluations are very important to learning, because the resulting processing routes selected by the brain affect what eventually happens to the information. One consequence that will be examined is how emotional processing creates stress on the neurons affecting learning. Other problems such as autism occur at the neuronal level and involve both emotional processing and attention. For example, in people with autism the recently discovered mirror neuron systems haven't developed properly and this contributes to the attention behaviors teachers see, making the autistic adolescent's life even more complicated. The implications of media violence and how this affects adolescent emotional behavior are considered as well. Another facet of emotions that will be explored is the significance of students making emotional connections with the lessons at hand and with their teachers. The chapter follows up with what educators can do, with suggestions of how to help students develop those emotional connections. The degree to which emotional connections are built and affect motivation is reviewed in Chapter 5.

Chapter 5 looks at motivation, one of the most difficult educational issues, which is a ubiquitous problem. Without motivation, adolescents will drop out of school. Educators face student motivational issues on a daily basis. Many educators suggest that motivation is *the* problem and that if they can get a handle on motivation, the rest of teaching and learning will be much easier. Much of Chapter 5 explores what we can do about adolescent motivational processing through our teaching practices that promote or defeat motivation. Fundamental motivational principles are explored, such as the role of the teenager's belief about whether his or her efforts will have any effect on the lesson's outcome, and how autonomy, in which the student selects what tasks to engage in, affects performance. A teacher's belief about his or her own effort in teaching the adolescent is also explored. Closely related are the strategies adolescents will employ based on what they believe about their personal competence. The role of setting achievable goals, the use of models as examples, and feedback are all part of this exploration.

Chapter 6 looks at the concept of intelligence. A number of theories that affect educational practices are reviewed. Explicit theories, such as traditional IQ, and implicit theories, such as Gardner's multiple intelligences, Sternberg's successful intelligence, and emotional intelligence are examined in turn. The IQ, a traditional measure of intelligence, is closely related to how fast information is processed and maintained in the brain. The use of different intelligence measures and their effects on adolescents, such as when students apply for admittance to colleges, benefits for special education, or scholarships, is discussed. What educators can do to expand the range of student learning capabilities, how emotional intelligence may facilitate appropriate social behaviors, and how to use intelligence successfully are also presented. Closely related to IQ is how the brain consciously maintains information in the mind. This involves the brain's processes of working memory, which will be explored in Chapter 7.

Chapter 7 begins the examination of memory in its multiple forms. The curious properties of sensory and working memory affect our lives, and our students, moment by moment. Chapter 7 briefly discusses sensory memory, which is linked to some of the initial processes of pattern detection and attention described earlier. Then the properties of working memory are examined, along with many instructional strategies suitable for adolescents that build on the weaving together of attention, emotion, and motivation, as discussed in previous chapters. Working memory is one of the most important brain processes to affect adolescent learning and performance. The overlapping regions of the brain used for working memory and intelligence are discussed, along with two major models of working memory that describe how information is processed on its way to becoming consolidated into long-term memory. A number of instructional strategies targeted for the teen mind and that accommodate working memory are presented, along with suggestions for teachers about how to develop strategies for addressing working memory that will be needed for specific lessons.

Chapter 8 discusses the establishment of long-term memory and its consolidation and maintenance. I consider how teachers frame questions or "Google" the brain to find the memory that both the student and teacher want. Causes of different types of memory errors are also explored. With long-term memory, the various structures of the brain and all the processes described in earlier chapters, such as perception, attention, emotion, motivation, and working memory, come into play. This chapter will explore how different types of memory make use of different brain structures, and in continuing to follow the problem of what educators can do, we'll examine how teaching can incorporate a little-used form of memory to significantly assist adolescents in school. I explore how some memories are more quickly consolidated because of their emotional context, while memories for other information, even when reviewed hundreds of times, are still unreliable. Also explored is the relationship between adolescent sleep deprivation and memory consolidation and how consolidation is affected by adolescent computer use and texting habits. Taking a longer view, the chapter will re-visit and expand on how information that finally gets processed into long-term memory will affect our students' performances both in school and later throughout their lives. I present procedures that teachers can use to develop their own personal applications in lessons that help adolescents build a retrievable memory, the essence of much learning. All of these instructional strategies, progressively built through the chapters, aim toward adolescent performance and measuring it, which is the subject of Chapter 9.

Chapter 9 focuses on study practices and assessments, the goals that the assessments tend to represent, and what assessment goals are conducive to better learning and teaching. I consider assessment in the context of brain development and whether assessments are age-appropriate, and I introduce some new designs for assessing that can provide better information. I also take a broad look at matching instruction and review practices to the assessment. Using the brain development model introduced in Chapter 1, we also explore how educators might design better application questions. For traditional testing, such as multiple-choice tests, we will review strategies that work best. Study-review practices that adolescents can apply from class to class are also presented. For schools shifting to more computer use, a high school note-taking template that can be easily incorporated into school programs will be introduced, along with ways to use cell phones and other digital equipment in study processes. To assist the busy teacher, I present a lesson design analysis, with each step paralleling key points of research, to enable a teacher to quickly track a multitude of details in order to facilitate better instruction from initial planning to final assessment. The lesson design analysis stems from the guiding belief that implementing neuroeducation can provide better direction for instruction and interventions and can predict when learning will be more likely to occur.

In Chapter 10, we look at the future, the learning problems that are emerging, and how the traditional landscape of the classroom is changing to include the digital classroom, and even virtual classrooms around the world. The chapter also considers the possible impact of neuroeducation of adolescents in other learning areas, ranging from driver's education and experiential-outdoor education to the military. I also examine what educators might learn from the video game industry, new interventions that are being considered, and the implications of new research tools. Finally, I consider the potential impact of neuroeducation on college instruction and teacher preparation within schools of education.

Key Points and Recommendations

- ***Neuroeducation is created from the common grounds of cognitive neuroscience, cognitive psychology, and education.*** Each is concerned with thinking and learning and each approaches problems with a different perspective. By combining their efforts in a reciprocal fashion, greater understanding of how thinking and learning occurs can be achieved. Different scientific communities working on the same problem usually ignore each other, but understanding the brain is such a complex endeavor that it takes efforts from multiple disciplines to address and understand the problems. However, neuroeducation is just starting out, and at the moment there is not an equal partnership. Educators, both in the schools and especially the colleges, need to form partnerships with those in the other areas of research.

- ***Our brain is involved in virtually everything we do.*** Every action inside the body is either directly or indirectly going to interact with the brain, from the food we eat to the genes that are switched on or off. Similarly the environment outside the body also has a substantial effect on the brain; otherwise we would not be attempting to educate a person. In like fashion how we treat others, or how others treat us, can profoundly affect how the brain functions. The direct results of those relationships are seen in the thousands of "self-help" books that have been published.

- ***The more we know and understand about how the brain works the better we can design our instruction, communication, and assessments.*** This is the essential premise of neuroeducation: We can use the information to more intelligently guide our actions and policies. As the examples illustrated, the lack of fundamental knowledge can have a devastating effect on staff and hence on students. With the appropriate use of basic principles, we can facilitate learning in students.

- *The effect on the brain when learning is indirect.* If we use a particular teaching intervention we don't always get the result we want because we don't understand the effect of the multitude of other variables. Interventions do affect the brain, but we are not always sure how. Clinical studies typically don't provide information about actual practices. A direct cause and effect can often be buried by a multitude of processes and variables going on in the brain and in the classroom. This is why teachers should work with researchers to find out more precisely what happens. Collaborative partnerships help researchers focus on crucial problems faced in the classroom.

- *The brain is extraordinarily plastic in its ability to process information and continuously change in response.* It is the ability of the brain to change that permits learning. No change means no learning. This dynamic quality means that we also need to use newer methods of analysis to design studies and understand interactions with the actual teaching.

- *Learning is a dynamic process; it doesn't take place in fixed stages as many assume.* The learning process is uneven but follows distinct patterns for each cognitive skill area. We should expect to see uneven progress, and often a drop in performance when the type of thinking changes, even within the context of the same subject. With direct and continued teacher support students can develop considerably greater cognitive thinking skills than if they are left to their own devices.

- *Our vision or lack of it should not limit another's learning.* Let learners find their own limits; don't assume limits and structure a lesson that will hold students back. Lessons should be designed to allow students to stretch as much as they are capable by using multiple approaches. Don't assume that a student is dull because the grades he or she previously earned were poor. We need to help students blossom, not clip their wings by assuming they can't do something. By providing goals that are incrementally more advanced, and by treating students as people, not as idiots, teachers see that a number of students will likely demonstrate unexpected talents, skills, and knowledge.

- *Most traits in the brain have multiple genes affecting them.* In high school, many of us learned classic Mendelian genetics where one gene determined one trait, but one trait is actually the result of the combination of many genes. The brain is affected by thousands of genes. But the genes are like musicians performing a symphony. They can produce multiple sounds and harmonies, but each player is active at different times and to a different degree.

- *How the brain works is measured indirectly.* Only in very rare circumstances can we make direct observations with a few neurons and a learning activity. Consequently many investigative processes are used to understand a problem, but that also means solving problems is complicated. Any given lesson will involve many enormously complex processes involving many parts of the brain, but at different times and to different degrees.

- *With learning, the brain physically changes.* Physical changes in the brain at the cellular level are repeatedly observed (although the major folds, or structure, of the brain don't change). By detecting these minuscule changes, we can learn what affects learning.

- *With optimal support, a student reaches considerably higher levels of cognitive skills.* A teacher's continued direct involvement, using a variety of instructional strategies, can produce great differences in students' thinking skills and can help students reach the higher levels of abstract thought and problem solving. Computer programs cannot provide appropriate guidance at the higher levels of thinking. It remains an open question of whether virtual schools will be able to elevate students' cognitive skills without an instructor being directly involved.

- *When optimal support is missing, a student will see a lower level of development in his or her cognitive skills.* If a student doesn't develop cognitive skills to a very high level, there also may be significant implications for society, because problems today are more abstract, complicated, and not easily understood on a simplistic level. This is not a new issue but was first discussed in a report titled *A Nation at Risk*, released in 1983. The inability to discern complicated relationships through abstract thinking at a higher cognitive level suggests poor learning or misunderstanding may result. Another implication is economically related; our students are less able to compete in the global market. A society that fails to understand the problems at hand places itself at greater risk in making inappropriate decisions. We must adequately address complex issues such as climate change or genetic engineering. Poor thinking skills also have personal consequences, such as negative influences on employability, bad health decisions, or being taken advantage of in a digital age. A final implication is that the lack of higher thinking skills may also play into how much mental processing we have to draw upon in old age. The longer we can maintain mental health and maintain independence, the greater our personal freedom and the less the cost will be to our families. We don't yet have sufficient research to answer these important issues. For educators, developing higher levels of cognitive skills touches on one of the most basic reasons for the value of neuroeducation; the more educators know and understand, the better we can design lessons and improve teaching. If we accomplish that goal, it can help our students to make more informed and better decisions.

- *There is variation in development, even within the individual student.* Cognitive skills do not progress smoothly from one stage to another; instead, the development of cognitive skills within the student is uneven. It progresses in fits and starts, sometimes purring along, then sputtering when a different type of thinking skill is required. Traditional grading and standardized tests provide virtually no indication of where the student's cognitive development is, even within the context of a single subject. The unevenness of development has implications for assessment design and our expectations of performance, which will be discussed in Chapter 9.

RESOURCES

Battro, A., K. Fischer, & P. J. Lena. (2008). *The educated brain: Essays in neuroeducation*. Cambridge University Press.

Fischer, K. W., & M. H. Immordino-Yang. (2008). *The Jossey-Bass reader on the brain and learning*. San Francisco: Jossey-Bass.

Marcus, G. (2004). *Birth of the mind: How a tiny number of genes creates the complexities of human thought*. New York: Basic Books.

Organisation for Economic Co-operation and Development. (2007). *Understanding the brain: The birth of a learning science*. Paris: Centre for Educational Research and Innovation.

CHAPTER TWO

Foundations for Learning

From Neurons to
Maintenance and Communication

Most everything in my brain,
someone else helped put there
—Unknown

The Building Blocks of the Brain

If we are really going to understand how students learn, we must also understand the brain and its neurons. The brain is made up of an estimated 100+ billion neuronal cells that occur in more varieties than in any other organ of the body. The activity of the neurons and their supporting glial cells is the business end of the brain, where the learning takes place. Neurons that make up the outer surface, or cortex, of the brain compose a layer only about 3–4 mm thick. The cortex or, more properly, the neocortex has six layers (Thompson, 2000), which undergo the dynamic growth changes discussed in the previous chapter. The cortex is commonly known as the "gray matter," and, in general, the more neocortex there is, the greater computational power the brain has. To increase the computational power of the neocortex, it appears that more neocortex is needed, but limited skull growth also restricts the space for the brain. The problem of increasing the cortical surface that is needed for more thought is solved by the creation of deep folds, which simultaneously generate a larger surface area while not increasing the volume of the skull. If the neocortex were flattened out, it would cover about three and a half sheets of typing paper (Matousek & Petersen, 1973). As we will see, the adolescent brain is adult in size, but not in function.

While there are more types of neurons than any other cell type in the body, each with different shapes and functions, the descriptions that follow are of parts common to all neurons. The neuron cell has three major parts: the cell body, axons (very long nerve fibers that send out signals), and dendrites (the tiny spindly structures that receive signals; see Figure 2.1). Within the cell body is the nucleus, which contains the genetic information for synthesizing proteins into neurotransmitters along with organelles, which are many tiny structures that perform a large number of essential cell functions. When a neuron receives information in the form of a tiny electrical impulse, it changes the activity of the cell. If there is sufficient stimulation to pass the information along, then an electrical impulse called an *action potential* is generated, which travels down the axon to other neurons.

The action potential is an all-or-nothing impulse. Imagine a mousetrap that either triggers or doesn't; there is no halfway, or weak, trigger. The electrical im-

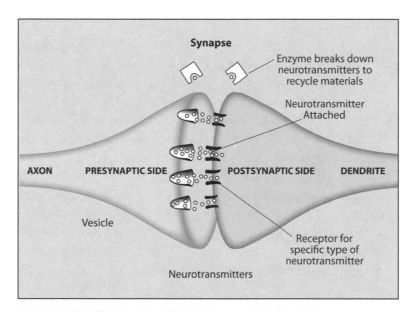

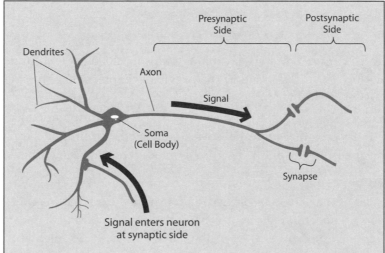

Fig. 2.1. Learning takes place at the neuronal level. Signals are transmitted down the axon triggering the release of neurotransmitters across the synapse. Memory appears to be built in the synapses.

pulse either has sufficient energy to trigger a signal, or there is no signal because action potentials come in only one form: They do not vary from weak to strong. The "strength" of a signal, traveling at about 200–300 mph, is determined by the frequency at which the neurons fire (Ward, 2006). Every second, hundreds of impulses travel down an axon to a flattened terminal on the *presynaptic side*. The synaptic terminal is where neurons transmit their signals to other nearby neurons. This location, where the signals transfer from one neuron to another, is where the key parts of learning appear to take place. There is a tiny gap between the flattened terminal and the dendrite of the next neuron. This gap is called a *synapse* (see Figure 2.1). When the electrical impulse travels down on the surface of the axon, the electrical signal converts into a chemical signal at the synapse. These chemical signals, called *neurotransmitters*, occur in more than 100 forms. When they are in the bloodstream, some of the same neurotransmitters are known as hormones (Gazzaniga et al., 2009). The neurotransmitters collect at the end of the flattened dendrites into tiny packets called vesicles. The vesicles move rapidly to the surface at the end of the axon. Once there, the neurotransmitters are released to diffuse across the tiny synapse gap to the next dendrite on the *postsynaptic* side. The dendrite on the postsynaptic side has receptor sites that can receive the signal. The receptors are proteins that make large pores or channels in the cell membrane, through which the neurotransmitters can enter. These channels stay closed until the proper stimuli trigger their opening. *The combined processes of the firing of the neurons, the movement of neurotransmitters, and the building of protein receptors and their maintenance are important because they are a major portion of making memories, resulting in learning.*

Although complicated, educators may advance the adolescents' learning by using specific methods of instruction to trigger changes in the neurons that result in learning. Many of these changes must occur at the synapse with the neurotransmitters. Let's take a closer look at some of the processes going on there.

Some neurotransmitters, such as acetylcholine, cross the synapse gap to excite a neighboring neuron, making it more likely to fire and continue passing on the signal. The acetylcholine acts like a "go" signal. This is excellent if the adolescent needs to use the signal to continue some action, but what if continued action would be harmful? It turns out there are other transmitters like GABA (*gamma-aminobutyric acid*), which can function like a "no go" or stop signal and thereby inhibit the neuron from sending signals further on. Neurons have chemical signals that switch them on or off, and it is not unusual that something in the environment, such as a specific instructional method, provides the stimulus to create the chemical signal.

Not all neurons switch on at particular times; they carry all manner of information. Neurons in specific regions carry only the information related to a specific task. For example, the type of information carried is largely determined by its origination: sound information comes from the cochlea of the ear, and visual information comes from the eye, which stimulates the neurons that are connected to those areas. The wiring of one neuron does not connect to all other neurons everywhere in the brain, but they do make thousands of connections to nearby neurons. Neurons may have anywhere from 1,000 to 10,000 synaptic connections, making up to around 100 trillion synaptic connections in the brain, but most of these are localized connections. However, some of the neurons do reach out and connect to relatively distant areas of the brain. This happens below the thin surface of the neocortex in which a given section of the brain is wired to many other areas by long axons. Together, these long axons make up the "white" matter of the brain. The front of the brain connects to the back while one side of the brain connects to the other side. The cortex on the surface also has axon connections to structures deep within the brain.

The Creation of Memory

When a learning event occurs, the stimulated dendrites on the neurons grow tiny *dendritic spines.* The spines are on the receiving or postsynaptic side of the neuron. Hebb (1949) proposed that when a synapse is activated at the same time the post-synaptic side is active, the connection is strengthened. A popular phrase about this is that "neurons that fire together wire together." This suggests *that if a neuron is actively stimulated or repeatedly fires particular circuits, it results in a stronger connection.*

Effective lessons that are designed to create stronger memories and better performances actually make use of this neurological concept. How the strengthening occurs at the cell level is still controversial, but it seems to involve a process called LTP, or *long-term potentiation* (Bliss & Lømo, 1973). The LTP process is a major candidate for memory building. LTP appears to involve creating more neurotransmitter receptors (called NMDA, or N-methyl-D-aspartate receptors) in the postsynaptic membrane. On the postsynaptic side, calcium and magnesium ions (an ion is an electrically charged molecule) play key roles in opening the channels to continue receiving and transmitting the signal (Gazzaniga et al., 2009). The idea is that if the neurons are stimulated, then more receptor channels are built to receive the signals. That same neuron is now more sensitive to any further stimulation. If the student keeps on using the same concept or lesson in a way where the neuron receives continued use, then the synapse strength is maintained, and the student's memory is easier to retrieve (that is, use it or lose it). The problem for both educators and researchers is to find out just how the brain creates and maintains memory and what are the most effective ways to do that. Obviously, that is no simple thing to accomplish. Adolescents from middle school on up have the experience of forgetting things they thought they knew well. What happened to the memories?

The principle of "use it or lose it" may provide a broad picture of what teachers might do to keep the memories of lessons more intact in the adolescent brain. However, not all lessons and tasks are equal: Memories for some lessons are lost while others only partially fade. LTP is a part of the key to memory, and maintenance of NMDA receptors and LTP is under intensive study. Teachers and students want to know why memories fade and what they can do about it. For the student this means the development of metacognitive skills, while for the teacher it requires more understanding of the mind/brain system. To complicate issues, sometimes a desired memory is present but inaccessible. Everyone has had the experience of something that was forgotten earlier suddenly "popping" into his or her head. The problem is figuring out what happened to those memories, so corrective action can be taken to make them more accessible. Although the chemistry of memory and learning is still largely a mystery, strategies are emerging to help everyone with these problems, and each of the subsequent chapters will focus on different brain processes and strategies that facilitate learning and memory. To understand how teaching strategies affect the brain, it is necessary to start in the location where learning and memory are taking place. With adolescents, the stage for learning was prepared years earlier.

Because memory and a key portion of learning apparently reside in the synapse, the growth of synapses, including the growth of more dendritic spines, is important. The process of growing the synapses is synaptogenesis. Neurons and their synapses start growing well before birth and reach their maximum density in the 15 months after birth. During infancy, neurons in different areas of the brain lack specialization. As the neurons undergo specialization during adolescence, it appears the underused or understimulated synapses are pruned out (Huttenlocher & Dabholkar, 1997). The pruning doesn't occur everywhere at once, which corresponds well with the cognitive development patterns of maturation that were described in the first chapter (Fischer, 1980). When the overabundance of unused synaptic connections is pruned back, cognitive skills become more refined in regards to governing attention, regulating emotions, controlling impulsivity, and anticipating consequences of particular actions (Giedd, 2008). As different parts of the brain continue to make connections with each other, more capabilities come online. These changes significantly impact teaching and student performance both in and out of school. When connections for skills remain unused, they become weaker and may dissolve or eventually be lost. If the brain is to maintain learning, the connections that hold the learned material must be used. For the brain, learning a lesson is rarely a onetime event. Memories of skills and knowledge stored in networks must be routinely accessed or adolescents face diminishing returns on their memory.

One aspect of the maturation of the brain profoundly affects adolescent performance. The white matter, underlying the neocortex, provides connections to other areas of the brain. The neurons of the neocortex are usually limited to communicating with nearby cell layers. These cells have no insulating cover to keep the signals from fading. If a signal must travel a greater distance, a sheath is needed around the axon in order to protect the signal. As the brain matures, the neurons in the "white matter" below the cortex develop a sheath of myelin. Myelin is made of special fat cells wrapped around the axon, and myelin keeps signals from fading out as they travel from one place to another. As the myelin sheath grows, the more distant areas of the brain finally establish connections with each other. Before the insulating myelin sheath was in place, the signals did not make it through very often. Multiple sclerosis is a disease wherein the myelin sheath is damaged, and signals are not

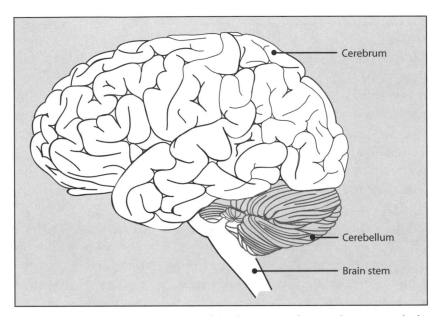

Fig. 2.2. The three major parts of the brain are the cerebrum, cerebellum and brain stem.

properly sent or received in the brain. Because the wiring inside the brain primarily consists of these myelinated cells connecting different regions of control or processing, we need to explore those different regions. In adolescents, the slow growth of myelin contributes to a number of behaviors that interfere with learning.

Navigating the Brain: The Major Landmarks

When we look at the 3-and-a-half-pound convoluted lump that is our brain, several features are noticeable. There are three distinct regions. There is the large *cerebrum*, housing much of our control over movement, emotions, personality, vision, and speech, as well as other processes (see Figure 2.2). The cerebrum has two hemispheres (right and left) with duplicated regions; however, there are some differences in function between the lobes and hemispheres. This does not mean someone can be considered as right- or left-brained (see neuromyth #1 in Chapter 1). A second region lies at the posterior of the brain. Tucked underneath the cerebrum at the back are two tennis-ball-sized structures that make up the *cerebellum*. The cerebellum helps to fine-tune muscle movement to help control balance and motion and also affects emotion. Th*e brain stem* is a third region that merges upward from the spinal cord, and it regulates many of the processes that we generally don't think about, such as respiration, hunger, blood pressure, and sex drive/response. In the next section we will explore each of these regions in more detail.

The Cerebrum: A Brief Tour of Key Functions

The higher-order thinking occurs in the cerebrum, although other parts of the brain are also influential. The cerebrum has developed four lobes in each hemisphere (see Figure 2.3). I'll describe the primary processes of each lobe, although some processes are found in both lobes because of the brain's redundancy across the hemispheres. Remember, simply knowing where something occurs in the brain doesn't explain how it works.

The cerebrum has right and left hemispheres, each made up of four lobes: the frontal, parietal, temporal, and occipital. The boundaries between the temporal and frontal lobes are well defined by a deep fissure, but when we look at the parietal, occipital, and temporal lobes, there is no fissure that makes a clear physical distinction. The function of the cortical tissue determines where the boundaries are, and the only way to find that out is by testing. The functions of the different lobes are described next.

Starting in the posterior (at the back of your head) is the *occipital lobe*, which is covered with the visual cortex that processes visual information. Within the occipital lobe, information is coded for visual properties such as motion, color, orientation, and luminosity, but the occipital lobe does considerably more than that. There are many specialized pathways within the occipital lobe. For example, motion and color are processed in different areas (Zeki, 1993). Consider the significance of vision for reading, a difficult task. A student must see the letters, note their orientation, where they are located spatially, recognize them, and perform a host of other processes. Part of reading is processing the positions of the letters and words. Recognizing the positions of objects involves the *parietal lobe*, which is located above the occipital lobe. Some of the information from the occipital lobe is processed along two pathways: one provides information on recognition ("what") and the other provides information on location ("where") (Ungerleider & Miskin, 1982). The parietal lobe helps you to orient information from the world. Orientation can be where the letters are in a sentence or where your body is within the environment.

In the parietal lobe, there is a section of folded cortex called the *somatosensory strip*, which is specialized for sensing each part of the body. A fold in the cortex is called a *gyrus* and a groove between folds is a *sulcus*. Between the parietal and frontal lobes is a particularly deep sulcus that marks the boundaries of the front and back portions of the brain. On either side of this sulcus are gyri that make up the somatosensory strip that regulates movement (see Figure 2.3).

The somatosensory strip extends from the top (dorsal) side downward. The gyrus on the parietal lobe is where you sense much of your body. However, the cortex that is devoted to processing and controlling the body parts is not equally allocated. The brain uses the face and hands to detect large amounts of information. They have correspondingly more neocortex to handle the information. On the other hand, the neck and shoulders detect less information and consequently need less neocortex dedicated to them. Immediately adjacent to the somatosensory strip, but in the next lobe forward, is a gyrus for directing movement or action: This is the *motor strip* of the *frontal lobe*.

The frontal lobe is the most anterior part of the brain. Part of it rests right above the eyes behind the forehead. Many educationally significant "higher-order" think-

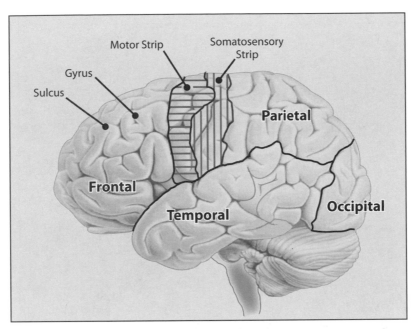

Fig. 2.3. Four lobes of the cerebrum. The somatosensory strip of the parietal has the body parts "mapped" into specific areas of the strip. Immediately adjacent on the frontal lobe is a corresponding motor strip which exerts motor control over the movement of those body parts.

ing processes take place here. Much of the adolescent's executive decision making takes place in the frontal lobe, which directs or inhibits the actions to be taken. Deep inside the frontal lobe are other folds of neocortex that help regulate attention, working memory, emotional control, impulsivity, reasoning, and personality, as well as some areas that facilitate reading and speech. The very anterior end of the lobe is the *prefrontal* lobe, and ours is radically different from that of other primates. Ours is bigger and seems to allow a much greater range and depth of processing in thinking. The prefrontal lobe has more recently evolved, and in the maturation process, it is among the last to myelinate in the course of our development, thereby profoundly affecting adolescent behavior. Some regions of the prefrontal lobe do not come "online" until a person is well into their twenties; this may be why ill-considered youthful actions are relatively commonplace. In looking back upon those years, it is with mild surprise that many of us survived them at all. It seems clear that an adolescent's ability to think through the consequences of his or her actions was not yet in place because the wiring was incomplete, a common characteristic in adolescent brains.

The *insula* is another area of the brain that also develops with experience. It lies deep in the frontal lobe. Have you ever had a "gut" feeling that something isn't right? The insula is highly active in these circumstances. When you feel physical pain or watch a football player get mashed and you wince, the insula is involved

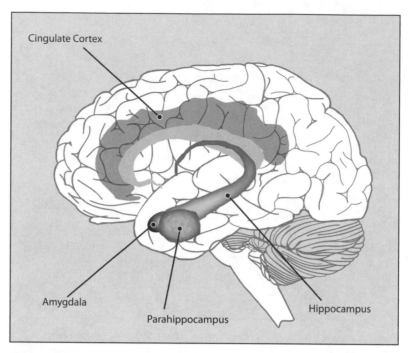

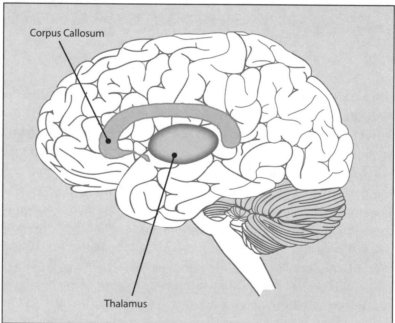

Fig. 2.4. (top) and Fig. 2.5 (bottom). Major interior structures of the interior of the brain. The corpus callosum is the communication connection between hemispheres. The thalamus re-routes information to various areas of the cerebrum. The amygdala, hippocampus, cingulate cortex, and parahippocampus are involved in emotion, attention, and memory formation.

with those feelings and perceptions (Singer et al., 2004). The frontal lobe has important linkages to other lobes as well.

On either side of the brain are the *temporal lobes*, which have many crucial connections to the frontal lobes and other areas. The temporal lobe handles initial emotional evaluations and early memory formation, both of which are continually involved with the executive decision making going on in the frontal lobes. Two structures found inside the temporal lobe are also critical to learning. One is the *amygdala*, which works with the emotional significance of information, which includes the processing of fear-pleasure responses, problem solving, and memory. Right next to the amygdala is the *hippocampus*, a curving structure that resembles a type of seahorse. The hippocampus is essential for the initial building of new memories (see Figure 2.4).

The final structure that educators need an awareness of is the *thalamus*, centered deep within the brain (see Figure 2.5). Almost all incoming information is channeled through this central structure, which acts something like a computer hub or switchboard; it re-routes information to the appropriate networks in the various lobes.

The Hemispheres of the Brain

Both hemispheres of the cerebrum have the same four lobes; these provide slightly redundant systems, though still help to process information. The right hemisphere controls the left side of the body, and the left hemisphere controls the right side of the body. The hemispheres communicate with each other through a connection called the *corpus callosum* (see Figure 2.5). When an individual has severe epileptic seizures that medicine cannot control, it is sometimes necessary to sever the corpus callosum, or split the hemispheres from each other. When researchers performed these split-brain operations they discovered that each hemisphere could function and learn independently, though each hemisphere was unaware of what the other side was doing as it processed information in slightly different ways (Sperry, Gazzaniga, & Bogen, 1969). The hemispheres also differ in the functions they carry out. These are summarized in Table 2.1. Of these, the most noticeable functions are the language centers, which are primarily in the left hemisphere. However, there are some popular misconceptions about the hemispheres. It is common to attribute the right hemisphere as being more "creative," and the left as being "analytical": this is a gross oversimplification and a neuromyth.

In the following section, the perspective narrows from the broad functions of the brain and starts to focus on some of the specialized functions that are carried out by portions of the brain. Here, we explore what educators can do about those brain processes to influence adolescent performance. For education, some of the most basic brain functions involve maintaining brain health through proper nutrition and exercise and fine-tuning the communicative processes by which so much information is acquired.

Table 2.1. LATERALIZATION OF HEMISPHERES	
Left	**Right**
"Interpreter" system that looks for patterns to assemble explanations of events in order to facilitate a proper response	Global information Ability to see how one object influences or relates to another
Memories for abstract and categorical information	
Lexicon (meanings associated with specific words)	Lexicon for language processes
General comprehension of language	
Dominant for speech production	Very limited/rare speech production
	Emotional tone for language (prosody)
Abstract or categories of memories	Superior visual and spatial processing
Voluntary facial expressions Spontaneous facial expressions	Spontaneous facial expressions

The Educational Connection

A number of characteristics about the brain and its processing of information have been presented, but how do these apply to education? In this section, we will explore two major mind/brain connections with education that have great potential to affect learning. The first part explores some general relationships between nutrition, health, and learning. In the second part, the focus narrows on the role of communication—speaking, reading, and writing—as one of the critical components of successful education, because it affects most subsequent learning.

Maintaining the Brain: Nutrition and Exercise

Thinking requires energy, and the resting brain consumes approximately 20–25% of all our available energy, a disproportionately huge amount because the brain is only about 2% of a person's body weight. An improper diet, whether in terms of caloric intake or an imbalance of types of fats, vitamins, and minerals, affects the brain because the brain is made of what we eat. From that perspective when we look at what adolescents eat, we begin to get an idea that their choice of foods may be something less than ideal.

Brain foods? What can we believe?

In workshops people frequently ask about "brain food." The public hears a lot of conflicting information, and there are untold numbers of websites and more health food stores than can be counted, all making claims that some particular substance, diet, or extract will boost brain power. Let me put it plainly: There is not a particular brain food, vitamin, or extract that will do miracles or boost brain power. None will make significant differences in a healthy individual's performance that researchers can consistently substantiate. However, overall diet can affect how well the brain functions. The problem is sorting through all the claims and research, because many findings regarding diet appear to conflict. Health food supplements are difficult to assess because there is an almost total lack of careful research on the effect of many brands. However, many people believe supplements make a difference, and the placebo effect, the mere desire or expectation to feel better, can have a profound beneficial influence (Benedetti, et al. 2006). Who hasn't heard the claims about someone's Aunt Minnie who took an extract and now feels wonderful? About a decade ago there were a number of TV advertisements that heavily marketed gingko biloba. The public spent untold millions on it, but gingko biloba makes no significant difference in preventing dementia or Alzheimer's or in helping people with those afflictions (DeKosky et al., 2008; Dodge, Zitzelberger, Oken, Howieson, & Kaye, 2008). If a person's diet is seriously deficient in some particular way, and many adolescent diets are out of balance, then some vitamins, extracts, supplements, or changes in fat calorie intake *may* produce a change. I've seen it in my own family, but in most cases the diet had been seriously out of balance.

A cautionary note about health food supplements is in order. Millions of people use them as alternative medicine, but there is no uniform standard for quality or testing, if they are tested at all. The active ingredients may be quite different from what the label claims and a consumer has no way of knowing. Also, the relationships between dietary supplements as preventatives are weak, and few studies have been carried out on adolescents. Consequently, changing diets is not risk-free (Tomlinson, Wilkinson, & Wilkinson, 2009). Changes in diets or medications should only be done under the supervision of an appropriately licensed health care provider. Still, the cheapest and arguably the best route an adolescent can take toward diet-affected brain health is a well-balanced, age-appropriate diet. I'll briefly review what the brain/mind needs for more optimal function.

Carbohydrates

The glucose is the fuel for the brain and is absolutely essential for thinking, although the sugar needs to be released steadily and not all at once. When the brain lacks the glucose fuel, it doesn't think as well; a person is slower and the thinking is foggy. Insulin, produced by the pancreas, helps to regulate the glucose levels in the blood. If an adolescent eats a sugary, high *glycemic* breakfast in which sugars are quickly released, such as cornflakes, raisin bran, bagels, Cocoa Puffs, Cheerios, or puffed wheat, the blood sugar may spike and then crash. While the glucose level is high, an adolescent's thinking is fine, but when it crashes, there may be hypoglyce-mic conditions. The pancreas is stressed into releasing too much insulin when there is a sudden load of glucose from food. The massive release of insulin can rapidly reverse the high glucose levels, plummeting the student into a hypoglycemic state where the sugar is generally below 53 gm/dl, which is not good for thinking at all. When a student is hypoglycemic he may feel feverish, lightheaded, very pale, wob-bly, and disoriented. This may last around a half hour or so. The exact glucose levels for hypoglycemia vary with the individual (Cryer, 2001). Usually a small amount of fruit juice will bring sugar levels back up to normal in about 15 to 20 minutes.

A low glycemic breakfast produces a more constant supply of glucose, allowing the brain to work more evenly. Low glycemic foods include nonfat yogurt, skim milk, cherries, apples, bran cereal, natural muesli, and oatmeal (Brand-Miller et al., 1999). A proper diet avoids the problems of fluctuating glucose levels, particularly if the *glycemic load* is considered in meal plans so sugars are released constantly. Gly-cemic load (GL) combines information about the size of the food portion with how fast it will release sugar into the bloodstream. *The lower the glycemic load, the slower the sugars are released for that portion of food* (see Appendix A for a list of glycemic loads). Foods with GL at 10 gm or lower are more ideal, while foods that score a GL of 20 + should be avoided when possible or eaten only sparingly. This is more useful than simply knowing how fast the sugars are released (called the *glycemic index*).

Generally, having some protein first, such as from eggs, before the carbohy-drates, slows down the absorption of the sugars and helps to keep glucose levels stable. Eating complex carbohydrates, with their long chains of sugars rather than the simple sugars that make up so many of today's cereals, also slows the release of glucose. It takes more time to break down the complex carbohydrates to the simple glucose. Simple sugars, found in fruits (such as fructose in corn syrup), high-energy drinks, and energy bars, are very rapidly broken down into glucose and absorbed. These foods can create a tremendous glycemic load, rocketing the glucose levels in the blood first up, then down, when insulin kicks in. *An adolescent's performance improves not only when she has a breakfast, but when the glucose is available to the brain in a steady manner from cereals with lower glycemic loads* (Gibson, 2007; Ingw-ersen, Defeyter, Kennedy, Wesnes, & Scholey, 2007). What the brain needs in order to fuel its thinking is a steady source of glucose. Using a food's GL to plan meals is simpler than trying to figure out which foods have complex or simple sugars. Meals designed properly with lower GL can reduce the potential for hypoglycemia, im-prove athletic performance, and also reduce the probability for diabetes, cancers, cardiovascular disease, or obesity.

Fats and oils: Omega 6, Omega 3

The bulk of the brain is made of fats found in the myelin sheath, and the adolescent brain is built from what an adolescent eats, which may not be too encouraging. While there are a number of significant fats related to brain function, all of which are influenced by diet, several are especially important. These are the Omega 6 fats made from linoleic acids (LA), and two types of Omega 3 fats, EPA and DHA made from apha-linoleic acids. (DHA is a fat and should not be confused with the steroid DHEA.) For a properly functioning, growing adolescent body, just any fat won't do. The body and brain need specific fats and that excludes almost all fried foods and fatty red meats that are commonly in the teenage diet. Additionally, the body can't convert one fat into another kind: An Omega 6 cannot be changed into an Omega 3. For optimal function, the diet should be in balance regarding the amount of Omega 6 to Omega 3. Historically, our diets may have been in the near ideal ratio of 1:1, but now it is not unusual to find an Omega 6 concentration 20 to 40 times greater than Omega 3 (Schmidt, 2007). With today's fried foods, adolescents tend to eat foods high in Omega 6 fats and low in Omega 3.

Foods high in Omega 6 are common cooking oils, such as oils of safflower, sunflower, sesame, and corn plants. Omega 6 foods often include donuts, ice cream, french fries, onion rings, milkshakes, potato chips, butter and margarine, cheese, bacon, and steaks.

Foods high in Omega 3, with EPA and DHA, are fish, such as atlantic cod, haddock, halibut, mackerel, pink salmon, sardines, sea bass, rainbow trout, bluefin tuna, skipjack tuna, mussels, and scallops; plants, such as green leafy vegetables and avocados; and foods made from or containing nuts, such as candlenut, hemp seed oil, soybean, canola, and algae oils (which are important for vegetarians desiring a nonmeat source of omega 3), flax, flaxseed oil, English walnuts, brazil nuts, and chia seeds.

Having the correct types of fats is important because they affect brain development and maintenance, not only in adolescents but also for the fetus and growing infant. An expectant mother is a baby's only source of crucial fatty acids. A healthy baby needs a healthy mother. For a pregnant teen, the effects of eating foods with Omega 3 have been linked to their children having higher IQ scores; without proper levels of Omega 3, children have an increased risk of lower verbal intelligence (Hibbeln et al., 2007).

Proteins

The adolescent body is still growing and needs about 0.8 gm of protein per kg (or 2.2 lb; National Academy of Sciences, 1989), while athletes need about 1.2–1.8 gm/kg (Tarnopolsky, 1988). Proteins are the source of the 21 necessary amino acids. Complete proteins, such as meats, supply all 21 amino acids. Plants supply proteins as well, but not all 21 amino acids at the same time; consequently, a carefully selected variety of plants must be eaten to obtain the necessary amino acids. When protein is consumed, its amino acids are reassembled under the DNA's direction to build vital enzymes for running the body. Many enzymes directly affect the function of the neurons of the brain. Sources of protein include red meats, fish, eggs, dairy products, nuts, and beans.

Table 2.2. ESTIMATED CALORIE REQUIREMENTS FOR ADOLESCENTS				
Female	**Age**	**Sedentary**	**Moderately Active**	**Active**
12–19 years old, mean caloric intake = 1,993 calories	9–13	1,600	1,600–2,000	1,800–2,200
	14–18	1,800	2,000	2,400
	19–30	2,000	2,000–2,200	2,400
Male	**Age**	**Sedentary**	**Moderately Active**	**Active**
12–19 years old, mean caloric intake = 2,686 calories	9–13	1,800	1,800–2,000	2,000–2,600
	14–18	2,200	2,400–2,800	2,800–3,200
	19–30	2,400	2,600–2,800	3,000

Source: Institute of Medicine of the National Academies (2002).

Caloric intake

Carbohydrates, fats, and proteins can all be converted into energy. Nationwide, the caloric intake is on the rise and physical activity is declining as witnessed by the increasing problems of obesity in youth. The amount of calories an adolescent needs depends on his or her level of activity. There is a brain/mind connection because the amount of calories consumed affects an adolescent's fitness, which, in turn, impacts academic performance. Eating too many calories without enough appropriate physical activity leads to poorer health, and that corresponds to poorer academic performance. *An adolescent who is generally more physically fit and active typically performs better academically* (J. Ratey, 2008). Those who are less fit, overweight, or obese often do more poorly. However, it is difficult to start exercising, let alone maintain being physically active, when a person is overweight. *Establishing proper dietary habits during adolescence is important, especially if they did not have a proper diet earlier in childhood.* Establishing new dietary behaviors is difficult because of the incomplete growth of the brain's frontal lobe, thus contributing to impaired decision making and general lack of thought to future consequences. Unfortunately, unhealthy dietary choices and eating habits may extract a harsh payment later in life by profoundly impacting on adolescents' physical and cognitive health as they become adults. Listed in Table 2.2 are the estimated energy requirements through adolescence.

Vitamin, minerals, and antioxidants

Blood tests, in particular a *metabolic profile*, can reveal if vitamins, critical minerals, or other nutrients are out of balance. If there is a possibility of a deficiency in the diet, the physician may recommend age-appropriate vitamin supplements. However, the necessary vitamins can often be obtained more inexpensively by purchasing fresh food, especially vegetables and fruits, as opposed to buying special and expensive supplements. Another important food characteristic is that many foods retain far more of their helpful properties if they are not boiled but are eaten raw or steamed. Having school meals not heavily laden in fat and starches has helped, too, but there is considerable room for improvement, especially by using certain types of fats and foods with a lower GL. Occasionally, a number of mental problems or disorders, such as depression or ADHD, can be successfully addressed by precise changes in diet based on a metabolic profile. *One of the first things that a physician or a psychologist may recommend is to adjust the diet. It is the simplest thing a person can do, and it is usually the easiest change,* although the evidence for improvement in a broad population is not well substantiated at this time (Tomlinson et al., 2009). This lack of a general improvement for the general population highlights a critical point and what is a new approach to mental health (Leyse-Wallace, 2008). Mental health issues and their underlying causes are unique and what works for one individual, especially with a diet, often will not work for another, but properly diagnosed dietary interventions can be very helpful. There are easily hundreds of chemical dietary and brain interactions. Broadly speaking, these will fall into different categories of intake, uptake (absorption), utilization, and metabolic responses, among others. A change in any of these may change a person's mental health. The theory goes like this: The brain is made of chemicals, which interact with each other, so a large number of mental health issues are the expression of imbalances of brain chemistry. If you change the brain chemistry (through diet, supplements, exercise, or medications), you can change the mental health issue. By using a metabolic profile, a physician can create an intervention for the individual's identified chemical imbalances instead of relying on a shotgun approach of generalized dosing with medicines. If the problems persist after dietary change under the guidance of licensed health care professionals, other tested interventions should be considered.

Many of the brain and nutrition books and Internet websites make numerous associations with all sorts of mental disorders and general cognitive function. While very modest effects are sometimes observed, the linkages found by research are still rather poor. Unfortunately, to complicate matters, research results about the connections between adolescents, diet, and the brain are even rarer; we simply don't know much yet. Hence, there is reluctance to make many dietary suggestions in respect to the brain.

Most adolescents do not consume enough Vitamin A or C, particularly if they smoke. Additionally, adolescents are frequently deficient in many B vitamins, and girls are frequently low in calcium and iron (Kretchmer & Zimmermann, 1997).

Besides a potential iron shortage when girls menstruate, other minerals such as zinc and magnesium may be in short supply in the adolescent diet. These minerals help to produce enzymes used in the neurons, and magnesium has recently been confirmed to play a more basic role in memory creation than previously believed (Slutsky et al., 2010). Vitamin D is necessary for appropriate bone growth, and vitamin E affects cell reproduction. Both vitamin E and Omega 3 are major antioxidants.

Antioxidants are chemicals that help absorb the DNA-damaging free radicals produced by stress. Damage from free radicals can accumulate over time. Reducing this damage lowers the risk of Alzheimer's Disease or dementia, as well as a more immediate lowering of cardiovascular damage, especially for those adolescents with some genetic risk as indicated by their family history (Small, 2002). However, the overall health benefit of becoming more fit also helps cognitive processing. Educators can do a simple and informative dietary survey by having the students place a number by how many times a week they eat each food, and then discuss it with them.

A number of fruits and vegetables are also excellent sources of antioxidants and have been measured for their ability to absorb free radicals. Some receive ORAC scores for Oxygen Radical Absorbency Capacity (USDA, 2007). Some of the better foods are listed in Table 2.3. Because there are several methods of calculating absorption of free radicals, the foods are not ranked by ORAC scores.

Table 2.4 lists known dietary influences on the nervous system. What is apparent in the table is that many of these affect pregnant women, fetuses, and young children. Why are they included within a work about adolescents? First, the adolescents we see may have been subjected to such dietary influences by their parents or when their mothers were pregnant. Second, there are a significant number of teenage pregnancies, and as new parents, teenagers don't know much about their own diet let alone about prenatal care. Third, teenage parents also need to know what their dietary lifestyles may do to their children. Educators and counselors may be their only sources of information. In an era when most people follow exceptionally poor diets, this is another necessary piece of information for having mentally healthy children.

Alcohol

Alcohol abuse by adolescents is not unusual. Beyond the well-known effects of alcohol on teenage driving, and its associated high death rate, there is also now evidence that binge drinking causes permanent damage to the attention systems (Tapert, in press). Equally serious is alcohol's extraordinary ability to deplete the entire range of vitamins (A, the B series, C, D, and E) and the Omega 3 and 6 fats, as well as reduce critical minerals such as magnesium. Alcohol also interferes with the glucose levels of blood, which increases the risk for diabetes. Simply put, if the adolescent wants a better functioning brain, he or she should steer clear of alcohol.

In summary, adolescents (as well as adults) need to stay away from heavily processed foods and fried foods, while significantly increasing their consumption of

Table 2.3. FRUITS AND VEGETABLES WITH EXCELLENT ANTIOXIDANT PROPERTIES

Berries
- Blackberries
- Blueberries
- Cranberries
- Elderberries
- Currants (raw)

Apples
- Dried
- Granny Smith (raw)
- Red Delicious (raw)

Vegetables and Beans
- Artichokes
- Black beans
- Red kidney beans
- Pinto beans

Nuts
- Almonds
- Pecans
- Pistachio nuts (raw)
- Walnuts

Other
- Plums with peel (raw)
- White raisins
- Dried pears
- Prunes, dried and uncooked
- Many spices

fresh, leafy green vegetables, fruits, and fish rich in Omega 3. Adolescents' caloric intake seems to be rising with a concurrent decrease in physical activity, which creates a very worrisome trend toward obesity. That combination is not only poor for general health, but poor for the brain as well.

Table 2.4. DIETARY INFLUENCES ON THE NERVOUS SYSTEM

Amino Acids and Proteins
A constant supply of amino acids is needed for brain proteins in the first 2 years. Amino acids are the precursors to neurotransmitters and must be present in order to build all the neurotransmitters.
A lack of protein and energy results in deficient mental development, and stunted growth. Supplements can be beneficial.

Vitamins and Minerals
Vitamins and minerals are essential for normal brain function.
Vegan mothers who breastfeed may have infants at high risk for lack of B12; children who are vegans should possibly be given B12 supplements.
A diet deficient in B vitamins may contribute to dementia, memory loss, and depression in older adults.
Excess vitamin A in the fetus can lead to major abnormalities.
Deficiency in folate may contribute to defects in the fetus's neural tube.
Deficiency in iodine may cause major brain damage.
Deficiency in iron may cause impaired cognition and poor psychomotor development. It is one of the most preventable deficiencies.
Vitamin E may be helpful for some brain disorders and for the absorption of free radicals.
Newborns with jaundice may be treated with riboflavin to reduce toxicity of bilirubin in the brain.

School meals

As with so many things with the mind/brain systems, there is not a direct connection between what is served at school, beyond having a good breakfast, and cognitive performance. Diet is one more piece of the complex puzzle that creates the mind. Approximately 30–40% of children in the United States are overweight and obese. Of these, about two thirds will become obese adults and will then decrease their life span by approximately 5 to 20 years (Miller, Rosenbloom, & Silverstein, 2004). If too many calories are consumed (not enough calories burned, suggesting a lack of sufficient exercise) this will create overweight or obese students. The diet/obesity problem may be connected to academic performance.

When we consider the problem a bit further, it rapidly becomes more complicated. About one third of the calories are consumed at school at breakfast and
lunch programs (Neumark-Sztainer, French, Hannan, Story, & Fulkerson, 2005).
The foods made available are often fatty foods like french fries. Nearly 81% of the
schools in the United States exceed the recommended fat levels for foods (Gordon et
al., 2009). Compounding this problem is the availability of foods that compete with
USDA-sponsored school meals. These foods may come from vending machines, or
students may pick other fat-laden, high-calorie foods or eat at fast-food restaurants.
There are just too many calories available in the wrong types of foods at schools and
this contributes to students' weight gain.

Overweight kids, as well as many others, do not get sufficient exercise. The
amount of time that all kids spend sitting in front of some sort of digital screen (using computers, playing video games, texting) is growing (Carr, 2010). Kids prefer
digital entertainment to playing or doing something physical where there is body
movement. We cannot make a clear link at this time between meals, obesity, exercise, and cognitive performance, but portions along this chain are being linked to
each other in research (Brown & Summerbell, 2008). What schools can do is remove
or limit vending-machine snacks and sodas; reduce the availability of french fries,
other potato-based foods, and fried foods; and make healthy foods more prominent
and more attractive on campus so students do not leave school at lunchtime (Budd
& Volpe, 2006). Fortunately, educators can do something about the level of physical
activity their students have. The level of physical activity by a student does have
significant beneficial effects on the mind/brain systems and is explored next.

Movement and exercise

The brain has nerve extensions going out to the farthest reaches of the body where it
retrieves information and sends new commands back through other neurons. Movement that elevates the heart rate helps to maintain brain health with the added benefit of simultaneously keeping the rest of the body healthy, too. Exercise in adolescents and schools in general is not at levels that facilitate better cognitive function
(Hedley et al., 2004; J. Ratey, 2008). From 1991 to 2003 student enrollment in physical education (PE) in the United States fell from 42% to 28%. A parallel but opposite
trend to the decrease in physical activity was a tripling of overweight youths to 16%
of the population after 1980 (Centers for Disease Control and Prevention, 2004). In
the next section I will explore how the brain benefits from exercise. John Ratey,
of Harvard Medical School, has said that "exercise is the single most powerful tool
you have to optimize your brain function" (2008, p. 245). He has also suggested that
exercise improves learning on three levels. First, it helps to create a mind-set that
facilitates improvement in attention, alertness, and motivation. Second, it stimulates
neurons to make new connections to each other and to create more receptors for
a chemical called BDNF (brain-derived neurotrophic factor), which contributes to
stabilizing memory. Third, exercise stimulates stem cells in the hippocampus to develop new neuron cells (Colcombe & Kramer, 2003; J. Ratey, 2008).

Hundreds of studies and several large meta-analyses have found that academic performance and cognitive performance improve with exercise, and certain types of exercise produce greater benefits. Exercise has positive effects on cognition across the life span. In contrast, many adolescents' poor health decisions are reflected by their obsessions with fast food and lack of exercise, and this continues to be a topic of urgency among health care professionals. More than 170 studies have found exercise to have significant positive benefits for students' cognitive function, and this applies across different ethnic and economic groups (Chomitz et al., 2009; Etnier et al., 1997; Sibely & Etnier, 2003). Not all PE activities will produce gains academically and cognitively. The nature of the activity is very important. Many educators probably recall PE games where sides were chosen and the dreaded embarrassment for the poor kids who were picked last. "Loser" is what many thought of these kids, including the kids being picked last. PE classes that increase both cognitive and physical fitness don't have to have "losers." Rather than competing against each other, where it is not uncommon for some students to sit out and be uninvolved, students can measure their performances against themselves.

What should the exercise do for the student?

First, let's examine some important characteristics exercise should have if it is to help students cognitively. Vigorous exercise is better than moderate exercise in respect to higher academic performance (Coe, Pivarnik, Womack, Reeves, & Malina, 2006). John Ratey's review and recommendations in *Spark* (2008) on exercise and the brain summarize that *beneficial activities are those that combine an elevated heart rate with complex movement and the acquisition of a skill. That is important. The elevated heart rate is in reference to the student's personal heart-rate performance.*

To know the beneficial levels for an individual, the instructor needs to know the student's maximum heart rate. This is done by measuring the heart rate with a monitor strapped across the chest, as the student is exercising, which also allows the student to self-monitor. Some models will also automatically record the rate while engaged in various activities. Many brands are available. The kids do not have to be stuck on a treadmill. They can engage in many activities while wearing the monitors. There are slightly different iterations on how to figure the maximum heart rate, but generally it is 220 hpm (heartbeats per minute) minus age. For example, if you are 35 years old it would be about 220 - 35 = 185 hpm. For a 16-year-old, it would be 220 – 16 = 204 hpm. These are *general* guidelines. The actual program should be reviewed by a coach, trainer, or physician before starting.

What does the elevated heart rate do for the brain? The heart rate triggers different reactions that affect neurons. John Ratey (2008) compared walking, jogging, and running. When a person starts to exercise, blood flow is shifted away from the brain to the muscles, which have an immediate need to receive glucose and oxygen while simultaneously removing cell wastes generated by the increased activity. One consequence is that a person can't learn difficult material during the exercise; the re-

Table 2.5. SAMPLES OF EXERCISES OR ACTIVITIES WITH COMPLEX MOVEMENTS		
Team Sports	**Individual or Paired Sports**	**General Fitness**
Volleyball Flag football Basketball Rugby	Climbing cargo nets or rope ladders	Step aerobics Tai chi
Water polo	Rocking on an exercise ball, simultaneously stacking cups or jogging or lifting small weights while balanced on an exercise ball	Weight lifting, or lifting small amounts of weights while in an out-of-balance position, with spotters
Soccer	Sport rock climbing (when done properly this can be very aerobic; games of adding or eliminating moves can be done)	Cardio kickboxing
Tennis (pairs) Badminton Table tennis	High rope courses	Orienteering and fell or hill running without trails up steep gradients
Swing, line, square dancing, Scottish Highland Fling, or sword dancing	Slack line walking, similar to a tightrope, but only inches off the ground	Tap dancing
Floor hockey	Balance beam	Gymnastics Resistance training
	Biking Unicycle riding	Yoga Pilates Stretching

Table 2.6. SAMPLE EXERCISES WITH LITTLE OR NO COMPLEX MOVEMENT (SIMPLE REPETITIONS)
Jumping jacks
Squat thrusts
Many weight/strength-training exercises with barbells when the same form of repetition is used, such as curls, lunges, leg extensions, pull-downs, bench presses, pull-ups, chin-ups, laterals, and lifts (with some thought, and advice and direction from a trainer, these maybe slightly modified into complex exercises with out-of-balance movement if using a low weight)
Skipping rope, if this is done with exactly the same skip or hop (however, this is easily varied by making the skipping more difficult)

sources aren't available. During exercise a cascade of reactions is occurring; many key hormones and enzymes are being made that are especially helpful to learning and building nerve connections. However, right after the exercise more blood shifts back to the brain and prefrontal cortex where so much of the higher thinking goes on and it brings with it many of the important chemicals. The amount of benefit received appears to depend on the level of exercise, something like the old saw "no pain, no gain." Vigorous walking (a low-intensity level of exercise) pushes the heart to about 55–65% of the maximum, which is enough to start promoting positive changes. Jogging lifts the heart rate to a moderate level of about 75–85% of the maximum. At this level the exercise starts tearing down tissue and rebuilding. Chemical signals are released for triggering the growth of more blood vessels which facilitates cell growth and neurogenesis (J. Ratey, 2008). These signals include vascular endothelial growth factor (VEGF), which helps to consolidate memory and fibroblast growth factor (FGF-2), which helps stimulate LTP and memory formation.

The brain produces natural antioxidants, which help to reduce DNA-damaging free radicals, all without the aid of pills when there is sufficient exercise. A free radical is a highly reactive chemical that occurs naturally, or it can be man-made and found in products such as in cigarette smoke. If cells are to work correctly, damage to DNA must be avoided. In the nuclei of cells, free radicals may act something like bullets ricocheting around, randomly damaging sections of DNA. The more free radicals there are, the sooner the damage accumulates to a point where the body's cells aren't working correctly. Antioxidants help mop up many free radicals and slow down the damage. Common antioxidants are vitamins A, C, and E, but these should be taken at recommended levels.

The next level of exercise includes shorts bursts of high intensity such as sprints and running or walking steadily and rapidly up a very steep hill, which can push the heart to 75–90% of the maximum but at a rate that an adolescent can keep up for 40–60 minutes. However, one of the greatest benefits of the exercise is the production of BDNF, which John Ratey has described as "Miracle Gro for the brain" because of its widespread beneficial effects (2008, p. 40). BNDF affects increased synaptic growth, affects learning and LTP, and links movement, thought, and emotions. A nonprofit group that has incorporated these cognitively beneficial exercise strategies in schools is PE4life, which also participates in several university research programs. PE4life has developed a program used by adolescents in public schools and this has demonstrated significant benefits for the students. The program includes a comprehensive book with workouts, strategies, materials needed, and a CD (PE4life, 2007). There are a number of successful school examples of the academic benefits being derived from carefully designed PE programs. Perhaps the most well-known program is found in Illinois's Naperville Central High School where its cardio program is designed to help improve classroom learning.

Another side benefit to increased exercise is greater production of serotonin, a key mood stabilizer. It changes attitudes. An international test of student math and science skills called TIMSS found Naperville to be first in the *world* for science and sixth in math. While team sports are still played, *the emphasis is on students getting their heart rate up into the target zone and keeping it there for a while.* (See more precise training recommendations in PE4life, 2007.) Not only did students become more fit, but they also shifted focus *to achieving personal bests with the nice addition of improved academic performance.*

Unfortunately, not all exercise-activity programs work equally well, and some of their claims are based on faulty and thoroughly discredited science, yet they are still popular. Brain Gym's claims appear to a number of researchers to be based up three theoretical categories: neurological repatterning, cerebral dominance, and perceptual-motor training. *None* of the simplistic dimensions of focusing and centering as interpreted by Brain Gym and on which they've built their program have demonstrated increased learning. Their claimed links to specific academic gains are disputed and not supported by peer-reviewed research (American Academy of Pediatrics, 1968, 1998; Arter & Jenkins, 1979; Cohen, 2005; Hyatt, 2007; Kavale & Forness, 1987; Kavale & Mattson, 1983; Mayringer & Wimmer, 2002; Mohan, Singh, & Mandal, 2001; J. Ratey, 2008; Salvia & Ysseldyke, 2004). *Therefore, it appears that ritualized movements to improve academic performance may be a neuromyth. However, this does not suggest vigorous movements lack benefit, but the necessity of specific types is questioned.*

When my graduate students did an in-class investigation about a myth regarding a connection between cognitive performance and oxygen levels, the myth didn't hold up, and the results surprised us. The graduate students performed a Stroop effect test, where we measured their accuracy in naming colors and the corresponding levels of oxygen saturation in their blood before any exercise. The graduate students then performed a standard PE activity called a step test for 1 minute. We immediately conducted another Stroop effect test while measuring their oxygen levels. What we found was the oxygen levels remained at saturation (99%), demonstrating no change. Lower levels of oxygen did not play a role in their performance, but of more interest was their cognitive performance after exercise. We expected more errors and more time would be needed to complete the task. The Stroop task was finished about 30–40% faster and with considerably fewer errors. Subsequent experiments with the little 1-minute activity demonstrated the effect of increased naming speed and accuracy lasted about 30 minutes. The in-class physical exercises supported Dr. John Ratey's propositions about vigorous exercise's beneficial effects as he outlined in his book *Spark*. A precise exercise regimen that a school must buy is not necessary if educators pay attention to the principles involved. The only necessary cost is a single book that can thoroughly describe the changes needed, such as those recommended by PE4life. Given what is known about the benefits, or the lack of them, an educator's valuable class time is probably better spent in vigorous complex movement for a few minutes several times a day than in engaging in ritualized movements that do not affect brain processes. A program that is based on faulty, discredited, and simplistic science cannot be recommended in good conscience.

Communication

As we have seen, neurons are specialized into different systems located throughout the brain, and they are maintained, in part, through nutrition. This creates a foundation where newly acquired information is manipulated by the processes that make up learning and from which new skills emerge. Other aspects of those processes, including attention, emotions, motivation, and various forms of memory, are layered onto and then become part of that foundation. At the same time these complex processes weave together and influence one another and this allows communication, one of the most basic skills involved in learning, to emerge.

When adolescents arrive as our students, their communication skills are already shaped by long histories. A considerable portion of how educators gauge students' learning is based upon some form of their ability to communicate. If an adolescent has deficits in communication, it is likely to impact his or her academic performance. Other neural-cognitive processes will certainly affect performance as well, and those will be the subjects of different chapters in turn. However, because communication is the vehicle for both the acquisition and expression for much of learning, we will consider it next.

In addition to the health of the body and brain, communication is a fundamental cognitive process that affects adolescents and has the power to shift students' potential for success. Communication—more specifically reading, writing, and acquisition of a second language—has an enormous effect on adolescents' academic performances, let alone their futures. The communication struggles that teenagers face were first begun years earlier. In order to understand their current problems, and interventions for persistent problems, we must also explore the acquisition of communication skills.

Spoken language, reading, and writing

Everyday educators make assumptions about their students' ability to communicate effectively. When students do poorly in school, it is not unusual to find problems in their communication skills. Being able to communicate a wide range of information through written and spoken language quickly and accurately is clearly advantageous. The significance of this becomes only too obvious if you're in a foreign country and don't speak the local language. The following example illustrates the assumption that the brain has the ability to swiftly and accurately communicate.

High in the Andes of South America, a group of adventurers needed to have some equipment packed out from their base camp by some of the local people. However, there was no common language between the adventurers and the locals, who used Quechua, an ancient Inca dialect. To make the situation more difficult, there was no one to interpret. A sign language was improvised on the spot. It was a demanding dilemma. How would one convey, without a single word in common, that they needed burros to carry out equipment 10 days from the present? It would make an interesting challenge for students to communicate an abstract idea along with needs for something very tangible, such as the need for four burros. Everyone laughed at the clumsy attempts to understand each other. The locals were motivated because they could earn some good money for the use of their burros. After more than an hour of creative pantomimes, wildly gesticulating arms, drawing in the dirt, and helpful noises all resembling a badly played game, the adventurers believed the locals understood that they should arrive 10 days hence. But they weren't sure, and with some anxiety they trekked off into the mountains. However, the efforts paid off, and the locals and their burros showed up right on time.

Breakdowns in communication create problems for everyone: whether it occurs between a student and teacher, an employee and a boss, or one country and another country. Wars have started in part because of poor communication. With education, communication is pivotal, and with the ethnicity of our population shifting rapidly, where many parents and students are non-English speakers, acquisition of a second language is of paramount importance in many schools, as well as for future employment.

A number of systems have evolved in the brain that facilitate communication, and these directly and indirectly affect education. Physical actions, the different memory systems, the limbic (emotional processing) system, attention, and communication are among those that can provide us with potentially useful insights and interventions in learning. Communication skills have such an enormous influence on students' reading and writing success that it is imperative for educators to understand what happens in the brain that impacts the students' communication performance. I will first examine how events early in life continue to impact the adolescents' communication, followed with an exploration of reading and writing problems such as dyslexia, and I will then describe interventions for the adolescent.

The brain has evolved specific areas for processing language. Other primates have the same areas for processing sounds, but they are not nearly as well developed when compared to our brain. These structures in the brain are now specialized for producing language. Two of these language structures are in the left hemisphere, which, broadly summarized, are Broca's area (for producing words and names) and Wernicke's area (for handling word meanings) (see Figure 2.3). Both areas are also involved in higher levels of thinking (Bookheimer et al., 1998; Thompson-Schill, Aguirre, Esposito, & Farah, 1999).

Plasticity of the brain and language

Much of an adolescent's educational performance depends on the language skills that are acquired early in life. The ability to communicate through language, reading, and writing is the foundation of a student's education. A student who has difficulty using spoken language or written communication is potentially at greater risk for academic failure, which highlights the importance that educators need to have some understanding of these fundamental skills.

The brain's ability to acquire new information means the wiring connections are changing. If the connections could not be altered, learning would not be possible. This ability to change and learn is called *plasticity*. A neuron's ability to change affects all the rest of the processing in the brain, from emotional control to memory. A student's success in school or success as an adult is impacted by the changes in the brain. When a baby is first born, the brain is highly plastic, and the brain's acquisition of language skills is greatly influenced by what happens to the growing child, which in turn influences the student's ability to use language and to read as an adolescent. It is necessary to first look at what happens earlier in life in order to better understand some of an adolescent's reading and language problems.

Beginnings of communication

The brain starts to specialize its responses to language very early in life. During infancy, both hemispheres of the brain display sensitivity for language processing (Mills, Coffey-Corina, & Neville, 1997) but this shifts to the left hemisphere's temporal and parietal lobes by around 13–20 months as the infant's brain grows. There are also changes in sensitivity that can later affect adolescent language performance. For example, babies who are not yet speaking can distinguish between sounds such as "r" & "l," but this ability can be lost after 10 months (Gopnik, Meltzoff, & Kuhl, 1999). However, in testament to the brain's plasticity, a native Japanese speaker can later learn to distinguish the "r" and "l" sounds, but it is not easy (McClelland, Fiez, & McCandliss, 2002). The changes in plasticity also demonstrate there are periods of greater sensitivity in the brain's growth process. It is not, as sometimes is claimed, a severely limiting window of opportunity, which, if missed, is forever lost. However, learning a second language is easier if done before adolescence. Learning a second language later is not a closed door to learning but is a more difficult one to pass through. *It is a neuromyth that there are critical periods during which certain skills must be taught in order to be learned, because they cannot be learned later.*

Many public schools don't offer a second language until students are in middle school or high school. Offering the language later, as students begin adolescence, makes the acquisition more difficult for the brain, because the brain has lost some of its sensitivity to sounds. In order for the language skills to develop fully, specific circuits of the brain must be modified by appropriate language stimulation. Early exposure to language by parents, caregivers, or preschool teachers serves as a catalyst affecting the development of reading skills (Hart & Risley, 2003). If exposure to language occurs during the periods of sensitivity, how the brain processes language information is changed. For example, grammar is easier to master when started earlier (Neville & Bruer, 2001). When a child learns a second language between the ages of 1 and 3, the brain processes it in the left hemisphere, just as a native speaker would, almost as if it were a single language to the brain. After age 3, even as early as about 4–6 years old, the brain recruits more resources to process the language, and both hemispheres are called in to help process the second language (Organisation for Economic Co-operation and Development, 2007). Generally, the earlier schools or parents start children on learning a second language, assuming it is taught in an age-appropriate manner, the more effective it will be. For example, teaching a second language by using grammar abstractions (this is a noun; this is an adjective) does not make sense with younger children because those concepts are beyond their understanding. The grammar approach in teaching a second language is one of the problems encountered in many secondary schools. The abstract levels of understanding parts of speech are beyond a number of the students; they don't even know the parts of speech in English. However, they are perfectly capable of learning a language fluently when immersed in it as demonstrated by hundreds of thousands of youth who have learned different languages without being taught rules for formal parts of speech.

Accent is partially the result of learning the language after most of the brain's sensitive period has passed. If children learn the sounds (phonology) before early adolescence such as age 12, there is less accent because the brain can more easily distinguish the sounds (Neville & Bruer, 2001). Their sensitivity to hearing phonemes is different later. Unfortunately, schools create a much greater burden for the learner's brain by starting second languages in middle school or high school, a time when the brain has significant deficits for processing the grammar of the new language. Consequently, the brain must use other learning strategies incorporating different neural circuits, making the task considerably more difficult (Fledge & Fletcher, 1992).

When students enter adolescence, they begin to write more and tend to use the speech patterns they have learned at home. Disparities in their backgrounds may generate major hurdles in both reading and writing performance. The problems are compounded even more if the child must pick up English as a second language to communicate in school. When parents use a large variety of words, children tend to learn to use those words automatically and still acquire more words easily. In a word-impoverished home, or in a home where the diversity of words is considerably lower, babies and children learn fewer words because they are spoken to less frequently or with only the same limited vocabulary. This creates a situation where the word-rich become richer, and the word-poor fall even further behind (Hart & Risley, 2003). The differences in vocabulary and word variety do not get better with time but may worsen because many schools do not consistently devote much actual time to learning vocabulary, which, in turn, affects the student's reading (Wolf, 2007). For example, if a child from an impoverished background hasn't been exposed to a concept such as gravitational pull in their native tongue, it can be even harder to learn in the new language because there is not an already established concept to which it can be linked.

Reading: Brain plasticity in action

A brain that is learning to read is engaging in a remarkable feat. The linguist Steven Pinker noted, "Children are wired for sound, but print is an optional accessory that must be painstakingly bolted on" (quoted in McGuiness, 1997, p. ix). When a child learns to read, the process changes his or her brain physiologically as well as intellectually—it is never the same again (Wolf, 2007). For instance, if a person reads in two different languages, two different areas of the brain may be involved. The reading process and parts of the brain involved are not identical from language to language (Tan et al., 2003; Wolf, 2007). The brain does not use the same circuitry when reading Chinese characters versus English letters, which, of course, complicates helping a person with a reading disorder even more. For example, when a bilingual reader had a stroke, he lost the ability to read in Chinese but not in English (Lyman, Kwan, & Chao, 1938). Two different areas of the brain were involved.

Neurons also assist in the reading process for specific visual tasks; some work with lowercase letters, and still others may be used for diagonal lines (Gazzaniga et al., 2009; Kosslyn et al., 1993). As noted about the occipital lobe, networks of cells function together for a specific task without activating other networks, again illustrating the principle of neurons that fire together, wire together (Hebb, 1949). Taken as a whole, the environment in which children grow up, the diversity of vocabulary they are exposed to, and when they learned the phonemes or sounds of their native or new language in addition to other variables all affect their fluency in reading. As Maryanne Wolf observed in *Proust and the Squid* (2007), the learning brain, if it is going to read, must take older areas of the brain and establish new circuits and uses for them, even though they were originally genetically directed for different jobs.

When we listen to a language that we do not speak, it is like hearing different sounds in rapid-fire delivery. There are no spaces or acoustical cues to give any hint on where one word ends and another begins. Sounds that make up words have been analyzed for many languages. The smallest intact unit of sound is called a phoneme. If "phoneme" sounds odd to your ear, think of the word "phone" as in telephone. The sound's root word is the same. Languages based on alphabets use phonemes that are represented by letters or a small group of letters, such as "e" and "ph" for the fuff sound. In reading, we need symbols that we can understand to produce the sounds for words of our language. English readers and speakers use 26 letters; Chinese readers and speakers use about 4,000 characters to achieve the literacy to read newspapers or books. ChinaCulture.org (2009) reported that about 49,000 characters have been developed since the early dynasties and cuneiform, one of the very earliest written languages, used about 900 symbols. Writing and reading are difficult processes. Writing requires greater precision in selecting words to express our thoughts, to say as precisely as possible what we really mean. Writing, as Vygotsky (1962) observed, creates a powerful connection between the writer and reader through the words that were used.

In reading, the brain must also recognize patterns and make new networks. As it does so, some networks become specialized and strategies develop for analyzing patterns. Patterns are evaluated by the limbic system to determine if they have meaning, and by placing different values on the information we generate feelings about its significance. All the while, the external environment is relentlessly bombarding the brain with new information. Part of students' environment is the world their parents create and raise them in, and it seems to place an indelible stamp upon children's reading abilities. Hence, it is important to review what happens to the students' minds before educators see them in school.

The environment and the nature of children's early exposure to books can impact them for most of their lives. For example, the availability of books affects reading skills. It is difficult to learn to read and learn about the world if a child doesn't have something to read. Poor kids, growing up in Watts, had on average less than one book in the family, low-income families had about three books available to their kids, and the affluent over in Beverly Hills had roughly 200 books available in their households (Smith & Constantino, 1997). The difference in books available for reading extended to the classroom libraries as well: Poorer schools had only about 50 books available, and wealthier schools had close to 400 books, nearly an eightfold difference. Not only are the differences in the number of books available for reading striking, but the long-term effects on reading comprehension and vocabulary are significant, too. By the time book-deprived children reached sixth grade there is a gap with their well-read peers of roughly three grade levels (Biemiller, 1999). The poverty in books and language can create vastly different forms of childhood. The children miss out on stories being told, dreams being fulfilled, and millions of spoken words that could enrich their lives. The underprivileged children are handicapped academically before they ever start school. Their vocabulary is more sparse, fewer words are spoken, and spoken words are more often negative: "Don't do that"; "Stop that" (Hart & Risley, 2003). Another potential effect concerns the emotional connections a child or any learner makes with reading. If an emotional link isn't made quickly with either reading or the lesson, what follows is likely to be a struggle. In reading, Wolf observed that "emotional engagement is often the tipping point between leaping into the reading life or remaining in a childhood bog where reading is endured" (2007, p. 132).

Research continues to produce a better understanding of the brain, which facilitates the design of more effective reading interventions. The brain is loaded with old hardware built up from eons of genetic patches that must meet the constantly changing demands of running a BlackBerry, the iPod, mp3 files, or Blu-ray discs. The demands on the brain are enormous, and sometimes it doesn't work quite right. For years I believed the neuromyth *that dyslexia was some mysterious process in reading where a person reversed the order of letters, or flipped them around* where a *b* might look like a *d,* and that slowed down the reading. I was wrong.

When the brain doesn't get it right: Dyslexia
Cultures around the world place great value on literacy; it is immensely important

to the success of students and to their respective societies. An illiterate society is also an economically handicapped one. How literate adolescent students are and their ability to read and write fluently plays a vastly important role in whether the student continues on with education or drops out through frustration. While dyslexic students often become better at decoding words, they need support throughout all their educational years. In the following section, I will explore the nature of dyslexia, how it is detected and tested, what the adolescent needs from teachers or tutors, and various forms of support that may be given to the student.

Dyslexia is a neurobiological disorder where there are problems with accurate and fluent word recognition and poor encoding and spelling, making reading, writing, and math difficult, even after instruction, though the person may be otherwise normal in respect to abilities and intelligence (Lyon, Shaywitz, & Shaywitz, 2003). Dyslexia is a problem that presents many faces and there is no fully agreed-upon definition (Wolf, 2007). The double-deficit hypothesis currently provides the two best predictors of dyslexia in younger students (Fawcett & Nicolson, 2001). Basically, if a person has these two specific problems, they are more likely to have dyslexia. One of the deficits is poor awareness of phonemes or sounds, which is essential for building a foundation in figuring out words. The other deficit is slow naming speed. For instance, a student may have one or both deficits. He may know what the name is for each of a variety of colors, but is unable to rapidly say their names (Denckla, 1972; Denckla & Rudle, 1976). The naming deficits also include not just names but also letter symbols, or any other symbols.

Being able to say a name is also significant for forming a memory. This is important even for students without dyslexia. The brain can't easily retrieve and spell or say a name that was never pronounced, because there is no network to access. This makes saying the names in vocabulary exercises important. The language arts, social studies, and sciences often introduce strange names to the students. By carefully modeling the pronunciation of the name, and doing it as a brief whole-class activity, no one has to suffer the embarrassment of stammering through it and mispronouncing the word in front of everybody.

With nearly 2.5 to 5% of all students being dyslexic and potentially at higher risk for dropping out, how does one detect and determine who needs support? There is no simple way to determine if a student has dyslexia just by observations in a classroom because many of the traits that teachers see in students may also be caused by other disorders such as Attention-Deficit Hyperactivity Disorder (ADHD). Approximately 10–20% of dyslexic students also have ADHD (Shaywitz & Shaywitz, 1991). There are, however, a number of traits that, if present, should serve as warning signs that the student's processing might be amiss and the student should be formally evaluated. Some of these include when a student

- Mispronounces names or parts of a name;
- Performs poorly on multiple-choice tests if timed; however, does better with extended time;

- Struggles to retrieve words (c.g., "it was on the tip of my tongue");
- Prefers to use simple and easy words to spell when writing;
- Is inarticulate in expressing feelings or emotions;
- Had difficulties with childhood reading and spelling;
- Makes wild guesses in recalling everyday words;
- Has difficulty following oral directions;
- Has poor metacognitive skills in respect to sounds;
- Can write but cannot read;
- Has difficulty blending letter sounds together;
- Has hearing problems;
- Uses finger to keep place while reading; becomes extremely fatigued from reading;
- Has normal intelligence but can't comprehend written material;
- Takes more time and has more difficulty copying information from board than other students;
- Has slow reading fluency (speed); takes considerable time to read a sentence or paragraph;
- Has difficulty in recalling spelling of words;
- Takes a very long time to complete in-class assignments (and it's obvious he or she is not stalling);
- Omits words or whole lines while reading;
- Has sloppy handwriting; misspells the same word in different ways;
- Is resistant to change; can be inflexible or rigid;
- Is slow to name letters, familiar objects, colors;
- Can be easily distracted; or
- Can decode words, but has little comprehension.

Just as *there is no simple method to use in class to determine who might be dyslexic, there is not one test or standard that can be used to determine whether a student is dyslexic.* Generally, dyslexia is difficult to identify because it can't be completely disentangled from other neurological processing problems (Hunter-Carsch & Herrington, 2001). Because dyslexia exists in subtypes that result from a variety of problems in brain circuitry, a battery of tests will need to be administered by a school psychologist. Many schools that determine whether a student is dyslexic by using how much discrepancy there is on their tests with a normed population will likely miss a number of students or disqualify those who are also in genuine need of support and are dyslexic. Part of the problem stems from the vagueness of Public Law 94-142, which describes whether a student is eligible for support services. Where a student lives and the interpretation of the student's level of discrepancy often determine who qualifies for support. Actual criteria are not uniform from school to school. Many schools use a student's level of performance on test scores to identify handicapping conditions. Unfortunately that strategy ignores the neuropsychological and perceptual functions that better describe the student's needs. Feifer and De Fina

(2000) strongly suggest that schools not use discrepancy as a standard. They noted that there is lack of agreement on what constitutes a discrepancy. The discrepancy process ignores early identification of the student, thereby increasing the harm and deficiencies. It is not clear what form of IQ measure should be used, and it fails to distinguish between poor readers and dyslexic readers. Perhaps one of the worst things is that the discrepancy process promotes waiting until a student fails before interventions are started. There is no single assessment that is fully adequate for determining dyslexia. Measures from most of the areas in the list below are generally necessary.

- Intelligence (evaluate for levels and patterns of performance)
- Phonological awareness
- Rapid naming tests
- Verbal memory tests
- Naming subtests
- Visual-spatial skills
- Set shifting and attention

What dyslexic students need from their teachers

Dyslexic students will need support and encouragement throughout their entire educational careers because dyslexia is something that cannot be cured. Emotional involvement from the teachers and other students, showing they genuinely care, can motivate the student. Students don't want to be treated as stupid or talked down to. They want staff to actually hear what they are saying (Palfreman-Kay, 2001). The support staff is in a partnership in discovering what works, using alternative pathways in the brain. Students want staff to have a better understanding of the disorder and to have staff with better preparation or training. *Students will have to discover for themselves what strategies presented by support staff will work best; it is an ongoing task achieved in close cooperation, as the support staff and students explore the accommodations together* (Klein, 2001). Labeling a student as lazy and then doing nothing to support the student does not solve problems. Too often, staff members will write off a student with a label, as if it explained everything, and then ignore the student. Dyslexia is a neurological disorder, not a literacy problem. Because the process of reading, writing, or even math is ponderous, students will need more time to produce academic work. Some students find that computer-assisted reading or having a staff member or peer read the material out loud can be of tremendous help.

The success of the student is largely dependent on the support he or she receives from the teacher or support staff (Gregg, 2009). For a dyslexic student, the reading instruction should be in the hands of an appropriately trained teacher or support staff with specific in-depth training for dyslexia. Unfortunately, that is frequently not the case. The differences between the dyslexic and others rapidly increase with each succeeding year if there is not adequate support (Goulandris & Snolwing, 2003). Although there will likely be a considerable initial gap between the reader and his or her peers, an intensive support program should be maintained even if the gap should close (Shaywitz, 2003). The teacher needs to have sufficient knowledge to know when to change the pace, repeat or slow down, or to find alternative explanations, which can only be accomplished if she is frequently interacting with the dyslexic student (Klein, 2001). A common mistake is to withdraw intensive support when the student appears to be making steady progress. Shaywitz (2003) notes that if the student is not identified early, as is the case for many adolescents, the student may need between 150 to 300 hours of intensive instruction, approximately 90 minutes per day almost every day for 1 to 3 years. There should also be a constant flow of communication between the classroom teacher, aides, and support staff.

The staff also needs to be genuine with the students by showing they care about the students as people (see Chapter 3). Both teachers and support staff should provide encouragement and instill confidence in the students. However, they should not allow the students to manipulate them or stall and wait for the aides to do all the work for them. One of the classic problems is for the student to rely so much on a trusted support staff person to explain the assignment later, that he or she ignores the teacher. Such students incorrectly believe success lies outside their control (see Chapter 5 on motivation). **For the benefit of all the students, the instruction and advice need to be explicit for writing, reading, and math assignments.** The instructions should be written on the board, given orally, and checked for understanding. When different learning strategies are being presented, your advice also needs to be very clear. The support staff should help the student understand that they are providing academic guidance, not counseling. Support staff also need to provide feedback to the teacher concerning whether the pace is too fast or complex, or whether the assignment needs to be scaled back so it is not too lengthy but still addresses the core academic issues.

Potential accommodations are listed in Table 2.7. These will need to be determined and formally laid out in the individual education plan (IEP); however, it is not necessary to wait for months to crawl by before implementing some of these.

Most intervention programs do work, as Shaywitz observed. "The specific reading program chosen from among them is far less important than the provision of systematic, explicit instruction in phonemic awareness and phonics, and teaching children how to apply this knowledge to reading" (2003, p. 263; Skottun & Skoyles, 2002).

Summary

The brain's ability to be plastic by altering connections and their strengths with other neurons allows the brain to learn a language and to read and write. While there are periods of sensitivity, these are not limited windows of opportunity. Learning still occurs, such as for specific sounds, but it is more difficult. Consequently the acquisition of a second language is recommended to start as early as possible, well before adolescence. Unlike spoken language, reading and writing have only recently come to the brain, necessitating that regions of the brain originally evolved for other

Table 2.7. SAMPLING OF ACCOMMODATIONS FOR DYSLEXIC STUDENTS
For Reading
Extra time, quiet room, text to speech (TTS) software, e-text (electronic text), enlarged print, optical character recognition (OCR; converts print to digital text for downloading), concept maps, reader guide, annotated text, think alouds, interpreter, visualization strategies, note-takers or scribes, embedded e-text supports. (Note: *The use of colored reading filters, also known as Irlen filters, lack empirical support and is probably a neuromyth.* They are *not* recommended for dyslexic students.)
For Writing (including handwriting, spelling, syntax, and composition of text)
Extra time, quiet room, shorter assignments, scribes or note-takers, audio voice player, embedded e-text supports, word processor, speech to text (SST) software, mouse options with Microsoft accessibility resources.

tasks be co-opted into handling all the chores of written language. The environment a student grows up in can severely handicap him or her if books are not available. A reading disorder, such as dyslexia, is a neurological problem that occurs across all literate cultures. It is complex and hard to detect with just classroom observation, necessitating a full battery of tests to evaluate the adolescent. Unfortunately, difficulty in detecting dyslexia causes many students with reading problems to be overlooked until well into their adolescent or adult years, significantly impairing their chances for success. Students with dyslexia need long-term support and the close involvement of staff who should both understand the disorder and have the appropriate training. The quality of the staff support is paramount, but the student must also have the development of phonemic awareness, use of phonics, fluency, and ability to apply those strategies to reading.

Key Points and Recommendations

Nutrition

- ***The lower the glycemic load, the slower the sugars are released for that portion of food.*** Much food has a high glycemic load and will release glucose too rapidly, causing the blood sugar levels to first rise and then fall. Foods with complex carbohydrates have lower glycemic loads and release their energy at a more steady rate. Use Appendix A for glycemic loads.
- ***An adolescent's performance improves not only when they have a breakfast, but also when the glucose is available to the brain in a steady manner from cereals with lower glycemic loads.*** A breakfast balanced with protein to slow down the release of glucose and carbohydrates

helps fuel the brain steadily throughout the morning, contributing to higher performance. The brain needs fuel throughout the entire morning to achieve an optimal performance.

- ***The bulk of the brain is made of fats found in the myelin sheath, and the adolescent brain is built from what an adolescent eats. The diet should be in balance when it comes to the amounts of Omega 6 and Omega 3 fats.*** Adolescent diets (as well as adult diets) tend to have far too many saturated fats and Omega 6 fats. Fried foods found in many fast-food stores tend to use saturated fats or those that are not Omega 3 fats, thus supplying large amounts of the wrong kind of fat plus a huge number of calories. The improper fats make it more difficult for the brain to function optimally. There should be a balance between the intake of Omega 6 and Omega 3, which are largely obtained through cold-water fish, or some algae. Additionally, the Omega 3 fats act as antioxidants, slowing down DNA damage.

- ***An adolescent who is generally more physically fit and active typically performs better academically.*** Being fit helps to generate a number of brain chemicals that facilitate brain function and contribute to academic performance. Vigorous exercise should be a daily routine throughout adolescence and into adult life.

- ***Establishing proper dietary habits during adolescence is important.*** Parents essentially are the models for proper diet. If they don't eat appropriately and direct how their children eat, the students rather than the parents establish the dietary habits. Good nutritional habits need to be instilled consistently and throughout childhood.

- ***In neurons, the movement of neurotransmitters, building of protein receptors, and their maintenance are quite important because these combined actions are a major portion of the processes of making memories.*** If any of these processes fails to function properly, the signal may be interfered with. If the problem is widespread, then disabilities may result.

- ***If a neuron is actively stimulated or repeatedly fired in particular circuits, it results in a stronger connection.*** Many learning practices are based upon this principle of neurons that fire together, wire together. Neural circuits that are frequently used become more stable. If the circuits for the memory of a concept, or way of thinking, are repeatedly stimulated and used, then information in the networks is easier to retrieve as well.

- ***Adjusting one's diet may be the easiest and cheapest route to addressing some issues, such as ADHD.*** Carefully review the diet; making it balanced will potentially improve overall health if not reduce some symptoms of a disorder. Exotic and expensive supplements have not shown any cognitive benefits in research except when there has been a deficiency in a diet. Consider a blood test and metabolic profile to address mental health issues, as these can help the unique individual problem. Some supplements have been found to be harmful (even fatal) because they have unregulated amounts of active ingredients.

Exercise

- *Exercise, with complex movement, should elevate the heart rate and be measured against the student's own personal heart rate.* Complex movement creates a greater challenge for the brain and helps to improve balance. Many of the complex movement activities are done individually and can be continued throughout life. They are not dependent upon team sports having winners and losers.
- *Exercise programs should accelerate the heart rate to appropriate levels, and if maintained for a suitable time they can impact academic performance.* There are now many studies showing the academic benefits of exercise students receive whether in PE or recess in addition to general health. It is extremely shortsighted to curtail or eliminate either PE or recess in order to gain time for studying for high-stakes tests. Students of *any age* need physical exercise breaks in order to maintain their cognitive levels.
- *Vigorous exercise should be done before academic classes in order to help generate chemical changes that facilitate learning and improve general health.* The changes in brain chemistry need to have been triggered before the onset of the cognitive demand of the classes in order to derive the benefits. This appears to take advantage of the growth hormones that are in the system after a period of exercise.
- *Students should monitor their own heart rates and have a PE teacher or trainer to supervise and track performance.* Improvement is measured against their own prior performance, not against others. The outcome is not dependent on whether the team is having a good or bad day. The individual can see on a monitor just how well he or she is doing day by day. By focusing on the individual's performance we can potentially benefit cognitive/ academic performance as well as improvements in general health and emotional well-being. This also means the out-of-shape and overweight kids are also measuring their gains in their own heart rates, not how fast they ran or how well they placed. It is important that students get their heart rates to the target level and keep at levels they can maintain. This works for overweight kids to top athletes. This also helps to create a positive emotional shift in outlook—whether the person is overweight or not.
- *Aerobic activity precedes or is combined with complex movement.* The goal is to get the heart rate up and use many areas of the brain, through continuous complex movement, not only using rote, repetitive movements. Even in older adults, meta-analysis found cognition benefits were attained from aerobic exercise (Angevaren, Aufgemkampe, Verhaar, Aleman, & Vanhees, 2008).

- *Use complex movements that require that new skills be learned and where movements incorporate constant adjustments.* The brain is highly involved in the quality of its performance.
- *Everybody should be active; no one sits out.* That has been a traditional problem with many programs because several people, often those who need it most, are sitting out or avoiding activity. By using the heart monitor and measuring against their own performances, people cannot avoid seeing what their own hearts did. Everyone is active; the issue is not how well the team did but the improvement of individual cognitive performance. Remember, team cognitive performances are not tested on SATs or state standards tests.
- *PE programs should not dropped or reduced, but should be increased before core academics.* The idea of physical play, breaks from the academics, where there are brief periods of elevated heart rates works well not only in elementary but in middle school and high school (Chomitz et al., 2009). This will be visited more extensively in Chapter 3.
- *All activities must be properly supervised, especially including those listed in the complex movements, as there is risk for potential for injury as with any activity, especially with kids or older adults.*

Communication
- *Grammar is easier to master the earlier it is started.* Mastering concepts or becoming aware of them in one's native language makes it easier when they are encountered in a second language.
- *There is less accent if sounds are learned before about age 12 because they can be more easily distinguished.* If a new language is acquired during adolescence it becomes more difficult for the brain to process sounds, and accents become more pronounced.
- *To create a memory for a name, help the students say it correctly.* Names that can't be pronounced do not form memories that can be used to spell or say them later. Students may recognize the written name, but they can't generate it on their own. Teachers should model it several times before students attempt it.
- *Early screening testing for reading problems and detection of dyslexia is important for the child's success throughout his or her entire educational experience.* This can potentially save the child a lot of heartache while opening the doors to have a chance at success.
- *Give continual reading support.* Students benefit from continued reading support and it helps to reduce the reading gap, but only if both parents and teachers don't stop the support.
- *Reading strategies should not be approaches that concentrate on either phonics only or whole words only; the brain uses multiple systems.* Programs that emphasize only one or the other are seriously shortchanging

the students. The brain processes both larger sounds (such as words) and smaller units (such as phonemes).

- *Dyslexia occurs across all languages.* However, slightly different areas of the brain are involved from one language to another, illustrating Pinker's idea that language was added on by the brain co-opting areas whose original purposes were different and not necessarily specifically evolved for reading.

- *Start a second language as early as possible.* The more thoroughly a child knows his or her native tongue, the easier it is to pick up grammar and proper speech in a second language.

- *There is no simple method to use in class to determine who might be dyslexic, and there is no one test or standard that can be used to determine whether a student is dyslexic.* Educators need to be alert to the many traits of dyslexia and closely work with the students. If they suspect a student has reading problems, testing should be started promptly. To wait is to increase the likelihood of failure and increase the difference in reading with their peers.

- *Dyslexic students will need support and encouragement throughout their entire educational careers.* It takes time to build their decoding skills. It is likely there will always be a gap in their fluency compared to others, but they can build excellent coping skills, especially in their area of work interest.

- *Students will have to discover for themselves what strategies presented by support staff will work best.* It is an ongoing task achieved in close cooperation as the support staff and students explore the accommodations together.

- *The success of the dyslexic student is largely dependent on the support he or she receives from the teacher or support staff.* Without support staff the dyslexic student probably will make only marginal gains. Staff need to be thoroughly trained in the nature of the disorder and in the interventions and appropriate accommodations.

- *Staff also need to be genuine with students by showing they care about students as people.* The emotional connections that develop between staff and students can be very powerful in motivating students (see Chapter 4).

- *For the benefit of all the students, the instruction and advice need to be explicit for writing, reading, and math assignments.* Complex, multistep instructions or advice is hard to follow for any adolescent, but especially for those with reading disorders, because their brains can track only a limited amount of information (see Chapter 7). It benefits all students to keep instructions simple and clear, available in multiple modalities, and to review them before activities start.

RESOURCES

Feifer, S., & De Fina, P. (2000). *The neuropsychology of reading disorders: Diagnosis and intervention workbook.* Middletown, MD: School Neuropsych Press.

Human Kinetics. (2007). *PE4LIFE: Developing and promoting quality physical education.* Champaign, IL: Human Kinetics.

Langley-Evans, S. (2009). *Nutrition: A lifespan approach.* Oxford, UK: Blackwell.

Leyse-Wallace, R. (2008). *Linking nutrition to mental health: A scientific exploration.* Lincoln: iUniverse.

Ratey, J. (2008). *Spark: The revolutionary new science of exercise and the brain.* New York, NY: Little, Brown.

Schmidt, M. (2007). *Brain-building nutrition.* (3rd ed.). Berkeley, CA: Frog Books.

Shaywitz, S. (2003). *Overcoming dyslexia: A new and complete science-based program for reading problems at any level.* New York: Knopf.

Spafford, C., & Grosser, G. (1995). *Dyslexia research and resource guide.* New York: Allyn & Bacon.

Wolf, M. (2008). *Proust and the squid: The story and science of the reading brain.* New York: Harper Perennial.

CHAPTER THREE

In the Beginning

From Pattern Detection to Attention Systems

Any man who can drive safely while kissing a pretty girl
is simply not giving the kiss the attention it deserves.
—Albert Einstein

Or in the night, imagining some fear,
how easy is a bush suppos'd a Bear?
—William Shakespeare, *A Midsummer Night's Dream*, Act 5

It was foggy. We were in a white, featureless haze on a glacier in the Yukon, the nearest town over a hundred miles away. The ground held no horizon with the sky; this was a whiteout. So few were the features that even two feet in front of me I couldn't tell whether the glacier surface was flat, sloped uphill, or down. My eyes strained to pick out any texture at all to tell me what I was skiing on. Morgan was tethered to me by a rope. Suddenly he yelped as he started to disappear into a nondescript grayish slash that was hardly different from the rest of the snow. At Morgan's startled exclamation, I turned and saw in an instant, with chilling horror, that the gray slash continued into a yawning crevasse on our immediate right. We couldn't tell if the crevasse was 30 feet or 30 inches away, but it signaled extreme danger as Morgan, a highly experienced mountaineer, nearly fell in. In the foggy whiteout, our hearts now thumping madly, we both looked around and finally saw an almost imperceptible pattern of other gray slashes, indicating we were in the middle of a dangerous section of glacier with thinly covered crevasses (Schenck, 2003, p. 25). All that information—the yell, the sudden recognition of the crevasses—was taken in and processed in just an instant. How had the brain processed all the information and linked it with appropriate memories that quickly? Some of the brain mechanisms that process recognition are still unknown but a number of hypotheses have been advanced. In order for educators to create a more successful learning environment, it is helpful to understand how recognition and attention work together.

The Need for Pattern Recognition and Attention

As in the glacier story, detecting patterns is clearly needed to help us survive, to orient where we are in order to figure out what we can do, but first a person must detect the pattern so it can be placed in context and appropriately compared with other information. In other words, if the brain can recognize a pattern correctly, it can make predictions about what we should do next (Cherry, 1953). But sometimes that recognition system fails. However, failure to detect patterns most likely means that the problem cannot be solved, at least not with the approach that is currently being used. When a student looks at a math question and is unable to detect a pattern, she is stuck and does not know what to look for. The problems rapidly multiply. If students do not quickly find patterns they recognize, they don't know what procedures to use. Frustration is often the result and they simply give up. A different approach may be in order. Re-explaining the same way, only more slowly, may be worthless, as the same unrecognizable pattern is still present. Attacking the problem from a different perspective may facilitate recognition and get the student started.

In perceiving an object, the brain must address two fundamental questions: "What is it?" and "Where is it?" Answering those key questions about the properties of attention allows the adolescent to respond in a more appropriate manner of what to do next.

Properties of the Attention Networks

If the student can't pay attention to the lesson at hand, there is almost no chance of it being learned and becoming a memory. Paying attention is not a simple process of either, yes, the student is paying attention, or, no, she isn't. Most educators have had the experience of seeing the students looking toward them, perhaps even smiling, but their minds are disengaged from the teachers' words. Disruption of the attentional processes at any number of places can result in the lesson being lost. Divided attention, or the cocktail-party effect, is a classic example that illustrates some of the attention systems properties for a teacher. At a party, or in a classroom, you can ignore the busy environment about you and focus on just the conversation. However, your brain is still monitoring the surrounding activity. Attention is selective. Should someone nearby mention your name, the brain can immediately disengage your attention from listening to the person in front of you and reorient it to the conversation that mentions your name, never moving your eyes from the person in front of you. All the while, you can nod your head and say, "That's interesting," but never hint that you've mentally left the conversation. Teachers do the same in the classroom. I first learned about this with my second-grade teacher. She had a reputation for having eyes in the back of her head, and as second graders, some of us believed it for a while. We really wondered how she could be writing on the chalkboard and know when we were messing around. She had covertly shifted her attention, monitoring us, and we were none the wiser. The problem for our students (or staff in a meeting) is that they are sometimes embarrassingly caught with their attention diverted and have no idea what is going on. Our attention systems are simply limited in how much we can focus on. Information that a student can't attend to is usually poorly processed, resulting in a considerable if not total functional loss of information (Cherry, 1953). A variation of the ability to attend to one task and miss significant information was illustrated in a series of revealing experiments by Simons and Chabris (1999).

A class of teenagers watched a video clip of two teams of basketball players: one group of three in white t-shirts, the other group in black t-shirts. Both passed basketballs back and forth within their respective groups and around each other. The students were instructed to count the number of passes made by the team in white. During the short video clip, there were a few strangled laughs and efforts to keep quiet. Some of the nongiggling class members threw questioning looks at their fellow students as if to say "What is going on?" Later on, it was revealed that, in the midst of the video clip, a person in a gorilla suit strode among the players, stopped dead center, faced the camera, and pounded his chest and strode off. Half of the class never saw the gorilla, and the others tried to keep from laughing. When the clip was discussed, several people exclaimed, "No way!" They didn't believe it; it couldn't have happened. The clip was played again, this time with no one counting the number of passes. There was an exclamation of surprise when people realized what they had missed. Typically 50% will overlook seeing the gorilla. Attention systems are limited and these properties have major implications for adolescent education. This suggests sizeable portions of the population miss significant information when their attention system is momentarily interrupted.

The ability and the processes involved in paying attention are derived from a series of networks spread across different lobes of the brain (see Figure 3.1). There are three major processes: visual orienting, detecting events, and maintaining an alert state. In the Posner and Raichel (1994) model, one of the first networks involved in processing attention concerns *alerting* where irrelevant background information is suppressed, freeing up more mental resources that will be needed for establishing and maintaining vigilance. A second attention network involved is called *orienting*, where the networks are primed to be ready for more information from a location in the environment. The third network, *executive control,* takes the multiple networks that process information and choreographs them into an organized set of processes that allows encoding information in order to make sense of it.

But why doesn't some information rise to a level where the student becomes aware of it, such as in the cocktail-party conversations or with the gorilla in the middle of the basketball players? What can educators do to avoid students missing important information? And what about subliminal learning? To address these practical issues, we need a little more information.

Attention also seems to have at least three major properties that stem from the

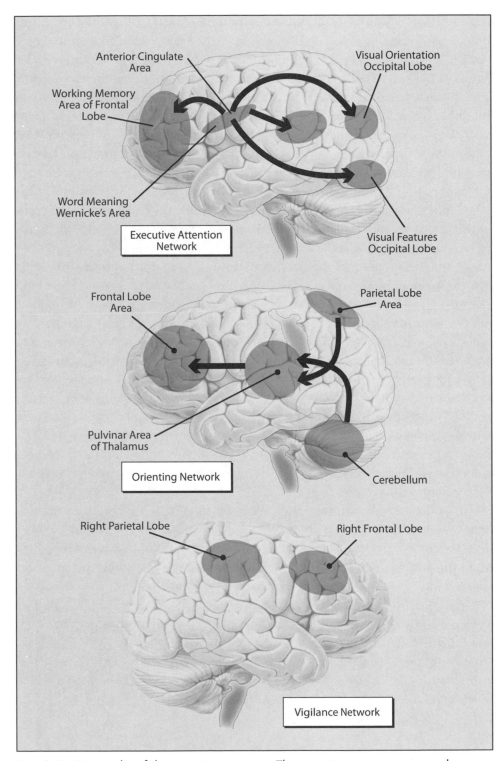

Fig. 3.1. Networks of the attention systems. The attention systems are made up of the three general networks, the executive, orienting and vigilance, which function together in directing a person's overall attention.

neural networks. *Selection* from the orienting and detection, *vigilance* from maintaining an alert state, and *control* all spread across the brain through a variety of networks. The brain's ability to coordinate these properties will impact a student's daily activities that involve perception, voluntary recall of information, and development of skills (Parasuraman, 1998). An important ability for an adolescent to develop is maintaining attention on the task at hand while simultaneously ignoring distractions. This is *sustained attention,* and it is often lacking with students with ADHD in classroom settings; however, when a personal, emotional connection has been made with the activity, then their attention can be riveted for hours. I will explore issues concerning ADHD and interventions for this disorder later in the chapter. Another important property of the attention system is the brain's facility for spontaneously grouping disparate pieces of visual information (Rubin, 1915; Wetheimer, 1923). An example of this is shown in Figure 3.2.

The emerging property of the dots that seemingly organize into vertical or horizontal groups may be the result of how the attention system works. When we try to focus on a single dot, our attention appears to spread out to the other dots that are similar, resulting in either vertical or horizontal groups (Driver & Baylis, 1998). These visual, self-organizing properties are called Gestalt groupings, and in teaching it is not uncommon to group things such as pictures or concept maps so they are more naturally organized. An awareness of Gestalt groupings and some of their properties can facilitate directing a student's attention. Another property that relates both recognition of patterns and attention is "popout." A person can be generally aware of some patterns, but in an apparent narrowing or tightening of focus of attention a person can zoom in on a single object or feature where it suddenly pops out into their awareness (Nakayama & Joseph, 1998), having crossed a threshold in consciousness.

Probably the most useful model of attention to date is the tripartite model by Stanislas Dehaene (Dehaene, Changeux, Naccache, Sackur, & Sergent, 2006). As in the examples of the gorilla and the cocktail party, the brain has different levels of states or awareness in attention. The differences in attention appear to arise

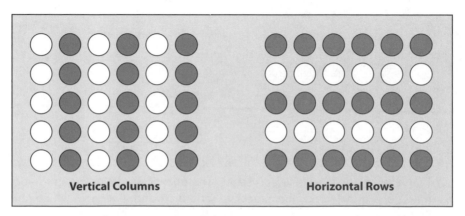

Fig. 3.2. Gestalt organization of dots.

Table 3.1. STIMULUS FACTORS		
Brain State	**Conditions**	**Result**
Subliminal	Weak stimulus + unattended	No awareness
	Weak stimulus + attended	No awareness
Preconscious	Strong stimulus + unattended	No awareness
Conscious	Strong stimulus + attended	Awareness

from combinations of stimulus strength, availability of information, and conscious control of attention. Incoming information that is processed but of which a person remains unaware is called *subliminal.* However, a person cannot access that information, despite the multitude of claims on the Internet. Subliminal information can, however, influence what a person becomes aware of, but research has not found any demonstrable way to use it to make changes in complex learning, as many claim (Pessiglione et al., 2008). A second state is *preconscious processing* where the information is just strong enough to trigger processing by the brain, but the brain is not directing its attention to it; thus, a person may remain unaware of some information, as in the gorilla experiment. The third state is *conscious processing* (awareness), in which the stimulus is strong enough and amplifies to the point that a person becomes aware. Information is not equal in stimulating the brain, so simple attention to that information by itself will not rise to a level of awareness. To bring things to a conscious state of awareness requires the stimulus factors and conditions shown in Table 3.1.

If the conditions in the classroom are not right for capturing the student's attention, it doesn't raise either the stimulus or attentional processing up to a conscious level. Adolescents will remain unaware of what we want them to notice. That doesn't mean their attention systems are offline. They are aware of other things, such as their latest covert text message, or friends two rows over, just not the teacher or the lesson. The consequences of redirected attention can be, of course, disastrous for learning.

When the attention systems divide or redirect to another task, there is a drop in the encoding of information, and memory for the original task is much lower (Naveh-Benjamin, Guez, & Sorek, 2007). This strongly suggests that if teachers are to create useful learning so that information can be encoded into memory, then the brain must actively pay attention to the learning event (Craik, Govoni, & Naveh-Benjamin, 1996). Studies on divided attention also found that learning tasks, which required deeper and more thorough processing, were also the ones most interfered with when attention shifts. Deeper processing requires more of the brain's limited mental resources. With some of the attention shifted away from the deep processing, there are insufficient resources left to thoroughly encode information into memory (Craik, 1982). Interrupting students when they are focusing on a lesson should be avoided. It is difficult for the brain to regain its rhythm of processing.

Encoding depends on attention. The brain's attention systems must be sufficiently directed toward the learning event so the information can be encoded into memory and have a chance of becoming learned. Achieving a state of awareness is only a start in building the memory, because that awareness must also be maintained and the encoding processes are part of that maintenance. Like attention, encoding weaves several processes together. It is not a single process following a set formula where if a student does a specific practice then he or she will produce a memory of a particular quality.

The student who is texting (which seems to have replaced passing notes) as well as the other student receiving the text has their attention divided. The texting student is attending to the lesson, but only fleetingly. Any other task that he engages in at the same time results in a significant decline in memory. To establish a retrievable long-term memory, the initial processing and thinking about the learning event are especially important. The student needs to actively think about what is going on, and that requires a very large amount of attentional resources (Naveh-Benjamin & Jorides, 1984; Tulving, 2002). Simply stated, *there is no such thing as multitasking where we can pay equal attention to multiple things at the same time; this is probably a neuromyth.* There are very few individuals (1 in 40) who do not experience a drop in performance when multitasking (Watson & Strayer, 2010). For the rest of us, however, the prospects of multitasking effectively are poor to fatal.

However, people do talk on the phone, write, or play video games all at the same time. Even though they appear to focus on all those different tasks, they still are unable to give full attention to all the tasks at the same time. A person can only truly *pay attention* to one thing at a time. What a person is actively thinking about involves something called working memory, which will be discussed in Chapter 7. But I'm getting ahead of myself. Let's examine how these properties of our attentional systems play out in the learning environment.

Summary

The brain has different systems devoted to attention: some process where the information is, others process what it is. These neural systems are located across the brain and are not concentrated in any one area. Information may be detected, but a person is not necessarily consciously aware of it. The stimulus must be strong enough to rise into awareness. The amount of mental resources available for attention is also limited. There is only so much of the mental resource to go around and no more. The more a person concentrates or focuses attention, the less there is of that attention available for other tasks. The more tasks a person tries to handle, the fewer resources there are available. Multitasking with equal attention to all tasks is not possible.

The Educational Connection

The impact of divided attention on education is hard to underestimate. It happens to teachers and students alike every day, and this can greatly decrease their productivity. Like the staff members in a workshop who are grading papers and also using their laptops to surf the net, or students who are paying attention to the cute new kid and not to the lesson, it happens at all ages.

When attention systems are divided and resources spread too thinly, what adolescents are able to learn, or what they can produce, suffers. It is even more of a problem for those who have ADHD, because their attention systems are not functioning in a helpful way in most educational practices. However, there are some blunt, hard facts educators must also face here. *Many of the daily teaching practices do a lousy job of helping the brain's attention systems maintain their attention. It is more than classroom management. Capturing, directing, maintaining, and sustaining attention at an appropriate level is one of the fundamental keys to learning.* As so succinctly stated in Thom Hartmann's *Attention Deficit Disorder: A Different Perception,* "I'm not inattentive, you're just boring" (1997, p. 77). Remember that a student's attention systems are working and paying attention, but it may not be the teacher or the lesson that has captured and held his or her attention. This does not suggest that educators are to be entertainers, but they need to raise their own attention system's awareness level of what their students' systems are doing, and sustain that monitoring of both their own and their students' attention systems. *We should pay attention to inattention.*

Music

A curious feature of divided attention is its connection to music. Many students like to listen to their mp3, iPod, or CD players. Countless interviews over the years with my own students suggest that many *are using music as an audio wall to screen out distracting noise.* Interestingly, in math, all students benefited from the slight additional stimulation by having their favorite music played (Arnold, 2001). Because students with ADHD (as well as others) are frequently distracted by music with lyrics, I permit only instrumental music to be played. With lyrics there is a strong tendency for the students to start listening to the words and to shift their attention away from the task at hand. However, it is not clear whether listening to lyrics in another language is distracting. Observing students through the years suggests it is not a problem.

Monitoring the students' individual players is logistically unreasonable, so I use a wide range of genres of music, and I play music during research or lab sessions and sometimes during reading assignments after I learn what works for a particular class. For some students, the selection of music will genuinely irritate them, resulting in poor attention on their lesson, so I will make appropriate accommodations for those students. In special situations, I permit students to use their own music, and then only if it is instrumental, although in reality it is easy for them to switch to some vocal music.

Sleep

Sleep is becoming a major issue because students lack a proper amount of it. Research indicates that sleep deprivation affects students' ability to sustain their attention. Students who sleep in class obviously don't have their attention on the lessons. Sleep affects their attention in school in at least two major ways. First is alertness, especially in adolescents because of the early hours at which schools start. *Adolescents do not function well cognitively until roughly 9 to 10 A.M.* Younger students can handle the early hours, but this changes as they reach puberty. Second, when kids have been up most of the night with computer games or other computer activities, their bodies need sleep. If they did not get enough sleep at night when they should have, their bodies will attempt to get it during class. Allowing adolescents to sleep just one hour longer has produced noticeable academic gains (Lufti, Tzischinsky, & Hadar, 2009). For high school students, starting school later at around 9 to 10 A.M. is better.

Maintaining students' attention is an ongoing task from the moment they arrive to when they leave the instructor. Many educators seem to be unaware of the brain's natural need for stimulation, and consequently the direct planning for maintaining attention is often not considered as a part of any lesson plan. Ignoring the need of the adolescent brain for stimulation only serves to make learning more difficult. Fortunately, educators can employ a large number of simple strategies to help a student focus their attention.

Attention strategies work not only for those who have attention difficulties but also for the rest of the class. Because of that, the following section will start with a general discussion of attention strategies for all students, and in the section after that I then focus on students with ADHD, because there is a very high probability that the instructor will have students with significant attention problems. Students with attention difficulties, whether formally diagnosed or not, are like the canary in the coal mine. Often they provide early indications when there is not enough being done to address their attention needs. For example, changing the conditions slightly for many students can evoke a larger shift for other students whose mind/brain systems are more sensitive. A seesaw illustrates how such minor changes near the fulcrum induce larger changes at the ends (see Figure 3.3). In the natural world when the balance is upset, conditions at extremes are the most sensitive to change and are the first to exhibit a more dramatic shift. In the see-saw, a difference in the balance shows as wild swings up or down at either end, but at the same time a shift in balances creates only a modest change in the middle areas, where the bulk of the

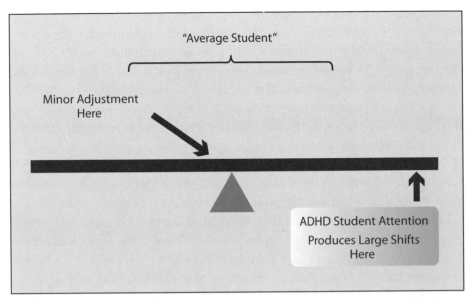

Fig. 3.3. Minor changes in classroom activities may create major shifts in attention behaviors of ADHD students.

population lives. If minor adjustments are made for the middle, it can produce great changes at the extremes.

Many natural systems function that way. Radical shifts in temperatures show up dramatically at the poles of the earth, but, like the seesaw, those toward the middle (near the equator) experience only slight shifts. The bulk of our students lay near this middle area in respect to attention. If a teacher does something different to stabilize the great attention swings at the ends, the students around the middle are also stabilized but they just don't show such dramatic changes. Hence, many of the interventions presented are well worth consideration for all students because their attention is still positively affected.

General Interventions for Attention

The following inventions are organized into strategies for the classroom: such as when students enter or leave, the environment itself, providing directions, lesson presentation, and class work. Additionally many of these strategies work with both older and younger students and will also help those who have ADHD. Because there are so many different ways to focus on student attention, *teachers should avoid overwhelming themselves by trying too many new strategies at once.* Every year I pick out a couple of strategies I want to improve on (never more than four, usually just two or three) and tape a list on my desk where it is visible only to me. This helps me to focus and improve on those areas. About halfway through a course I update these with new goals. The following discussion provides a broad overview of attention interventions.

In-class interventions for everyone

Establish classroom routines when students enter and leave. Although they are now in middle school or high school and should be more responsible, many adolescents are not prepared when they come to class. Using interventions is more effective than using consequences (Zentall, Moon, Hall, & Grskovic, 2001). Planning ahead and anticipating actions are largely prefrontal lobe processes, but most students are still developmentally incomplete and lapses may be more the norm. Their attention needs to be focused quickly on being prepared as they enter, before they get settled down and are tempted to go off-task. For example, when you greet them as they walk in, give them directions to immediately look at the screen or board. Make it routine. Write a list on the board in the same place every day, or project pictures of all the actual items they should be bringing (homework, notebook, textbook, pencils, calculator, planner, etc.) on the screen. There is no one right way to do this, but many students, especially at the beginning of the year when routines are being established, need to have their attention overtly directed to what they should have. Actually using a planner with a checklist of the necessary items, as a brief but routine all-class activity, helps the students to focus and see what they have overlooked. For some students, having a checklist or cues placed where they need it and when they need it is essential. That means the checklist is *not* inside the notebook or planner, but outside (perhaps laminated) on top of their planner, notebook, or locker door. *It's in the right place at the right time.* The checklist is a quick visual cue, and using it should become a habit of mind. If the list is laminated, and taped to their notebooks, the list can be repeatedly marked with dry-erase markers.

There are endless possibilities, but a list might include the following:

- Assignment planner (including key page numbers, phone numbers, and Internet URL addresses);
- Homework assignment (either handwritten, typed, or computer generated);
- Textbook;
- Appropriate reference materials (handouts, examples, readings, other books);
- Calculator; and
- Appropriate writing and drawing materials.

In a similar fashion, you should also establish classroom routines when students leave. Overtly review what they need to do outside of class; perhaps even stand nearby or next to students who have particular difficulties maintaining focus.

For each of the key items on the list, call on students to state what needs to be accomplished, such as that the assignment is clearly written, that they have its due date, and that they have the appropriate books. Also, help the students establish a ritual of getting assignments back into their proper folders, not just stuffed in the notebook or between book pages. This can be especially problematic. Students should also have phone numbers of other students, or the teacher, if appropriate. Additionally, they should have listed in their planner the URLs of Internet help websites. This routine should last perhaps one minute to get everything in order and it can help students immensely.

One way to make sure the checklists like the one presented above are actually completed is to have the students or an aide check a designated person's list or planner to make sure it is completed. It is also important that, at the beginning of the year or when semesters have changed, students should be reminded to check on what class they should be heading toward next.

Interventions for the classroom environment

Student attention is easier to maintain if a positive atmosphere is created by greeting students individually at the door, making them feel special and wanted (Zentall, 2006). Make sure that clear rules and routines are provided and attention is drawn to them by posting them and discussing them. Students who have attention difficulties will make themselves known fairly quickly. *These students (including those with ADHD) should be seated closer to the teacher.* When students have fewer choices there is often more talking. Providing even some simple choices can reduce the chatter (Bennett, Zentall, Giorgetti, & French, 2006). For example, have two different but immediate tasks they can choose between when they enter the classroom. One task might be to read a short article, or to solve a problem; another might be to answer some questions. The brain needs stimulation. A classroom environment that has activities that are stimulating and interesting but clearly related to the lesson can satisfy much of this need. Step back for a minute and reflect upon who is most active in your classroom most of the time. Is it the teacher or the student? Unfortunately, it is still common for most adolescents to have classrooms that are lecture centered. The teacher is most active, but it is the students who are the ones who need the activity. *The students' need to create their own stimulation is reduced when the environment provides it for them* (Zentall & Zentall, 1976). When students are actively involved in learning, the time seems to fly. If the class is dragging, it is a sure sign that student attention is probably wandering and is not providing anywhere near an appropriate level of physical activity. Remember, if the teacher doesn't provide the stimulus (and thus control where the student's attention is being directed), then the student's brain will seek out a stimulus, and it usually isn't the lesson. Rethink the activity level. Along with this, make sure students have space to move around in, with tasks located in different parts of the room so they move from one location to the next. This facilitates the much-needed periodic movement. Don't always have rows: Cluster seats in groups of three or four, make circles, use different workstations with each station having a different task. Active learning is the key.

Giving directions

To capture attention when tasks are changing, have routines that provide cues for students so they know a change is about to occur. Use novel sounds (like a party noisemaker or gong), or activities to provide the cue that a change is about to occur, especially with younger adolescents. Some teachers put on a special hat to signal the change, while others always stand in a particular location: Both are silent signals and with just a little practice students habituate to them. However, continuously using the same cue can be so routine some students no longer pay attention. It is likely these are the very students who most need to pay attention. So it is necessary to alternate the type of cue that signals an activity change. Also, when giving instructions, use proximity by standing near or next to those students who have difficulty with attention, so they may be unobtrusively checked to see that they have gotten and understood the instructions—even if a sound system is used (see next item).

When cueing, stop the current activity. When all eyes are on the instructor and students are quiet, provide the new directions. This works well with the entire range of adolescents. The instructions should be brief, uncomplicated, and accompanied by visuals or a model for students to look at if possible. Instructions should be specific and clear, without too many steps. Students with ADHD and those with working memory deficits will commonly miss information. If there is confusion, or students are immediately off-task, it is more likely because of the teacher's poor directions than just misbehavior. Be certain the instructions are understood. Vague instructions or too many steps are recipes for disaster.

"Get your things and start on the page. Be sure to complete all the questions." While that may sound initially fine, it is really rather vague. What specific "things"? What are they to be used on, or with? Which page, in what book or handout? Are there questions that accompany illustrations? Are there some questions whose wording is possibly confusing? Do those need to be reviewed, perhaps having the students making a special note or direction about the question? Where are resources located if they need them? More specific direction would be helpful. For example,

- "Students, eyes on me" [pausing . . . making sure she has their undivided attention].
- "For the next assignment the resources that you may need are located here."
- "We're going to work with handout #2, it looks like this." [Holds up the paper.] "Please find it, and check to see if your neighbor has the correct one." "Does everyone have it? Here are additional copies if you're missing the paper."
- "To complete this you will need [lists specific items]. Set those items on the desk now." [Teacher walks among the students and checks.]
- "Please look on your handout now, page 2, back side, question #13. [pause] Everyone found it?"
- "Okay, the wording is a little strange. Isabella, what do you think they are asking for?" [Isabella answers.]
- "Okay, everyone write down this rewording . . ." [Restates several times as needed and check to see if it is completed correctly. Remember, there will

be several students who normally will miss information because they can't process it effectively, and they won't necessarily get better. They aren't lazy; attention deficits and working memory problems are not always outgrown. They need to become aware of their difficulties and be coached in developing coping strategies.]

After capturing students' attention, check for understanding and have either those who have difficulty with attention or another student repeat back the instructions. Be sure to *follow up* by asking, "So, Henry, what will you be doing?" (Schenck, 2003). This allows the instructions to be presented three times: once by the teacher and twice by the students.

It invariably happens that instructions need to be adjusted. While a teacher should obviously have reviewed the directions to catch errors, some errors in the directions are commonly missed. It is vital to find and reduce as many of these errors as possible, because periodic corrections or updates to directions during the course of the lesson is an attention-memory destroyer for many students (and adults). *Avoid interruptions if possible.* First, interruptions are literally an annoying distraction for many people. It doesn't matter whether interruptions are from the instructor or announcements over the public address system, they interfere with attention and performance. When information or a stimulus overlaps, any additional irrelevant detail can reduce performance (Zentall, 2006). Students lose their place, their concentration is interrupted, and a rhythm or flow is stopped. A student has trouble recalling verbal details if her working information is constantly updated.

If the students must be interrupted, provide a context or category by directly drawing their attention to it (Voelker, Carter, Sprague, Gdowski, & Lachar, 1989). Here is an example: "Please stop [direct their attention]. Look at the drawing on the left page. Everybody found it? Good. There is an error on the drawing; the name crocodile should be . . . Show your neighbor to be certain all of you see it. [Walk about and check.] Anyone need help finding it? Okay. What are we to be doing now?" Then restart the activity.

Attention strategies during lessons

It is not uncommon that some students have hearing deficits, and students with attention problems often don't hear all the information. The use of a sound system with a wireless mic helps everybody to avoid missing what is said. Funding for such systems is sometimes available through the special education department because of special needs students in the classroom.

Have clarity! If a teacher is disorganized in the lesson, the student will likely be confusing and disorganized as well, especially if a student has ADHD. Using a verbal and visual outline facilitates the grasp of a concept. Consider having numbered points, but be consistent and use a standardized note form. Students' attention wanders when they don't know where the lesson is going. Provide the big picture, along with an overall guiding question, and use the question several times by referring back to it. This provides a framework and helps them to direct their attention. To maintain attention, consider having the students summarize their information, skills, or applications in direct reference to the big picture.

There always seems to be more material to cover than there is time, but blasting through the material produces little gain. *The attention systems of students may simply be overwhelmed if there is too much information.* Slow down presentations, be succinct, remember that less is more, and pause frequently so students can catch up on notes. This saves time in the long run because less re-teaching is needed. To assist the students' attention systems and still-developing metacognitive skills, directly note or point out what is important and what they should be writing down. If there is information to be memorized, provide meaningful categories to create organization. This may not only increase speed, but also may reduce confusion and create a specific "place" in memory to search when the information is later needed (Voelker et al., 1989). When a student may need help and to simultaneously reduce distractions for other students, you can encourage the student to use nonverbal cues or signals (besides the traditional raised hand), such as a card signal they can post on their own desk.

Interventions for class work

Class work does not always have to be seatwork! The brain needs stimulation; the body, no matter the age, needs to move. To help maintain attention in adolescents, allow students to stand while working. Many students are also distracted by noise, so allow the option of having them move to a quieter area or by using noise suppression earphones, or you can allow nonvocal music to be played in the background. To elaborate a bit more on this important point, the use of nonvocal music works well during rote practice, study sessions, or routine paperwork exercises with middle school and high school students (Abikoff, Courtney, Szeibel, & Koplewicz, 1996; Hallam & Price, 1998; Scott, 1970). I have used music in the classroom for more than 20 years with hundreds of students at the secondary level and have found it to be quite helpful for maintaining general classroom management. Other teachers have reported the same effects of using music. However, formal research is needed to better understand it. For fidgety adolescents, have them sit on beanbag seats, large rubber exercise balls, or one-legged stools (which also require balance and prevent slouching). This can produce extraordinary results in less than a minute. Their brain stimulation is provided by the constant need to adjust slightly in order to stay in the seat, yet it doesn't disturb the rest of the class. However, for many students there is a real need for larger body movements. In middle school this can be partially addressed by providing class jobs that have high status or real responsibility and allows the student to move around. For both middle school and high school, having periodic peer-tutoring sessions permits many students to move about. Allow students to be the "expert" tutors for selected tasks, and then rotate "experts" so many students (if not all) will have an opportunity to help others and move around while maintaining attention.

While all students have attention and movement requirements, some students' attention needs are different because their attention deficits were acquired through injury or were hereditary. Although the previous discussion and suggestions apply to most students, those with these types of attention deficits need additional consideration. Their numbers may account for 4–8% of the students in any class, and when considered schoolwide, that can be a substantial number of adolescents. Their problems are even more demanding of the teacher, and a single student with ADHD can disrupt an entire class. It will be the rare classroom that doesn't have an adolescent or two who has ADHD. Later in the chapter, in the section on ADHD, those problems and needs will be examined more closely.

Note taking

Another aspect of managing student attention is in regard to note taking. Adolescent notes, even if students have been shown how they should take them, are often disastrous. Provide models of note taking with poster-sized samples of notes before and after. Because divided attention is such a major problem and students commonly miss some information, post outlines of lectures online or provide hard copies.

Note-taking skills are inconsistently taught in middle school and high school. Nevertheless, one technique that students rapidly become aware of is highlighting selected information. However, there are misconceptions about the effectiveness of the technique. Highlighting alone is of limited help to forming a memory (Bailey, 2002). Adolescents, including those in college, often don't know what is important and will highlight everything. This is a superb opportunity to teach metacognitive study where the students begin to develop an awareness and understanding of how they learn and of their reading comprehension skills (Zentall & Dwyer, 1988). One of the first places is to direct how they use their highlighters or underline important information or directions. Directing their attention to how to discern important information is a skill whose development is facilitated with guided practice. Here is an example of this guidance in more detail:

1. Copy two or three pages of material that is similar in difficulty, with every student having their own practice copies.
2. Using a projector, show the same pages and guide the students through identifying what is important. A simple rubric that specifies not only what they are doing, but also the quality level of the task would be helpful. (There are many online sources.)
3. The students mark what they think is important on the practice papers, using a rubric.
4. After students have made their first attempts, the teacher highlights or marks on the projected copy for their comparison.
5. Discuss what you're looking for and refer back to the rubric. If note-taking skills are truly valued, this practice should be done routinely for a while. Once or twice is probably not sufficient for most students.

6. However, there is one more *critically significant step that is usually over-looked by almost everybody.* REWRITE or type the highlighted or underlined information; don't just re-read it. The rewrite draws their attention again into an active process and reinforces that information in memory. For older adolescents, such as those in college, they can consider jotting *legible* notes in the margins or perhaps attach sticky notes either physically or electronically. These notes can be compiled into a physical rewrite to summarize the information (Boch & Piolat, 2004).

Between tasks or wait time

Attention wanders rapidly when students are shifting between tasks, because there are so many captivating distractions. Teenagers, just like younger students, need to have direction in what behaviors are acceptable in the classroom. They may be darlings in another teacher's classroom, and holy terrors in the next, especially if they lack direction during delays, or wait time. Teach them an acceptable physical routine that allows movement, such as standing, collecting materials, or tapping their foam-tipped pencils (Binder, Dixon, & Ghezzi, 2000). The class can also be differentiated by having self-paced tasks available to students who are not waiting for directions, but such tasks should be regularly monitored. Another strategy for younger adolescents during wait times is to have stress balls or squeeze balls or other objects that students can manipulate. Consider allowing students to correct assignments, read, or work on assignments for other classes.

Computers

Many students with laptop computers don't wait for the lesson to change as an opportunity to move off-task. They can shift their attention away from the lesson at any time to participate in more interesting games or to view material on the Internet through sites such as Facebook or YouTube. This temptation affects not only the student with the laptop but also those around them, even students at different tables if the screen is visible. Students' attention is indeed focused, but it is on the computer. In order to maintain their attention on the appropriate tasks, teachers should modify hundreds of years of traditional practice where they remained in front of the class or sometimes moved among the students. With students using laptops, it is necessary to monitor and teach from *behind* the students, so teachers can see what is on them. This requires a change in voice projection as well. More volume may be needed so students may adequately hear, because many students are facing away from the teacher. The teacher should also carefully note what is showing on the computer screen's bottom edge, so you can see what pages they have open but are concealing. There is monitoring software that can see what sites students have open, and these have the ability to freeze unwanted pages and close them. However, such software is considerably less than 100% effective and still "buggy." Even so, students have a number of ways to go around server-based restrictions by using "backdoor" entries. With each new technology, new ways to be off-task emerge.

Some students will invariably get off-task with even the best teachers. Reprimands should be given quietly, firmly, and *without emotion*, and should not draw other students' attention (Abramowitz & O'Leary, 1991). Students hate being humiliated (as does anyone) because their pain continues long after the reprimand. Go over to the student, kneel down, maintain eye contact, be within one meter but not "in their face," and quietly redirect the student's attention. Other students will know what is going on, but if this proximity technique is also used for when students need help, then reprimands become less of a whole-class issue where everyone's attention is shifted off-task.

Other students enjoy the power they get with attention and may attempt to bait the teacher. Avoid putting your "buttons" on display. Some students, especially those who are oppositionally defiant, will search for your buttons and push very hard until they are rewarded with your explosion. It can be difficult to handle, because most of us have sensitive "button" issues. But the moment they capture your attention, and you react, especially negatively, such students have gotten their reward. At this point none of the students are attending to their lessons. Some tactics that can be used include ignoring the comment (which is clearly a judgment call depending on the issue); flipping the comment and, without emotion, making it a point of discussion; or smiling in response and then redirecting the comment.

Students With Attention Deficit/Hyperactivity Disorder (ADHD)

Adolescents who have problems are found worldwide and have been described in stories for hundreds of years if not longer. Students with ADHD are probably in every class, and their unregulated behavior can dominate what happens with other students' learning. The disorder is significant because it can impact students' own academic and life performances, and *it can also affect the entire class atmosphere. Educators need more knowledge about ADHD and what they can do, because ADHD affects everyone, whether one has the problem or not.*

Not everyone considers ADHD as a curse or as something bad. In a number of circumstances, *not* having one's attention jump from object to object, not constantly monitoring for changes, just following the same old routine, would be a fast way to become some other critter's dinner. Thom Hartmann (1997) presented this interesting perspective that ADHD can be, or has been, an advantage to many people. He suggested the possibility that many of our ancestors survived because of it. That raises the question of how can being a disruptive teenager, whose attention is often fleeting and seems endlessly disorganized, be an advantage? They create so much disorder in our neat, orderly classrooms. But they can also be highly creative and incredibly productive people, if they learn how to coax and regulate their attention to their advantage. Before I go on, a point of disclosure is in order here. I have ADHD, and I was completely unaware of it for the first 45 years of life, though it was apparently obvious to others. My perspective is not only as an active teacher working daily in the trenches of the classroom, but as a person who has to cope with the problems of attention on a 24/7 basis. But I digress. Can ADHD be *helpful?* (Eisenberg, Campbell, Gray, & Sorenson, 2008). Let me illustrate. A number of outdoor guides across the world who have ADHD have indicated there have been numerous occasions when their rapidly roaming attention kept their clients out of danger and avoided potentially fatal situations. If you're in a changing environment it pays to quickly notice changes as your life may depend upon it. However, some argue that too much is being made about ADHD, its significance, and how common it is, and that it is completely overblown. It is an important claim that needs to be examined.

Is ADHD Overdiagnosed and Overblown?

More than one parent or teacher has asked me, "Don't you think they're overdiagnosing ADHD?" TV pundits, with their latest moral outrage, echo the same. What is the story with ADHD, and are educators and health care professionals paying too much attention to it? I'll address the last question first. It turns out that most of the strategies that work well for assisting students with ADHD also work very well for other students, too. In the attention interventions described earlier, *all* of those interventions were found to be effective for students with ADHD. *If we can address the attention issues, pay attention to even some of them, and actively work with them, more students will benefit with fewer disruptions and greater learning.* Because all adolescents can potentially benefit from better direction of their attention systems, I will explore ADHD and appropriate interventions to some extent. However, misconceptions still abound about ADHD.

What Happens to Attention in ADHD?

There is not a lack of attention; it is that the systems that guide attention are not directing it in a manner that is typical for most of the population. The attention systems tend, in part, to be biased toward novelty (Allen, 1986). Because several systems in the brain are involved, multiple things can go awry in many combinations including those in Table 3.2 (Barkley, 1998; Robins, 1998).

These students can focus, but usually not in any one place for very long, although there can be some stunning exceptions when the task is really interesting to them. At those times, they can bring intense powers of concentration to focus for hours on a single task, but it may also be very difficult for them to break away, too.

Diagnosing ADHD

Earlier, I raised the frequently stated question about overdiagnosing. There is enormous misperception and misinformation about ADHD that lingers in part from unfounded claims and exaggeration that were pushed during the 1980s (Barkley, 1998, p. 33). To address the claim of overdiagnosing, let us examine just how common ADHD is.

The process of identifying ADHD continues to improve as diagnoses have gone through a number of iterations and psychologists and psychiatrists become more

Table 3.2. TYPICAL PROBLEMS FOR A STUDENT WITH ADHD

- Inability to keep focused (sustained attention); starts many projects or jobs but finishes few of them.
- Resistance to changing tasks (either in getting started or stopping).
- Socializing continuously but never getting started on a task.
- Always procrastinating until the last moment (and even then not necessarily starting on the actual task).
- Easily distracted.
- Frequently misplaces things, such as books, writing utensils, assignments, or keys.
- Remembers forgotten things shortly after leaving the room (the ADHD pirouette).
- Poor impulsivity control: Blurts out comments without thinking, frequently goes for the short-term reward.
- Doesn't pay attention to detail, rushes through homework, and misses critical details.
- Handwriting is often sloppy to illegible; writing neatly may be possible but takes excessive effort and time to accomplish.
- Talks a mile a minute, because he or she can't talk fast enough to keep up with his or her thoughts.
- His or her desk is vertically organized (if at all) and is very messy; litter is everywhere and piles up on the floor and in the locker.
- Zooms about and is constantly in motion.
- Is often attracted to emotionally stimulating activity, such as, danger, fast speeds, drug usage, and sex (especially so if co-morbid with Oppositional Defiance Disorder) (Barkley, Guevremont, Anastopoulos, DuPaul, & Shelton, 1993; Whalen, 1989).
- Will selectively focus on loud, action-oriented events (Cotugno, 1987).
- Attracted to other ADHD kids who are disruptive, argumentative, and fun to be around (Mrug, Hoza, & Gerdes, 2001; Whalen, 1989).
- Easily frustrated, often moody or easily agitated; responses can be aggressive physically or verbally.
- Often hears directions and knows what to do, but does not initiate action (Zentall, 2006).
- Tends to seek out high-energy or high-stimulus activities.
- Has chaotic organization (forgets where assignments are, papers are stuffed haphazardly between book covers, lockers, laptop cases).
- Generally has about 7–10% lower scores on IQ measures (causes are unknown) (Barkley, 1998).

These descriptions are only a general list and also tend to be observed more often in boys, and are not observed as frequently in girls, an important difference in diagnosing ADHD.

attuned to the expressions of the disorder. Over the last 100 years, the names for ADHD and mental health professionals' understanding of the behavior have undergone a series of changes. Each time the descriptions and intervention criteria become steadily more precise. The children were originally believed to have a major "defect in moral control," which I still run into in certain religious circles. This concept evolved later into the belief that they were brain-damaged (p. 4). The public is now beginning to accept that the brain can become sick, malfunction, or simply be different like any other organ, but that thought is still fiercely resisted by the insurance companies. It appears the number of ADHD diagnoses are rising for students and adults, but the actual level of occurrence is uncertain in part, because the major surveys of different populations around the world have not been repeated (p. 85). What is the actual situation then? Determining whether a person has ADHD is not a simple process, and although Table 3.2 lists a number of typical outward symptoms, *these are not definitive* because not all forms of ADHD are expressed in clearly observable patterns, especially by girls. For example, Nadeau, Littman, and Quinn (1999) found that in the commonly used Conners's Teacher Rating Scale—Revise L (Conners, 1997) only 7 items of 59 focused on ADHD traits more typical of girls, traits such as anxiety, depression, timidity, and problems with listening. The rest of the scale is more likely to pick up ADHD in boys. Without prior training, teachers are more likely to miss detecting ADHD for the girls because they can't easily recognize their problems. For example, 72% of the boys with ADHD were identified by teachers, but only 27% of the girls with ADHD were similarly identified. However, with practice, teachers can become capable of distinguishing girls with and without ADHD (Greenblat, 1994). Some of the traits more common to girls include being extremely talkative, giggly, and hyperreactive (Nadeau et al., 1999).

However, not all girls with attention problems are hyperactive. It was noted earlier that *we need to pay attention to inattention.* The shy, quiet girl, who seems to be withdrawn or avoids others, and may possibly be disheveled, often gets overlooked compared to the talkative, hyperactive girls, who may also rapidly flare up emotionally (Grskovic & Zentall, 2007; Nadeau et al., 1999). *Educators need to pay attention just as much to those especially quiet girls, because, although they are not disrupting the class like the hyperactive kids, they are probably missing out, too.* Along with being ignored in the classroom, these quiet girls with ADHD often get clobbered emotionally; they are rarely confident of themselves and wonder what is wrong with themselves. They don't have the same level of awareness and self-control as their peers do. Educators should look out for quiet but inattentive students, especially the girls who never participate. However, don't embarrass them or humiliate them when you discover they aren't paying attention; that is poor classroom management and does more harm than good. Educators should help, not humiliate, them to monitor their attention; the adolescent doesn't need further hateful baggage on top of a load she is already struggling to handle. If a teacher suspects a girl may have ADHD, or that the school is potentially missing this, educators need to take a hard, honest look at the *numbers* the school is serving, because the numbers of girls with ADHD should be occurring almost equally with boys. I would strongly recommend reading *Understanding Girls With AD/HD* by Nadeau, Littman, and Quinn. The book has a number of excellent checklists specifically for girls, which may help identify these overlooked girls even though the lists are not normed.

Occurrence

ADHD occurs in all populations around the world. It is not just a problem in the United States. The numbers being found are showing an increase, but the way schools, psychologists, and physicians are determining the occurrence is not the same. For example, in the early days of medicine, cancers were crudely identified, and little was known about how to treat them. As medicine advanced, surgery came into play, with excision of the tumor being a generic approach. As knowledge increased, more forms of cancer were diagnosed and different treatments with better outcomes emerged. Today, a diagnosis of cancer is no longer an automatic presumption of a death sentence. Similarly, the diagnosis of ADHD continues to evolve, as do the interventions. For example, some researchers use the criterion that the behaviors in question must also have been in existence prior to age 7, but there is no evidence to support that claim (Nadeau et al., 1999). Hopefully, further research will clear these discrepancies. The frequency of ADHD shifts with the type of diagnostic survey tool used, such as the older *DSM-III* or the more current *DSM-IV-TR*. The frequency also changes with the age of the person (age 4 to adult), gender, the ethnicity/genetic population (Asian, Western Caucasian, etc.), and subtypes (Gadow & Sprafkin, 1997; Pelham, Gnagy, Greenslade, & Milich, 1992; Szatmari, Offord, & Boyle, 1989; Zentall, 2006). The reported occurrences range from around 3% all the way up to 29%, but *an average, for all types, it is around 4.7–4.9% when using the DSM-IV criteria* (Bhatia, Nigam, Bohra, & Malik, 1991; see Appendix B). *DSM-IV-TR* is an evolving diagnostic tool; it naturally misses some things. For some time researchers have been aware that *the frequency of ADHD decreases with age to approximately 2.9% for males and 1.4% for females* (Barkley, 1998). However, there are still lingering misconceptions. A National Institute of Mental Health study in 2007 found that for a number of students with ADHD, the brain matures about 3 years more slowly than their peers (Shaw et al., 2007). Popular press articles gave the misperception that the problem was solved. What the press ignored is that a number of people do not outgrow it, and it is hoped that they learn how to successfully cope with their ADHD. There is support for learning how to handle ADHD through life, including some excellent coaching strategies, such as those by Nancy Ratey. Her strategies will be summarized in the interventions section later in the chapter.

In Appendix B are the formal criteria for making a diagnosis of ADHD. To be legal, a licensed psychologist, psychiatrist, or physician must perform the diagnosis. It is included here for educators' reference in order to broaden their awareness of what to look for. However, educators still need to be aware that many girls still are overlooked and never receive a formal evaluation.

Types of ADHD

If the school uses the standard surveys with *DSM-IV-TR* criteria and is careful with intake interviews in collecting the students' histories and has a thorough record of observations, both in class and out, *at least three forms of ADHD and possibly up to six may emerge:* inattentive without hyperactivity, inattentive with hyperactivity, or a combination. One problem is that these rely on descriptions of behavior, which makes it tricky to pick up with girls who have ADHD. Girls tend to be more of the inattentive type, and for most teachers, considerably more difficult to detect in a classroom (Biedman et al., 1999; Gaub & Carlson, 1997). Efforts are being made to see if there are any less subjective and more objective biological markers that might be used in making a diagnosis. The situation for objective measures is not perfect either. A number of studies using either SPECT or EEG scans have found that areas related to attention in the brain's frontal lobes were underactive compared to control groups (Lou, Henriksen, & Bruhn, 1984; Zametkin & Rapoport, 1986). As more research accumulates, researchers may find other subtypes of ADHD. Amen (2001), using thousands of SPECT scans, suggested that there are actually six forms, spread across the lobes; however, although his books and brain images show different patterns, these have not yet been thoroughly reviewed by others.

Genetics and ADHD

When we look at our children it is generally easy to see a correlation between their adult height and our own. If the father is tall, the son is typically tall; if the mother is short, the daughter may be similar in height. Heritability for height is well recognized, with approximately 81% probability that differences are influenced by genetics. Even intelligence is not as strongly influenced as ADHD is by genetics; for intelligence, the genetic component is roughly 55% (Amen, 2001; Willerman, 1973). However, when it comes to ADHD, genetic influence upon our children is even greater than for height or intelligence. *If individuals have a combined subtype of ADHD, the probability of passing on the ADHD genetic trait is around 92% to 98%* (Willcut, Pennington, & Defries, 2000). Amen (2001) reported that if both parents have ADD, then about 85–90% of his patients at his clinic will have ADHD. When I look at my own family, my parents, siblings, and two of my children, they seem to be perfect examples for describing ADHD. Clearly, there is a strong genetic tendency, with environmental or outside causes, such as a head injury, contributing to the remainder of ADHD. As of this writing, it is too early to tell, but I suspect that veterans of the wars in Iraq and Afghanistan who have been exposed to horrific blasts from improvised explosive devices will come to exhibit ADHD-like symptoms and will need help.

Interventions for Students With ADHD

Medical interventions

It is only 10 A.M. and D. A. is on this third 20 oz. bottle of Mountain Dew. Before the day is out he will have consumed at least two liters of "Dew." For D. A., this is normal and with it comes urgent, untimely requests for bathroom passes. If he misses his caffeine-sugar fix, he will be bouncing off the desks and chairs, impulsively tossing things around the classroom, definitely in motion. A time exposure photo would show him as only a blur with the arms invisible because they moved so much. D. A. appears to be self-medicating without his awareness of it, trying to get the stimulation that his brain craves. Medications, such as Ritalin or Adderall, are stimulants, while Strattera is a nonstimulant that blocks the reabsorption of critical cell chemicals related to ADHD.

With the appropriate chemical stimulation prescribed by a physician, a person with ADHD seeks out fewer outside sources to provide stimulation for the brain. For many, such medications work very well, as long as the dosage is correct and they do not miss taking their pills. I remember the day C. M. stopped taking his medication. I had not been informed that he was on any meds or receiving special services. A few weeks earlier I had identified him as a person who needed to be approached carefully, but his attendance was erratic so I had little time to establish a connection. The day he stopped his meds his behavior rapidly spiraled out of control in just a couple of hours. Since he had recently turned 18, he exercised his right to refuse medication, yelling and swearing in violent outbursts that there was nothing wrong with him. When he was on his meds, he was a wonderful, likable young man. A wide number of concerned staff made a variety of attempts to intervene, but it was like talking to a rock. Only a short time later he was in jail and his school career was over.

Nonmedication Alternatives for Students With ADHD

ADHD coaching

One major nonmedical intervention for students with ADHD is coaching. This requires a different mind-set on the school's part, because the school is taking a continuously active intervention. Imagine having a heart attack, and then without either knowledge or training, you are expected to operate on your own heart and fix the problem, even though you don't really know what is causing it. It is a rare individual who can learn to self-regulate his or her behavior without assistance. Like C. M., it is hard for someone to realize there even is a problem, because his or her own erratic behavior is familiar, and impulsive, inattentive behaviors are normal. Sometimes it seems schools and parents expect kids who have real problems with the brain's self-regulation of behavior to somehow correct their neurological problems without assistance. Coaching provides that assistance and guidance, and the easy-to-understand model that Nancy Ratey (2008) has developed works especially well. I had been using a method of coaching students with ADHD in my own school, but the Ratey model helped provide me with even more direction. Essentially in coaching, the student, the coach, and the parents become a team and develop a series of coordinated strategies to recognize and monitor the problems resulting from ADHD.

First, the student has to genuinely realize there is a problem and acknowledge it. Many students are painfully aware they are often in trouble for their actions, losing papers, forgetting assignments, not paying attention. For girls, depression, low self-esteem, avoidance, and nonparticipation often accompanies these problems.

Coaching is a commitment to the student for the long run. It works better if the coach is not one of his or her regular teachers or aides but is someone who can maintain a more objective "distance." The coach helps to create conditions where success can be achieved. This is accomplished through a partnership with the student and parents. Under the guidance of the coach, they all develop the structure that the student will need to succeed. It will be necessary for the coach and student to develop and agree upon a plan of an achievable immediate goal, not multiple goals, and long-term goals should also be identified. The coach utilizes the strengths of the student to help develop the strategies needed to succeed. Students or adults with ADHD often need structure, which is provided through the joint development of a plan in which specific problems are focused on. One of the first things to do is establish when the student will check in with his or her ADHD coach.

The plan, directed by the coach working with the student, helps to identify and prioritize goals, then the coach works on the specific actions that will be taken and monitored. For students with ADHD, the ability to manage attention, and not be distracted from important tasks, or impulsively launching into something more exciting, is difficult. Procrastination among those with ADHD is another major issue. Sustaining attention to get the tasks done requires effort, and procrastination typically occurs when the effort is not sustained. Consequently, one of the common overarching goals is to focus on time management, a skill that adolescents frequently lack.

Many students and adults wait until the last minute to start tackling important tasks. Look at how we shop during the holidays or file taxes; there are droves of people lined up trying to get things done at the last possible moment. Procrastination is one of the typical characteristics of ADHD. If a student is a procrastinator and appears to need to wait until sufficient stress has built up, the prioritizing, planning, and daily checking with the coach helps to develop accountability. Again, the underlying problem is how ADHD affects time management.

To help the student, a critical part of the time management plan frequently takes the form of daily checking in with the coach before classes start and again later in the day just before leaving school. Meeting places might be a learning resource center or library where the student can drop in to have materials and his or her day reviewed. Initial goals may be as simple as having the right books or having assignments completed, or perhaps discussing his or her progress in maintaining attention. If a student is identified as having or is thought to have ADHD, using the last period as a guided study period can be particularly beneficial. This is more than the typical "supervised" study hall where the teacher does not closely monitor the kids who really need to stay on task. The coach might be an ideal person to have available in such a class. In any case, the progress is continuously monitored, and periodically the coach and student reevaluate the progress on the tightly focused goals and make revisions as needed. If the initial goals are reached, the cycle starts over with identifying and prioritizing new goals, and developing the strategies needed to address them.

The coaching is not just a coach-to-student effort. Bringing in the appropriate teachers and parents is often essential to the student's success. To help teachers who are not the coach, consider having the student tape a typed checklist to his or her notebook, *and* locker door, *and* a different one for home. A list of general interventions was presented earlier in the chapter; even more specific interventions along with a short parental checklist follows the end of this ADHD section. Coaching is an ongoing process, not a one-shot deal. For a person with ADHD (including those who are teachers), learning to cope with the problem is a continual process. But teachers should be aware that changing the inappropriate ADHD behavior doesn't guarantee improved academic learning in adolescents, although it does seem to work better in younger children (Fantuzzo et al., 1992; Pelham et al., 1993).

EEG neurofeedback

This is a second, nonmedication intervention, which can be done either in school or in a private clinic. While still not common, more schools are making use of this intervention, and more medical schools are teaching about neurofeedback to physicians in training. Neurofeedback is a modified form of biofeedback that is designed to help specifically with self-regulation of the brain. Although its use as a mechanism of feedback has been around for nearly 30 years, it has only been in the past decade that schools have started to use this intervention. When a student goes off his or her medication it is all too often painfully evident and is typically disastrous for the student. If the right medications are determined they can provide excellent assistance in controlling ADHD, but they rapidly flush out of the body, so if the student misses taking medications, the teachers see the crash. Some parents and adults with ADHD are unhappy with some medication side effects. They don't like the drugged-up, haze effect that can occur, or they are philosophically opposed to having chemicals introduced into the body. It is often as a last resort that people turn to neurofeedback. The use of neurofeedback for people with ADHD and some other disorders is still contested by some primarily because there have not been the classic double-blind studies used with many medical interventions. Neruofeedback is not a cure: There is no treatment for ADHD that will solve it. However, a number of studies have suggested it is promising as an intervention (Arnold, 2001; Ramirez, Desantis, & Opler, 2001; Rossiter & LaVaque, 1995). In actual use, I've found that about 60–70% of the students with ADHD were responsive and demonstrated greater self-regulation of their behaviors, more so now that the technology has improved. I was initially skeptical. I had questions about what happens with this form of feedback and how much of it was a placebo effect. How does feedback from the brain work?

EEG neurofeedback passively records EEG brain waves from one or two sites on the scalp, which are processed by a computer and visual or audio feedback is given to the student when the right combination of wave patterns is reached.

Gradually the brain learns to regulate the wave patterns that are associated with ADHD behaviors. Measurements of the brain waves clearly show a lasting training effect. In treatment, the young children do not know the clinician is trying to get a change in their behaviors, nevertheless, the positive changes occur in many. There isn't an obvious placebo effect either. The process of neurofeedback was initially found with testing of cats that had epileptic seizures. In the course studying seizure medications during animal trials, it was learned that the animals could be trained to change their brain waves, resulting in fewer or no seizures (Sterman, MacDonald, & Stone, 1974; Sterman, LoPresti, & Fairchild, 1969). In time it was learned that the human brain could also learn to self-regulate to a degree so that a number of behavior problems improved, including those associated with ADHD, bipolar disorder, and panic attacks, and at the time of this writing, new procedures are being used to treat PTSD (Posttraumatic Stress Disorder). There are group studies and tens of thousands of case studies on the use of neurofeedback, reporting significant progress on ADHD and other symptoms, but it is not a panacea; it does not work for all mental problems. Like a pebble dropped in a pool of water, the ripples have the greatest effect on those things closest to the impact, and neurofeedback works better with some problems, less with others.

The effectiveness of neurofeedback appears to depend on several factors. First, a correct diagnosis is essential, because that suggests whether the treatment is appropriate and which brain locations to target. This can be aided by having a QEEG scan to more precisely determine which areas of the brain are over- or underactive. (A QEEG scan costs about two-thirds as much as an MRI scan.) Second, the skill of the clinician is critical. A person who is providing the intervention treatment should have a solid background in psychology, such as being a school psychologist, and while the training is short, it is very intensive, with advanced clinics needed to polish skills. Third, the quality of the equipment must be good. I know several practitioners who are using early, rather antiquated equipment and are able to get excellent results, but it takes a while. However, training the brain to self-regulate and retrain neural circuits that were years in the making is a gradual process and the newer equipment can affect the speed of the retraining process. Typically, it takes anywhere from 20–40 hours of therapeutic training in half-hour sessions spread over a semester. With the latest technology, results may be seen much more rapidly, taking as little as 4–10 hours of training to see helpful results, and perhaps up to 20 hours to stabilize the training, because not everyone's brain responds the same way. These two case examples illustrate some of the differences in response to training.

A. C. is a 5-year-old boy in perpetual motion and his attention is never fixed on any one thing for very long. This is coupled with ignoring his parent's directions, the inability to stop behaviors, and procrastination. His parents were greatly stressed by his behaviors. Although not formally diagnosed, he displayed most of the ADHD behaviors listed in *DSM-IV* when he came in for neurofeedback. With less than 5 hours of neurofeedback training A. C. started to be able to sit for long periods at a variety of different tasks, which had never happened before, and his "runs as if by a motor" behavior slowed to that more typical of other 6-year-olds. In 3 weeks he started responding much faster and more appropriately to directions given by his parents and other adults.

In contrast, B. F. is a professional, older middle-aged male with significant traumatic brain injury and many ADHD-like symptoms caused by the trauma. After a year with 45 hours of training sessions, 11 of his 14 major complaints had noticeably been reduced, and his quality of life significantly improved, making it easier for him to function professionally. Every brain has its own response; some will train faster than others.

The most powerful ADHD intervention approach I've seen is a combination of support from parents, a counselor, the student's physician, and a neurofeedback provider (school psychologist, counselor, or private clinician). It has been my observation that using single interventions alone, such as only medications, counseling alone, or neurofeedback alone, is less effective than a team approach. The team approach is achieved more easily through the schools, or college health services. Incorporating such interventions is a commitment of time, space, and resources. Ethically, once an educator starts working with students, I don't believe they can abandon them. If the services are provided through the school, there can be a large savings to parents. In a private clinic one is paying for the skills of clinicians and their time.

Classroom Attention Interventions for Students With ADHD

All of the general attention strategies described earlier can help the adolescent who has ADHD. However, they may also benefit from more specific classroom interventions.

For many students with ADHD, handwriting is an arduous process. It is not unusual for much of their writing to be illegible, especially if they are writing to keep up with note taking or attempting to complete an assignment on time. They can write more legibly but the effort, the amount of concentration it takes, is enormous, and it is often an exhaustingly *slow* and frustrating process. Allow the students to print instead of writing in cursive; it is both faster and generally produces more legible writing. One student of mine exhibited profound symptoms of ADHD. He tried to write fast enough to keep up with the thoughts that were rushing through his head, but he couldn't keep up. The scribbles resembled no language and even he couldn't read them. Later, when he was learning Russian, he started to write with his left hand when doing his translations. The concentration necessary for both the translation and writing left-handed forced him to go slower, resulting in clear, legible writing. Similar problems arise in speech when students are trying to express themselves fast enough to keep up with their speed of thought. For adolescents with ADHD, explaining or elaborating on how or why they are doing something can be very difficult (Saunders & Chambers, 1996). They may speak at an incredibly fast rate in an effort to get the information out before they lose track of it. Gently coach them, because the explanation process requires them to not only find their thoughts, but to also organize them in a coherent manner. The effort to stay focused can be very draining and frustrating. To help maintain their focus in writing assignments, consider having them use a storyboard so that they can illustrate what is happening. It assists students in organizing the information visually, allowing them to see if they've left out critical elements, while providing them with the needed stimulation. Make eye contact and praise (quietly) for their small successes. Developing control over their writing and speech are skills that are gradually built up.

The brains of students with ADHD appear to be understimulated. To provide that stimulation many bounce their legs, tap constantly, or fidget. One unobtrusive way to provide the stimulation is to allow them to doodle; it does not interfere with learning (Andrade, 2009). Providing them with foam balls to squeeze, sitting on exercise balls, and using only one leg to keep balanced all work well. Beach balls work well for providing significant movement for the entire class. The beach ball can be used soccer-style by dribbling it around the desks, but not by violently kicking it. This allows the students to refresh by briefly reaching a higher level of activity with accelerated heart rate and respiratory rate. For pencil tappers, place small foam balls on the tips of pencils. That way the tappers still get the stimulation from the tapping without noisily disrupting everyone else. When they are working through procedures, students with ADHD may need a quiet place away from windows or other students. To help them focus, allow them to self-talk as they work through the material. It often helpful to allow the students to use a foam ball at their desk.

Does the student actually know what the appropriate behavior is at this age level, or is it assumed? In my observations, we tend to assume that students know what appropriate behavior should be from middle school on. However, direct instruction may still be necessary. Students pick up very quickly what the real rules are by the way the class is conducted. If a teacher is inconsistent, they may find themselves in a quagmire, from bathroom requests to procedures for getting out and putting things away properly, such as putting chairs in place instead of creating what looks like an abandoned demolition derby of crushed cars.

With younger adolescents, making appropriate in-class responses is a learning process. At first, many students, not just those with ADHD, may need consistently high structure in how to respond in questions and in how to participate in discussions. They are learning the social rules that are not exhibited on TV (even though some adult TV pundits sometimes fail miserably at this, they usually do wait to respond, if gnashing a few teeth in the process). Discuss and lead students in what is appropriate: that they should not interrupt, and they need to wait to speak when they approach the teacher or others in a discussion. Give them consistent feedback, too; it takes a while to establish the new connections. As they learn the appropriate social roles, disruptions by students with ADHD tend to fall off and boys have more success at this than girls do (Zentall, 2006). Using smaller group work or computer-based assignments gradually moves the students toward being more independent and responsible as more choices and suggestions are provided.

Homework

With the ADHD student, homework is often a disaster. If they haven't forgotten it, or have the lesson only partially completed, it may be crammed in the books somewhere, emerging as a crumpled mess. Assistance in self-regulation at several points often helps. The first is to know when the lesson is due. Make a routine of posting the weekly objectives so the students know where they are headed. Also provide in both writing and on the board the details of their weekly assignments. As these become routine, the student will establish a ritual of looking at what is due or coming up. However, educators should not make the mistake of assuming students will always check these; assignments must still be pointed out. Second, have the student organize the assignments and class materials in a folder by date or topic. Both student and teacher should check it every day. This takes only a moment as the teacher moves among the students. Assignments can still get lost, so it may be advisable to have a place in the room where students file their finished assignments or back-up papers. Third, they need to complete the work. The use of study partners to periodically check each other's work is helpful. In reading assignments, students should read highlighted sections and take summarizing notes, which can facilitate their memory. However, highlighting alone will not help retention because there is no active processing of the material.

One of the ongoing problems with students with ADHD is incomplete assignments. It is frequently advisable to decrease the length of their assignments, because of their issues with time management. Carefully select problems that will demonstrate mastery, but do not leave so many as to overwhelm the students with difficulty. This potentially reduces frustration and allows the student to better sustain attention. If the educator is inclined to do this for all students, he or she should get honest feedback on how long the assignment really took, and then adjust accordingly in order to avoid being manipulated. Another approach is to provide computers or laptops for students to use instead of expecting handwritten materials.

ADHD assessment and tests

Like the homework assignments, it may be necessary to also adjust tests or other assessments; they may need more time, or shorter, more succinct assessments. One strategy to help reduce students' potential for distractibility when working on reviews or tests with multiple choice answers is to cross out the rejected answers, versus just circling the selected ones (Zentall & Smith, 1993). Assessments in other modalities, such as oral tests or demonstrations, may assist the student in staying focused. If impulsivity is an issue, consider the student having retakes, as the first assessment may not measure what they know.

Adolescents have histories that follow them, and these can create problems for them if they are trying to break away from past behaviors, because sometimes neither teachers nor students allow them to try. We expect them to be acting out, noisy, or disruptive, making it even more difficult for them to escape their past. But if they are asking for help, or when they attempt to add something to a group activity, don't ignore them. Make them a welcomed part of the school community (O'Conner & Jenkins, 1993). This also applies to disabled students. However, educators need to be aware of being manipulated by disabled students. Over the years, many students with learning disabilities have become dependent upon assistance (learned helplessness) and are skillful at having an aide or someone actually do their work for them. That doesn't mean you don't provide appropriate help but learn from other teachers or aides how much they actually need (see their individual education plans) and what their manipulation tactics might be.

Schoolwide support

For students to have their attention needs met, whether they have ADHD or not, schoolwide support is needed from both the staff and the administration. Ignorance about the brain's natural attention needs will compound the problems of students being off-task, being easily distracted with texting or mp3 players, or their minds merely out wandering about, lost to the lesson. Students' attention needs are often best met with movement. Support and encourage movement, perhaps through schoolwide rewards that provide everyone with whole-body movement, such as a little extra time for games, or a participation event for the entire student body. Working in an extra 10 minutes just for physical activities is a start. With elementary students, it was found that 30 minutes of activity each day, whether it was all at once or broken up, made a difference in student attentiveness, and that adolescents need movement as well (J. Ratey, 2009). The brain's need for movement doesn't decrease as students become older. Recess is probably one thing that should be retained throughout all levels of school.

Parental involvement

A student with ADHD will have a better chance of experiencing success if there is parental support; much too often it is a critical missing element. Parents have already struggled on the home front, but support and encouragement from the school that provides some real guidance can be helpful. This is not to suggest the school directs the parents in what to do. A heavy-handed approach rarely works, but parents can be coached, too. Help them out by providing them with models of what good note taking looks like, perhaps with a before and after skeletal outline. Discuss with them their children's need for structure that provides the necessary guidance. Parents actually using the checklist and examining their adolescent children's notes or assignments is part of that structure. Educators should also remember that there is a very high degree of heritability for ADHD, and so the parents may be rather scattered and disorganized, too. One idea might be to suggest the establishment of home routines. For example, suggest that the parents use a checklist and review it with their adolescents. There should be a specific place for books and papers *where they are always placed, without fail*. Otherwise, they quickly become scattered. The student should have his or her homework physically checked by a parent if at all possible. To assist parents, provide a simple checklist (which is nearly identical to the student checklist presented earlier) so they can check on their children before going to school:

- Has homework,
- Has books,
- Has writing paper, and
- Has pencils and pens ["writing materials" is too vague, they may forget the paper or the pencils!].

There is also the reality that many of these adolescents don't have adults to check in with them before they leave for school: this emphasizes the necessity of having a coach in place whom they check in with when they arrive at school. Chewing a kid out because he forgot his paper is not a very good approach. It's like blaming a disabled person in a wheelchair for not moving fast enough. It's not a choice: It's part of how his brain works, and he must develop better coping skills. Chewing a person out doesn't change his genes so he can grow new connections.

Here is a summary of ADHD support and interventions for teachers to use with the students:

- Use a coaching system.
- Consider EEG neurofeedback.
- Get students active in sports such as swimming, basketball, soccer, or rock climbing (see Chapter 2 for a list of complex movements) (Zentall et al., 2001).
- Develop a plan jointly for students with ADHD and for their parents (this works with other students as well, and can be accomplished in homeroom or with teacher/student advisees).
- Make counseling for students and parents available.
- Consider and implement medical/pharmacological interventions, as determined by a physician.
- Suggest nonmedical alternatives: ADHD coaching both outside of school and within the school; neurofeedback used in conjunction with counseling.

Designing Your Personal Application

This chapter suggested and commented on a multitude of applications, but where should an educator begin? One of the goals of this book is to move from theory into real applications, with all its complexities. Often one of the hardest tasks is to actually get started. At the end of some major chapters an exercise will be presented to assist the educator in getting the applications going. The approach used here is to work out applications for one or two lessons that have problems, not to tackle a unit with many lessons, because that can easily be overwhelming. Additionally, it will probably take a while to fine-tune the first lessons a teacher tries. We have to learn to walk before we run in these applications.

Think of one or two important lessons where there are problems with student attention. It can be an attention problem that lasts all period, or just a portion of the class time. Answer the following questions:

What are the students paying attention to?

What is capturing their attention or distracting them? Some of the problems may be partially addressed through consistent and fairly enforced rules and guidelines. For example, let them know the rules regarding the use of iPods, mp3 players or cell phones. If there aren't school rules for these, consider having the students set them on the desk tops, shut off. The distractions can be reduced.

What can you do to initially capture the students' attention? Look over the general attention suggestions throughout the chapter, and try to compile about four to five different ways to initially capture their attention. Doing the same thing each day will quickly become a routine that students pay less and less attention to unless there is a task for them to immediately and actively engage in. This might be lesson, a search activity, or some sort of challenge that organizes and keeps them active. In the ideal world this is the time when teachers take a role or get out the upcoming lesson. The reality is there will most likely be some students, possibly those with ADHD, who will need some direct supervision or coaching.

List a few examples of physical activities the students may engage in that directly relate to the lesson.

List a few examples of activities that require focused visual attention, such as visually comparing, or finding differences in patterns.

Expand on any of the above activities to include written or verbal descriptions, summaries, or any form of personal elaboration.

Describe a small group activity where each person takes a part for which he or she will be accountable.

Elaborate and explain in some detail what those attention-grabbing activities will be. Actually build one or two activities before you go further. It is important that you get physically started.

Maintaining attention is the next hurdle. No question about it; this will be a continuous hurdle for everyone. Attention strategies that work for one group of students may not work for the next. Tackling this is something like being a professional sports athlete: Your opponent is always there, yet always changing and adapting. So must you. Here are a few starters for adapting.

Review the strategies described under general interventions again and select the five you think will involve the most students.

Make a list of the strategies, perhaps on a card, and tape it to your desk or some other place to remind yourself.

Continuously reflect, What happened? When did their attention drift? Why?

Reflect on success. Perhaps the students didn't drift, and most paid attention. What was different about that lesson that held their attention?

Remember that the brain is naturally attuned to movement; use it to keep your students with you.

Key Points and Recommendations

There is no such thing as multitasking where we can pay equal attention to multiple things at the same time; that is a neuromyth. The brain cannot track multiple pieces of information with the same levels of attention. It can rapidly engage, disengage, shift, and reengage with different items, but the capacity of the attention systems is limited. Consequently, if too much information is coming in, portions of it will be missed. This is a common problem for many adolescents in middle school and high school, especially when more instruction is presented through lecture. More is not better, but is just more lost information.

Capturing, directing, maintaining, and sustaining attention on an appropriate level is one of the fundamental keys to learning. Teachers should actively work at getting students' attention, and actively focus on maintaining it throughout the lesson: That will reduce the number of students who will likely drift. There is no doubt that having students maintain attention is a challenging task. If the teacher is physically active, up and moving among the students frequently, students are more likely to pay attention. The old saying "One teacher on her feet is worth ten in the seat" is sound, and this goes for college instructors as well. Being trapped down at the front podium is considerably less engaging than being up in the aisles and interacting directly with the students, even in large lecture halls.

- *Pay attention to inattention.* Too often a teacher will overlook a student who is quiet but not paying attention. Any number of problems may be present: There may be another distraction, such as texting, listening to an iPod, to reading or zoning out. Teachers need to be alert to these particular students and be proactive with them, rather than letting the situation go until a disaster visits the student.
- *Nonvocal music can function as an audio wall to screen out distractions.* Be alert to how they respond to the music; some genres may agitate them or, conversely, put them to sleep. Allowing students to use their own music generally does not work, because it is easy for them to switch to music with vocals and abuse a teacher's trust.
- *Teachers should avoid overwhelming themselves by trying too many new strategies at once.* Master one skill before trying to add more. Become sufficiently adept at the new technique so that it has reached automaticity, and you don't have to think about it. Too frequently teachers become enthused and try too many changes at one time and perform mis-

erably on all of them. Just like the students, it takes a while for our own brains to become skillful. Allow yourself time to learn.

- *Adolescents are not functioning well cognitively until roughly 9–10 A.M.* The adolescent sleep-wake cycle is different from that of younger children. Adolescents become more alert and function at a higher cognitive level in mid- to late morning. Considering that many adolescents are also sleep deprived, whether from texting, computer games, or early morning sport practices, cognitively demanding classes probably should not be in the early morning, but closer to lunchtime.

- *Establish classroom routines for when students enter and leave.* The rituals provide boundaries for the students, and, when used properly, can quickly get students organized and onto tasks before the teacher has said anything, or help them check to make sure they not only have their assignments, but also the necessary materials to complete them.

- *Students who have difficulty maintaining attention (including students with ADHD) should be seated closer to the teacher.* This permits the teacher to more easily keep them on task, but they are also less prone to distractions presented by other students simply because their backs are to potential distractions. Additionally, the teacher can easily use proximity in an unobtrusive manner and move up to the students who are being distracted without embarrassing them.

- *Students' needs to create their own stimulation are reduced when the environment provides it.* A classroom where the kids are sitting, and essentially passive, provides very little stimulation for their brains. There should be a series (often more than one) of activities that are both physically and mentally engaging. Activities that involve movement, especially where the students move around several times, or where their heart and respiratory rates are accelerated, will frequently provide the necessary stimulation. If students' brains are insufficiently stimulated, students will typically create their own movements such as talking, texting, tapping, looking around, or engaging in other off-task behaviors. If several students become engaged in off-task behaviors, the lesson's activity level is probably needing life support. This is a major warning signal to the teacher that the lesson is failing to engage the students' brains. Rather than harshly reprimanding students, consider that your lesson needs immediate adjustment. Lesson CPR may be needed. Halt and change (or start) with a new direction and activity but make certain that all students are both physically engaged and moving.

- *Avoid interruptions if possible.* When a distraction is present, no matter what the source is, it is more difficult for the student to reengage at the same level of attention and same level of cognition if they have been interrupted. They also will frequently lose information. They will miss changes or forget what was just discussed. It is often necessary to pause and revisit the information that they were engaged with just prior to the interruption. That may mean asking several review questions to help them refocus. Because information is almost invariably lost by an interruption, it is imperative that lessons and handouts be reviewed prior to handing them out and instructional changes made then. If that is not possible, guide the students collectively to the corrections *before* the lesson or activity starts to eliminate or reduce any further interruptions.

- ***The attention systems of students may simply be overwhelmed if there is too much information.*** The attention systems are very limited in how much information they can monitor. If there is a barrage of information, major portions of it may be overlooked, or worse, intentionally ignored in the students' efforts to concentrate. Keep the lessons straightforward, using the old principle of KIS (Keep It Simple). The use of skeletal notes and graphic organizers will help the students maintain their attention in addition to keeping the teacher on track, too. It is still quite possible to insert interesting trivia or sidebars as the lesson progresses to avoid being dull.

- ***Students with ADHD can affect the entire class atmosphere.*** Because of that, the typical educator needs more knowledge about ADHD and what they can do to help students. ADHD affects everyone, whether he or she has the problem or not. The old saw that teachers spend 90% of their time with 5% of the students is probably true, and it is more likely some of those students have ADHD, though not all. The cliché of "forewarned is forearmed" is highly applicable. The more an educator knows about ADHD, its symptoms, the students' needs for stimulation, and the likelihood that students will create their own stimulation if the activity is too dull, the better the lesson designs will be.

- ***If educators address the attention issues, and pay attention to them or to even some of them, and actively work on those problems, more of the students will benefit with fewer disruptions and greater learning.*** The problems of maintaining attention concern all the adolescents. By being alert to potential problems *before* the lessons start, such as where a lesson may drag, when there is a lot of information to process, or when physical activities need to be incorporated, educators will be able to keep students focused longer. If regular disruptions, such as school announcements, have any kind of pattern, plan and adjust the lessons around those times. If that is not possible, create a routine with the students so they know to expect to have a brief refocusing activity or review immediately after disruptions. This might take the form of students being called upon to provide the review information, rather than the adolescents becoming totally reliant on the teacher.

- *Educators need to pay attention just as much to those quiet kids, because, although they are not disrupting the class like the hyperactive kids, they are missing out, too. Pay attention to inattention.* The noisy teenagers easily capture the attention of teachers, but the quiet students may be completely tuned out as well. They may seat themselves in an effort to be obscure. Girls who have ADHD will express it differently, and sometimes they are very quiet. Make a point to talk with those students, and use proximity so you can monitor whether they are following the lesson and are actively involved. Be certain to call on them every day just the same as any other student.

- *ADHD for all types occurs in around 4.7–4.9% of the student population when DSM-IV criteria are used.* A simple check on how many students have been identified may alert the educator if some students are being overlooked. If there are almost no girls identified, there is a strong chance teachers have missed them. For example, if there are 10 boys for every girl who is diagnosed, the school is overlooking the girls with ADHD, and those students are being underserved, missing out on some of their education. At least three forms of ADHD have been consistently identified and there may possibly be up to six, depending on the brain's activity. These values are not fixed. As better diagnostic tools emerge, we might see a shift in both the frequency and other subtypes of ADHD.

- *The frequency of ADHD decreases with age to approximately 2.9% for males and 1.4% for females.* Although the brain development of a student with ADHD lags by about 4 years from the regular student population, not all students outgrow ADHD. Even though many do learn coping skills, others will need support in developing those skills so they can succeed when they leave school.

- *The probability of inheriting ADHD is around 92% to 98% if individuals are of the combined ADHD type.* ADHD is an inherited disorder. Attention problems may be noticed with other family members, including parents. The heritability may complicate interventions on the home front. If the parents are in denial, or continue to have problems of their own, it may be difficult to enlist support, let alone actually see home interventions carried out.

- *The most powerful ADHD intervention approach is the combined support of parents, a physician (for the medications), a counselor, and a neurofeedback provider.* Working as a team, we can address more issues effectively than anyone by themselves. Each team member brings a different perspective, knowledge set, and experience to focus on the students' problems. Additionally, the comorbidity of ADHD typically means that other significant problems will emerge as ADHD or some other initial problem is brought under control. It is essential that the health care provider or team member has others ready to assist when these occur rather than suddenly having to seek assistance in a crisis. Additionally, the group effort can not only help the teen with ADHD, but the group often lends some support to each other to make sure the gaps that naturally crop up are more likely to be covered.

RESOURCES

Hartmann, T. (1997). *Attention Deficit Disorder: A different perception.* Grass Valley, CA: Underwood Books.

Ratey, N. (2008). *The disorganized mind: Coaching your ADHD brain to take control of your time, tasks, and talents.* New York, NY: St. Martin's Press.

Robin, A. (1998). *ADHD in adolescents, diagnosis and treatment.* New York, NY: Guilford Press.

Zentall, S. (2005). *ADHD and education, foundations, characteristics, methods, and collaboration.* Columbus, OH: Pearson Education.

CHAPTER FOUR

Emotional Processing

Any emotion, if it is sincere, is involuntary.
—Mark Twain

The students walked in, expectant, but not quite sure what they would find on the first day of school. Mr. D. had a reputation and his classes were different. When the students were seated, he introduced himself by writing his name on the board. For the students, it was all the usual stuff so far. Mr. D. paused only for a moment, but in that brief span, Alex, a student who had failed the class the year before, strode up to the board and wrote his name below Mr. D.'s, saying, "And I'm Alex, Mr. D.'s student assistant, and you better listen to what he says. He means it. I know the drill, he wants quality and you can do it. And," he pauses, looking at the students meaningfully, "don't ask Mr. D. for answers, because he forgets fast, I know, but *I* still remember. I won't be tell'um to you either, but I can *show you how to get* to the answers." The class was already different, and Mr. D. had yet to speak even three sentences. But this was unusual from even what Mr. D. typically did because Alex had completely surprised him by confidently and proudly introducing himself. Alex's self-introduction had not been discussed earlier. Alex went on to become a very real student teacher, using the same techniques that Mr. D. used, never answering a question directly but guiding them and using his own examples to illustrate his points. That he had once failed the class was soon forgotten because he had quickly moved on to become the in-class veteran, the resource and peer-teacher students would turn to for advice. Rather than dreading Alex as a returning failed student, Mr. D. was obviously pleased to have him back and welcomed him back even before classes had begun. Even though Alex failed, a genuine connection had been established the previous year, and both grew from it.

It had not always been that way. Years earlier Mr. D. approached the classes as if he were a drill sergeant going to war. One time he had to wait for a poor freshman who was lost, and late for his class on the first day of high school. When the bewildered and rather stressed student finally staggered into his room, Mr. D. then launched into a rehearsed but terrifying rage. The students sat frozen in fear, with deer-in-the-headlights looks. It was his intent to have established control and discipline from the first moment. It took Mr. D. years to realize that by building nonthreatening emotional connections to the students he could accomplish the same control and even push learning to a much higher level. Reflecting on this, he said, "I hate to think what I did to those freshmen; they certainly were too scared to do their best."

The importance of emotions in our daily affairs has been recognized across the world for a long time. If a person listens to the honky-tonk songs of country western music, they are filled with the feelings of those who'd been wronged, cheated upon, and lost love. Countless songs express emotions from other times and areas around the world. Many Irish songs are mournful laments about lost loves; even the Bible has whole books, such as Lamentations, the Song of Solomon, and the Psalms, that express emotional themes and the full range of human sentiment.

Emotions and emotional processing are essential to both our survival and communication within and between cultures. In common usage, emotion is the subjective interpretation of feelings in the body (Damasio, 1999; Ward, 2006). From the perspective of research, emotions are considered to be body states that result from a series of physiological changes or that function as an "action schema" (Lande & Nadel, 2000) to prepare the body to have particular responses to the environment, such as dodging threats, avoiding disease, approaching others, and mating with others. When we become aware of these emotional changes in our body states we call them feelings (Damasio, 1999).

Our expression of an emotional state and our ability to determine how someone else feels directly affect our survival (Hampson, 2006; Thayer, 2000). Part of this ability to read body states is called "emotional intelligence" (Salovey & Sluyter, 1997) and will be considered further in Chapter 6. When we want to communicate our emotions we primarily use facial expressions and body language.

However, adolescents don't have as much experience in their abilities to communicate with others. For example, in some photography classes there is an assignment where students are required to shoot four images of the same person expressing completely different emotions. The results are revealing. A number of teenagers thought they were showing different emotions with their facial expressions, but the rest of the students were unable to figure out what the emotions were supposed to be. In looking at the photos, some of the students were baffled by the expressions and other students thought they all looked the same. At that point, an "a-ha!" moment occurred. It dawned on a few students that how they expressed their emotions facially was completely murky to others, and that lack of clear expression contributed to misunderstandings. TV sitcoms and movies frequently base their shows upon our classic misreadings of others' emotional states. In schools, the situation has played itself out countless times between two adolescents. The girl glares at the boy, wrinkles up her nose, slams shut her locker, and storms off. The boy stands there looking bewildered, utterly confused, and hands outward as if begging for help, and says bleakly to his friends, "What'd I do? Is she angry?"

When people misread the facial cues (disgust in this case), they can have serious problems. This form of social feedback provides us direction in what actions to take or avoid. In short, the ability to interpret facial expressions accurately and the emotional information they represent are fundamental to human decision making. As children become adolescents, they become aware of how important that skill is, but even with experience adults continue to struggle with it as well. I still have problems accurately reading my wife's expressions, and most men I know have similar problems with their wives. As a result, husbands routinely find themselves in some minor (or major) difficulty if they cannot interpret body language correctly. I can tell when my wife isn't happy, but it is difficult for me to discern just which emotion is being expressed. Generally, females are better able to read emotions that we express on our faces (Hall, 1978, 1984; Hall, Carter, & Horgan, 2000). When there is only fleeting information to be seen, they are better than men in figuring out the emotion (Hall & Matsumoto, 2004).

Reading the emotions of those who are important in an adolescent's life is a survival skill; it makes up a crucial part of social feedback within family groups and cultures at large. For instance, failures in developing the skills to detect emotional expressions are part of the problems autistics have. Additionally, there are innumerable violent family conflicts fueled in part by poor reading of emotions. In the classroom, problems inadvertently arise when a student misreads a teacher or fellow student, or when a teacher is unable to discern what a student is expressing. As a result of the survival significance of understanding facial expressions, a specific part of the brain apparently evolved to help process facial stimuli, and considerable effort has gone into researching what happens. Understanding others' emotions is part of what makes us human.

The Brain's Processing of Emotion

There are about five emotions that humans seem to recognize across most cultures when we look at faces (Ekman & Friesen, 1976; Ekman, Friesen, & Ellsworth, 1972). These are happiness, sadness, anger, fear, and surprise. These emotions are processed through different areas of the brain. There does not appear to be a single system for processing emotion as suggested by the misleading term "limbic system," but rather a series of different brain structures that may process certain types of emotions independently of other structures (Gazzaniga et al., 2009). For example, the amygdala is involved in the fear response and it influences memory and is used in detecting sadness in facial expressions (Fine & Blair, 2000). It lies just in front of the hippocampus, which processes the memory (LeDoux, 1996). The insula, an area of cortex deeper in the brain, is used for processing facial expressions of disgust (Phillips et al., 1997), while happiness does not appear to be processed in any single location (Ward, 2006). (See Figure 4.1.)

Properties of Emotions

The six emotions listed above do not have distinct boundaries but vary along a continuum, and they are nuanced by having different levels of intensity (Gazzaniga et al., 2009). Imagine you open a food container that was left in the refrigerator long ago and a pungent odor of spoilage greets your nose. You turn your head away in disgust. On another day, you have the misfortune of munching on a stale potato chip. Disgust again registers, but the difference is one of intensity. The potato chip tastes bad, but the fuzzy green and unrecognizable container churns your stomach; the intensity level is much greater. How pleasant something is, from pleasant or good, to bad or very unpleasant, is called *valence*. The internal intensity, how soothing or agitating or exciting something is, is called *arousal* (Osgood, Suci, & Tannengaum, 1957; Russell, 1979). Both of these properties can affect later memory (Cahill & McGaugh, 1995; LaBar & Phelps, 1998; Ochsner, 2000), making certain events that had high valence and arousal easier to recall. If the dimensions of valence and arousal are used properly, as in experiential learning (discussed later in this chapter) they can be remarkably powerful in making a lesson easier to recall. Let's see how this might work by exploring what you remember about different past events.

- Do you remember your first day of school?
- Do you remember your first algebra test?
- Assuming you were not "chemically impaired," do you remember your twenty-first birthday?
- Do you remember what you were doing on September 11, 2001?
- Do you remember the first time a close loved one died?

Each of these events created different levels of valence, they were pleasant to unpleasant, and also generated different levels of arousal from soothing to agitating or irritating. Some memories may be fuzzy and blended with others, while other memories are distinct and easily recalled. If teachers designed lessons that intentionally built in valence and arousal, the lesson would be more easily recalled. For adolescents, emotions can profoundly influence how they recall information and how they act.

Negative experiences are often better remembered than neutral, everyday lessons because they create a valence that is unpleasant or agitating (Kensinger & Corkin, 2003). However, it is probably not a good idea to make learning unpleasant, unless a very specific lesson is being driven home, as in the military or with safety issues. *Emotions used positively can make learning events much easier to recall.* Too often an educator's daily lesson design creates a distaste for learning. That does not mean educators should entertain the students, but rather teachers should look

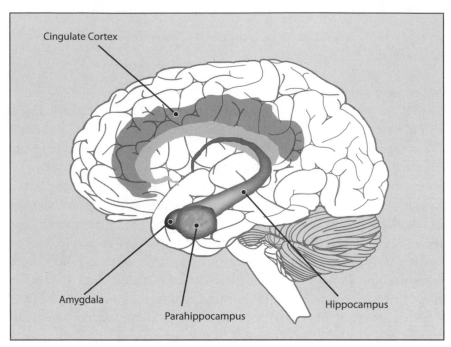

Fig. 4.1. Emotional processing structures. Some of the structures that are involved in emotional processing include Amygdala, cingulated cortex, insula (not pictured), hippocampus. Many of these structures are also involved with memory encoding, including parahippocampus.

hard and honestly at why so many students are disaffected with particular subjects, teachers, or school with respect to valence and arousal. It might reveal why so many adolescents are turned off by school.

The Effects of Stress

Many adolescents have experienced events with so much stress that they literally could not think or concentrate on even simple tasks, let alone sleep. When stress jumps to higher levels of intensity or lasts too long, it interferes with their ability to retrieve memories (Starkman, Gebarski, Berent, & Schteingart, 1992). Stress hormones change a person's bodily responses, including heart rate and respiratory rate. Both prepare the body for action. In small doses, stress hormones aided our nomadic ancestors because the stress would peak in a confrontation or hunt, and then diminish. Our bodies evolved to handle that. However, in today's world the stress load comes in and stays, with deadlines and lousy bosses that one cannot escape. Other stressors for many of our students who live in poverty may include where the next meal will come from or not getting shot at by a rival gang (Keenan et al., 1996; McLeod & Kessler, 1990). In poverty situations, students and parents alike are constantly responding to the crises; there are few or no resources in reserve to reduce the stress (Lupien, King, Meaney, & McEwen, 2000). In the recent severe recession of 2009, some were made homeless and some had no alternatives but to live in tent cities or cars, reminiscent of the Depression. When the stress levels stay high, there are too many *glucocorticoids,* such as the steroid hormone cortisol, in the system and in the brain. Too much stress while cause damage to the brain. With small or moderate amounts of stress, the glucocorticoids help to form memories, increasing long-term potentiation in the synapses, but when the levels rocket upward, there is interference with the memories (Sapolsky, 2008). Fundamentally, what occurs is that the neurons have two types of receptors for the stress hormones: one is sensitive to low levels of the hormones; the other is sensitive to a higher concentration. When the stress occurs, the brain believes it will need more food, so the glucose levels increase. After about 30 minutes the glucose levels drop back. The boost of sugar helps the body to work faster. However, if the stress continues, the second set of receptors is activated, but the sugar level is still low and may go lower still because of the glucocorticoids. Meanwhile the body, housing the brain, is still in a crisis. If the stress continues, more hormones are pumped into the brain and rest of the body. The result is that many of the dendritic connections atrophy and shrink, making it hard to access memories because there are fewer connections. Additionally, the stress increases the likelihood that a number of the hippocampal neurons will die (Magariños & McEwen, 1995; Magariños, McEwen, Flügge, & Fuchs, 1996; Reul & deKloet, 1985; Sapolsky, Krey, & McEwen, 1985).

One of the most fundamental survival responses involved in learning is our fear response, processed through the amygdala, and the associated memory of what triggered it is processed further by the hippocampus. Consider Mr. D.'s early years in teaching. He routinely terrorized his new students in order to gain classroom control and instill fear. I recall my own student years when I focused on what *not* to do in order to avoid being smacked by a meter stick or to avoid receiving a verbal thrashing. Concentrating on the lesson and learning was not nearly as important as just surviving. It was fear conditioning; the moment we entered that teacher's classroom, our stress and attention immediately jumped. When the conditions are particularly stressful, what students have learned may not even be available for their later use. LeDoux (1996) found evidence for two different types of processing that explain this. One pathway uses a more thoughtful analysis and a slower response, while a different "quick and dirty" pathway provides for an immediate acceleration of heart and respiratory rate and a fast response. The amygdala, functioning somewhat like a quick decision maker, crudely evaluates the incoming information as if it were asking, "Is this a threat to me or not?" The automatic quick and dirty response can save your neck or get you into even more trouble despite extensive training for just that situation. Let me illustrate. Navy fighter pilots are smart and highly trained to land on a relatively tiny, pitching, and tilting deck of an aircraft carrier. Furthermore, they have to do it at night when they can't see the surface they're supposed to land on. If they come in too high, they can't get the plane down to "home" and safety. If they come in too low, they slam the plane into the rear of the aircraft carrier at 150 mph, which doesn't leave much chance of survival. Laurence Gonzales, a fighter pilot, described how one pilot completely ignored multiple forms of communication from the carrier to wave off and not land. The pilot fixated on only one thing: getting down. He crashed into the back end of the carrier, tearing the plane in half, but fortunately he survived. The brain's quick and dirty, fast processing overrode the slower, thoughtful processing. Carrier pilots, Gonzales noted, are warned that they go into combat flight with only half their IQ, meaning that they often won't be able to think clearly, and time to reflect is not usually an option (Gonzales, 2003). *Fear or terror can automatically override well-rehearsed training.* In test situations, students' thinking can be so severely affected by fear that they may stumble on routine skills. They may react quickly instead of thinking calmly their way through the problem.

The Educational Connection

Students are often fear-conditioned in schools by particular instructors, but for many people the effects created by fear do not seem to fade. In middle school and high school, many parents never show up for parent-teacher conferences, or they do so only reluctantly. One reason I've heard from parents is that they don't want to return to a place where so many unpleasant memories were created. For them, school was not a place of experiencing success and preparing to enter the world; it was a place where the classroom frequently held the tyranny of terror. These parents end up avoiding even coming to school for their children. *Schools should be welcoming and safe. Teachers should actively reduce the fear and increase the safety for both students and their parents.*

There are simple, potent techniques to reduce fear in a classroom. *To reduce fear and change moods, smile as you personally greet the students and play music when they enter the room or during work activities, labs, or when class routines change.* The strategy of greeting students at the door means that you must have a genuine smile and make eye contact while you're doing it. This applies not only in the hallways but also in other student-gathering places, like the cafeteria. Teachers can create a mood in the classroom by using music to help regulate emotions. We've all experienced how music can change the mood in a movie. There are violins played in a romantic scene or a heavy, throbbing beat if something scary is about to happen. Some high schools pipe music into the halls when classes change. Think about it: the students are already using music to create a mood when they walk around with their iPods or mp3 players. The difference is the school is being proactive and using music to redirect the students. Music primes their brains for what is to come. Play a wide selection of music, because what works for one class may completely fail with another. Each class has its own personality. Eric Jensen provides a selection of CDs specifically for the classroom (at www.jensenlearning.com), a number of which I've found reasonably effective, though I supplement heavily. I have even found that rock and heavy metal songs can be rearranged into beautiful orchestral performances, much to my surprise (Vitamin String Quartet, 2009).

When the students are greeted, eye contact is made, and all the while music is being played, an emotional connection is starting to be made. It is a start but probably not enough. Build the emotional connection with your students. Dr. Robert Greenleaf, a friend and colleague, suggests, "Make the emotional connection first, then worry about the lesson." When students are processing information, the emotional context can influence the learning even much later. *Offhand remarks may carry considerable weight for students with very long-term effects.* They may be mulled over by the student for years, influencing his or her actions. The original comment might be either positive or negative, but students will remember some of those apparently little things the teacher thought of as inconsequential. The emotional perception of the lesson can stem from either the unintentional actions or comments the teacher has made or the content of the lesson itself. *The teacher's body language and tone of voice can increase the emotional significance for the lesson by displaying enthusiasm and creating anticipation and excitement for the student.* Enthusiasm can be infectious.

Experiential Learning

Experiential learning is a powerful way to link emotions, memories, and action because the student is literally immersed in the learning event, experiencing through many senses, and creating strong memories for what happens (Andreasen et al., 1999; Willis, 2006). Typically, experiential learning is found in outdoor recreation programs, which can teach crafts and historical skills and also sports, such as orienteering, cycling, mountain biking, hiking, backpacking, sport and rock climbing, and many other activities. Part of the reason experiential programs enjoy success is their excellent use of valence and arousal. Wilderness schools, such as the National Outdoor Leadership School (NOLS) and Solid Rock Outdoor Ministries (SROM), use experiential learning to hone their lessons to a high level (Cruickshank, 2009). SROM's approach is powerful, not just because of their religious message, but because they consciously work at creating linkages between action, emotion, and memory that their student clientele will be able to recall much later. They use high positive valence and an appropriate mix of arousal. In experiential learning, the student's whole body feels the consequences of decisions, moment by moment, day after day. As the name implies, they experience the learning, not just passively observing, talking about it, or doing a token lab exercise with minimal participation. Instead, students are interacting with fellow students in ways that create emotional bonds such as in rock climbing, where one student must implicitly trust their life to the rope-handling skills of the other student. Strong social feedback is in place and affects decision making. Thought and emotions can't be separated like Mr. Spock does in the old *Star Trek* series. Deliberate decisions are influenced by socio-emotional feedback (Immordino-Yang & Damasio, 2008).

Emotions, Mirror Systems, and Decision Making

The world that adolescents live in and their particular cultures impact the emotional states of their brains. This applies to both the students and the teacher. Those emotions and the ever-changing mental and body states weave into the brain's decision-making process. Different cultural rules can affect a person's emotions; certain actions will be disapproved of while others may cause embarrassment (Semin & Manstead, 1982). For example, in some cultures, eye contact with someone is frowned upon, as is standing up in front of a class made up of students from other cultures. For some Native American students, depending on the tribe, it is culturally inappropriate to make a child speak or make a presentation in front of a class full of nontribal members.

If people somehow separated their emotions from decision making they would be unable to function normally in any society. Worse, they would probably be in constant trouble, because making sound decisions depends on the emotional fabric. When the brain's emotional processing goes awry, so do the decision-making processes and the ability to function smoothly.

Just as a student's ability to read emotions in facial expressions affects his or her ability to communicate (Merten, 2005), there are other processes that appear to link emotional processing and decision making, which result in rational actions within a society. Apparently, something at a very basic level of processing called mirror neurons can help in understanding someone's actions (Oberman & Ramachandran, 2007). The mirror neurons help students to understand someone else's emotions, and that understanding starts very early in life.

When we smile at a baby, it smiles back; when a moody student grouses in a classroom, everybody changes his or her behavior. For example, some students become guarded in their comments, while others go silent and watch both the agitated student and teacher. When we watch a person run smack into a pole they did not see, we wince at the sickening thud. When a person comes in smiling, bubbly, we smile with her, and she lights up the room. Students use social feedback to recognize emotions and respond in a similar fashion. In short, they have learned to mirror back a behavior that they have seen. When people observe an action, the same areas of the brain that are necessary for the action become activated, even if they are just passively watching. For example, when we watch a painful collision of two hockey players on the television, we wince as if we felt the pain and tighten our muscles. The modeling is activating areas in our brain that we would need to carry out the same action (Iacoboni, 2008). The mirror systems help a person to communicate and make decisions (Immordino-Yang, 2008). A malfunctioning system, such as might be occurring in children with autism, severely handicaps functioning in society. What a person decides to do depends, in part, on his or her understanding of another person's actions. A person's decisions have a goal, directed by the mirror systems. If a student is unable to interpret another person's actions, and he can't understand what the other person intends, then his selected response may be incorrect. For example, if someone is unable to recognize the emotional communication expressed in the eyes because she does not make eye contact, she may just walk right over other people, stepping on them without acknowledging them, as some autistics do. Of course, it's much more complicated than that, but some models are beginning to help educators to understand the behaviors. The models may provide direction in their educational design of lessons.

How adolescents perceive something and whether it makes sense to them influences the actions they take. *Mirror systems enable us to better understand others' actions and make more appropriate decisions that make sense within a particular culture/society.* A student's perception is built from information taken in from the environment but this perception is also colored by the lens of memories. When the brain's mirror system combines streams of information with a choice of actions, the action that emerges is directed toward some sort of goal (Damasio, 1989; Klin et al., 2009). (See Figure 4.2.) The action the brain takes does not happen in a vacuum; it also needs to make sense in respect to the society that people find themselves in—hence, the role of social feedback. Social feedback that a student receives may inhibit or encourage further actions on the student's part. The mirror system helps a person to perceive and understand what the society that immediately surrounds them is doing or intending to do. Gawking up at the skyscrapers of New York and

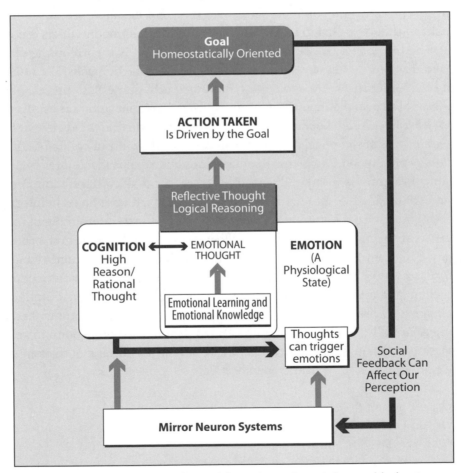

Fig. 4.2. A simplified, hypothetical flow chart of goal directed behaviors.

wearing a style of clothing that screams out that a person is a tourist may not always be the smartest of actions to take. The time-tested advice "when in Rome do as the Romans do" may help the person to adapt to the society.

These dynamic relationships between students' perception of the social context and the actions they take toward a goal suggest a basis for motivation, and one that will vary with each learner. In the classroom or learning situation, the lesson needs to make sense to the student in terms of the actions the student is going to take. That is where the lesson must "connect" to the student. It is probably more important that the lesson is meaningful from the student's perspective, rather than the teacher's. The lesson may have great significance to the teacher and overall learning, but if that understanding is so obscure or developmentally beyond the reach of the student, getting the student to take an action or to even attempt the problem may cause difficulties. We often see this reflected in the student complaint, "Where am I going to use this?"

Their perceptions are their reality. However, a perception of reality can be seriously skewed. How might a misperception look in a teaching situation? In my biology class, misperceptions are commonplace. Take the color of blood, for example. Students believe that oxygenated blood is bright red (arterial blood), which is correct, but that blood in the veins (without oxygen) is blue. That is incorrect: the blood is a dark red, not blue. They are shocked and argue that "in the books, the veins are colored blue!" Unfortunately, most books inadvertently perpetuate the misperception in their efforts to distinguish between veins and arteries and in most diagrams the color of veins is blue. Looking at veins through the skin and yellowish fat below the skin, along with the peculiarities of wavelengths of different colors of light, we see a bluish color. Blood from veins that has never been exposed to air (oxygen) and drawn into a vacuum is a dark red. To address this I try to draw upon their personal experience of having blood drawn, or show a video clip with the blood being drawn. Because their new conception is fragile, I follow up with reinforcing questions in order to establish a new perception. I have to look at the problem from the students' perspective in order to know what to do to change their misperception.

Teachers need to try to get into the students' heads and see how they perceive. As a teacher with a lot of practice, I don't always find it easy to do. To understand the teenagers I work with, I ask them to help me by giving me their feedback, sometimes formally, while at other times the questions are embedded in reviews or discussions. Although the questions change, here is a sampling of questions that may be used to probe the students' perspective.

- Why are we studying this?
- Why do you need to learn this?
- What was easy for you?
- What was confusing?
- What things did I do that helped you understand?

- Did having fellow students explain it help you?
- Give me a couple of examples of who uses this.
- Where might you use this information/skill? How can we solve problems with this?
- If you want to be _____, is this a knowledge/skill that might be required for you to complete the program?
- What can I do differently that would help you understand/demonstrate/ explain this topic?

Routinely addressing many of these questions before and during the lesson will help students make the connections. In fact, before the lesson formally starts, a brief student investigation into the topic can help establish the bridge. With feedback, a teacher can find where the gaps are and begin to address these.

Let's be honest. Some of these are very hard questions, and many teachers don't have answers to them. Educators have two tough questions they must answer for *every lesson* if they don't want to lose their students. Adult students vote with their feet. If the lessons are not meeting their needs, they walk; adolescents can't do that. *However, those students who cannot vote with their feet, vote with their minds and will turn them off during the lesson.* The questions educators must address are:

- What are the connections (and can students understand them)?
- If there are no uses/connections, why is this being taught?

Math is obviously one of the toughest topics to have students make connections with because its daily application to the average person is obscure at best. Educators often don't help matters. I once encountered a math teacher who could do an excellent job teaching how to do all the calculations, but he was unable to provide a single application for anything he taught. From the students' perspective they might as well be learning how to speak a dead language that nobody can use, or learning how to calculate footnote space at the bottom of a page using a 1910 typewriter. It might be interesting, but then what? It should not be surprising that the student perception on a topic might change when there is no connection. *Understanding how a student perceives a lesson can be used to help make better emotional connections between the student and the learning task.*

Emotional Processing and Autism

Autism is one of those conditions where the person has tremendous difficulties making emotional connections with others. The symptoms, such as lack of eye contact, are now being checked for in infants, but many parents don't pick up on the problems until the child is 2 or 3 years old (Kanner, 1943; Richdale & Schreck, 2008). While autism requires a medical diagnosis, some symptoms that educators should be aware of include the following:

- Fails to respond to his or her name;
- Is apathetic;
- Avoids or has little eye contact;
- Has great difficulty with change; wants to preserve sameness;
- Has preoccupied, repetitive behaviors; is anxiously obsessive for keeping a routine; lines up objects;
- Has an excellent detail memory for lists and rhymes;
- Relates well to objects but not to people;
- Generally has a lower IQ (Asperger's is a higher functioning form of Autism Spectrum Disorder [ASD]);
- Is socially isolated;
- Does not understand nuances of language such as teasing or sarcasm; takes remarks literally;
- Is tempted to smoke or drink in order to be more socially acceptable;
- Knows he or she is different but does not understand why; this often leads to depression;
- May be zealous about one subject and talk excessively about it. (Baron-Cohen, 2003)

What causes Autism Spectrum Disorder (ASD) is still under intense investigation. One major hypothesis by Baron-Cohen (2003) found evidence that the male brain goes to extremes in figuring out the rules for how a system works (systemizing) and that the female brain tends to develop more empathizing skills but can also skew to systemizing, but less frequently than males do (Hobson & Lee, 1999). There is also a disproportionate number of males who are autistic, roughly 10 males for each female, and the frequency of occurrence seems to be rising, although some of this could be due to better reporting. Heredity seems to play some role, but it is not clear just how. There is an emerging set of hypotheses suggesting the mirror neuron systems as part of the emotional processing are not functioning correctly (Dapretto, Davies, & Pfeifer, 2006). For example, when a student without autism imitates someone playing a stringed instrument, he imitates the person, whereas an autistic student imitates the action but fails to notice the style used. It was also found that the more severe the disorder was, the less active the mirror neurons were (Weiss, Fiske, & Ferraioli, 2008).

Parents trying to cope with such a daunting situation often grasp at many unsubstantiated claims and interventions, some of which are even harmful (Hanson et al., 2006). One study found as many as 74% of the parents were supplementing their children's training with treatments that had no research to back up their use. The parents were highly susceptible to fads and fashions but so are educators. One book, promoting *sensory integration,* was given the "Teacher's Choice Award 2006" from *Learning* Magazine (Notbohm & Zysk, 2004). However, upon examining how well sensory integration really stacked up, the intervention was not promising. The research studies were, in fact, equivocal, in which the "majority reported either no change, or adverse effects" (Weiss et al., 2008, p. 51; Gillberg, Johansson, Steffenburg, & Berlin, 1997; Kane, Luiselli, Dearborn, & Young, 2004). *Carefully check the intervention program; many popular ones have little or no research to support their claims, and some may actually be harmful to the child.*

Autism program interventions

When any intervention is recommended, it should have a foundation in credible research. What are worthwhile interventions that have a solid research base, and what should be avoided? As with most things about the brain, autism and Asperger's Syndrome are complex, and while exploring specific interventions in detail is beyond the scope of this chapter, a short overview of interventions both tested and questionable is listed in Table 4.1. When a school or parent is adopting an intervention, it is for the long haul because the student will likely need assistance for a very long time. Consequently educators need the best information they can get *before* starting the intervention and should thoroughly examine the programs listed before making the long-term commitment. Perhaps the most thorough and teacher-friendly autism intervention book at this time, with many ready-to-use ideas, is *Behavioral Intervention for Young Children with Autism* by Maurice, Green, and Luce. The interventions recommended are not single programs, but a variety that have met the standards of Applied Behavioral Analysis (ABA) by having thorough research and are not harmful to the student (Metz, Mulick, & Butter, 2005). The National Academy of Sciences' Committee on Educational Interventions for Children with Autism recommends that an education program for autism should include:

- Social skills for participation in family, school, and community;
- Expressive language skills;
- A functional symbolic communication system;
- Increased engagement in developmentally appropriate play and adaptive behaviors;
- Fine and gross motor skills that are developmentally appropriate;
- Cognitive skills;
- Reduction of problem behaviors and replacement with appropriate behaviors;
- Development of independent organizational skills and behaviors for success in the regular classroom;
- At least 25 hours a week of active, intensive instructional programming;
- Small training groups that are small in size, repeat and plan training, and include parents and family. (Lord & McGee, 2001)

Autistic adolescents are not the only ones whose emotional processing goes awry. In this age, where adolescents have grown up being exposed to all manner of things

TREATMENT PROGRAM	RESEARCH RECOMMENDATIONS	REFERENCES
Table 4.1 AUTISM TREATMENTS		
ABA (Applied Behavioral Analysis Treatments)		
Discrete Trial Training (DTT)	Instructions are clear, repetition, practice & immediate reinforcement	Wiess, 2008
Incidental Teaching	Naturalistic, builds generalization Imitation, spontaneous use of	Fenske, 2001, Hart, Riesley, 1982, Ingersoll, 2007
Pivotal Responses Training	Very important, may positively affect changes in untrained behavior. Self initiation, responding to multiple cues	Weiss, 2008, Fenske, 2001, Cooper, 2007, Koegel, 2003,
Natural Environment Training TEACCH	Better than typical Special Ed Has some research to support	Metz, 2005
Programs without scientific research support, or potentially harmful for Autistic children		
Auditory Integration	No Scientific Support Potentially Harmful	NY State Dept. of Health, Early Intervention Program, 1999
Chelation Therapy	No Scientific Support Side effects potentially harmful Kidney & liver damage	Roberts & Prior, 2006
Sensory Integration	No Scientific Support	Metz, 2005, Kay & Vyse, 2005, Smith, 2005
Gluten or Casein free diet	No Scientific Support Possible harm from malnutrition	Irvin, 2006, Metz et al. 2005
Music Therapy	No Scientific Research	NY State Dept. of Health, Early Intervention Program, 1999
Holding Therapy	No Scientific Research Potentially dangerous	Metz et al., 2005
Facilitated Communication	No research support/refuted	NY State Dept. of Health, Early Intervention Program, 1999

digital, their brains have also been bombarded by media laden with violence. The media exposure does affect the mind/brain systems. In the next section I examine some of those effects of media, especially violent media.

Media and Emotions

It has been long known that media, whether music or images on film or video, had the power to elicit emotional reactions. From drummers in the wars of long ago to the Scottish Highlanders' war pipes, music has been used to move, motivate, and stir the emotions. Music can stir up excitement, transforming a mundane scene into a heart-pounding event, as was discovered in the early days of silent films. The images also evoked emotional reactions. The World War II image of the famous flag raising on Iwo Jima's Mt. Suribachi helped to reinvigorate a country weary of war. Media can create powerful emotional states.

Media violence

The question of the effect of media violence on adolescent and young adult behavior came up in several discussions with my students both in high school and in graduate school concerning what is seen on TV and in movies and video games. The overwhelming response, slightly paraphrased, was, "I've played violent video games all my life and haven't killed anybody yet, and neither have my friends." There are fundamental errors in logic, not the least being that their sample of a couple of people does not generalize to the entire population. The other error is assuming that there is a direct cause and effect, which ignores the brain's complexity because usually multiple factors are present as illustrated in Figure 4.2 (Anderson, Gentile, & Buckley, 2007). What adolescents watch does affect their emotional state. Think of moviegoers when people leave the theater. Sometimes they were all somber after watching a film like *Schindler's List*. By contrast, recall the viewers' reactions after watching some lighthearted animation. Smiles all around, and everyone was in a talkative, happy mood. What we watch has an effect, but apparently, the effect can last over a period of time if the mind is repeatedly exposed to it. Let's briefly examine the findings.

The media that students watch and play affect emotions and violent video games affect emotions negatively. There is fairly strong evidence that increased playing of violent videos is associated with and contributes to higher levels of later aggression and violence. Despite the multitude of denials from the gaming industry, media violence can be linked to higher frequencies of aggressive behaviors and violence (Anderson et al., 2003; Gentile, 2003; Kirsch, 2006). A meta-analysis of a number of studies on media violence all demonstrated significant associations with violence and increased aggression. To be certain, there are also a number of studies that show mixed results, and sometimes no relationship (Williams & Skoric, 2005). Studies that follow game players over a longer period and would shed more light are not available yet. However, there are a number of studies that examined the total number of hours

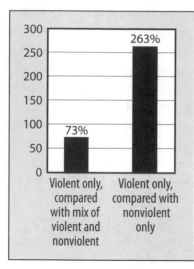

Violent video games are very effective at teaching aggression. In this study 2,500 children played multiple violent video games. There were 430 third to fifth graders, 607 eighth to ninth graders, and 1,441 older teens (avg. 19 years). The games produced greater hostile and aggressive behaviors after 6 months. The more they played, the more aggressive the behavior. There was an increased risk of high aggression by 73% compared with the students who played a mixture of violent and non-violent games. There was also an increased risk of high aggression by 263% compared with students who played only non-violent games. The games are superb at motivating to persevering to learn and master skills.

Fig. 4.3. Risk of increased aggressive behaviors after playing mixed violent and nonviolent video games and playing only violent video games.

playing violent media games, and overall they, too, have been linked to aggressive behavior (Anderson et al., 2007). For example, in a large study with over 2,500 students who played a mix of violent video games and nonviolent games, the risk for highly aggressive behavior went up 73% for students who played violent games when compared with students who played only nonviolent games. When the students played only violent video games, not a mixture, the risk for high aggressive behavior soared to 263% compared with the students playing nonviolent games (see Figure 4.3) (Gentile & Gentile, 2008).

The general pattern of increased exposure and increased violent or aggressive behavior seems to start early and even affect other cultures noted for their nonaggressive public behavior, such as Japan. In the Japanese culture there is a low rate of violence; however, even that culture has witnessed a lot of people playing violent video games and increased risk for aggression and violence like their American counterparts (Anderson, Sakamoto, & Gentile, 2008).

Violent video games are not going to go away, but there are several things educators and parents can learn from them. Before educators make suggestions to parents, they must be aware of what is happening on the home front. A complex social dynamic belies simplistic suggestions. First, parental oversight seems shoddy at the very best. One study found nearly 90% of the parents had no restrictions on how much time they allowed their children to play games (Walsh, 2000). Parents are present but seem almost completely negligent. Few parents really seem to check the ratings, with only about 15% routinely checking them (Gentile, Lynch, Linder, & Walsh, 2004), while nearly 53% never checked, and only about 20% intervened and stopped the purchase of the game because of the rating (Walsh, Gentile, Gieske, Walsh, & Chasco, 2003). Further compounding the problem is the so-called rating system, which doesn't match with parents' desires across society (Funk, Flores,

Buchman, & Germann, 1999). What is too much violence, gore, and sex for one set of parents is acceptable to others, and some parents even play the games with their kids present. Modeling can go a long way. There are other disturbing facets to the family dynamics. Many players stay up late into the wee hours of the morning, and the more they played the worse their relationships with family and friends became (Jackson, von Eye, Fitzgerald, Zhao, & Witt, in press; Padilla-Walker, Nelson, Carroll, & Jensen, 2009). Add the lack of sleep to school performance, and teachers see kids who are falling asleep in class or are unable to pick up any of the lesson due to exhaustion. Unfortunately, the phenomenon of sleep deprivation and computer usage is worldwide (Fischer et al., 2008). It is hard to learn and create a memory when you can't pay attention, and think, let alone keep your head up. None of this sounds especially encouraging but there are some things teachers can suggest for parents to do.

Overall, *parents need to become actively involved in the selection and playing of video games and have those games/computers in a family room where they can be monitored.* More specifically, teachers might suggest to parents that they:

- Be directly involved in the selection of what games are played.
- Have the computer/games in the living room where the children can be directly monitored. The bedroom can't be monitored.
- Make tough decisions and actively parent. The adolescent shouldn't be making or forcing the choices.
- Limit the amount of time playing.
- *Carefully* consider whether they want to go down the violent video game road. It is hard to turn off.

Educators learn from video and game playing

In games, adolescents are responding to challenges where they have to make choices, overcome obstacles, feel some autonomy, and gain immediate feedback regarding their choices. Additionally, the games use smart media to learn how the player is responding and it adjusts accordingly. The gore and violence does not make the game more enjoyable. Another potent aspect that I believe has been overlooked is that the experiential nature of game playing can be similar to experiential learning in the outdoor programs. As one person said, "When I'm moving through the game world, I feel as if I'm actually there" (Przybylski, Ryan, & Rigby, 2009).

Educators need to learn what video games do well: provide challenges to overcome, a series of choices, rapid feedback, some autonomy in the approach, and higher levels of thinking. Educators can also learn from video game design such as, "How are people learning?" For example, players have commented there is a visceral response in some situations, and what happened in those specific moments are very well remembered. What goes on in the brain at that moment in the game when we are simultaneously feeling a strong emotion? What can we do to improve educational or interactive media? Much of the educational computer material I've looked at is cumbersome and dull to the point of being stupefying. They are improving, but why is there such a difference between the games and educational material? The video game entertainment industry spends a lot of time, financial resources, and enormous effort on their designs.

Video games are also excellent in how they keep the players involved, all of which tie into motivation. They usually have attention-grabbing graphics. The feedback is virtually instantaneous. The player knows without anyone telling her if she made a mistake. There are progressive levels of challenge: sometimes incremental, sometimes with large jumps in difficulty. With the feedback and successes, players' skills are honed repeatedly. If they fail at the next level of challenge they can go back to a lower level. The player can self-adjust. Admittedly, the cognitive challenge tends to be rather low, but more games are emerging where the player must figure out the relationships and hidden rules. What can teachers learn from games? Several things:

- *Attention*: The lesson must captivate their attention. Graphics, music, and *movement* all help. Papers and worksheets don't move. The student needs to be the one moving. Students' levels of physical activity are declining nationwide.
- *Feedback*: The students need rapid feedback to help them assess what they are doing wrong. Students need to learn to evaluate information and at progressively deeper levels.
- *Opportunities*: There must be multiple opportunities to practice the skills.
- *Challenge level*: The challenge level is of the student's choosing, and it is progressive. Each level requires a slightly more refined set of skills/knowledge. But with each level of challenge the rewards are also greater.

All of these point toward motivation issues, which is the subject of the next chapter and will be explored there more deeply. However, if teachers will reflect on their lessons in regard to just these criteria and make adjustments, the student response is likely to be very different. We need to pay attention to what is working in the game industry.

Rather than criticizing the industry, educators should learn what adolescents respond to, and education needs to do more than that. There are a handful of researchers working on educational problems, but they haven't the resources of the gaming industry, which spends billions. One significant problem in either gaming or educational game design is the level of cognitive difficulty. Most popular video games reach only a low level of thought, while educational games need to reach more difficult, abstract levels and designing such material is difficult (Michael Connelly, personal communication). Whenever possible, preview the games, make use of instructional facilitators to check the video games/labs out (if your school has such personnel), or try to find reviews online.

Summary

Emotions affect learning, and learning is normally inseparable from emotion. Emotional changes within the body have varying degrees of intensity for how soothing or agitating something is, but emotions can also range from pleasant to unpleasant. In turn, these affect how well an adolescent remembers different lessons. If educators make personal connections with students, it facilitates student learning and performance. When the teacher's efforts are expanded to helping the student to make more and stronger personal connections with the lesson, then the lesson sticks more easily. Stress overload can not only interfere with learning, but it can also literally damage neuronal function. When the entire body is experiencing the learning, as in experiential learning, it readily produces lasting memories. Managing our emotional relationships with others is essential to both surviving and thriving in a society. An adolescent's perception, distorted or not, is that person's reality, and he will make decisions based upon that perception. Mirror neuron systems appear to be part of the fundamental processing of emotional information, which allows us to adapt emotionally to the world about us. A breakdown in that processing appears to be part of autism and Asperger's Disorder. An adolescent's emotional state is also affected by what she watches. Video game violence contributes across cultures to increased aggression from younger children through the adolescent years, as well as causing impaired relationships and sleep deprivation.

The Impact of Social Media

Across the world much of the current generation of adolescents is undergoing socio-emotional change spurred on by electronic media, which do not appear to have a precedent. Facebook, YouTube, texting, sexting (sending explicit images via cell phone), and cyberbullying all are creating shifts. It is too early to determine the outcome, but in addition to the media-related game-violence, a related issue of empathy may be emerging. A major meta-analysis of 72 studies and 14,000 students spanning over a decade found college students were becoming less empathetic, with nearly a 40% drop by standard measures (Konrath, 2010). Some individual studies have not found significant changes suggesting students may be no more self-centered than previous generations (Barr & Higgins-D'Alessandro, 2009). Why such a huge drop? At this time there is only speculation. For example, the drop might be related to how we use media. If a student didn't like another's attitude or comments and did not want to listen to them he or she could simply tune out, or literally turn off the media. Violent video may numb us to seeing and experiencing violence, so that we fail to respond when violence is real. Empathy and violence share some of the same neural circuitry (Moya-Albiol, Herrero, & Bernal, 2010). Social media allow students to avoid having to physically interact with real people, live with the consequences of their actions in the same local environment, and potentially grow from the interactions. However, the media create a world environment where there is often literally a physical disconnection with the consequences of media interactions. Students can cyberbully from a safe distance, but it seems only rarely are they brought to account. For a key facet of human-to-human interactions, the mirror neurons, which appear to be integral to developing empathy, now have a wall of disembodied media inserted into the developmental mix. Perhaps empathetic development is changing? To be certain, electronic media are powerful new variables in the socio-emotional world of adolescents, and the overall impact is not yet clear.

In the following portion, an activity is presented to help educators to make use of the information presented throughout this chapter. Many educators use this exercise successfully across the country. It will take some reflection, and perhaps looking back over a few of the topics, but it is well worth the effort for the benefits achieved in student learning and in teaching practices.

Designing Your Personal Application

Educators hear these emotional complaints by adolescents in every school: "This is lame" or "This is stupid. Where will I ever use it?" Rather than dismissing the whining complaint and saying, "You'll need it to graduate," explore it with the students. The emotional disconnect has reared its ugly head, and ignoring it will not help either you or the students.

This chapter presented a host of ideas, key points, and caveats, but to make them work, we must now figure out how to apply these to our own instruction. The process below helps to ease that work.

- *Identify a lesson or topic where the students have difficulty making connections between the lessons and their own lives:* What are the students actually doing or saying during the lesson? Be specific because their comments can help you identify what is missing for them. Their feedback is essential; we need their perspectives, so it is imperative that we really listen to what they are saying and why.
- *List examples of ways to make emotional connections with the students:* Do more than just think about the possible connections; it is necessary to write them down. Seeing them written down can trigger more ideas for you or your fellow educators. Try to establish a few connections for each of the areas listed below, but if you can't, ask colleagues for help. If you get stumped, go to Google and try adding the tag "practical use, applications, uses for, activities with, or fun" with your search topic. Even math will turn up thousands of ideas.
- *List physical activities that can be used.*
- *List visual, pictures, imagery that can be used:* To help, use Google Image to find about 15 to 20 images that illustrate the real application of the topic. Have students find their own pictures or bring them to class to show.

- *Develop an exercise that uses descriptions in either verbal or written form.* The images listed above can help launch short written elaborations or discussions by the students. That can help to start building the bridge between themselves and the topic.
- *Describe some social activities that use small groups, or even classwide activities.*
- *Select one or two of the most promising ideas you've listed above and take a hard look at them:* Reflecting back on the student comments, does the activity you've listed address their emotional need to connect and help build other units, or is it just an isolated event? If not, network with your colleagues and rethink.
- *Do the students have the skills/knowledge to do the task?* Will they need to be taught those as part of the activity or before? What are those necessary skills or knowledge?
- *Will the strategy work equally well with both boys and girls? Comment on possible adjustments.*
- *How will you know if the redesigned lesson was significant and helped to build emotional connections?*
- *DESCRIBE YOUR NEW STRATEGY. Be specific and work out as much detail as you can.* If you come up with variations, work those out as well to differentiate and reach more students.

Key Points and Recommendations

- *Emotions have different levels of intensity (arousal) and pleasantness (valence).* Lessons that don't evoke much of an emotional reaction are not likely to be easily recalled, but if the class had several lessons or exercises that were unpleasant the students are more apt to recall those, and these will possibly color their opinion of their entire class experience. Think about the classes that students "hate or love." How many pleasant memories can they recall, and which of those memories were more intense for them: the pleasant activities or unpleasant ones? Repeated anxiety and failure can lead to reluctance or even withdrawal in participation in those classes. If you want to build "attitude" think about the emotional climate of the class.
- *Emotions used positively can make learning events much easier to recall.* It is okay to have fun woven into the lessons. Some of the most important things can be indirectly reinforced and easier to recall if there are several fun memories that are associated with them.
- *Fear or terror can automatically override well-rehearsed training.* Students (from the very young through adults) may have consistently demonstrated during a period of nonassessment that they grasped the skills and concepts but may have a total collapse during the formal assessment

because of stress. Be alert to which students are prone to stress or "test anxiety," and consider alternative forms of testing. Is the test supposed to measure what they know and can do, or it also supposed to include working under high pressure? If the intent is also to see how performance is under such a stress load, were the practices repeatedly conducted under similar stresses? It might be appropriate for the emergency services and military, but how appropriate is it for your students? Remember that, under stress, most people, even very bright military personnel, can't think very clearly. It is *not* a "suck it up and be tough" issue (interestingly the military is adopting a stress training program). There are three issues: (1) Does the student know the material (how are you going to find out)? (2) are they supposed to be able to perform under high stress? and (3) what did you teach and train them to handle? As an educator, your role is also to facilitate and help students learn how to find the information and use skills. Gentle, probing questions asked one on one can gradually elicit the information and rebuild confidence, although it may be very difficult to do on that same day. If a student has a meltdown, what can be done to help the student avoid a future collapse?

- *Schools should be welcoming and safe. They should actively reduce fear and increase the safety for both students and their parents.* There are multiple approaches to making schools welcoming and maintaining safety, from using student or adult-senior citizen greeters or guides to the displays a visitor first sees. Also, use peer tutors, study buddies, and using music in the foyer or halls. Even when surveillance cameras are used, the amount of overt hazing changes.

- *To reduce fear and change moods, smile as students are personally greeted.* Play music when the students enter or during work activities, labs, or class changes. This is essentially the same as the prior key point with a few differences..

- *Consider having music playing in the hallways or offices* (notice that some dental and doctors' offices do this to reduce tension, as do stores and coffeeshops to put people in a better mood). Some of us naturally smile, and others do not. I have to remind myself to smile, but it is worth the effort when I receive positive student reactions. The old folk saying that smiles are contagious also applies to grumpy people, too. When you first see a student or fellow teacher, smile and offer a genuine greeting.

- *Offhand remarks may carry considerable weight for students with very long-term effects.* The valence of the remark plays into how it is perceived by the student. I've observed more students comment about a negative remark or tease that some teacher said more than any other form. You can also plant an occasional positive "offhand" remark, too. Positive comments made in passing, made either directly to the student or where he or she could overhear them, can change emotional response and involvement.

- *Our body language and tone of voice can display our enthusiasm and create anticipation and excitement for the student. Don't hide your enthusiasm!* Your excitement creates student excitement or at least greater attention. Sometimes it may be necessary to be a bit of an actor. For example, one teacher hated plants and found them particularly dull, but he worked at showing great interest and having "a-ha" moments in the class. The unexpected result was that a couple of students became botanists because of the interest sparked by the teacher who displayed enthusiasm. Educators and students are occasionally criticized for waving their arms around with gestures as they describe something. This helps learning. Be alive!

- *Experiential learning readily makes emotional connections because the student is literally immersed in the learning.* When the whole body is part of the learning, a mistake or the correct performance of a task often creates immediate feedback; the educator does not have to tell the student because he or she already knows. One of the beauties of this form of learning is that the teacher/guide is recast in the student's eyes as a person who helps. Their advice can be quickly tested with dramatic effect. The emotional impact can be quite powerful. For example, trust can be so strongly established with a partner that they will pair up for years. In some types of activities, lifelong partnerships have also become established between teacher and student.

- *Mirror neuron systems enable us to better understand each other's actions and make more appropriate decisions that make sense within a particular culture/society.* These fundamental levels of processing are part of our ability to process emotional information. Errors in the system, such as for those who have autism and Asperger's, can have devastating effects.

- *Their perceptions are their reality.* The students' perception may be skewed, but perceptions often play into how they make their decisions. By talking with students, not just to them, and also routinely asking for feedback, teachers can get a better handle on a students' perception. A visit to a student's page on MySpace or Facebook can be rather enlightening (or disturbing).

- *If educators understand how a student perceives a lesson, they can use that perspective to help determine where to start making better emotional connections between the student and the learning.* In turn, this can lead to better-designed activities and lessons. Standard old cookie-cutter lessons leave many students hungry for something else. Adapt those lessons to the students' backgrounds.

- *The media that people watch and play affect emotions, and violent video games affect emotions negatively.* Emotions are changed by what students see and hear, but teachers can be proactive in the classroom by controlling the selection of music. Having a special night for parents on how their children learn could be a way to introduce information about the potentially harmful effects of violent video games and a place to address upfront the myth of "Well, I played violent games and didn't kill anybody."

- ***There is fairly strong evidence that increased playing of violent videos is associated with and contributes to higher levels of later aggression and violence.*** We're not going to stop the consumption of video games, but teachers need to help parents become aware of what is happening with behavior and these games. Some parents, though not enough, do not permit game playing until homework is completed, but there is still a problem of how late the kids are up playing the games. Sleep deprivation and a crash in student performance are often the results.

- ***Discussing video game and computer usage by students is a place where teachers need to help educate parents, whether in parent-teacher conferences, PSAs, one on one, or in a major parent night presentation. The message needs to go out. Parents need to become actively involved in*** the selection and playing of video games and have those games and computers in a family room where they can be monitored. Parents need to actually parent rather than allow the TV or a computer game be substitute babysitters. The children learn, but the lessons they need to learn about how to function in society are not the ones being taught.

- ***Educators need to learn what video games do well.*** The better games grab the players' attention, have challenges to overcome, provide a series of choices, give rapid feedback, allow some autonomy and multiple opportunities, and progressively increase the knowledge and skills demanded. Four criteria—attention, rapid feedback, multiple opportunities, and progressive level of challenge—can be adapted to regular classroom lesson designs. Pressure needs to be placed both on university game design programs and educational game suppliers to incorporate at least better autonomy, interesting challenges, adaptability of the programs, measurement, and higher levels of thinking in addition to better feedback.

RESOURCES

Anderson, C., Gentile, D., & Buckely, K. (2007). *Violent video game effects on children and adolescents*. New York, NY: Oxford University Press.

Damasio, A. (1999). *The feeling of what happens: Body, emotion and the making of consciousness*. Orlando, FL: Harcourt.

Matson, J. (2008). *Clinical assessment and intervention for Autism Spectrum Disorders*. Oxford, UK: Academic Press.

Maurice, C., Green, G., & Luce, S. (1996). *Behavioral interventions for young children with autism*. Austin, TX: PRO-ED.

CHAPTER FIVE

The Multiple Roles of Motivation

The task of the modern educator is not to cut down jungles,
but to irrigate deserts.
—C. S. Lewis

Educational achievement is not equally important across the classes and cultures. For many students, using the lure of academic performances or grades is not a way to reach them; a different approach will be necessary. When it comes to motivating students, teaching is more often like an art: Some of us are Picassos, and some of us are still finger painting. Fortunately, we all can learn more.

Tracy's Story

Tracy dreamed of being a cartoonist, but she avoided doing most of the art assignments that would broaden her skills. She had zero social skills and was unkempt and unhygienic. Because she did not expand her repertoire of drawing skills, her quality of drawing never improved. When asked why she didn't take some courses that would help her toward her dream, she replied, "I might fail." As a result she didn't even attempt the courses that would help her, and she sat doing nothing in the other classes as well. She was defeated before she started. The fear of failure had captured her.

Sarah's Story

Sarah walked down the hall, flashing a smile and calling out greetings to other passing students. She limped slightly on her right leg, and she cradled a few books in her smaller right arm, which had some paralysis. Like many students, she wasn't fond of math, but she held her own in the sciences, earning mostly B's. Sarah was similar to many students: She didn't have a lot of confidence, even when she had demonstrated adequate skills in various classes. She would avoid work if she thought a teacher's aide would do it for her. On the surface, this is not unusual for kids who have gone through school receiving special services. Too often they became dependent as they manipulated well-meaning aides. But there is one remarkable difference. Sarah was missing half her brain though none of the kids and few teachers knew about it. I visited with her recently. She still had the self-conscious smile, but she wanted more out of life than her grocery job and she was making plans to get a better job. She had motivation issues, but despite her very real limitations, she was still striving. She believed she had the power to do something about her current situation.

The Emotion and Motivation Connection

Over and over again in motivational research and texts, twin themes emerge. One involves making connections between the teacher and student, and the other is helping the student make emotional connections with a subject or task. Motivation has an emotional foundation. One perspective is to consider that motivation is fine-tuning the emotional linkages. Peel back the various motivational theories and you'll find basic emotional processes. From that perspective, motivation seems to be a manifestation of emotional states.

Theories About Motivation

There are multitudes of ideas on how to motivate; it's one of those concepts that everyone has an opinion about, from TV pundits to preachers, from parents to children, and many will gladly share with you if you ask, and sometimes even if you don't ask. Threats and accusations almost never work to motivate either a child or adult to do his or her best work. They might get a person started, but the moment the threat is gone the work usually plummets. Research has produced a swarm of theories as well. Only a thumbnail sketch of major theories will be provided here, with a concentration on practices that work. There is no single correct theory, or one set of best practices. Each theory and its respective strategies works particularly well for motivating under the right conditions. Rather than choosing one tool from our motivation toolkit, we need to see what other tools exist and how we could use them.

As we observed in the previous chapter on emotion, motivation and emotional processes are woven together. Despite Tracy's overwhelming fears, students like her also have other feelings of anger, pleasure and joy, in other words, emotions. Motivation seems to be an extension or expression of various emotions. It is hard to separate motivation and emotion, but that wasn't always believed to be so. For centuries, one of the most common methods was to provide the tried-and-true stimulus of a carrot-and-stick approach, and to see if the students produced the desired response. One of the very first recorded examples of students learning to read and write was that they were being "motivated" by beatings (Y. Cohen, 2003). To many people that approach seemed to make sense. Watch a lion cub do something wrong. The mother swats him sharply with a paw, sending the cub tumbling. Our reactions are often similar but sometimes with disastrous results. Untold thousands of parents were told not to spare the rod or we'll spoil the child. When my son was young, my wife and I did not yet know he was profoundly bipolar and had ADHD, and we knew nothing about the brain. Our preacher told us to literally beat the child until we broke him. We were to beat the sin out of him. Thankfully, we didn't. Motivation is more complicated than can be solved with a physical or verbal beating, especially if you want students to continue to learn on their own. In the previous chapter we examined how high stress can literally damage the neurons in the brain and reduce performance. The motivation strategies we choose need to improve performance and to increase and maintain the learning even after the instructor is no longer present. Motivation should help build a lifelong learner.

The stimulus and response concept was introduced over 100 years ago with Thorndike's Law of Effect (1898) and was built upon by Hull (1943, 1951) and B. F. Skinner (1974) in the field of behaviorism. The belief was that if we used a specific consequence the behavior preceding it would change. In other words, the behavior or action was reinforced by the result. A baby cries and the mother picks him up every time. Soon the baby has learned to associate increasing the crying with a favorable consequence of being picked up, and so the baby uses crying to exert some control over his immediate world. In a similar fashion, the lion club learns that certain behaviors will earn it a painful thumping, so it learns to avoid those specific behaviors. This is known as *reinforcement theory*.

Skinner took a very narrow view of the theory to explain all behavior. If we greatly simplified the theory, it would describe a mechanical process of learning: If a person did some specific action, then we'd see a very specific response (Stipek, 2002). Behavior, it was believed, was caused by external events. The 3-pound lump of neurons between our ears that makes up the brain was not considered necessary. Researchers assumed that if some process could not be directly observed or measured (and most brain processes couldn't be) it wasn't involved. Emotional processes and their expressions, such as feelings, values, beliefs, and aspirations, were taboo topics among psychologists until fairly recently. This began to change when cognitive neuroscience started demonstrating that the brain is intricately involved with emotions and subsequent actions.

Reinforcement theory provided educators with some of their first specific motivation strategies. For example, if students were too noisy, blurting out answers rather than quietly sitting and raising their hands, they would be punished by being assigned to detention. Or if a teenager turned to whisper to the student next to her, a whack of the meter stick was used to extinguish the whispering behavior. We now understand that the emotional process of fear is highly involved. On the other hand, good behaviors or performances might be rewarded with a smile or compliment. But even that turned out to be a double-edged sword because the poor adolescent so blessed with the compliment would be taunted by his peers for being a teacher's pet or for being a brown noser.

Gradually, it was discovered that reinforcement theory could not explain a number of behaviors; somehow, thinking or cognition was involved. If a person thought she would be punished or rewarded, then she would change her behavior. Why would that happen? Personal experiences or seeing others in similar situations helped people to form *beliefs or expectations* of what might happen next (Atkinson, 1964). For instance, if I say the multiplication tables 20 times, then I expect to do better on the test. The belief is that a certain number of repetitions will influence the student's action. *Cognitive motivation* theories emerged.

By having an understanding about what students believe or what their perceptions are about the consequences of an action, we can better design the lessons or activities. As with Tracy's belief that she might fail, a belief can quickly defeat a student, or conversely, generate enough confidence for the student to persevere. If educators understand a student's beliefs, they might be able to focus in and identify the source of some of the problems. For instance, Tamara has started to say that she believes she is poor in math because she failed a fractions test, and now she won't be able to achieve her goal of getting into college. Upon careful questioning her teacher finds that she doesn't understand what a denominator is. By restructuring math activities into small, reachable steps, Tamara's belief about her math ability gradually changes.

Beliefs about ability, value, or how worthwhile the effort is as well as the pleasure derived from succeeding in figuring out the problems were all found to influence student performances (Eccles et al., 1983). Together, these involve theories on *expectancy and value, intrinsic motivation, goal theory, attribution and locus of control* among others, but all of them are about *internal* mental states. For example, the students may have a common goal but the reasons for striving for it can be completely different for each student. For one student it may be to maintain a higher grade, while for another it might be to master some skill involved. How teachers set the goals for the students can have an immense effect on the attitude for the entire school. In my work with different schools across the country, I repeatedly observed a clear distinction between public schools and private schools. Public schools were almost invariably focused on test scores, especially those tied to the No Child Left Behind law and related standards. In the private schools I encountered, there was typically an entirely different emphasis on learning, not on testing. If the students learned their skills and mastered the knowledge sufficiently, later test performances were fine. Students were able to drive toward their test goals by concentrating on the learning and what they believed they could do.

The Educational Connection

When students leave their formal education we hope they've become intrinsically motivated so that they continue to learn and develop higher levels of mastery and derive pleasure from those efforts. Getting there is another matter. How do educators motivate a student? We've heard the cliché "You can bring a horse to water, but you can't make him drink." However, we can create a thirst by changing the conditions before we even bring out the water. Even though teachers don't have the control they might wish for to help their students, they are not powerless. In the last chapter I asserted that one of the first things teachers can do is change the emotional climate, which stems from *self-systems theory* of our need to feel socially connected and have a relationship. Closely allied to that is another motivational aspect called self-worth, which is the feeling of how the person is valued (Covington, 1992). Building those initial connections is part of the foundation for motivation.

To organize these theories into functional strategies, I will use three questions posed by Stipek (2002) to construct the framework that helps to build motivation:

Can I do this?
What do I need to do in order to succeed? Is the task worthwhile?
   (Do I want to do this task?)
Why am I doing this task? (Can I also explain the skill I am learning?)

Can I Do This Task?

Embedded in the question of "Can I do this?" are a series of other questions that must also be planned for if the student is to enjoy success and gradually build up intrinsic motivation. Some of these include, What is the goal? Am I smart enough? Do I have the necessary skills? Is there a model to see what is involved? Before we can address these, we must also consider the task through the perceptual lens of the student. How does she perceive the task? What does she believe?

The question of being able to do the task revolves around what the student believes she can do. The goal that is set out and whether the student believes she even has a chance of obtaining that goal can powerfully influence academic effort. This is the concept of *self-efficacy*, demonstrated by the idea that we make judgments about ourselves in how capable we are in organizing the task and carrying out the actions needed to reach the goal (Zimmerman, Bandura, & Martinze-Pons, 1992). To build a student's sense of self-worth, you need to make personal connections with the student and continue as if you were building a scaffold. Add one piece at a time in helping the student to believe she can actually do the task at hand. What follows here are the pieces that compose that scaffold to build the belief that she is capable and can achieve her goal.

Who Is in Control?

Motivation has many faces and they often blend into each other. When a student or adult thinks about who is in control, who has the power or capability to do things, he or she is considering the *locus of control*, or LOC. It is an extremely important aspect of anyone's perception. It may range from "I'm powerless, so there is no sense in doing anything, it will make no difference" to "I can affect the conditions, I can really do something about this situation." All of these thoughts color our perceptions and subsequently affect our actions. The LOC is a facet of motivation that seems to work at several different levels. Many things can affect a student's LOC, and by knowing what these are and knowing what power we have to change them (including our own teaching LOC), we can create better conditions that a student will need to become more intrinsically motivated.

Stipek (2002), Pintrick and Schunk (2002), and others have offered many insightful comments on the significant effect that autonomy has on motivation. *When students know they have options they tend to perform better*. Autonomy is probably affected indirectly by the student's level of cognitive development. The options provided to the student should be within his current range of ability, and he should also be made aware of the responsibilities that go with each option. With autonomy comes an internal LOC, that he has some control and, with it, a sense of empowerment. It may take repeated exercises along with coaching and guidance before the students realize they have significant control over outcomes. If students are to become intrinsically motivated, it is essential to move them beyond their usually mistaken belief that they have little or no control, along with blaming others for their outcome (an external locus), to a belief that their actions actually affect the outcomes (Rotter, 1966). Students begin to signal this when they initiate actions, adjust their responses depending upon what happened, and acknowledge that they can do something to change the outcome. We traditionally summarized this new LOC perspective as "taking responsibility." Even though the TV court shows with real plaintiffs and judges are edited to show the more dramatic cases, I still find it amazing to see adults who deny any responsibility for their actions. If their expressions are genuine, some of those people are still unable to grasp the concept that their actions (or lack of them) have real consequences.

Autonomy

Autonomy is also influenced by the culture the adolescents grow up within and the degree of autonomy permitted by their parents can have a major impact. Some parents are highly controlling; fearful of the world, they may desire to protect their kids by controlling as much as possible. If parents keep tabs too closely and have emotionally insecure children, those children tend to be more susceptible to conforming behaviors, peer pressure, and crippling self-consciousness (Ryan & Kuczkowski, 1994). When teens have basic emotional needs that are not being met by their parents, they often feel more insecure. In the processes of attempting to bolster a sense of self-worth they sometimes become excessively materialistic. What they wear and their style of dress and who they hang out with are important, and they are more likely to become involved with risky sexual and drug behaviors (Kasser, Ryan, Zax, & Sameroff, 1995). The parents who allow only limited, if any, autonomy and offer poor support for relationships often end up inhibiting adolescents' development in several areas. This effectively backfires because their children have not fully developed the skills to make them capable of adapting and functioning in the world.

These teens haven't had sufficient opportunity to build up their self-regulation skills and are easily influenced (La Guardia & Ryan, 2002).

The popular cultural views say that when adolescents are coming of age, or in the process of "breaking away," and they become more rebellious, that this is a time when parents should back off so teens become more independent. Yet it is at this time that teens are still building values, gaining their identities, and further developing their relationships with their parents. If the parents are cold, uncaring, rejecting, or unrealistically demanding, the adolescents' autonomy needs are not being met. It is then that a student may erupt in frustration because of excessive controls exerted by family or culture. Most adolescents will express independence, a desire to be separate, and rebellion to some extent, but these reactions don't always have to occur (Blos, 1979; Ryan & Lynch, 1989; Steinberg & Silverberg, 1986). When parents and culture are supportive, creating the feeling of belonging and a willingness to allow them some choices in what they do, then the issues stemming from rebellion are less likely.

In the classroom: Teacher and student autonomy

The fear of losing classroom control weighed heavily on my mind as a beginning teacher, and over the years many new teachers have expressed those same worries to me as well. One of the most terrifying things for me was to give up some control and provide the students with more autonomy. But when teachers are also warm and supportive, and they take that scary step into the unknown and give students more control, students generally respond by being more intrinsically motivated and developing greater confidence in their skills (Deci, Schwartz, Sheinman, & Ryan, 1981; Ryan & Grolnick, 1986). Student performance was partially based on the belief that the students could do better when they had some choice in which tasks they were going to try. When solutions were based on the students' perspectives, students displayed greater curiosity and desire in working on the task. This is illustrated by presenting problems that are more open-ended and where there may be more than one possible solution. Students are encouraged to try out their ideas: "Let's see what happens." For example, most of us have had the experience of a soda can being dropped and, if opened, the soda comes arching out like a fountain, making a mess. However, if the can is chilled, then shaken up, the chance of a foaming disaster can be averted. There are several possible solutions, and the student can try any or all of them and see what happens. He may simply wait to see if time makes a difference, he may tap the can immediately and see if that makes a difference, or he may try some combination of waiting and tapping. The idea is the student is in control: He chooses what course to take. The teacher may lead with some questions to get the student to think about outcomes, but the student still is in control. He is beginning to build his LOC, and the teacher can springboard from here to other activities to continue building the student's confidence and his sense of whether he can do it.

Controlling teachers typically use social comparisons such as grades for rewards and punishment, or external praise or pressure to keep things going as they wanted. But this often results in lowering the students' motivation toward achieving mastery, decreasing their confidence regarding their abilities, and creating a lower self-worth. (A telling trait about these teachers was revealed if they were controlling outside of class, too.) Such teachers remind us of drill sergeants, and they have problems even trusting other teachers with minor tasks or favors. Learning under these teachers, students' motivation takes even more of a beating. The students are less intrinsically motivated, feel even less competent, thinking, "Now what am I going to get yelled at about?" and have lower self-esteem, thinking, "I'm not very competent." Heavy-handed teacher control moves students away from being intrinsically motivated. There is more shallow or surface learning because of the orientation toward top grades and because of social comparisons (Midgley, Anderman, & Hicks, 1995). The depth of understanding is poorer. The nationwide emphasis on high-stakes standardized tests, which function as report cards for the student, teacher, and school, can negatively affect the entire school, including high-achieving students. The emphasis can move students away from being intrinsically motivated (Ryan & La Guardia, 1999). The rising emotional needs of the adolescent, especially regarding autonomy and belonging, can be compromised as schools are forced to use increased controls in response to their emphasis on testing, with intrinsic motivation being the casualty.

An important but usually unstated aspect of motivation is that the LOC applies to us—the teachers or administrators—as well. The personal beliefs we have about students' capabilities can be used to build their skills if we believe the students can learn, but it can also potentially hurt the students' efforts if we think they can't (Parajes, 1996). When teachers label students as "lazy" it often indicates that the teachers have finally "quit" on the student and are no longer looking for how to reach them. Mel Levine (2003) argued that the issue is not that the student is being lazy but that the student has "output failure." The student has a natural desire to learn, but something, often multiple things, changed his or her desire until the student produces little or nothing. Too often, I encounter teachers who simply have given up out of frustration. The students may not turn around for you, but the work you do may see fruition with students in a later class. You may not get to harvest the crop, but your actions are watering seed and fertilizing the ground. "Little Joe" is an example.

Little Joe failed in class after class in middle school. He was the classic "loser." Almost every teacher tried for several months or more before becoming exhausted and they stopped making the extra effort. Stories about his nonefforts were legend. For whatever reason Little Joe had not dropped out of school by the time I saw him in 10th grade. Assignments were rarely completed; test scores usually ranged from F's to the rare low C. He was not exactly a success story. He had the stereotypical track record with the courts and local police. In tenth grade some teachers were on their last legs of making any extra effort with Little Joe. The concept that no child will fail, which produced students who worked the system to delay assignments, was not working. The teachers were reaching exhaustion. One day something "snapped" in Little Joe, and a crucial threshold in self-perception had been reached. Little Joe didn't want to be at the bottom anymore, hearing the painful, snide remarks aimed at him. An extraordinary effort on his part took place. Average grades, or even a 95%, was no longer good enough. He wanted the top score and strove to work for it. His grades changed in my class to a consistently high 90%. Little Joe became my top performing student. He was competent, and he enjoyed that feeling, smiling, even happy throughout the day. His outlook changed, because he had gained a sense that he could do something about this performance. His LOC was now internal. One day he entered class looking crestfallen; he had a shattered look on his face. "I have to leave." He was being court-ordered out of class. It was a gut-wrenching break for both of us. He was growing daily in my class, and we were both exhilarating in it. Being raised like many men, I was taught to have a pretty tight control over my expressed emotions (and all the baggage that goes with that approach). But my tears welled up, as we gave each other farewell waves, our body language mutually projecting dejection and great sadness. I asked Joe that if he ever got back into town he should please stop in and see me. A few years later he did. Joe was starting to put his life together; he still had an internal locus of control. Joe is a rare example, but he illustrates a significant point, that *all those earlier efforts by other teachers sometimes bear fruit.* It just happened that he blossomed in my class, and I was lucky enough to witness it.

Never quit on the students, no matter how agonizing it is. It doesn't mean they aren't accountable, but we must continue to do what we can in building that intrinsic motivation. We can make a difference in our students and in staff, but we must be proactive and continuously work at it. I'm no saint; I have feelings, too. I become very frustrated at times when students fail to produce, but I would never take my anger out on the students. They can be held accountable, but you cannot terrorize them. This isn't the "old days" where a teacher could beat a kid for noncompliance or "attitude." If they are working out of fear, what happens to their efforts when you are not there? I try to determine the reasons for "output failure." Is the student displaying learned helplessness? What are their beliefs about how they learn, their failures or successes? I've got to find the key to the student. Sometimes I quickly can, though usually it takes a lot of effort. But the kids are worth it, after all; their futures are generally what is at stake. With today's economy, their effort or lack of it affects not only themselves, but the whole economy if they've neither the skills nor motivation to learn and persist in their efforts.

Likes and Interests

When students reach puberty and move into adolescence, their interests and likes shift. As they enter into middle school or junior high school, social activities and sports may be what they like, but their perspectives about what interests them, or what they feel is really important, can be quite different from what teachers assume. When young adolescents rated four activities, school subjects that were perceived as difficult, subjects such as math came out as the second most important. Sports dropped to the bottom, and at the same time their self-esteem initially dropped lower during this transition to a different type of school structure (Wigfield, Eccles, MacIver, Reuman, & Midgley, 1991). Their deeply felt recognition of what is important and what interests them may not always be what teachers see displayed.

Rewards and Intrinsic Motivation

Should educators give rewards? Aren't rewards harmful? This is still controversial; evidence has accumulated for both sides of the question. With the public and legislatures focused on test scores, and their thinking that test scores are the equivalent to learning, some schools try to motivate students by paying them for higher test scores. However, when the goal is oriented toward high-stakes tests, it moves the adolescent away from intrinsic motivation to the extrinsic view of "What's in it for me?" Visions of Wall Street greed conjure up the thought, "It's all about me." Well, it may be, but it's what skills and knowledge people will pursue on their own that will meet their both immediate and long-term needs. One argument suggests that because we pay laborers wages, why not students? In some conditions, rewards inhibit intrinsic motivation, effectively sending a message that the teacher is responsible for motivating the students because they would not otherwise do the task. A reward must be obtained. It sounds a lot like the traditional concept of a labor contract. "If you do this, I'll pay you that." And when the pay runs out, the laborer (student) quits. There is no autonomy, the laborer-student does not have a choice and she is very unlikely to continue without the reward. No desire to learn is developed (Lepper, 1973; Ryan & La Guardia, 1999). It is fairly common in schools for many students to judge their self-worth by their ability to successfully compete for grades. However, that is a self-defeating behavior if educators are truly striving for intrinsically motivated lifelong learners (Covington, 2002). Developing lifelong learners who can learn and adapt is not what public education is currently set up to do. There are times students do need just the boost that a reward can provide, but I would suggest *if rewards are used, that teachers be judicious in how big the rewards are or how often they are given*. Covington (2002) has recommended that rewards be plentiful where *anyone can earn them* if the quality of personal performance or workmanship meets the rubric, and that there are different types of rewards available. Autonomy should be encouraged through the student's own independent expressions. There are, of course, some caveats. If rewards are too frequent or too plentiful, their motivating power rapidly decreases. Even when based on self-improvement, if the reward is to satisfy the student's desire for a grade improvement rather than a love of learning, the student will become less motivated. Students should also have some autonomy to modify a task to create deeper personal connections and to make it more personally attractive in regard to challenge and expectations.

Developing a Locus of Control

In trying to navigate the maze of competence, greater LOC, self-improvement, and student desire, I tried the following strategy with my high school students. My students had just finished a short but intensive unit about the brain and building a retrievable memory. The students found the unit personally fascinating and fun when they engaged in a variety of simple but dramatic experiments. However, I had a hidden agenda. Part of the unit task was to apply the newly learned strategies in studying for their test on the brain. Therefore, we actively worked at using those strategies. Most of the students aced the test with the average score at about 98%; the lowest was a solid 88%. Even so, the most important issue before me was to get them to apply those learning and study strategies to other courses, so that they could discover that the strategies not only worked but that they had the power to make them work within themselves. They had an understanding of which strategies were personally more effective and could choose from these (meeting the need for autonomy). They could actually use the strategies effectively (building competence and locus of control). Finally, I selected a goal or challenge I believed was within their grasp. If they could improve their test performance by at least 75% toward just the next higher grade by using the memory and learning strategies on a test of their choice *but in a different class*, they could also use a percentage of the test improvement as extra credit in my class. I hoped this would be a win-win-win situation, higher grades in two classes, and I hoped they would learn that the strategies worked in other classes and with other teachers, in addition to reinforcing the brain unit of my own class. Certainly I was aware of the potential hazards of grades being a goal, but I was trying to change their perceptions of their competence and control. Fifteen students with a wide range of abilities decided to see what would happen. The average performance increased 18% over prior tests, with the lowest being a 15% gain. They were mildly surprised; the techniques did work in other classes. The next year a follow-up and refresher was planned for those students to facilitate transfer. In my own classes, I followed up with a short reflection exercise, with the following questions:

- What did you do to make the unit easier to learn?
- Was there anything dull in the lesson, and what strategy did you use to keep your mind from wandering?
- What could you change in your own actions to help you more with that dull portion?
- Describe the personal links or connections that you made to help you learn for the test.
- What were the most effective strategies for studying for this test?
- How did having this opportunity to boost your performance affect your view of _____(fill in the class or subject)_____ ?

Within the complex world of motivational processing, there are many crucial questions yet to solve. For instance, why did students seek those particular rewards, and not others? What meaning does the use of rewards convey to the student? What is the effect of cognitive development on the perception of rewards? Why are educators resorting to rewards? (Has something "failed"?) What is the impact of the institute's orientation on student motivational needs, and what can be changed?

The over-used phrase "paradigm shift" comes to mind when we begin to view and think about things from a totally new perspective, especially on what is possible. The historic election of Barack Obama as the first black president has potentially created a shift in the locus of control for many of the disenfranchised, though if that actually happens it remains to be seen. If students believe the outcomes depend upon their own actions, they make changes. Of course, there are many inspirational stories and an untold number of motivational speakers trying to shift the LOC. Getting anyone, student or teacher, to that point of change where one can initiate and exert control is one of the most important challenges we have because there is no one magic bullet that solves the problem. Several methods have been developed to measure LOC (Connell, 1985; Crandall, Katkovsky, & Crandall, 1965; Skinner, Zimmer-Gembeck, & Connell, 1998). These are useful in getting an idea of what students believe about LOC, and thus where educators need to concentrate in their efforts not only in lesson designs, but also in schoolwide efforts and building community relationships. The problem is, it is not possible to collect all the measurements we'd like at any given time, but key information can be accumulated over the course of several years. One place to start is to collect data in a semiformal manner. The following section will explore some of these methods.

Competence: Am I Smart Enough?

Self-doubt

Self-doubt continually assails some of us while others are only occasionally afflicted with such questions. Although a person's perception is his or her reality, everyone's perception is commonly skewed a bit. Feeling competent is another crucial element to developing people's intrinsic drive, breeding the self-motivation that will propel them forward more confidently into life's unknown. These are issues of belief. Is it within my power to control? Am I competent enough? It doesn't matter whether students are in sixth grade or graduate school, sometimes they don't realize they are already competent because they currently feel inadequate to the task. This is another opportunity for genuine positive feedback and not platitudes.

If an adolescent makes a claim that he understands the assignment but can't get going, or is quickly lost, the teacher needs to help him determine piece by piece just he they can do, and then zero in on the areas where he starts to falter. It is bit like detective work, but the search area is in the mind. In the opening of this chapter, Tracy didn't believe she had the intelligence or skills, and there was nothing she could do about it either. She thought she had no control, so she gave up even before starting. She believed she had no competence and repeated efforts failed to shake this belief. It is relatively commonplace for the student to stubbornly cling to a belief, no matter the evidence (Schmitz & Skinner, 1993). The tenacious refusal to accept new evidence and a model to explain it will be explored further in Chapter 8. *The feeling of being competent is nearly as important as competence itself.* A person feeling competent will likely experience more pleasure, creating an emotional linkage related to valence. The respective cultures we grow up in also influence our perspectives (Gladwell, 2008; Stipek, 2002). Think about math students who may squeak by and then are assigned to the next higher level course. What do they really believe about their skills, intelligence, and competence? These are more than simple internal LOC issues. There are a variety of sources that may influence their beliefs, each with a different degree of influence. In Table 5.1 is a brief survey that helps identify self-handicapping strategies.

Table 5.1 SELF-HANDICAPPING STRATEGIES

Instructions: This is handed out to the student. His or her name is not necessary. The responses can be used to develop a self-awareness and may also be used as a point of class discussion. Students should not add the scores; numeric totals are not meaningful.

Response options:
1 = not at all true   2 = usually not true   3 = sometimes true
4 = frequently true   5 = very true

- Some students put off doing their work until the last minute so that if they don't do well on their work they can say that is the reason. How true is this of you?
- Some students purposely don't try hard in school so that if they don't do well they can say it was because they didn't try. How true is this of you?
- Some students fool around the night before a test so that if they don't do well they can say that is the reason. How true is this of you?
- Some students purposely get involved in lots of activities. Then if they don't do well on their schoolwork, they can say it is because they're involved in other things. How true is this of you?
- Some students let their friends keep them from paying attention in class or from doing their homework. Then if they don't do well they can say their friends kept them from working. How true is this of you?
- Some students look for reasons to keep them from studying: not feeling well; forgot my books, papers, pencil; my schoolwork is at a friend's house or in their car; having to help parents; taking care of brother or sister, etc. Then if they don't do well on their schoolwork, they can say this is the reason. How true is this of you?
- Some students will play video or computer games to avoid doing homework so they can say they forgot about it, or didn't have time to do their work. How true is this of you?

Adapted from Urdan, Midgley, & Anderman, 1998, p. 120. Copyright American Research Association. Reprinted with permission.

At the end of an assignment, conduct surveys either formerly or indirectly as a reflection exercise. Ask students to review the amount of effort they actually made, and perhaps compare it with other tasks and the effort made on those. Additionally, have them consider how well they performed on tasks where they had considerable practice or experience. Finally, ask them whether they could put in more effort or practice, or if there were outside conditions that influenced how well they performed.

When we reflect on the results of a performance, such as a theatrical play, test, or even an athletic scrimmage, we tend to believe that certain factors played a role in the outcome. When we look at performances, it is not unusual to make errors regarding the influence of a particular source. "The refs were lousy! We were home-teamed!" "I kept those Washington politicians from raising the taxes." We frequently see this tendency to bias expressed by politicians, athletes, and even some teachers or students, among others, who take too much credit or deny what they actually did. Students and parents may claim that the grade depended upon who they were, or on whether the teacher liked them. Sometimes bias is displayed with the thought, "Isn't that right, don't you agree? Everyone thinks so," where we attribute our own belief as being the same as everyone else's. The perception about what is the cause is more formally described in attribution theory (Pintrick & Schunk, 2002; Weiner, 1985, 1992). There may be a series of sources that influence performance such as effort, difficulty of task, student mood, ability, effort, who the teacher was, fatigue, and so on (Weiner, 1986). The influences may be grouped into three intertwining dimensions, all affecting what we think is the cause. One of these dimensions is *stability*, whether the underlying cause is unchanging, relatively stable, or changeable. If a student believes he or she does not have the ability, or he or she is not smart enough and that it won't change, those beliefs will likely have a negative influence on the motivation to work harder. In turn, this may lead to a feeling of hopelessness. On the other hand, if the student believes that hard work or effort makes a difference, and one can become better or smarter, he or she will be hopeful and is more likely to work harder. *Our task as educators is to create situations to facilitate and reinforce the student's belief that effort can make a positive difference.* For example, I used my lesson on the brain and memory to create a situation where students' belief that their efforts would make a difference was progressively reinforced first in my own class and then in others. A second dimension of attribution theory regards the *locus* of the influence: whether the influences came from within the person and were caused by their own actions, or if the results were influenced by outside causes. The locus is further influenced by how consistent or stable those influences are. For example, a student might have done poorly because she didn't study but realizes that the disruption of studying was caused by the rare event of having to move from her house. She is not likely to have that problem continuously. (However, homeless children have the opposite problem; continually moving is more likely to be a unchanging or stable but negative influence.) The third dimension is *control*. Can the student exert any control over the conditions? Do their actions make any difference? Going back to the lesson where I taught the students a simple model of how memory works, the in-class demonstrations and experiments helped established that they could exercise control. It might take a series of small activities to establish the groundwork where they see that they do have some control.

Building competence

The great feeling of competence and the security it creates becomes a foundation where students become more interested in their schoolwork, believing that they will be successful. When students succeed in a challenge that was just beyond what they had accomplished earlier they experience the emotional feeling of pleasure, and maybe even exhilaration. The tasks must be "just right," neither too hard nor too easy (Harter, 1974; Stipek & Seal, 2001). When tasks meet those conditions, students feel more competent. However, these Goldilocks criteria will vary from student to student. A task that is too easy for one student may be too difficult for another. This is another place where creating various levels of challenge becomes important. Deborah Stipek described how to determine whether tasks meet the "Goldilocks Test." I have adapted criteria for my own "Goldilocks" Test based on Stipek's work (Stipek & Seal, 2001).

- -

THE GOLDILOCKS TEST

Too Easy

The task was very rapidly finished, even by students who normally take a long time.

They found the task easy.

No extra effort was needed; they did not need to look up answers, research them, or consult about the questions.

Are the top students usually getting nearly perfect scores time after time?

Does the student get excellent grades, yet never seems to study?

When the student actually encounters a real challenge, does he or she rapidly become frustrated and not know how to tackle the problem?

Too Difficult

(This is harder to determine. The teacher should quietly visit with the student, using an investigative approach, not an inquisitor approach.)

Does the student avoid even starting, or does he or she put the assignment off for as long as possible?

Does the student do a variety of other delaying tasks?

Does the student ask or attempt to get someone else to do the work, or does he or she immediately copy the entire assignment from another student?

Does the student have the rubric but even figure out how to get the first step going?

When the student is asked to explain how to do the problem or task, does he or she have any idea how to solve it?

Does the student lack the necessary skills? Probe methodically through the skills he or she needs and see whether he or she has each one that is needed.

Does the student flounder even with serious effort despite his or her skills and does it appear that he or she does not know which direction to pursue? (Is the activity developmentally appropriate*)

*The tasks that have an appropriate challenge are ones just beyond a student's current level of difficulty. However, if the task requires a new cognitive skill level that developmentally a student has not yet grown into (see Chapter 1), he or she may be completely baffled. For example, in an honors high school biology class students had successfully negotiated some difficult and complex genetic problems. When the genetic processes were applied to classical evolution questions that the public frequently gets stuck on, they successfully applied the principles to predict and explain what would happen. However, when they were asked to provide a more advanced genetic explanation at the core of many misunderstandings, they were unable to make the connections. The problem and presentations were changed several times, even using completely different analogies without reference to evolution, but with no success. However, just 1 or 2 years later the same students were able to use the basic logic that was beyond them earlier and were able to march right through the problem using the reasoning principles to make the appropriate applications. Upon analysis of several years' worth of student responses to the problem it appeared the students had been given a problem that was developmentally just beyond their reach (see the section on cycles of cognitive development in Chapter 1).

- -

Getting to Know Your Students

Teachers need to know and understand students better than just trying to appeal to them on some emotional level. From the perspective of teaching daily in the trenches of public school, my colleagues and I bemoan getting information that we wish we had known sooner. It happens every year. About 4–9 weeks into the year, and sometimes much later, we finally learn who has problems with reading or math, who hates writing or can't spell, who reads at a third-grade level, or who has a home environment where just surviving is a major feat and doing homework is an absurd expectation. Had we known such information earlier, our lessons could have been more accurately tuned. That would allow us to refine critical lessons to meet some of the more urgent needs, especially complex or difficult lessons that might demotivate students. What might that information look like and how would it work? Over the course of several years my fellow colleagues and I have assembled information we'd like to know *before* the school year starts, or at least have available during the year. To preserve confidentiality, the access to the information would be available only to their current teachers and authorized personnel, while information regarding special services or disabilities would be available only as permitted by law. Our intention is to have the learner profile tied into the electronic-computer grading system rather than a 20-pound mound of paper filed away in some office. In Table 5.2 is what our staff would like to have available. Obviously what is permitted will vary from school to school. Notice that it goes well beyond simple IQ and test scores, and touches on issues related to motivation.

Learning Styles Are Neuromyths?

Reevaluation of the published research indicates too few controls and too many variables (Pashler, McDaniel, Rohrer, & Bjork, 2008). If educators were to accept learning styles as published, it would mean that each student would have multiple learning styles for different subjects, different teachers, and different times of day. What that really says is that there is no single learning style that can be relied on for a student. Like some neuromyths, there is a lot of hype: Whole businesses are founded on these ideas, and when carefully examined there is found to be little rigorous substance.

What is the goal? What are you asking me to do?

We are naturally curious and from infancy we explore our worlds; we want to learn, but schools have a tendency to crush that curiosity in many students (Levine, 2003). As discussed in the chapters on attention and emotion, it helps tremendously if teachers are able to capture and maintain their students' attention with emotional connections. Curiosity, novelty, and using the unexpected all help to make that initial but tenuous connection. Creating a level of interest high enough to pique the adolescent's curiosity, with just slight stress, may help to keep the neural networks active. Too much stress, as we've observed, is not good but too little stimulation or a boring lesson can cause neural networks not to function well either (Berlyne, 1960; Pintrick & Schunk, 2002).

To help the student answer her own but unstated question about whether she can do the task, educators need to be very clear about what they are asking the student to do. The student should know what is being expected of her. The goal must be clear, not vague (Locke & Latham, 1990). *The challenge or difficulty of the goal must also be neither too easy nor too difficult.* For many beginning teachers, making sure the assignment is at the appropriate level of difficulty is a monumental challenge, and it continues to be, even for veterans. This is where a form of differentiated instruction can be used. *Have several levels of difficulty available for a particular lesson from which the students can choose, or post models that demonstrate several levels of challenge.* That is easily said: I've heard workshop leaders express it a number of times. However, for teachers, the real issue is time. *Staff need to be provided time with guided instruction in order to actually develop some of the things they learn about*, which I will briefly comment on in the following sections on motivation and staff development. To start, I'd suggest selecting only a single, really important lesson or two, especially lessons where students are too bored or are frequently overwhelmed. Develop several levels of challenge in those before moving on to others.

Table 5.2. THE LEARNER'S PROFILE

School Observations/Measures

Summary of proficiency levels in all areas
Lexile scores/reading
PAWS (statewide assessment)
SAT/ACT
MAP (measures of academic progress)
MAP comments/recommendations
AWMA (automated work memory assessment)
DIBLE, RAN, or RAS scores and profiles for reading
Hearing (central auditory processing/CAP)
Writing skills
Vocabulary usage and consistency
Logic/reasoning skills
Metacognitive skills
Seating recommendations in classroom/bus
Computer literacy level
Activities
Group skills
At-risk status (also free and reduced lunch)
Books available at home?
Interventions tried (note success, or lack of)
Hygiene
Health issues

*Learning styles are not included because substantial meta-analysis has demonstrated that learning
  styles do not exist. There are learning style preferences that might be used to help maintain student
  interest. Even though there are hundreds of web pages, countless workshops, and published studies,
  the studies on learning styles, when carefully evaluated, failed to meet the standard of quality
  research with appropriate controls, and research design (Pashler et al., 2008).

Motivational Issues

Plays/socializes with other students, or isolates himself or herself?
Willingness to work with others
Likes or dislikes
Favorite activities
Extracurricular interests
What he or she thinks is important for the future
Other interests
Button issues (topics that are especially sensitive, either positive or negative)
Facebook and Myspace address/links
Friends (who they hang out with)
Home environment (living w/parents, grandparent, foster parent, self-supporting?)
Parent/community involvement with student

Other Concerns

Based in part on Marzono's 11 influences on student learning and neuroeducation/developmental research
  from Fischer, Dawson, Petitto, and Wolf.

- -

CAVEAT: MOTIVATION AND STAFF DEVELOPMENT

The teachers and paraprofessionals also respond to some of the same fundamental motivators in staff development. What is the goal? Is it achievable (especially considering the element of the amount of time needed)? "What do I need to do to succeed?" assumes that the staff consider the staff development worthwhile. Basic motivational needs apply to staff as well to the adolescents we teach. That should not be forgotten.

- -

Long-term or distant goals should derive naturally from a series of short-term goals. Although we might design lessons with the end in mind, a series of intermediate goals that allows students to use their just-learned skills helps them in task orientation, self-regulation, and overall motivation (Lens, Simon, & Dewitte, 2002). If the goal is too large or distant, such as a science fair project, paper, book report, or a large time-line poster, the students can quickly lose interest or feel overwhelmed. Break up the lesson so it has a series of close or immediate goals so that the students can see or measure their progress while moving them to the larger goal. For example, with longer projects, have periodic checkpoints. In science fairs, or writing reports, each portion of the project should have a specific goal and time to be completed. With writing, the steps might be figuring out the theme; an outline; a rough draft; checking the project for voice, conventions, and word choice; and a polished draft. The checkpoints can be used for seeing if the students understand and for any necessary mid-course corrections or re-teaching. Each of the intermediate goals should have a clear due date. The idea is to make a series of small obtainable goals. We don't want to throw the kids in the water and see if they sink or swim; they need coaching and feedback as they learn.

Why am I doing this?

Of the underlying motivational questions, why the student is to engage in some learning activity is perhaps one of the most important, and, in the United States, this question is one of the most difficult for teachers to address. Another way of asking the question is, "What is the goal and what does it mean for me?" Having a goal that is personally important (more salient), and where a student can see progress is probably significant to students and teachers alike. Judging by student feedback, one of the most successful forms of teaching that addresses "Why am I doing this?" is experiential learning.

Field Investigations or Experiential Learning Versus Field Trips

When students have immediate goals in mind, such as collecting information during a field excursion, or where they are physically immersed in the learning experience, it is easier to keep students involved. Field trips where students are passively looking and the significance is drawn out only later in discussions can create problems when goals are vague or progress toward them is delayed. When a sequence of tasks is accomplished and key lessons are grasped *during the activity,* where students can monitor their own progress, the result is more motivating than working toward a goal that is announced or discussed a couple of days after the trip. The delay in time can contribute to their minds being off-task and potentially raise issues of "Why am I doing this?" or "Is this worthwhile?" Experiential learning tends to be more continuously rewarding in a natural manner, providing rapid feedback about the quality of their effort. Because the student is wholly immersed in the learning, and new experiences can build immediately upon prior experiences, the effect is felt bodily. The student engages in self-reflection, which can be guided by the instructor, and the student's new concepts can be self-tested and re-evaluated in a continuous cycle. Students are more likely to experience a natural flow where their desire to learn is fostered by their involvement, and time seems to fly by. Experiential learning can be extraordinarily powerful and life-changing; I have seen that it profoundly changed the direction of my life as well as the lives of at least eight of my students. If I had the opportunity and means, experiential learning would be my choice of an instructional method.

"You'll need to know this when you grow up"

"I know you don't see it now, but you'll thank me later." How many times have we said that? What does that mean for the adolescent right now? For most students, when you're "grown up" is a lifetime away. They really might need to know this lesson, but teachers aren't likely to succeed with such instant turn-offs. Even with older adolescents, with a more mature sense of time and goals, their lessons need to have a value they can relate to right now, meaning that *they can immediately see how they can use the lesson now rather than later*. For most people that need for relevancy doesn't seem to go away. With teenagers, we're signaling to them that we don't have any immediate use for this lesson, and it has no apparent value to them, at least right now, so they should get ready for a dull lesson. This is the wrong message. Brophy observed that teachers explained the relevance of the lesson only 1.5% of the time, and when introducing a lesson *none* of the 317 teachers in the study said the lesson would even help them develop useful or enjoyable skills (Brophy, Rohrkemper, Rashid, & Goldberger, 1983). Is it any wonder that kids start becoming seriously unmotivated by the fourth or fifth grade? The younger the student, the more he or she lives in the here and now. Their perception of time is quite different, and even a large number of adolescent students can't relate to distant goals. Our challenge as educators is to find a way to help them to connect with the lesson *now*.

Are we there yet? The perception of time

We learned in Chapter 1 that the frontal lobes are among the last parts of the brain to mature and that youth have a difficult time with anticipating consequences. One way to consider anticipation may be how they process time. For young children, next week is so far away it might as well be forever; for those with ADHD the future may be only right now. Students actually experience time differently (De Volder & Lens, 1982). During adolescence, students' experiences of time range widely from very short to very long and can significantly affect their performances. While this difference in perception may be related to prefrontal lobe growth, students who are more motivated attach greater value to distant goals; those who don't value the distant goals, such as many vocational students, are less motivated. If a student's perception of the future is a short time away, and his or her life revolves in the here and now, he or she often cares little for the school's focus on a more distant future. That future doesn't exist or he or she is unaware of it (Lens et al., 2002). For these students extrinsic resources may help motivate them because they can more quickly see the external result. One thought is that studying more easily overloads their working memory (see Chapter 7). However, there is an additional problem. During the initial start-up of a task, these same students are vulnerable to distractions. Think about students who usually favor the vocational tasks. They are often hands-on, project-oriented where one can see the results quickly and where they can steadily monitor their own progress in an almost continuous fashion. Their feedback and orientation is extrinsic but often sufficient to keep them going on long-term projects as long as they can see steady progress.

Feedback

Feedback is based on the student's actual work and is done privately in either written or verbal form. Use feedback to advance students' performance and hold them accountable. *Do not broadcast their results by posting scores, even with numbers or initials.* That shifts the goal away from a focus on learning to a competitive grade performance, and in such an atmosphere, there can be more losers than winners. Additionally, a goal that shifts to a grade performance also typically shifts away from the love of learning (Stipek & Seal, 2001). Feedback should be constructive, clearly noting what they did well, and specifically where and what they need to improve on. Make sure to recognize the effort they have put into it. The lack of feedback is also a signal. When teachers ignore a student and his or her work or effort, it telegraphs to the student that his or her work is not important or is wasting the teacher's time, or that he or she probably can't improve (Stipek, 2002). Sympathy can also be counterproductive. Stipek (2002) observed that teachers feel sympathy when they believe a situation is beyond the student's control. The message of sympathy suggests that there's nothing the student can do about his or her performance and he or she may lose confidence. Why bother with more effort if it's not going to get better? The perception is that the locus of control has shifted to some external source.

Feedback is a time to encourage, redirect, and coach, but not to crush. Teachers can use the feedback to redirect student attention, help them analyze what happened, and coach them on what they can do. That doesn't mean teachers say only positive things for fear of squashing the student's self-esteem. *Adolescents can take criticism if it is constructive and tactfully delivered* (Braumeister, Campbell, Krueger, & Vohs, 2005). Point out that mistakes are opportunities to learn, and follow through with some direct coaching. Being brutally frank about what was done poorly usually backfires. You can be honest without being brutal.

Should a student finish an intermediate task early, and to the quality level indicated by a rubric, he or she can be rewarded with a form of positive feedback. This might include some free time, perhaps more computer time, or a visit to the library to look at some magazines. For example, within a photography class some students select problems that vary considerably in difficulty. It is not unusual to find that some must go back and reshoot, which results in projects that are completed on different days, but all students have the same final completion date. Some students need significant help from the teacher or another student with advanced computer skills, and others motor right along on their own. However, all the students have been made aware of several posted options they may choose from when they finish. *They have a reward menu they may select from if they finish early with quality work.*

If the goal or task is perceived as being worthwhile then the student is more likely to see personal connections with the task and how it can be used or fits in with some other larger goal. If those critical connections have been made, the next question to address is what the student needs to do in order to succeed. What skills and knowledge are necessary, and how hard is the challenge? Using either a physical example or a person demonstrating how the tasks are to be accomplished will address many of these unstated concerns.

Provide a model

For many students the skills they actually put to use will provide them feedback about their competence, but some still completely miss the connection between their competence and the tasks they've completed. This is not unusual in math and writing. *Vague praise, such as "nice job, well done," is of little help.* It provides no direction. If they have more precise information, such as a model to look at or watch where they can make comparisons, it can be of immense help in building student competence. Models can range from a person performing a task to something students can directly examine such as procedures used in a task, posted themes, essays, or reports written at various levels of quality. For many students *the model also represents a goal, a level of expectancy.* The model provides a variety of cues that have meaning to students and helps them to direct their actions (Toleman, 1949). When a person watches a model, a fundamental processing system in the brain called the mirror neuron system (described in Chapter 4), is also engaged. The mirror system appears to help us learn how to mimic a physical action that has never been seen before and thus can be extremely helpful in student learning (Bandura, 1969; Iacoboni, 2008; Rosenthal & Zimmerman, 1978).

Observing a model can strengthen a student's direction of action, or weaken it. For example, students watch a fellow student of much greater ability in PE class who fails to execute a particular movement. The rest of the students are not encouraged by what they saw and are less likely to attempt the action. However, watching a student model can also be very empowering. For example, in a math class students were having difficulty figuring out how to set up a geometry problem. Armijo, who was noted for being rather average and obviously not the class brainiac, had a flash of insight that made the problem come quickly together. The teacher had him go around and help other struggling students, but gave Armijo *explicit instructions to not directly give away the procedure or answer*. Armijo as the student "teacher" showed the other students a similar problem and then asked a series of leading questions. One by one, the remaining students discovered the relationship. Armijo beamed with pride. This was cool, and his enthusiasm soared. The rest of the kids took on a newer attitude that "if Armijo can get it, I can, too."

The teacher continually functions as a model, both in class and out of school. Often in our curricula there are units that teachers don't get especially excited about. If we display that lack of enthusiasm, the students rapidly pick up on it. If we are enthusiastic, bursting with energy, interest, and excitement, students pay better attention (Perry, 1985). Rapport also increases and students enjoy that section more (Abrami, Leventhal, & Perry, 1982). The teacher's enthusiasm can have unexpected results. In one case a student's parent was her teacher for a particular subject. The parent/teacher found the unit personally dull but worked at overtly displaying excitement, pretending interest in the topic, even outside the classroom. The parent/teacher did this so effectively that her child developed a keen interest, majored and took a degree in the topic, never realizing her parent/teacher found it personally boring. Modeling is a powerful tool that affects students in many subtle ways.

Properties of Effective Models

Attention: The model captures attention and holds it.

Similarity: The model and goal or procedure share an obvious similarity (Bandura, 1986).

Salience: Those models with little personal value are not remembered (Schunk, 1987).

Competent: The model is competent, the person knows what they are doing, or it displays an accurate example (Schunk, 1987).

Easily Observed: Important steps, or characteristics, of the model can be easily seen; guided practice facilitates complex procedures; students are able to demonstrate and verbalize all critical knowledge, skills, and behaviors (Pintrick & Schunk, 2002).

Credibility: The person practices what he or she preaches. If he or she is seen to act differently in a similar setting, he or she may be considered to be a hypocrite (for example, TV figures, preachers, politicians, athletes, or teachers who say one thing publicly and do the opposite privately) (Bryan & Walbek, 1970).

Enthusiasm and Excitement: The message is consistently energetic, has a higher level of interest, and incorporates fun and curiosity.

When using models, point out and review the problem areas to the adolescents where the model does not exactly match the current situation. In many cases, some of these adolescents are now cognitively astute enough to have noticed some discrepancies. These differences are excellent points of opportunity to teach and develop application skills. *Have competent fellow students of the same level of ability as the rest of the students demonstrate or explain*. Break up the class into small groups. Have one student from each group be taught by the teacher. Then those student "teachers" quickly review, demonstrate, or model the task, and finally the students as teachers then return to their original groups to instruct their peers. Rotate student teachers so each person in the group has the opportunity to become the "expert" on some part of the lesson. Students really enjoy the empowerment that stems from their competence. This works well in many science, math, and social studies classes. Peer teaching is very powerful and has the additional benefits of allowing the teacher to spend more time closely monitoring how the students are mastering the challenge at hand (Schunk, 1987).

For the older adolescent who is either in college or in a remedial "adult education" class, most of the motivational strategies presented earlier, with slight variations in respect to age, also apply. Wlodkowski (2008) developed a number of strategies that can be used with adults. Variations of these, with comments, are summarized in Table 5.3.

Summary

Motivation is the natural extension of emotional processing and the making of connections between the learner, the knowledge, and skills that the instructor wishes adolescents to learn. There are strong environmental or extrinsic factors as well as internal factors that together create the chemistry of motivation. Fundamental questions that the learner asks, such as, "What use is this to me? Can I do this?" and "What skills and knowledge do I need?" underlie much motivation. In turn, we find that the adolescents must often be guided in realizing they control most of their learning. However, some things are outside their locus of control. Helping students believe they have some control can be accomplished through autonomy where students have some choice. Along with this, students need to build their competence across a variety of skills. New tasks should be just a little beyond their current level of performance. This is more readily accomplished by learning about their interests and getting to know the students' learning habits. To keep students from being discouraged, clear and obtainable goals should be presented. A student's perception of the future changes developmentally from the right here and now to stretch gradually toward weeks, and even months later. In the meantime, lesson goals should be broken up and be more immediate. Long-term goals can appear overwhelm-

Table 5.3. MOTIVATION STRATEGIES FOR OLDER ADOLESCENTS

1. Connect with your learner by sharing something you find valuable. (This begins to create the emotional connection.)

2. Demonstrate your desire to help older adolescents learn. (This reinforces the emotional connection and addresses the competency issue of "Am I smart enough?" by telling them you're there because you want to help them. You're their partner and coach.)

3. Introduce yourself and have others introduce themselves. (Do this face to face.)

4. Mirror their perspectives, styles, and common interests. (Mirroring is one of the most basic levels on which we connect.) Be as genuine as possible; find common ground and talk about it.

5. Explain your reasons for specific requirements or criteria. This helps to establish the credibility of the assignment and potential significance to their lives.

6. Create a positive environment; address concerns, fears, and work to eliminate these.

7. Provide conditions for success. Use study groups; share phone numbers; point out related workshops and books; tell where to find computer assistance and writing centers and other tutoring sources; and clarify your availability. Also make use of handouts, emails, peer comments, editing, wordsmiths, and disability resources. Provide clear goals and set schedules.

8. Treat them like adults, even though they may not have reached full cognitive development. Do not be imperious, condescending, or authoritative. None of us knows it all.

9. Guide and inform them on how they learn and how their mind/brain systems work. Use that to build up other forms of instruction and learning modes. Give them greater ownership by increasing their understanding of what works in learning (and what doesn't work).

10. Let them know they are in control. Guide and encourage them. Help them to correctly link their efforts with their successes.

11. When there are misconceptions or erroneous beliefs, address them positively and tactfully. If the beliefs involve motivational problems (I'm not good at math, I can't write well, etc.) discuss them and learn if these are perspectives common to the class or just individual locus of control problems. If beliefs are strongly held, be aware of how the brain processes information. (See the decision-making model in Chapter 8.)

12. Direct students with similar interests toward each other.

13. Be supportive and encouraging. Facilitate the formation of study groups.

14. Use different modes of instruction and different levels of challenge (differentiated instruction), ranging from computer-assisted instruction, small group and cooperative group studies, multiple sources, checklists for guide self-study, and audiotapes and videotapes/DVDs.

15. Models should be relevant and should demonstrate the appropriate level of challenge.

ing, even to adults. Teachers are sometimes tempted to use rewards to motivate students, but these can cause numerous pitfalls and so caution is advised. Timely feedback should be provided to students, and it should also be very clear what needs to be improved upon. Peer instruction from someone at the same level of ability can be especially powerful. For the older adolescent, many of the same fundamental motivational principles apply, with some differences adjusted for age.

Designing Your Personal Application

There are numerous approaches to trying to motivate adolescents. In the broad sweep, a teacher may target the entire year, or focus on smaller lessons or units. Some gifted individuals can succeed with many students across the years, but others of us may be less talented and might focus on working on a lesson at a time, eventually building an overall tone or spirit. In either case some serious reflection is probably in order, but it is important to recognize there is no standardized solution in motivation that works for all adolescents. All students are different, and they learn differently and are motivated differently. I would suggest starting with smaller lessons and see if motivation can be built from there.

- Identify several lessons where students don't appear to have the motivation either to get going or to see the lesson through. Motivation will be closely linked to the personal emotional connections the students make with the lesson.
- With the chosen lesson, the next and perhaps one of the most difficult tasks is to determine what aspect of motivation is lacking. Besides considering the small selection of motivation areas presented in this chapter, interview a range of several students away from the class. Their perspective will shed light on the direction the motivating actions need to take. What to focus on in the interview is next.
- List their beliefs about how they think they learn, what they are capable of, and the degree to which they believe they can change their learning. Besides those, list the interventions that would address each one of the beliefs or perspectives. Some of their beliefs might suggest metacognitive skills that need to be developed. (This is explored further in the next chapter.)
- The selected interventions must now be woven into the lesson. It is all too easy to fall into a negative frame of mind while working out the possible interventions with thoughts like "That won't work because . . ." Move past the negative tide. Have you actually tried that intervention, in conjunction with other strategies? It is especially important to elicit the students' input and demonstrate that their comments and feedback make a difference. The students themselves just might provide some of the solutions. It is not just the words they use but what they really mean by those words; it is

what they are really telling you about the lesson and their condition.

- Finally, as the interventions are being drawn, will the students be worse off if the interventions don't work? If things would be no worse, and it were possible to improve them, go forward and attempt it. However, be sure to get student feedback immediately after the lesson: What worked well? Why do they feel that? What was most interesting? Why was it interesting? What didn't work? What was slow or boring? What would they do to make that part better?

Key Points and Recommendations

- *When students have options, they perform better.* They buy in to the assignments more because they will tend to pick tasks they feel more competent in and that they can perform reasonably well. This autonomy applies for all ages. We like the feeling of empowerment where we have some say in what we are supposed to do.
- *When we label a student it often carries unintended baggage with it.* Too often the label is hurtful, and when educators hear it from other teachers it can change their expectations. For example, if we've heard that Chris is lazy, or Kendra is a thief, we look at and treat those students differently the moment they enter the room. The problems arise if we reinforce those preconceptions. We expect Chris not to work, and we may not be proactive in making sure he is working like everyone else, or we are wary of giving Kendra any responsibilities. It doesn't mean we turn a blind eye to them either and allow them to fail; rather, we should be proactive and immediately work on creating the conditions for success. Some students have worn a very provocative T-shirt that says, "I'm not what you label me." Indeed, be wary of labels.
- *A locus of control (LOC) applies equally to teachers and to students.* We can change the student's actions, behaviors, and beliefs in their ability to effect change. But if a teacher doesn't believe he can make a change in the student, then he should probably get out of teaching, because changing the student is what teaching is about. A brain that isn't changing isn't learning. Teachers can model the LOC by demonstrating personal responsibility by cleaning up the room, organizing material, and working with the students to implement changes. Even taking a few minutes to help students organize their notebooks is a start.
- *Never quit on students.* This is undeniably hard, but this is what we are here for: to help the students, to guide them. Teaching goes beyond being a clock puncher. Remember that if you're working with youth or young adults, their frontal lobes are not completely online yet, and their judgment and anticipating consequences of their actions need to be influenced through your direction. If you don't provide direction, who will?

- *Be judicious in using rewards; they should be neither too big or frequently given but should be available to everyone based upon personal improvement.* There are considerable opportunities and dangers in using rewards, so caution and fairness are strongly urged.

- *There should be clear, specific goals.* Vague goals are frustrating. Students and staff don't know what they should be doing, or whether their actions are of any value and they're just wasting time. Goals should be clear and the older students should recognize when they've achieved it. Younger adolescents may need more direction and assurance. Posting a rubric or a model and reviewing it are essential to bringing clarity to the goal. Check for understanding by asking medium- or low-level ability students to state what the goal is.

- *The challenge or difficulty of the goal must not be too easy or too difficult.* For beginning teachers this will likely be a challenge because of simply trying to find out what level to make the material. One way to reduce the problem is to take the commercially made tasks and rewrite a couple of items into two or three levels. Gradually add to these. Don't attempt to rewrite a number of lessons all at once unless you've got some time to reflect because you can simply work yourself into the ground. Pace it; don't race through it.

- *Goals should have several levels of challenge to be more developmentally appropriate and to avoid boring the student or overwhelming them.* In writing materials to new levels, just edge up the difficulty a bit. It you attempt too large of a leap it may be developmentally beyond the student's reach.

- *Staff need to be provided time for guided instruction to actually develop some of the things they are told about.* I've seen entirely too many workshops where excellent material was presented, but the staff (including me) were given no time to actually design lessons and implement them. Having time to take the ideas, work them into a design, and reflect and discuss them with our fellow teachers with the guidance of the workshop coach is badly needed (and usually missing).

- *Goals should be broken up into a series of immediate, attainable sections that allow the students to clearly see or measure their progress.* Even if students seem competent, many will naturally put off a task until the last minute, especially when it comes to reports or major projects. Having a series of smaller steps that will be graded reduces the procrastination. Recall that adolescents normally have difficulties with anticipating the future. Set the students up for success, not failure. A series of checkpoints also allows for mid-course adjustments and coaching, resulting not only in more on-time assignments but also achieving a higher-quality performance. Post the schedule of checkpoints, and remind the students when a deadline is approaching.

- *With adolescent students, we need to design the lesson so they can immediately see how they can use the lesson now or later.* Students need to see value in the lesson, not just because they are told to blindly obey and learn it. Their perception of time becomes important. For adolescents, the idea of the future may be a week or a month away; longer periods are difficult for them to conceive. The second part, and equally important, is designing the lesson so the students see how they are going to use it. What role will it play in their life, and is that role important to them? That is obviously the most difficult task. The more we know our students the more likely we can find a way to help make the connections.

- *Feedback on performance should generally not be in a classwide format but should be provided in private.* There is the possible exception of art class critiques, where students explain what went well or didn't, and the teacher guides with commentary. When teachers privately acknowledge their effort, students may respond positively. Unfortunately, for some teachers, when a student has done so poorly, or has an "attitude," that student becomes a nonperson. The student or his or her work is completely ignored. Other students pick up on this teacher behavior as well. Ignoring students doesn't motivate them to change their effort, and this may be counterproductive.

- *Kids can take criticism.* Criticism, if constructive, can be handled by adolescents. High school arts classes are good examples. Students may research the style they were attempting and explain with examples what they were trying and what they attempted. The teacher may note what worked and why and what didn't work. Ask the students what could be done to improve their work rather than simply telling them what to do. This approach also may work by asking, "What could you do to improve it?" "How might that look?" "What might you try to . . ." "OK . . . Let's try that again, or on the next one try that idea you had and see what happens." This shifts from directing the student to having the student suggest his or her own ideas (greater personal involvement) and giving the student more autonomy.

- *Feedback can be in a positive form of a reward with structured free time with some choice of activities.* When the students know they have some choice of activities if they finish early some will work harder in order to have the extra time to work on something else. Heaping more problems on them because they finished early is often perceived as a punishment unless it is an option that allows students to explore because of their personal interests.

- *Provide autonomy, where students have some choice in the direction and level of challenge.* This is similar to feedback but represents an important fundamental need as the student grows older. Having some choice positively influences a student's intrinsic motivation. Students are more likely to work harder, longer, and do better when they can choose.

- *The feeling of being competent is as nearly as important as competence itself.* This harkens back to the idea that if students actually believe they can, they have a much better chance of actually accomplishing the goal because they also put in the effort that will be needed. Many of us were introduced to this concept as a moral story when we were very little ("The Little Engine That Could" or "The Pony Engine": "I think I can, I think I can").

- *The educator's task is to create situations to facilitate and reinforce the student's belief that effort really can make a positive difference.* Plan a short series of slightly progressive learning events where the students will have success. Follow up the lesson with a reflection activity where the students not only are guided in making the connections on their recent task, but where they project to the next task, creating a level of expectation just slightly above where they are currently (see the next Key Point immediately below).

- *Tasks should be just above students' current level of ability, or "just right," but should also be developmentally within their reach.* To reduce frustration and likelihood of failure, differentiate the tasks into progressive levels of challenge. It doesn't have to be a completely different task, but the new level of difficulty can be embedded in the current learning task as a natural progression. Make sure the students have the option (autonomy) to try to work with harder material. Determining the appropriate challenge level is more difficult when teachers lack prior experience with a particular age level of student (either in middle or high school). Look at material already written and then slightly modify those with a few more levels of difficulty. Don't try to reinvent the wheel. Additionally, get feedback from the students about the challenge. Who found it too easy, too hard, and why? Do they have any ideas of how to make it different?

- *Vague praise, such as "nice job, well done," is of little help.* Comments on returned papers can be powerful. Use specific comments on what they did well and what they need improvement on. For example, "Kelly, you're coming along, and with a bit more effort you'll do much better. You explained #3 and 4 very well. You were thorough and clear. But look at question #5. You need to tell us more information about why it happened. Make sure you write about who, what they did, and when they did it." Teachers are pressed for time and may have large classes, so writing thorough feedback is practically impossible. Use only a few phrases or a couple of sentences at the very least. Further, don't use red ink! Students will get nervous if they see a huge amount of red written in the margins. Prepare the students before you hand back the papers. Let them know you've written specific, guiding comments to help them improve. You're their coach! Gradually it may not be necessary to write so much. But this is feedback they need in order to know what to do and what to change. Time spent on these personalized comments shows that the teacher actually reads *all* of their work, and that she cares. It can be some of the most productive time a teacher can spend with students.

- *The model also represents a goal or a level of expectancy.* The model provides students with a tangible target: "This is what a medium-quality model looks like" or "This is the lowest level that will be acceptable." Also, show higher-achieving students what they need to rise to. We do this all the time in the arts and sports. The student can see the differences. In some respects, models can be considered a visible rubric where the quality of the outcome can be directly observed.

- *Observing a model can strengthen a student's direction of action or weaken it.* "I saw what happened to my sister; boy, I'm not going to do that!" Students can see positive or negative results and will usually adjust. However, it is sometimes necessary to also point out specifics that the model did well or did poorly, and explain or demonstrate again how that influenced the result.

- *Do not directly give away the procedure or answer.* The moment we give a student an answer, they stop trying to solve it or think anything further about it. Generally, we should almost never provide a direct answer. When they are frustrated, consider leading them quickly toward the answer. If they still can't discover it on their own, perhaps try a prompt of, "Consider _____ or _____. What do you think that will do? Tell me."

- *The teacher continually functions as a model, both in class and out of school.* Whether teachers like it or not, students see and note any discrepancies between what they do and say. It can be in the hall or the mall. A teacher in public is a teacher on display. For some students it comes as a shock that we are real people and that may help or hurt our ability to impress upon them back in the learning environment. It is the old saw: "Practice what you preach."

- *Have competent fellow students of the same level of ability as the rest of the students demonstrate or explain.* Students of the same ability level are viewed as more credible than the class brainiac. Students can relate to each other, and often speak in terms so they can understand each other more effectively than the teacher. Peer teaching has long been understood as a powerful way to reach students, in addition to multiply how many people are teaching.

RESOURCES

Heckhausen, J., & Dweck, C. (Eds.). (1998). *Motivation and self-regulation across the life span*. New York, NY: Cambridge University Press.

Pajares, F., & Urdan, T. (Eds.). (2002). *Academic motivation of adolescents*. Greenwich, CT: Information Age Publishing.

Pintrick, P. R., & Schunk, D. (2002). *Motivation in education, theory research, and applications*. (2nd ed.). New York, NY: Pearson Education.

Stipek, D. (2002). *Motivation to learn: Integrating theory and practice*. (4th ed.). Englewood Cliffs, NJ: Prentice Hall.

Stipek, D., & Seal, K. (2001). *Motivated minds: Raising children to love learning*. New York: Owl Books.

Wlodkowski, R. (2008). *Enhancing adult motivation to learn*. (3rd ed.). San Francisco, CA: Jossey-Bass.

CHAPTER SIX

Intelligence
Different Ways of Being Smart

Every generation imagines itself to be more intelligent
than the one that went before it,
and wiser than the ones that come after it.
—George Orwell

A milieu of cultural beliefs shapes what we think intelligence is,
and that determines whether it can be objectively measured, or not.
—Jeb Schenck

Jim strode along through the trees in Yellowstone National Park, with a collection of graduate students and others trailing after him trying to see what he was seeing. He stopped and bent over to examine the ground more closely. "See that?" He was pointing at an undistinguished pile of manure that people noticed only because they wanted to avoid stepping in it. He swiftly noted many things about the smelly little pile. He described what the animal ate, probably the species (grizzly), and a host of other details most people never notice, let alone look for. It was another page to read in the book of Yellowstone, one pattern among countless others that helped tell a story. If measured by the multiple intelligences criteria, Dr. James Halfpenny had an extremely fine-tuned naturalistic intelligence.

Teachers hear allusions to intelligence all the time. "He's really smart, but sometimes he does something really dumb." What we are saying hints at what we think intelligence is, but the conception of intelligence varies across the world, and there is no agreed-upon definition of intelligence. The concept is important because it generally concerns a person's ability and skills to solve problems considered important to a particular culture. That perspective of ability and skills to solve problems as it relates to adolescent education will provide our framework in this chapter.

A Global Perspective

Our respective cultures and their traditions influence what we think is intelligent. What passes for intelligent in one culture also depends upon the approach used to address problems. From a practical standpoint, if there are problems to solve, using a particular skill or knowledge set and knowing how to appropriately function in a specific society is intelligence. Wearing shorts and a broad straw hat is considered by some as ideal dress in the hot western United States but the same clothing approach in the Sahara is less effective and will create problems. It is not considered a smart way to dress both by locals and by those with experience in desert travel. How to solve problems in a particular culture is just one way to consider what is intelligent.

Figuring out intelligence, who had it and who did not, became important around the world a very long time ago. Nearly 1,400 years ago in China it was learned that inherited leadership didn't necessarily produce the best civil servants (R. Thorndike, 1997). An official testing system called *ke ju* to select the top government appointees was in place by 598 A.D. Applicants were tested in two to five subjects, on anything from agriculture, politics, economics, to military affairs (Encyclopedia of China, 1985). The value of having smart, well-trained leaders was of considerable importance to the governments. The method of determining who was most suited was not random. Before 234 A.D. Zhu Gelian set down seven guidelines in his *Book of Mind* (*Xin Shu*) (Lin, 1980). One of the very first selection systems to consider individual differences, and types of intelligence, was developed by Spain's Juan Huarte de San Juan in 1575. His book *Exam of the Talents for Sciences* considered intelligence to be a set of mental abilities (Ferna dez-Ballesteros & Colom, 2004; Huarte de San Juan, 1575). When educators hear "He's not very bright," many typically assume the unstated belief that they now have an explanation for the student's performance, and tend to limit their expectations for that student. But such labeling doesn't offer an understanding of the student's real capabilities. Determining whether the person is bright does not predict how well that person will actually perform when he uses rational thought in a natural world (Stanovich, 2009). To complicate matters, a student's implicit beliefs about his or her own intelligence predicts math performance, demonstrating how his or her beliefs affect motivation and resulting effort. Keith Stanovich observed "[everyday usage] of the term intelligence is an utterly inconsistent mess. It is a unique confluence of inconsistent terminology, politically infused usage, and failure to assimilate what science has found out about the nature of human cognitive abilities" (2009, p. 7). Does being intelligent really mean someone is smart? How are teachers to make sense of being intelligent or smart?

Figuring out solutions to our problems is important, and trying to determine who can solve them is a major ongoing task in many organizations ranging from corporations to the military and university graduate schools. How to determine who is smart and what we mean by it are entirely different problems. For our adolescents who are taking intelligence measures there are three potential immediate effects:

1. Qualifying for special services, either remedial, or gifted and talented assistance.
2. Awarding of major scholarships, which are heavily dependent on modified IQ tests such as the SAT and ACT along with placement in military jobs using the ASVAB.
3. Letting parents know whether schools are succeeding or failing at educating their children.

Implicit and Explicit Theories of Intelligence

Educators harbor a mixture of ideas about the definition of intelligence. The following section will broadly summarize theories that have major impacts on education. These usually take the form of formal, or explicit, theories, such as the intelligence quotient (IQ), and lay, or implicit, theories, such as our personal conception of intelligence. "Oh, she's got an IQ of 124," would be an example of an attempt to explicitly measure a person's intelligence. However, we are more likely to use implicit theories, such as, "She's very sharp. She can figure out anything we do in school." Intelligence is not simply an idea described by any single theory. Rather, intelligence is a set of very complex, interacting functions that arise from a bewildering variety of processes that yield no single definition (Demetrious & Papadopoulos, 2003). If educators are to make appropriate use of intelligence to help address student learning, it is important to understand the underlying concepts that influence so many of our educational practices.

The most traditional of all the intelligence concepts is the explicit theory of the IQ. Significant research on explicit theory led to the modern versions of the IQ mental tests, which were developed in the late 1800s and early 1900s by Alfred Binet, Robert Yerkes, and Lewis Terman, among others (Binet & Simon, 1905; Terman, 1919, 1921; Yerkes, Bridges, & Hardwick, 1915). The echoes of these views are still found today in formal testing. In the following section we'll look at some of the origins of IQ-based theories.

Explicit Theories of Intelligence

Spearman's "g"

In 1904 Alfred Binet was beginning to develop about 30 tasks that attempted to validate teachers' observations of those who could not learn or would not learn. It was never meant to be a full measure of intelligence, although aspects of it are still found in the Stanford-Binet test (Binet & Simon, 1905). In nineteenth-century America massive waves of immigration were occurring and there was a perceived social need to sort out students who lacked ability from those who had it, to be used in part to make selections for admissions to elite schools (R. Thorndike, 1997). A number of problems with the testing instruments were quickly observed in the procedures used for scoring intelligence. The IQ was an effort to address these problems. There have been many uses for traditional intelligence tests, including the identification of special needs students. Today, we base much of our special education and special needs laws on these traditional theories, but there have also been abuses of the intelligence concept over the years, including discriminating against nonwhite races regarding admittance to schools (Gould, 1981; Kamin, 1995; Thomas, 1995). The theory was thought to help explain why "smart" parents had "smart" kids and supposedly "dumb" parents had "dumb" kids (Herrenstein & Murray, 1994) by using the recently discovered Mendelian genetics. The understanding of the mind then was relatively simplistic.

Charles Spearman introduced a theory of intelligence with two factors: "g" for general use in reasoning, and "s" for specific factors that changed with experience (Binet & Simon, 1905; Spearman, 1904). Spearman's g consisted of many academic-like tasks, making it a fairly restricted measure. When more natural tasks were added, the g factor was significantly weaker (Gardner, 1999; Sternberg, 1997b, 1999). The test could not predict performances in the natural world. One aspect about measuring g was that speed in problem solving made a difference in scores. Some people can process the problems but only quite slowly. That distinction in processing speed may permit a student to qualify for special services.

In the early part of the twentieth century, science was illuminating all sorts of mysteries, from uncovering the infinitesimally small particles within the atom to exploring the vast expanses of the universe. The belief that science could solve other mysteries also extended to the mind, where measuring intelligence testing was believed capable of "measuring innate talent and as providing a way to solve society's problems" (R. Thorndike, 1997, p. 10).

However, as early as 1920 Thorndike was having problems with Spearman's g. Thorndike believed intelligence was incredibly difficult to determine, and it couldn't be measured by a single quantity (g). "Intelligence is not one thing, but many" (E. Thorndike, 1920, p. 287). Defining intelligence had already become like opening a Pandora's box.

Gf-Gc: Crystallized and fluid intelligences

A considerable refinement of g are the concepts of crystallized (Gc) and fluid intelligences (Gf) developed by Horn and Cattell (1966), and these still figure prominently today. Cattell and Horn suggested there were probably nine distinct intellectual abilities, including those that were classically measured. Crystallized intelligence (Gc) is made up of increasing factual knowledge built up from experiences that are unique to each individual. Fluid intelligence (Gf) is made of reasoning processes found across the population (Carroll, 1993; Horn & Noll, 1997). Gc increases with age, and then peaks as a person's memory begins to falter, while Gf displays a gradual decline after the late teens. Stanovich (2009) observed that the Gf/Gc theory is the most comprehensive to date, with extensive scientific validity. Today, thinly modified forms of g theory tests are represented in the SAT, ACT, ASVAB (military), and GRE tests. How a student performs on any of these often impacts his or her educational and higher employment goals, which I will explore further in the section titled "The Educational Connection."

The Flynn effect: Changes in IQ

A curious pattern has been observed in IQ test scores. After refinements the scores should be stable from generation to generation. The world's population shouldn't be getting either smarter or dumber, but the IQ results keep rising. IQ tests have a mean score of 100, and each standard deviation is 15 points higher or lower. IQ scores from 85 to 115 would account for about 68% of the population. A genius score was usually considered a score of 145 or higher. But across the world IQ scores kept on inching upward and continue to do so even today. Every couple of decades the tests must be re-normed because the mean keeps climbing on classic intelligence tests, as much as 18 points on WISC and over 27 points on the Raven Progressive Matrices test. The phenomenon, called the Flynn effect, has been observed in country after country (Flynn, 2007). Are we actually getting smarter? If we are actually getting smarter, then by projecting the trends backward into time we face the absurd idea that our great-grandparents were all mentally feeble and should not have been able to cope with the merest rude existence. Obviously, that is wrong. In a careful analysis Flynn found we really weren't getting smarter but were staying the same in key problem-solving abilities. Flynn (2007) suggested changes in how we reason underlie the increase as more people shift from concrete rule-bound thought to a more flexible scientific style of thought. Mental tests are not perfect; they are our best attempts, as one researcher put it, to use "19th century concepts of intelligence with early 20th century methods of analysis" (Stein, Dawson, Schwarz, & Fischer, 2009).

The Flynn effect is not an arcane academic issue; it can have profound consequences for our students. *Because IQ measures must be re-normed, thousands of students are affected, potentially changing who qualifies for different types of services, as well as creating a huge financial impact.* The Flynn effect changes the numbers of students who qualify for different programs, and this impacts the social fabric of the community, from those who will qualify for special services or gifted and talented programs to the type of sentencing teenagers receive who run afoul of the criminal justice system. Billions of dollars are spent annually on students who qualify for special services. Tens of thousands of students may now qualify for services if they score lower than average. Conversely, if they don't score high enough, as they need to do to perform certain jobs in the military, they may fail to qualify for specialized training programs. Additionally, there is the stigma of labels. Parents want to avoid having their children labeled mentally retarded, or given other euphemisms such as developmentally delayed or mentally deficient (Baroff, 1999).

In America there seems to be a love-hate affair with testing. We want quick answers, and we have come to believe that tests can provide the information. In our

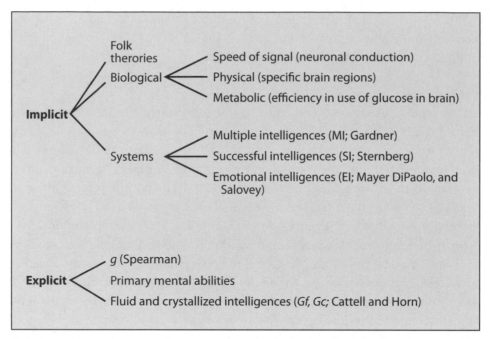

Fig. 6.1. Major theories of intelligence include Implicit and Explicit forms, each with their own variations in how they are measured.

drive for improvement and accountability, we generate more laws and regulations, many requiring still further testing. But the love affair is one-sided; kids and teachers complain about the endless treadmill of tests. Some states spend about 5 to 6 weeks of the school year just conducting assessment tests to meet federal, state, and local requirements, losing more than 35 teaching days. Much of this is the direct result of schools not having a theory of learning to suggest the guidelines for administrators. With too many assessments, it is garbage in, garbage out. A theory of learning tells educators what they should be looking for in learning and assessments.

However, new approaches have emerged because intelligence theories left so many unanswered questions. Education has now reached a state where numerous skills and abilities are claimed as forms of "intelligence." This expansion of "intelligences" to incorporate problem solving in the natural world helped to fuel more implicit theories of intelligence.

Brain scans suggest that g processing uses a variety of similar regions in the brain, but there is no single center for intelligence (Jung & Haier, 2007). Many of these are the same regions used in *working memory,* and there is a very high correlation between Gf and working memory. Working memory is what a person can consciously hold in the mind as he or she thinks and solves problems. It appears that the more a person can hold in the conscious mind and juggle, the higher the person's Gf and ability to solve problems. Interestingly, a few studies suggest it may be possible to train our working memory to process more, improving Gf. However, past training efforts have generally little if any effect on fluid intelligence, and there is no improvement in solving unrehearsed problems (Jaeggi, Buschkuehl, Jonides, & Perrig, 2008). A basic question is whether *Gf* is a firmly fixed form of intelligence. Although there are a number of video games on the market and numerous Internet advertisements that claim to improve working memory, only CogMed, a computer-based training tool developed from solid research, has shown any skill improvement that successfully transfers to the cognitive problems we need for *Gf* (Green & Bavelier, 2003; Holmes, Gathercole, & Dunning, 2009; Holmes, Gathercole, Place, et al., 2009; Smith, McEvoy, & Gevins, 1999).

Rational thought

Stanovich observed, "When we measure Gf we measure a critical aspect of the engine of the brain, but not the skill of the driver" (2009, p. 51). The skills Stanovich referred to are more than our ability to solve problems as measured by *Gf*. The component missing from traditional intelligence tests is the ability of the person to engage in rational thought. For example, a simple version of reflective thinking is illustrated by a syllogism, a form of a logic problem. The problems in reasoning use frequently pop up in politics and religious arguments. If a person is not careful, and immediately agrees with the arguments that seem right, serious errors in the conclusions can be made. Some brief examples illustrate a few of the problems.

Major Premise 1	All humans are mortal.
Minor Premise 2	I am human.
Conclusion	I am mortal.

In this form of reasoning the conclusion is true *only* if the first two statements are also true. And that is where we must be very careful. If either of the first two premises is not true on even a technicality, then the conclusion is false. For example:

Major Premise 1	All trees need food.
Minor Premise 2	Mike needs food.
Conclusion	Therefore, Mike is a tree.

The minor premise, "Mike needs food," cannot come from "All trees need food" because Mike is not a tree! The reasoning is more than simple cause and effect: "If this happens, then this will result." Without careful thought, incorrect decisions can be easily made, and having greater *g* intelligence will not always produce a correct solution.

To solve such higher levels of reasoning students must learn to think reflectively, or "outside the box" so to speak. These advanced reflective reasoning skills are teachable and are briefly reviewed later in this chapter. In the following section I will examine Stanovich's model to explain what happens.

Reflective thought

Two types of processing are typically used in the *g* model of intelligence. We are already familiar with how the amygdala and the rest of the limbic system will automatically evaluate information, helping to generate the emotions. Automatic behaviors can be innate, such as jumping when you see a snake, but some actions can be learned so well they become automatic. Reaching a level of automaticity, as in learning to shift gears in a car without having to concentrate on it, is often desirable because it makes the cognitive load on the brain lighter, freeing up more brain reserves for other tasks. The brain apparently shifts to a default state of low cognitive effort whenever possible. In the classroom I have seen this default state where the brain is in an "idle" position. The brain's engine is running but is not in gear and cannot process much of a load. The brain is working on only the simplest of tasks. Stanovich calls this Type 1 processing, or TASS for the Automatic Set of Systems. A brain using TASS doesn't call upon someone to consciously make a decision. TASS will make the decision, and the brain can process a number of light cognitive loads simultaneously. Most of us can chew gum, cross the street, and avoid running into people all at the same time. However, there are times when automatic processing isn't such a good idea, and a person needs to consciously override its decisions. For example, a bully verbally assaults another student and throws a punch. The assaulted student might respond automatically with his own punch, which would be TASS processing. But such a response would need to be overridden if the bully is twice his size, just waiting for an excuse to beat the kid up. In that circumstance it probably would not be very wise to throw a punch. To override the impulse requires

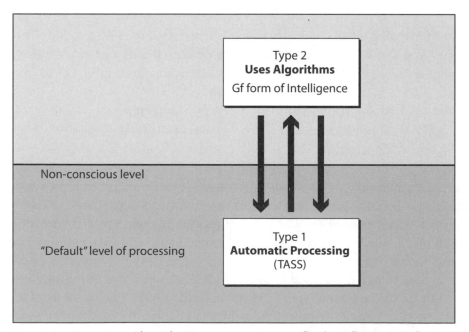

Fig. 6.2. Type 2 or Algorithmic processing using fluid intelligence (Gf) to override impulsive, automatic TASS actions.

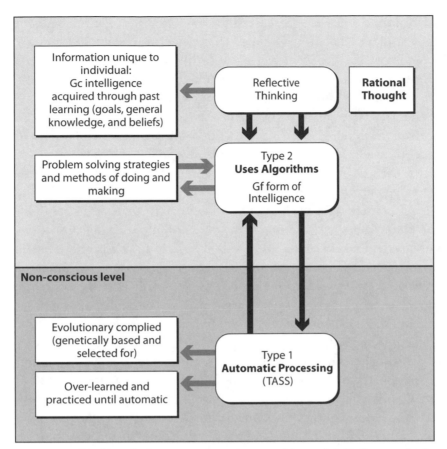

Fig. 6.3. Third level of processing in Stanovich's model. Reflective thinking and rational thought represent a third level of processing but it is not considered in classic g intelligence theories. However, use of reflective thinking better explains how we solve problems than g theories of intelligence. Reflective thinking can be taught.

other areas of the brain that are involved with *Gf*, or fluid intelligence. The mind instead uses a second type of processing called Type 2, the algorithmic strategies (see Figure 6.2).

When multiple regions of the brain need to override TASS processing, the brain literally needs more energy because the cognitive load is now heavier and greater effort is needed. Under these conditions the brain can process only one major problem at a time. There isn't enough reserve to take on another major load because the brain is using most of its resources in a series of algorithms to solve the current problem. Let's go back to the bully and the kid. The bully throws a punch and the kid ducks (automatic, Type 1 response). The simple strategy would be to retreat to fight another day. This is *Gf*, Type 2 algorithmic processing. This type of intelligence produces a "correct" result but fails to solve the larger problem of the kid's loss of "honor" by running away. It is necessary to have more reflective smarts. The traditional dual processing model combines automatic Type 1 processing with the

Type 2 algorithmic processing that constitutes *Gf* intelligence, but the model doesn't adequately explain what is happening. That's when we hear, "He's smart, so why did he do something so obviously stupid?" Without a solid model of learning and intelligence to guide teachers, educators don't know what they should be trying to teach the students. *Gf* can't be taught, but *reflective thinking* can be. This third type of processing has been proposed by Stanovich (see Figure 6.3).

The reflective mind uses *Gc*, or crystallized intelligence, which is made of accumulated knowledge and whose content is unique to each individual. Traditional intelligence tests do not measure *Gc*. Our student, being picked on by the bully, draws upon his knowledge of surveillance cameras. He is reflecting, although doing it fast. He withdraws, with the bully following, then he yells at his assailant, "Look! You're on the camera!" momentarily distracting him, allowing him to run, making his escape. He used past learning to temporarily solve his dilemma. To briefly summarize, *automatic, or Type 1 TASS, processing appears to be the brain's default in thinking where the brain will do as little as possible. Several cognitive tasks are handled at once with Type 1 processing. Higher cognitive demands on the brain involve Gf, and only a single task can be handled at a time, but even so reasoning errors may still occur because reflective thinking may be absent.*

In solving problems our brain's default response is to use Type 1 automatic processing whenever possible. When adolescents consider a selection of possible answers, they will typically generate a simple prompt response after they find an answer that seems to confirm the information, thinking, "Yes, that agrees with . . ." Using this simplistic confirmation approach can lead to incorrect responses as was demonstrated with the syllogism example of Mike and the tree. Everyone has these tendencies because of the way the brain seems to be wired (Stanovich, 2009). *We do not normally look for things that will make a conclusion or decision false. We are wired to seek evidence to confirm or support a conclusion.* For example, to step back away from standard thinking and deeply reflect on *what would make the information or conclusion false is not what the brain normally does.* That approach to problem solving requires methodically looking at what will falsify a particular conclusion; it is what science routinely does but is little understood by the public. It's not the typical way of thinking and is rarely taught in schools. However, when people are trained in it, such problem solving works. For most, analytical problem solving (learning to check and see what will make a conclusion false) is a skill that must be taught. It can potentially correct many reasoning errors. This skill in determining which conclusion is false does not depend on traditional IQ either. *Those with higher IQ scores make the same reasoning errors as everyone else will unless they are given directions on solving the problem.* In other words, if adolescents encounter reasoning problems in real-world situations that require rational thought, a higher IQ is no safeguard from making reasoning errors. For example, the simple wording of a question can alter people's responses even though they think they are being fair and ethical (Stanovich, 2009). Take, for example, the question of choosing a healthier energy bar. Which of the following will people more likely respond to?

Zoom energy bars have 7% saturated fats.
Zoom energy bars have 93% unsaturated fats.

Both are the same. Younger students may rapidly choose but others have learned to briefly pause and reflect before they respond.

If a person's brain is wired to process automatically and decide without using reflective reasoning, it suggests that such processing is inherited. This provokes the question of how much of intelligence is inherited and how much is a reflection of the student's environment? I will explore that next.

The heritability of intelligence: Genetics

In the 1990s the publication of *The Bell Curve* set off a firestorm regarding race, intelligence, and public policy (Herrenstein & Murray, 1994). A raw nerve had been touched. Politicians, using crudely oversimplified science of intelligence loaded with misunderstandings, jumped to justify taking particular actions or to advocate dropping some social program. Nature versus nurture arguments became rampant because they affected basic political philosophies. Political views divided people into two camps. One group thought people should be given assistance because their environment gave them little chance, and another group felt that people should be left to suffer the consequences because their present circumstances were mostly the result of their own decisions. Politicians, when they considered science at all, used highly flawed interpretations of how intelligence worked. Was the environment contributing to a student's poor or exemplary performance, or was intelligence mostly inherited? It turns out neither the environment nor the genes that students inherit is solely responsible for molding intelligence; instead, the influence seems to be a combination of genetic inheritance with environment. Intelligence is created from both nature and nurture. But how much does each contribute? If nature really influences intelligence, then the student's environment, both in school and out, on the streets or home, is potentially changeable by educators. Thus by changing the student's environment it should be possible to alter and improve intelligence. Research, especially studies of twins who have been separated and raised in different environments, suggests about 50% of intelligence is due to genetics and the other 50% is due to a host of environmental conditions (Bouchard, 2004; McArdle & Prescott, 1997; Plomin & Rende, 1990). This suggests that education and genes both have effects on intelligence.

A little background on genetics is needed here. A single gene almost never controls a single trait, especially for something as convoluted as intelligence. A whole suite of genes probably affects the genetic contribution to intelligence. More important, just because a person has a combination of genes for a general trait does not mean that the trait will be expressed. For example, a person may have a set of genes for a specific disease, but the disease does not develop. Sometimes to switch on a gene it requires something outside in the environment as the triggering event. It is incorrect to blame the parent's genes for all the child's intelligence just as it is also incorrect to say that intelligence is due to the environment a child happens to grow up into. To have a better understanding of what educators can do about intelligence will require a little more exploration of the intelligence theories.

Implicit Theories of Intelligence

A number of researchers were finding that *g* inadequately measured how well people functioned outside narrow academic parameters. As a result, three more educationally significant theories were developed, and each is outlined here. They are multiple intelligences (MI), successful intelligence (SI), and emotional intelligence (EI). These additional approaches were also accompanied by a trend to call most any skill at which a person can excel as an "intelligence." There are problems with using such labels. A number of researchers believe that the implicit forms described here are not really intelligence at all, but instead are abilities or skills whose measurement is not clear. We can only roughly describe optimal behaviors as in Gardner's MI, or Sternberg's SI. Another problem is the public's perception of intelligence. Calling something an "intelligence" places the skill in question on a more equal footing with the traditional intelligence *g* (Stanovich, 2009). The intelligence label also has been used as a motivational tool. For example, Gardner (1983) had an idea of the ways a person can be smart that have helped to positively change many students' conception of their abilities. Whether or not these labeled skills are "intelligences," they do help us to better understand our students' abilities to solve problems under different circumstances.

Multiple intelligences (MI theory)

Howard Gardner's MI theory is perhaps the best known and most widely employed of the non-IQ theories of intelligence, and it is probably one of the most misinterpreted and misunderstood, too. MI was introduced in 1983, and it now includes about eight relatively distinct multiple intelligences as opposed to IQ's single g, or *Gf-Gc*'s two. Gardner was not the first to propose a variety of intelligences. Guilford's work (1967) implied there were possibly 120 abilities. Gardner (1983) believed intel-

---

Table 6.1. MULTIPLE INTELLIGENCES

- **Linguistic:** writing and reading
- **Logical-mathematical:** solving mathematically based problems
- **Spatial:** knowing how objects fit or are related to each other in space
- **Musical:** composing, performing music
- **Bodily or kinesthetic:** being physically athletic (performing gymnastics, dance, and traditional and nontraditional sports)
- **Interpersonal:** interacting with people, social skills
- **Intrapersonal:** understanding oneself
- **Naturalistic:** discerning patterns in the natural environment

Table 6.2. IDENTIFICATION CRITERIA FOR MULTIPLE INTELLIGENCES

- Distinctive evolutionary history associated with adaptations to environment
- Exceptional individuals with specific extraordinary skills
- Brain damage that isolates or impairs specific skills
- Core skills or a set of core skills necessary for a specific intelligence
- Obvious development of intelligence, from novice to master
- Supportive cognitive research
- Supportive psychometric data
- Potentially can be represented in a symbols system

ligence was indicated by the person's ability to solve problems or create products that are valued within a culture. Table 6.1 lists the intelligences suggested by MI theory and is followed by a series of criteria in Table 6.2 that could be used to identify these intelligences.

Multiple intelligences allow a student to demonstrate in multiple ways his or her skills or abilities. MIs do suggest which methods for learning are preferred by the student. There are many self-administered surveys available on the Internet to help identify the multiple intelligences that a student might possess. These may show trends in a person's interests and areas of particular strengths; however, they lack validity to allow us to make real judgments because the criteria are subjective evaluations. Even so, MI theory has been able to trigger significant positive shifts in education. MI moved many educators away from using one principal instructional method for all students. Instead, MI encourages the use of multiple modalities within a unit or lesson. Gardner's concept of intelligence relies on literature reviews and not empirical testing, which makes it rather difficult to validate. Like other intelligence theories, there are debates about whether the designation of "intelligence" is really a talent or an ability (Sternberg, 2004).

Successful intelligence (SI theory)

Robert Sternberg observed that to be successful it took more than just a high IQ. No one denies that the IQ plays a significant role in thinking and success. However, the IQ emphasizes analytical processing, which dominates in schools, often making the lessons uncreative or not explaining how problems have any practical value (Sternberg, Ferrari, Clinkenbeard, & Grigorenko, 1996). The result has been a glaring inadequacy of IQ theory to explain why some people are more successful and others with high IQ scores could be dismal failures. To address the problem Sternberg developed the concept of successful intelligence (SI), which goes beyond traditional cognitive skills of the IQ. SI provides a usable theory that helps to explain that success can be achieved through evaluation of information, generation of novel solutions, and the application of solutions to achieve a desired outcome. SI also provides a potential way to develop the reflective thinking skills that Stanovich proposed.

Sternberg's SI theory proposes that all aspects of intelligence have some common processes including the ability to adapt to and modify the environment to achieve personal or societal goals (Sternberg, 2010). To successfully adapt, people need to know their strengths and weaknesses, and how to adjust them in order to take advantage of their strengths and compensate for their weaknesses (Sternberg, 1997a). This is the concept of "know yourself," as formalized in the theory.

To adapt successfully in the world, SI theory holds that three key abilities are needed:

1. *analytical,* which is needed to evaluate and understand the nature of the problem;
2. *creative,* which is needed to generate new ideas and options for solving the problem at hand; and
3. *practical,* which is needed to acquire and use essential knowledge in or to make effective use of the options.

SI is significant to most learning environments because of its emphasis on abilities to make practical adaptation beyond the IQ. Because SI helps educators to understand more of what makes a person successful, its use may open doors for students and it does not seem to function as a gatekeeper as so often happens when selections are based on the IQ. SI abilities, such as evaluation and making applications, can be trained and learned. Therein lays the educational significance, which I will explore in "The Educational Connection" section.

Emotional intelligence (EI theory)

The public and popular press became aware of emotional intelligence (EI) in 1995 with the release of Daniel Goleman's book. The concept of emotional intelligence had been originally proposed in research by Mayer, DiPaolo, and Salovey (1990). As with many properties of the mind, defining EI is difficult, creating problems both for research and the making of any practical applications. Measuring EI, like MI, is challenging because it cannot be described with much precision, which has provoked further questions about whether emotional intelligence exists. However, the evidence for EI is accruing.

There are two dominant concepts regarding EI. The model by Mayer, Caruso, and Salovey (2000) is along the traditional vein of intelligence, which considers EI an ability, and hence objectively measurable. They describe *Ability EI* as having four different but related abilities:

1. The ability to accurately recognize, identify, and monitor emotions in yourself or others, and express them appropriately;
2. The ability to use emotions to facilitate such tasks as creativity and problem solving through directing of attention;
3. The ability to understand emotions, and how they can transition to other emotional stages in certain situations; and

4. The ability to manage, or self-regulate, their own emotions in order to achieve a better outcome, such as the ability to control oneself in stressful situations.

Ability EI appears to be a form of emotional intelligence that has an objectively measurable ability and is supported by growing number of validation studies. The more commonly known *Trait EI* (emotional intelligence as a trait), popularized by Goleman and Bar-on, is questionable because of the theory's considerable overlap with personality theory and reliance on self-reporting. Trait EI relies on the self-perception of the individual. Bar-on defined it as "an array of non-cognitive capabilities, competencies, and skills that influence one's ability to succeed in coping with the environmental demands and pressures" (1997, p. 14). This view has significant common ground with the well-researched personality trait theory such as the "Big Five" model of extraversion, neuroticism, openness, agreeableness, and conscientiousness (Davies, Stankov, & Roberts, 1998). If there is a lot of overlap between personality traits and EI, then Trait EI has little utility as a research tool on individual differences (Saklofske, Austin, & Minski, 2003). However, other researchers consider both Trait EI and Ability EI as two different sides under the same conceptual umbrella of emotional intelligence. EI should be able to include a wide collection of psychological constructs such as emotional understanding, empathy, social cognition, and emotion regulation (Qualter et al., 2007). To a number of researchers, Trait EI is simply repackaged personality theory. In addition to duplicating much of personality theory, Trait EI also has problems lacking support in key validity research, as well as having considerable inconsistency because of its reliance on self-reports (Davies et al., 1998; Gannon & Ranzijn, 2005; Perez, Petrides, & Furnham, 2005; Warwick & Nettlebeck, 2004). Though Goleman and Bar-on's Trait EI concept is better known and more popular with educators and the media, *great caution is in order when using it, and making predictions*. The lack of distinction with personality research renders it questionable if one is using Goleman and Bar-on's concepts.

Ability EI has also come under fire because of validity concerns (Brody, 2004). However, the Mayer-Salovey-Caruso model, as tested by MSCEIT (the Mayer-Salovey-Caruso Emotional Intelligence Test, version 2), has increasingly demonstrated more crucial validity data that distinguishes it from personality and intelligence (Rossen & Kranzler, 2009). Although Ability EI correlates slightly with the *Gc* form of intelligence, it is beginning to appear to be measurable and a distinct construct, unlike Goleman and Bar-on's Trait EI. Even so, further research to validate each of the four branches of Ability EI remains (Akerjordet & Severinsson, 2009; Lyons & Schneider, 2005; Mestre, Lopes, Salovey, & Olarte, 2006; Rode et al., 2007, 2008).

Trait EI is the type of emotional intelligence most commonly referred to by educators and the media, and unfortunately, many have accepted a number of wild and unsubstantiated claims as truth. A number of the claims about Trait EI serve to illustrate the problems when a concept is quite fuzzy, can't be accurately described or measured, or has taken on another area of research and renamed it. An idea might make intuitive sense, but often the claims don't hold up in respect to how the brain works when research peels away the fluff to see what really lies underneath. That tendency to latch on to popular but unvalidated ideas creates enormous practical problems for those who are trying to make much-needed improvements in how our students understand, interact with, and cope with each other.

A biological basis for EI?

Chapter 4 on emotion noted that mirror neurons are essential in processing information expressed by others and that a significant portion of that processing is the ability to recognize and understand emotional information, such as facial expressions. EI incorporates the ability to properly discern emotions being expressed by others. The development of mirror neurons is necessary for processing facial and body expressions, suggesting, at least in part, that some of the emotional intelligence is found in the neurological structure of the brain. One manifestation of defective wiring and synapse development that involves mirror neurons and emotional processing is autism. Autistic youth have feelings, too, but they have tremendous difficulty in reading the emotional cues that people normally present, and consequently they are often unable to respond appropriately.

The Educational Connection

The idea of intelligence in some ways resembles a vast forest that has been known only for a short time, though stories of the existence of the forest abounded for thousands of years. Nonetheless, there is much to learn about in the uncharted areas of intelligence, especially when compared to the areas first explored in the past 100 years. As educators, we'll consider the traditional explicit theories, the newer implicit theories, and examine how the theories are actually being used as well as their potential to change teaching. The educational connection will start with the more traditional intelligence theories and then move into the implicit theories with a number of teaching suggestions.

Explicit Theories: IQ

Traditional intelligence measures, such as the IQ, have considerable widespread use as a way to select or qualify individuals for various programs, and in assigning a certain legal status. The IQ concept also influences how we measure learning in many state assessment tests because they often measure only a narrow range of traditional skills and knowledge found in IQ measures. There are also a number of very similar tests or instruments, and those who make use of them range from public and private education, colleges, military programs, businesses, and the medical field.

In education programs, IQ testing may be used to determine who qualifies for special education and disability programs, and gifted and talented classes. The 1975 Education of All Handicapped Children Act requires all public schools to provide education training and services to all children. Children under 6 years old may receive services, including helping them with their language skills and socializing. For ages 6 to 18, the educational emphasis typically shifts toward improving academic performance and assistance in acquiring basic living skills. The nature of that emphasis is determined after a series of evaluations, typically including IQ measurements that have been reviewed by a committee made of teaching staff and experts. Their recommendations usually become part of an Individual Education Program (IEP). Later, the Individuals with Disabilities Education Act (IDEA) was passed to require that disabled students also receive the least restrictive settings for their education.

For colleges, IQ-like measures, such as the SAT and ACT, GRE, and other exams, are used with varying degrees to determine who gets admitted, who qualifies for honors programs, and who will be awarded scholarships. In the military, the ASVAB is the initial instrument to sort out who qualifies for various job positions, although they do conduct extensive further testing for jobs that require great intelligence, such as becoming a pilot.

Additionally, the medical and legal fields use IQ measures. In medicine, they are part of the diagnostics used to measure cognitive damage. This has a bearing on the legal rights of adolescents, as the scores help to determine mental competency, independence, qualification for support services, and the type of sentencing adolescents receive for crimes committed.

Our public concept of intelligence also influences how the political arena holds public educators accountable with the famous (or infamous) Adequate Yearly Progress report. Essentially, the belief of what makes a person intelligent affects the overall educational design that each state uses. For example, many state assessments narrowly focus on analysis and problem solving (the traditional facets of the *Gf* portion of the IQ), but the assessments may largely ignore in-depth exploration, creativity, and applications to the real world as suggested by using either an MI or SI orientation.

For educators, implicit theories have value beyond just academic theory. They have practical implications for how lessons are taught and measured. If the theories are used with some thought, they can improve student performance. Practical applications of MI, SI, and EI are explored next.

Implicit Theories: Multiple Intelligences

The goal of this section is to help the educator develop instruction using an MI approach because it facilitates breaking free of the lecture, drill, and kill routines. Of no less importance, the use of MI seems to encourage educators' natural employment of the skills and knowledge presented in the previous chapters of this book, which can result in even more powerful lessons. Ultimately, the students are the beneficiaries of well-designed MI lessons and assessments. However, teachers need to be aware of what they can and can't do.

A cautionary note

Since it was proposed over 20 years ago, MI continues to be debated about as to whether the intelligences exist or not because the theory generally lacks broad empirical evidence (Morgan, 1992; Stage et al., 1998; Waterhouse, 2006). Additionally, the widely available inventories or MI surveys that purport to tell us our intelligences, whether for adolescents or adults, are not validated either. However, the theory has a significant and practical impact on students in secondary education, though it is largely ignored by educators within higher education (Barrington, 2004; Kezar, 2001). What MI did was help educators realize that students can learn in multiple ways through different modalities. But it is not clear whether using MI helps with traditional academic assessments, which lean heavily on linguistic and logic skills. One relevant problem is whether traditional assessments even accurately measure what a student has learned. Those questions still linger.

As an educational philosophy, MI is powerful because it provides a conceptual framework for developing instruction that can successfully reach more students by embracing a broader range of teaching methods. The result is that MI frequently energizes and empowers both the student and educator. In that vein, MI is unusually potent and is definitely worth considering. Whatever instructional method that is chosen, the educator must always bear in mind his or her learning goals and should select methods that work best for the adolescents. The selected method of instruction should have techniques that capture and maintain attention, create emotional connections, build motivation, and develop metacognitive skills. Using such an approach for lesson design can result in more finely tuned teaching throughout the adolescent years. That is a tall order, but if teaching practices can also make use of MI's vast repertoire of skills, and as long as academic gains are achieved, I would suggest using it. If there is a performance drop by the use of any teaching method, then the methods and the assessment used both need reconsideration in light of the goals.

Identify learning goals

With MI, the range of potential instructional methods is extraordinary. To keep things in focus, I would suggest that clear, measurable learning goals be determined first, and then determine a variety of specific instructional strategies that also make use of the student's strengths or learning preferences. This also causes some instructors to use MI as an excuse to justify their standard instructional strategies as appropriate, and they therefore never change anything.

For any lesson, the goals or end result must be kept clearly in mind. What do you want the students to know, do, and *think*? The reality is that many lessons frequently have two or three goals. To illustrate, we first might want our adolescent students to be able to demonstrate the depth of their understanding of the topic. A second goal would be to develop their metacognitive skills about how they learn best; a third goal would include building motivation by using the activities in the lesson to change their beliefs about their abilities. In order to make better use of the student's learning preferences when using an MI approach, it is helpful to conduct an MI survey.

Survey the students and yourself

The MI survey serves primarily to build a student's awareness of his or her learning preferences. Although those results are not precise, it helps point both the educator and student in a general direction that will most likely encourage the student and generate more attention to the learning tasks. As I noted earlier, these unvalidated surveys represent only the student's general views on how he or she currently learns. The student is still developing metacognitive skills. As such, *the surveys are not diagnostic* in suggesting precisely what instruction will work best for that student, because we don't have that capability.

Not only should the student take the survey, but the instructor should as well, because it often reveals a teacher's tendencies in designing lessons and assessments. For example,

- Are your personal MI strengths also the ones that your lessons tend to emphasize? Look at what seem to be your strengths, and compare them with the way the lessons are designed.
- Are you avoiding the MI areas in which you are not strong or comfortable with?
- Do the assessments also lean toward your natural learning preferences, and do you avoid personal weaknesses?

The MI survey can be an excellent reflection of the educator's approach to instruction, and by inference, suggest what an educator might do to make classes richer, more engaging, and better learning environments. Many MI surveys are available free through the Internet, with some variation in results. They serve as a *general* guide to preferences. The survey can assist in developing the students' metacognitive skills. As students become more sophisticated about learning how they learn, other aspects about how the brain learns can be introduced to reinforce their personal efforts. Discuss with the students what they learned about themselves, their lessons, and what their teachers did. Students can become partners in the process and actually help build the rubrics (and, for added measure, have them analyze which MIs a proposed activity is using).

Keep the results accessible, because it is helpful to refer to the survey when students want to fine-tune their efforts and when you wish to adjust future lessons and conference with the students or parents about their performances. In the following section we will briefly examine descriptions of the MI and possible activities that may be used.

MI descriptions and samples of activities

- *Verbal/linguistic intelligence*: Using language, and words, often with sensitivity. Activities emphasizing this might include writing stories, essays, opinion pieces, news articles, blogs, tweets, haiku, poetry, a movie script, or a teaser for a story; reading aloud; doing crossword puzzles; word play with metaphors, analogies, symbolism, similes, and jokes; rewriting assembly instructions so they can be more easily understood.

- *Logical/mathematical intelligence:* Working with abstract patterns, discerning relationships, and solving problems. Activities emphasizing this might include sequencing; sorting; classifying; conducting surveys; analyzing patterns; making predictions; writing explanations for different kinds of math problems; using GPS clues for a scavenger hunt; playing Sudoku, chess, or calculator games; developing their own Sudoku problems; writing or breaking ciphers.

- *Musical/rhythmic intelligence:* Using rhythms, melodies, and awareness of pitch, tone, and nonverbal sounds. Activities that utilize this may include writing and performing a song; singing nursery rhymes; listening to music of different cultures; demonstrating different genres of music; playing Guitar Hero; dancing.

- *Visual/spatial intelligence:* Observing form, color, shape, and texture; making art; graphing; problem solving; and remembering by using images. Activities that utilize this may include direct or indirect manipulation with technology, such as building models, sculpture, painting, drawing, sketching; creating concept maps, posters, time lines; designing puzzles; using CAD; experimenting with digital photography, video/film projects, scrapbooking, and graphic design layouts.

- *Bodily/kinesthetic intelligence:* Having a great awareness of the body and enjoying movement around, through, and with objects, and manipulating objects. Activities that utilize this may include learning by doing, or being hands on;using tools, building/repairing; tasks requiring eye to hand coordination (science labs such as pipetting, dissection, gel electrophoresis); acting, role playing, storytelling, miming, and charades; experiential learning; outdoor games; sports/athletics in all forms, including balancing, puppeteering, dancing, choreographing.

- *Interpersonal intelligence:* Verbal and nonverbal communication, or social-group skills. Activities that utilize this may include teaching, coaching, tutoring, discussion, conflict resolution, developing compromises or mediating, helping to lead or participate in community-based decisions, politicking, creating positive relationships, role playing, problem solving, leading, organizing.

- *Intrapersonal intelligence*: Being conscious of their own feelings, what motivates them and how well they know themselves. Activities that utilize this may include journaling, writing an autobiography or memoir, working on metacognitive skills, self-assessing, reflecting, describing personal skills or preferred learning styles, working on personal bests, creating genealogy-family trees, setting and working toward goals, planning trips, personal time lines, cooperative learning.

- *Naturalistic intelligence*: Observing and discerning patterns and relationships in nature. Activities that utilize this may include noticing natural patterns or relationships in nature; finding similarities, or differences between organisms in the natural world; identifying, sorting, and classifying rocks, minerals, plants, weather, or any natural object or process; building a collection of natural things; describing food seasoning from particular plants; predicting how climate change might affect where or how they live, videotaping a zoo animal; photographing seasonal changes, taking care of plants and animals; blogging about the best nature videos or programs; taking a travel adventure.

Strategies for building the lesson and a reality check

Ease the new instructional strategies into the lessons. A teacher's own mind is easily overwhelmed if there is too much to monitor all at once. Work at polishing the new skills before rapidly adding still more to your load. When planning a unit or lesson, *select just a few of the MI preferences to concentrate on*. It will take time to become proficient with using the new forms of instruction. *Gradually* develop more units, and refine them with student feedback and performance results. Later units can incorporate other kinds of MI. By doing so, it provides students a variety of ways to learn the concepts and skills, and they can explore new approaches to thinking about things through their learning strengths. MI areas for which the student is not as strong become occasions where the student can be coached and guided into strengthening those skills.

There are many ways to develop MI lessons. I present one set below, but it is certainly not the only one. For an excellent work that demonstrates a full range of strategies, consider Thomas Armstrong's *Multiple Intelligences in the Classroom* (See Further Reading at the end of this chapter).

Start with the identifying goals of the lesson, and use the results of students' MI surveys for a perspective of their learning preferences. *After selecting a lesson, choose a couple of MI strategies that capitalize on your students' MI strengths. As you rotate through more lessons choose a few other MIs in order to build their skills in those areas as well. A specific lesson does not need too many MIs. Trying to incorporate too many MIs in a lesson is self-defeating. There may not be enough time, and there probably are not enough resources to try everything.*

Checklist

Select two or three MIs that meet the widest variety of student needs, using their MI preferences from the surveys.

Keep the learning goal in mind. Can you adequately use the selected MI areas in developing productive activities?

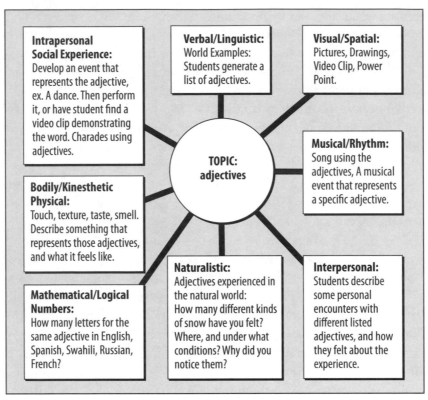

Fig. 6.4. Sample mind map using MI. In actual practice, not all the MI areas need to be used in a single lesson design.

Keep a short, brief list of the MIs on hand (taped to your desk, posted on the wall) for quick reference. Lack of time is almost always a problem, so consider Googling your lesson topic, or the specific intelligences for ideas.

Use the sample MI activities listed above as a starting point to brainstorm your own lesson.

Mind map approach

Getting started is sometimes the most difficult part. One way is by using a mind map (or concept map) as shown in Figure 6.4 and filling in just a few ideas for the targeted MI learning preferences. The details for each MI can be worked out in the next step. The MI planning template is available to copy in Appendix C. Remember it is *not* necessary for each lesson to have every MI. Target only a few MIs for a given lesson, but use other MIs on future lessons to avoid overusing the same MIs.

MI lesson description

In the next part we add substance to the possible activities that have been brainstormed and listed in the mind map. Several of the MI preferences that the students identified earlier can provide a framework for the activities as they work toward the sample goal of learning about adjectives.

Sample lesson in language arts, grammar: Adjectives

The goal in this lesson is to learn that adjectives are descriptions of something. The lesson will use four MI areas: verbal/linguistic (writing), musical/rhythm (musical jingles), visual/spatial (drawing, storyboard, photographs), and bodily/kinesthetic (touch, dance, pantomime).

In this lesson students will use a Tic Tac Toe, or Choice Board (shown in Figure 6.5), with nine activity choices about adjectives that make use of different and sometimes overlapping MIs. This permits differentiation and different levels of challenge. Students will select two choices to complete.

Feedback loop and MI

The effectiveness of lessons can be evaluated at three levels. These are the learning goals, the different MIs that were used, and student reflections.

Goals: Evaluate what worked in the lesson and why. Formally check to see what was *retained 2 or 3 weeks after* the lesson by having students use any of the 8 MIs and briefly demonstrate what they know and understand. Do the students still know why, and can they give you other examples?

Track MIs used: This shows which MIs are receiving heavy use, or too little use, and make adjustments accordingly.

Student reflections: Go beyond the teens' surface performance. What did they think was the most important? Where were emotional connections made? Did

Write a short movie review with an adjective in every sentence. *(Verbal/Linguistic)*	Make up a jingle to advertise a new theme park that describes how fun it will be. *(Musical/Rhythm and Verbal/Linguistic)*	Create a series of dance moves or pantomimes that demonstrate three different adjectives about a particular theme park ride. *(Bodily Kinesthetic and Musical/Rhythm)*
Draw what a person will feel when they go on a theme park ride. *(Visual/Spatial)*	Story board a 15-second TV advertisement that uses three adjectives. *(Visual/Spatial) and Verbal/Linguistic)*	Write a TV advertisement that pitches a product using 5 adjectives. *(Verbal/Linguistic, Bodily Kinesthetic, and Visual/Spatial)*
Make up a list of 10 adjectives. *(Visual/Linguistic)*	Find 4 things/objects that the adjective "rough" would apply to. *(Visual/Spatial and Bodily Kinesthetic))*	Find or shoot 6 photographs that match three different adjectives, and describe why each photograph is an example of each adjective. *(Visual/Spatial, Verbal/Linguistic)*

Fig. 6.5. An MI choice board. The student chooses one of the boxes for their activity. Each box represents a different MI.

the lesson affect student motivation and attention? Did the initial enthusiasm continue? How do they view their learning skills now? What do they need to strengthen?

Developing reflective thinking

Reflective thinking is a part of critical thinking skills, but it asks the adolescent to be more precise in analyzing what has happened, or may happen, and to follow up by evaluating alternative explanations. For example, is the proposed explanation likely to happen? What will make the proposed explanation unlikely or false? Looking at what will falsify an explanation distinguishes this type of reasoning. This also calls for the student to appropriately apply his or her newly acquired knowledge in fresh circumstances. This means the student is using active, considered thought, not reactionary thought. To some extent, prior knowledge and a student's level of cognitive skill development will influence reflective thinking. Are the students able to see the linkages between different ideas? This ability to see linkages or have basic insights may be a developmental issue. It may especially crop up around 15 to 16 years of age in the areas of math and science. The model of reflective thinking in Figure 6.6 incorporates elements of Stanovich's reflective thinking and Sternberg's SI, which is discussed in the next section.

Reflective thinking as a set of thinking skills can also be considered a form of metacognition. Other aspects of metacognition are discussed in Chapter 9. To facilitate the development of reflective thinking:

- Provide students time to think and consider ideas;
- Guide the students with a series of questions that direct or lead them to consider alternative explanations;
- Evaluate and judge those other explanations;
- Provide appropriate background information, as well as resources (print, web, images, etc.);
- Provide an emotionally supporting or encouraging environment so students feel safe to learn and try out ideas (take small risks);
- Consider using small groups of three with guiding questions to be discussed, and analyzed, that facilitate their exploration of the problem;
- Go beyond the standard knowledge level of who, what, where, when, why, and how: The basic knowledge provides the foundation from which to springboard forward into deeper thought;
- Let students critique, judge, explain, evaluate, compare, and contrast in their analysis; and
- Encourage students to investigate and analyze other ideas and incorporate advice and suggestions from co-learners and teachers.

Implicit Theories: Successful Intelligence

In Sternberg's view, thinking skills that are most needed in life are frequently not

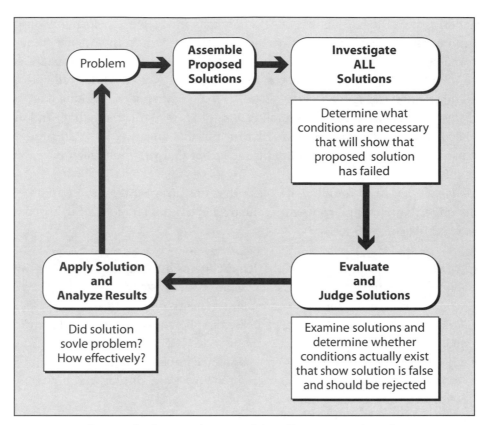

Fig. 6.6. Reflective thinking and Successful Intelligence combined into a problem solving learning cycle.

what we teach in school. Even after all the research, schools still tend to teach two principal skills: those that are memory-related (recall, recognize, and memorize), and abstract analytical skills (evaluate, judge, compare and contrast, and analyze). Educators still load up their students with information that has almost no use. Conventional IQ tests focus on these but in the real world of success, such tests predict only about 10% of the variation. The tests do a lousy job with most student variation in thinking skills. As Sternberg asked, "What happened to the other 90%?" (2010) Those memory and analytical skills will be needed to succeed in many jobs, but significantly more abilities will be needed. Those abilities, *memory-analytical*, *creative*, and *practical applications*, can be taught by using verbal skills, quantitative-numerical skills, multiple choice with figures to select from (not just words), and essays. Superficially, this may sound similar to Gardner's MI, but these may be more objectively measured.

Students whose skills are identified and then matched to an instructional program experience more success. When that was done with the successful intelligence approach where students were allowed to learn the material in SI's three different ways that took advantage of their strengths, they also performed better on traditional multiple-choice, memory-based assessments (Sternberg, Torff, & Grigorenko, 1998).

Considering how the brain grows developmentally in Chapter 1, Sternberg observed that many students' ability to learn and the level at which they learn frequently don't match (ibid.). The difference is our instruction. Additionally, SI appears, so far, to work with any group of students, particularly those who don't do well with traditional instruction (Grigorenko et al., 2004). What might applying SI look like?

Each of the three overarching intelligences of SI (analytical, creative, and practical) has a series of potential tasks. The concept of SI suggests that educators alternate using the different types of intelligences, not that we must teach every lesson three different ways.

Analytical teaching would create tasks that encourage students to analyze, critique, judge, compare and contrast, evaluate, and assess. The following list contains some examples of such tasks:

- *Analyze* the training strategy of Michael Phelps as compared to swimming Olympians before 1950 (physical education and history).
- *Critique* the artistic style of impressionist Claude Monet (art).
- *Judge* the fairy tale of Cinderella, describing how its message is relevant today.
- *Compare and contrast* the 2008 presidential campaigns of Barack Obama and John McCain, with examples of how they were similar, and how they were different (social studies).
- *Evaluate* the claim that the world is flat. Discuss mathematical evidence that supports the claim and mathematical evidence that makes the claim weak (mathematics).

Creative teaching would have tasks that encourage students to create, invent, discover, imagine, suppose, and predict. The following list contains some examples of such tasks:

- *Create* a different representation or interpretation of an artwork that uses the same subject but with a new perspective, or use of different media (art).
- *Invent* a language board game that uses nouns, verbs, and adjectives from Spanish (foreign language).
- *Discover* the pattern of hurricane intensity and temperature of ocean water (earth science).
- *Imagine* a slide show (or PowerPoint) where the pictures are used to illustrate music. What music would you choose and what pictures or photographs would be selected to pair with the music? (music and art).
- *Suppose* you asked to add a character to a TV series. What series would you select and what kind of character would be it be? (theater)
- *Predict* how lifestyles would change if we run out of petroleum (science and social studies).

Practical teaching means the students gain the opportunities to apply, actually use or practice with, implement, employ, and make practical use of what they know. The instruction must go beyond being potentially practical for the students, but should actually meet the needs of the students. The following list contains some examples of such tasks:

- *Apply* the recipe for making a salad to making enough for two dozen people (food and consumer science).
- *Use* your knowledge of engines to fix a lawnmower (mechanics and science).
- *Implement* your organizational skills in helping organize the science lab (science).
- *Employ* your computer skills in installing programs or teaching a fellow student a graphics skill or word processing skill (computer, language arts).
- *Teach* the use of a cell phone by helping parents learn how to text.

Implicit Theories: Emotional Intelligence

The idea that people have emotional intelligence, and that our ability to use it influences our daily interactions throughout society, is intuitively appealing. Also, the belief that these abilities or skills can be improved upon has been seized by the public and many educators. Regardless of the validity of either Trait EI or Ability EI, the concept has impacted education. In the following section, I will briefly discuss several factors that influence education's use of EI.

EI and political factors

Legislatures in both the United States and United Kingdom attempted to push forward the goal of providing children with a better start through, respectively, the No Child Left Behind (NCLB) Act in 2002, and in the Children's Act in 2004. As happens within the political arena, policy makers "have rushed to embrace emotional intelligence without considering the scientific basis of this work" (Qualter, Gardner, & Whiteley, 2007). At the same time the idea of EI resonated with many educators because it offered hope to students who were emotionally struggling. Neither the public nor educators waited for the slower scientific verification, potentially creating an environment ripe for new neuromyths. EI was a natural fit with education because many of the most important emotional competencies and skills are learned in a school context. But how is that fit going to work?

Trait and Ability EI

The two perspectives, Trait EI and Ability EI, might potentially influence education because of the basic premise that the mind/brain can be changed through teaching. As with the *g* form of intelligence, this introduces the nature versus nurture argument again. In order to know whether EI training should even be attempted, it is necessary to learn if EI is nurtured by the environment. If EI undergoes changes as student develop, then environments like home life or school should have an impact, and then hopefully EI might respond to some sort of training.

Genetic and social factors

Some facets of EI are probably inherited, such as the ability of infants to recognize and respond to emotional signals, or a person's temperament, adaptability, and social skills (Izard, 2001). How much of EI is inherited remains murky because there has been no research like the classic twin studies to distinguish many of the nature versus nurture questions as in other fields of intelligence.

In respect to education, one of the most important aspects of EI is socialization and whether the environment influences the development of EI. With adolescents, socialization skills are immensely significant as teens explore the new dynamics brought on with puberty. Parenting is believed to be one of the strongest influences, and, for adolescents, the foundation is laid in childhood where they learn how to become competent in their identification and regulation of emotions (Mayer & Salovey, 1997). For example, in the socialization process there appear to be four emotional competencies that are affected:

1. Development of a child's empathy and emotional regulation, related to the quality of attachment with their caregiver.
2. Emotional understanding, pro-social behavior, sympathy, and style of responding to negative impacts, related to the parent's expressiveness and sensitivity to the child's emotions.
3. Development of self-regulation, related to the type of home environment in which they grow up in: authoritative versus permissive; supportive versus nonsupportive; autonomous versus controlling.
4. Awareness of emotions and social competencies by child, related to openness of family discussion about emotions.

While these few generalizations can be substantiated, researchers are clear about their *inability* to say more regarding what EI training will accomplish (Zeidner, Roberts, & Matthews, 2002). Despite trainers' claims, there is simply a paucity of research.

In Chapter 4 on motivation, I noted that an adolescent's perception is quite important, and his or her coping skills can affect experiences and subsequent perceptions. The definitions of EI suggest having appropriate coping skills is very important. Adolescence is a period where life is roiled with distress and anxiety. Having EI coping skills to handle the turmoil can contribute to adolescents' life satisfaction and success. The properties of Trait EI imply that the students' experiences also influence their perception, suggesting to some researchers that training ought to have some impact on EI as well (Qualter et al., 2007). As educators, many of us have witnessed the unfortunate teenager having a meltdown during a test. Emotional stress can be debilitating and can directly affect a student's academic performance.

Confrontations with a bully, not making a team, absent parents, no food, and no safe place to sleep are a few of the emotionally distressful situations that are linked to a substantial body of research. A person with greater EI competencies should be better equipped to cope with those highly distressful situations. However, the hypothesis claims that a person with a higher level of Ability EI, and that adolescents who have training to develop it, will have greater academic or life success. It suggests a more socially competent person will have better relationships with peers, and better social skills may directly affect the number of encounters that are successfully managed emotionally (Aber, Jones, Brown, Chaudry, & Samples, 1998; Greenberg, Kusche, Cook, & Quamma, 1995; Qualter et al., 2007). However, educators should be cautious. Claims that socio-emotional learning programs improve academic achievement scores or school performance (Goleman, 1995), or "that emotional intelligence is a better predictor of success in school" (Aronson, 2000, p. 102) remain unsubstantiated. *Although EI is unable to predict academic/life success at this time, improving these assumed EI competencies are reasons behind the efforts to teach skills.*

Teaching EI

There are many socio-emotional learning programs, but researchers are not aware of any that focus just on Trait or Ability EI. Some programs appear to be overinclusive, intuitively based, and idiosyncratic; these are unlikely to experience success. Since none appear to be exclusively working with EI, they should at least be explicitly based on some components of EI. Listed here are a few programs that have some documentation.

- *U Think*. This program from the United Kingdom is a free 2-week, interactive computer course that can be downloaded. It provides rapid feedback and allows the student to repeat the skills exercises. The program appears to help to develop EI and socio-emotional learning skills. It is undergoing validation studies, but the initial long-term results appear to be promising. Teachers who will be involved should actually go through the computer exercises themselves. This will give teachers an interesting reflection on their own EI skills! At this time, U Think appears to be the most promising of those trying to address EI.
- *Improving Social Awareness-Social Problem Solving Project*. Some skills in this K–12 program are in common with EI, including self-control, stress and anger management, developing an awareness of feelings, and coping with emotions. Long-term gains were still present 6 years later, with lower levels of antisocial and self-destructive behaviors, as well as higher pro-social behaviors (Elias et al., 1986; Elias & Clabby, 1992).
- *Resolving Conflicts Creatively Program (K–12)*. This program trains students in skills in controlling impulses, self-regulating anger, developing an empathic understanding, and learning to identify personal negative feel-

ings when in a conflict. About 87% of teachers reported positive student impact, and 92% of students reported feeling good about themselves after going through the program (Aber et al., 1998).

Many social skills training programs do not make reference to emotional development. A significant problem educators face is what is actually in the training program. EI researchers recommend training but fail to specify how to accomplish it. Because educators simply don't know what programs, or parts of programs, work or for how long, caution is urged. *Any program under consideration should be viewed as a long-term investment not only in the students, but in staff energy and time. Since school resources are limited, the proposed program should be given a thorough review by both the staff and administrators who will be involved.* Listed below are some suggestions for selecting a training program in this buyer-beware situation.

- Is the training based on the Ability EI model or the Trait EI model?
- How is this training different from personality training?
- Does the program explicitly describe for which EI components that interventions will be taught? (Does the program align with any of the four components of the Ability model? If so, which ones?) If the program is based on the Goleman Trait model, what specific aspects (such as coping) of it are being focused upon?
- Does the program start with basic emotions (e.g., happiness, sadness, anger) and proceed to more complex emotions (e.g., guilt, pride, jealousy)?
- What specific practices and behaviors does the training hope to achieve in staff, in students? How do educators know these practices and behaviors transfer?
- Are the practices developmentally appropriate?
- Can the program be immersed in regular curriculum, or does it require a special class for students?
- Does the program target the entire school, K–12? If not, do not expect lasting changes because support is needed throughout a student's development.
- Are students given opportunities to practice emotional skills for both classroom and nonclassroom contexts?
- Are there plans for professional development and ongoing supervision that is more than a token effort by staff who must also have sufficient knowledge, skills, and expertise?
- How will success be measured in the school?

Summary

The value of having an intelligent workforce has been recognized for centuries, but determining who those people are has been a problem. Underlying that problem is the lack of agreement on what it means to be "intelligent." Even today there is still no agreement. Educationally, the traditional IQ, as exemplified by *Gf* and *Gc*, still plays a major role in the adolescent's life because it is used in various degrees for determining who gets into various programs or schools and who receives scholarships. The traditional IQ, however, is not immutable as demonstrated by the Flynn effect. As societies have learned to think more critically, IQs have steadily drifted upward when not adjusted. However, it has long been observed that the IQ is limited beyond its use in identifying students who are struggling in traditional academics. Three other major theories have emerged: multiple intelligences (MI), successful intelligence (SI), and emotional intelligence (EI). These theories attempt to describe other properties of how a student can be smart, and each has problems with accurately describing and measuring these intelligences. Additionally, there is continued debate about whether these theories are actually just lists of skills. Nonetheless, each influences how educators approach instruction. MI has generated considerable interest and helped teachers to realize that students can learn multiple ways outside traditional approaches and that they may excel in these other ways of learning. SI suggested three types of intelligences (analytical, creative, and practical), all of which may be taught and produce measurable differences in student performance. Reflective thinking, as an extension beyond the traditional IQ, is believed to be a very important and teachable skill that seems to compliment SI. But adolescents also need to learn how to get along with each other and in society at large. This involves EI. EI has two major variations: Ability EI and Trait EI. Ability EI has better evidence for its existence, but is not nearly as well known as Trait EI, as espoused by Goleman. Trait EI overlaps with many characteristics already measured by personality theory, and it is questionable whether it is distinguishable from those theories. Adolescents could also benefit from better socio-emotional skills. Existing programs offer limited training but they have yet to be validated.

Key Points and Recommendations

- *There are two major types of explicit intelligence.* There is *Gc*, which is accumulated knowledge, and *Gf*, which is our ability to solve problems. The traditional IQ test measures *Gf*. However, there is no consensus on the definition of intelligence. *Gf* is an attempt to objectively quantify the processes of classic problem solving. What is meant by being intelligent varies with the culture. Which students qualify for special services, gifted and talented programs, and scholarships is often based in part on *Gf*. *Gf* is helpful in identifying students who have difficulties with traditional academics but provides little useful information about later student success.

- *The Flynn effect means that IQ measures must be re-normed, affecting thousands of students and potentially changing who qualifies for different types of services, as well as creating a huge financial impact for schools and communities.* The IQ has been shifting upward about 3 points per decade, possibly due to changes in how we approach problem solving. Because IQ ratings are involved in many decisions that affect adolescents from school to the judicial system, using outdated IQ measures may affect the outcomes of the decisions. Too much weight should not be given to the IQ. It is but one measure of many dynamics that can be considered.

- *The reasonableness of the argument is not what determines whether a conclusion is correct. Flawed logic can produce very reasonable conclusions, but they are still incorrect. Rather, the conclusion entirely depends on whether it can be drawn from the premises. That requires reflective thinking, which is not the normal way of processing for the brain.* It is very important that adolescents become practiced with the thinking skill of looking for alternative explanations or solutions, or explanations that will show the conclusion is false. This is commonly seen in the scientific method but doesn't need to be so formal. The adolescent should consider, "What will demonstrate or show that this particular conclusion is wrong?" rather than immediately accepting a solution. Failure to routinely engage in such reflective thought may lead to disastrous solutions. Reflective thought is also closely related to the learning cycle used in experiential learning in which actions and their consequences are frequently evaluated, reflected upon, adjusted, and tested again.

- *Automatic, or Type 1 TASS, processing appears to be the brain's default in thinking, where the brain will do as little as possible.* Several cognitive tasks are handled simultaneously with Type 1 processing. Higher cognitive demands upon the brain involve *Gf*, and only a single task can be handled at one time; even so, reasoning errors may still occur because reflective thinking may be absent. There are many skills that need to become automatic for the adolescent, such as command of math facts, basic math processes, writing, and language so mental reserves are available for more demanding tasks. However, students also need to learn the cues for when to disengage and think or reflect about what they should be doing next. While doing as little as possible mentally may be the norm, adolescents need to learn to automatically shift into reflective thinking on routine tasks as well so they learn to think beyond the surface responses. Adolescents begin to do this when they challenge their teachers about rules. Use these challenges as an opportunity to begin applying their emerging reflective thinking to other problems.

- *Multiple intelligence allows a student to demonstrate in multiple ways their skills or abilities.* An approximation of which MIs a person may have is accessible through free Internet measures, but none of these are validated. MIs do suggest which methods for learning the student prefers. The significance of MI is how it encourages teachers to use other modalities and not place limits on how their students learn. For the adolescent, it allows him or her alternative ways of demonstrating not only what he or she knows, but the depth of his or her knowledge. As adolescents are still trying to find and create their identities in the world, the use of MI may allow them to explore how they learn and to more adequately allow themselves to learn through other ways of learning.

- *When modifying a lesson, choose a couple of MI strategies that capitalize on your students' strengths as determined by their personal MI surveys.* As you rotate through more lessons choose a few other MIs in order to build their skills in those areas as well. A specific lesson does not need too many MIs. Trying to incorporate too many MIs in a lesson is self-defeating. There is not enough time and probably not enough resources. Gradually develop lessons that use different MI strategies. Reflect on the lesson and determine which students appear to be left out or not responding to the traditional method of delivery. Consider which MIs might be used to help reach those students to engage them.

- *The concept of successful intelligence, as developed by Sternberg, goes beyond traditional cognitive skills of the IQ.* It provides a usable theory that helps to explain that success can be achieved through evaluation of information, generation of novel solutions, and the application of solutions to achieve a desired outcome. Successful intelligence also provides a potential way to develop reflective thinking skills that Stanovich proposed. The importance of SI is that it can be taught, and by using the skills students can be more successful. SI provides an approach to instruction that allows adolescents to elaborate and learn in depth, and those SI thinking skills can be applied to many areas.

- *Teaching successful intelligence requires three major tools: analytical teaching, creative teaching, and practical teaching.* In each of these the adolescent is an active learner. Analytical teaching involves the student in analyzing, critiquing, judging, comparing and contrasting, and assessing. Creative teaching encourages the student to invent, create, discover, imagine, suppose, and predict. Practical teaching means the students are given the opportunities to apply, use, implement, employ, and make practical use of what they know.

- *EI cannot presently predict academic/life success; improving EI competencies are reasons for the efforts to teach skills.* Despite some claims, EI can't make such predictions. However, having appropriate emotional skills is very important to the adolescent in his or her desire to be accepted. Alienation, depression, and suicidal thoughts are problems for many adolescents. Be alert to students who lack the skills to cope with these problems. Consider modeling, explaining, and role playing to help students develop their skills.

- *The Ability form of EI appears to be a form of emotional intelligence that has an objectively measurable ability, and it is supported by a growing number of validation studies.* The more commonly known Trait EI, popularized by

Goleman and Bar-on, is questionable because of the theory's considerable overlap with personality theory and reliance upon self-reporting. Caution is urged with using Trait EI, especially the claims that it can be trained for, primarily because Trait EI may not be a distinct mental property. Ability EI may be more useful in evaluating an adolescent's emotional skills. It is important to remember that adolescents don't have all the skills in place and are in the process of learning to self-regulate their emotional thoughts and actions. At this time most training programs appear inadequate in respect to addressing EI.

- *Traditional intelligence measures, such as the IQ, have considerable widespread use as criteria in selecting or qualifying individuals for various programs, and certain legal status.* The IQ concept also influences how we measure learning in many state assessment tests because they often measure only a narrow range of traditional skills and knowledge found in IQ measures. Regardless of how a teacher may feel about the IQ, it is important, and does have a place in helping alert educators to students who are likely to have problems with traditional instruction and reasoning. However, educators should not place limits on what students can learn or may attempt. Let students find their own limits rather than having them imposed upon them.

- *Any program that is being considered should be viewed as a long-term investment, not only in the plan to teach students, but in staff energy and time.* Since school resources are limited, the proposed program should be given a thorough review by *both* the staff and administrators who will be involved. A program should have regular follow-up and its incorporation should be routinely checked if it is to be truly valued by the staff.

RESOURCES

Armstrong, T. (2000). *Multiple intelligences in the classroom*. (2nd ed.). Alexandria, VA: ASCD.

Stanovich, K. (2009). *What intelligence tests miss*. New Haven, CT: Yale University Press.

Sternberg, R., & Grigorenko, E. (2007). *Teaching for successful intelligence*. (2nd ed.). Thousand Oaks, CA: Corwin Press.

CHAPTER SEVEN

Working Memory and the Beginning of Memory Formation

So many versions of just one memory, and yet none of them were
right or wrong. Instead, they were all pieces. Only when fitted together,
edge to edge, could they even begin to tell the whole story.
—Sarah Dessen, *Just Listen*

Teachers are in the business of making memories, and sometimes the most trivial things that are said or done in an offhand way are remembered for decades by our students. The challenge for teachers is to know when they have made a memory, whether it is intact in the student's mind, and what they can do to retrieve it when needed.

The following story is an example of how to know whether this is successful or not. At one point, some students were still getting to their seats; a few had gotten out their writing materials when the teacher began to give directions for the lesson. "We're going to look at plate tectonics today. That's in the next chapter, 4. You're to read from page 96 to 104, do the review questions sections 1 and 2 and chapter questions 1, 2, 3, 5, 6, 8, and 9. Any questions?"

Most students got out their textbooks. Three students immediately started asking others what they were supposed to do. Then other students began asking the teacher questions. "What pages? Are there questions we have to do? Do we do all the questions at the end of the chapter?" Their working memory was overwhelmed almost immediately, and confusion was apparent across the room. Having knowledge about how working memory functions can reduce potential disasters and increase student performance noticeably.

The Significance of Memory

Memory is essential to human survival, but it is also very important to remember significant moments, such as when you first asked your future partner for a date.

What would happen if you could not recall where your money was kept, or even more important, where food was stored, or who your friends or enemies were? Without help, a lone person would not last very long. Many adults have a hard-enough time trying to remember where their car keys are, or, if they are older, where the car is parked or the day of the week. On the other hand, students also forget things like assignments and test dates but not who their friends are. If they are playing a video war game, they are able to remember a half-dozen pieces of information so a video opponent doesn't kill them. In Chapter 1, a working definition of learning was presented as *a series of processes that includes the acquisition of stimuli that are represented in neural connections and that are consolidated while still remaining in dynamic relationships, creating networks of information that are retrievable as memory.* The adolescent is utterly dependent in this fast-changing world on accurately retrieving information from the brain's memory stores. The brain is constantly comparing new information against older memories in order to make decisions and sort information.

The human mind seems to have a number of forms of memory with boundaries that are not always distinct and with hidden properties that affect a student performance. Memories are grouped by their retention time. Some types last only seconds, other forms last minutes or longer. In this chapter, we'll explore the briefer forms of memory such as sensory memory and short-term memory, and will then concentrate on working memory.

Although these shorter forms of memory last but a moment, they are of considerable importance. As discussed in Chapter 3, if educators want students to remember information or skills for later use, that information generally must be paid conscious attention to or it is unlikely to make into a lasting memory. While it is true that some unattended information can make a lasting memory, most of the lessons are designed and delivered in such a way that the information must be actively attended to in order for our adolescents to retain it. Short-lasting memories are important for a second reason: There is a high correlation with the *g* form of intelligence and working memory. A student who can actively hold more material in his or her mind can often solve problems more easily because the information is immediately at hand from his or her memory store. He or she does not have to rummage around in memory as much to find the crucial piece of information. How these brief forms of memory work, and what educators can do in light of these characteristics, is of tremendous importance because these memories influence much of a student's academic performance. We'll begin with sensory memory, the briefest form of memory.

Sensory Memory

Sensory information is always the newly acquired information that comes streaming in through our senses, such as a visual image or a sound, and lasts only milliseconds to seconds. Certain sounds may last up to around 10 seconds, which helps a person in repeating words just said, and in linking the sounds into patterns, like musical

Table 7.1. TYPES OF MEMORY			
Memory Type	**Other Names**	**Duration**	**Consciously Aware**
Sensory	Echoic (auditory)	Up to 9–10 seconds?	No
	Iconic (visual)	Up to ½ second	No
Short-term and working		Seconds to minutes	Yes
Long-term	Nondeclarative (procedural and motor skills)	Hours to years	No
	Declarative (facts)	Hours to years	Yes

notes within a melody. Visual information is held in memory for an even briefer time, lasting approximately 1/16 to 1/2 of a second. If you've seen home movies from a bygone era, they will occasionally flicker if the projected still image lasts only about 1/16 of a second (hence the old name, "flicks"). When the displayed image lasts for an even shorter time, say 1/25 of a second, the images appear to blend together and move. This happens because the memory for the image is around just long enough before it fades and the next image appears without a time gap between seeing the images. Sufficiently important information may be passed on to the next phase of processing, which is working memory.

Working Memory

Working memory is composed either of a limited amount of information retrieved from longer-term memory or of information that has just arrived from our sensory inputs, which our mind maintains and manipulates over a short time period. Working memory can also be a combination of new sensory information and older long-term memory.

Working memory has properties that incorporate visual and auditory information, as well as executive decision functions. Because of the complexity of the brain's cognitive processes, the definitions of working memory will vary slightly with the context of the situation. In a simplified form, working memory is the information that you're *thinking* about right now. A person has a conscious choice to attend to the information, whether it is based in sound, space, or both. At any given moment, the amount of information being consciously thought about is rather limited, and that is

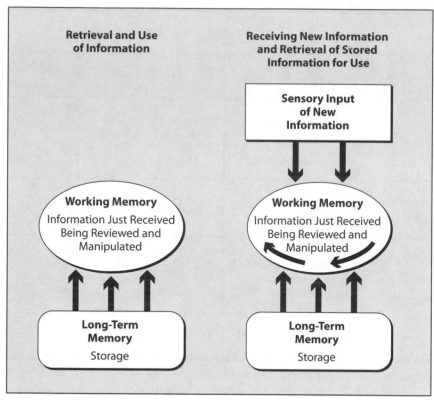

Retrieval and Use of Information

Receiving New Information and Retrieval of Stored Information for Use

Sensory Input of New Information

Working Memory
Information Just Received Being Reviewed and Manipulated

Working Memory
Information Just Received Being Reviewed and Manipulated

Long-Term Memory
Storage

Long-Term Memory
Storage

Fig. 7.1. Two basic conditions of working memory. One is where information is retrieved from memory and then manipulated or thought about. A second condition is where information from both the environment and from memory are both being reviewed and manipulated.

normal. This limited capacity of working memory has a considerable impact upon a student's successful learning. If adolescents have very little information available to them, it is harder to connect the dots if they cannot keep enough information in mind to see how the dots link together. Consider reading the last sentence. In order to make sense of it or any other sentence, the mind must actively maintain the information all the way through to the end of the sentence. That is the problem with really long, run-on sentences, or sentences with highly complex text. Students can forget the details of what they were reading about by the time they get to the end of the sentence. Two mini experiments will illustrate this.

Read the first set of numbers, then cover it and write those numbers in the same order.

5 7 3 9

Now try the next series of numbers, also covering it while you re-write the numbers.

6 3 9 1 5 7

Now try another series, covering it and writing those numbers down.

$$8\ 4\ 5\ 3\ 1\ 9\ 5\ 8\ 2\ 7\ 7$$

Look at your lists and compare them with the original sets of numbers. As the sequence became longer, it was more difficult to recall the information correctly. The working memory capacity was reached or more likely it was exceeded on the last sequence. The information rapidly faded. Now try the next experiment.

Read the numbers listed below from left to right as you would normally read. Cover the first set and write the numbers in reverse order.

$$6\ 2$$

Next, try this set of numbers, cover it, and write them in reverse order.

$$7\ 2\ 4\ 5$$

And, finally, read this set of numbers left to right, cover it, and write them in reverse order.

$$8\ 7\ 6\ 1\ 4\ 3\ 9\ 2\ 7\ 5\ 6$$

How well did you do? Were the numbers more difficult to recall in reverse order? The mind had to hold onto the information long enough for you to "look at it" and then manipulate the sequence, and finally to write the reversed sequence. As the cognitive demand upon working memory became greater, the capacity simultaneously diminished. The more difficult the cognitive task, the fewer items of information the mind can handle. Any distractions occurring at the same time increases the difficulty still more. Working memory is limited. Your mind is able to juggle only so much, and then it is overloaded.

Educators are well aware of a working memory phenomenon where students forget part of the instructions, or in higher-level classes where they have difficulty in note taking while trying to follow a lecture. For example, when students of middle school or high school age first learn to take notes, they shift their attention from listening to writing the notes, and they miss the lectured information. On the other hand, they may attentively listen but fail to write any notes. Because of this, when I have to lecture, I routinely pause to allow students to catch up, and frequently I'll ask them to state back a key word before going on. I'm trying to reduce the load on their working memory. In either case, significant amounts of information can be lost to the student if I were to continue lecturing right along. This highlights the importance of working memory: It is central to the student's learning.

Significance of working memory in learning

Working memory has immediate relevance for adolescents because it affects their performance moment by moment. If educators have an understanding of how working memory functions, they can make a number of practical adjustments that will help the entire range of students in their classes. Teachers will have a better idea of how to pace lessons, when to stop to avoid overload, and when to begin a short, quick review. Additionally, if working memory data are available on individual students, such as from the AWMA (Automated Working Memory Assessment—see Resources at the end of this chapter), it will help a teacher better distinguish whether a drop in student performance is related to working memory issues as opposed to poor attention or motivation. For example, a student may do well at the beginning of a task but could rapidly go astray because she has forgotten key information that would guide her. If teachers do not know who those students are ahead of time and they are overlooked, students' academic success is endangered. Although working memory is not part of a formal diagnosis for language impairment, dyslexia, or ADHD, it is a common problem to all of them, which further compounds the students' challenges in coping or overcoming their developmental disorders. Having working memory data can facilitate the identification of students who are academically at greater risk. For example, short-term memory, which is only the amount of information stored, may be normal, but a poorer working memory places these students at considerably greater risk for very low performances in math and English. Traditional academic performance is better predicted by working memory than by short-term memory (Gathercole & Alloway, 2008). In brief, teachers can use their understanding of how working memory functions in students to avoid overloading them with too much information. With such an understanding, teachers can develop routine practices that will reduce how often students are overwhelmed. A number of strategies will be explored in "The Education Connection" later in the chapter.

Differences between short-term memory and working memory

There are a number of differences between short-term memory and working memory, and those differences affect our approach to learning. The duration of memory is very brief for both. However, short-term memory does not actively manipulate the information in thoughts. Information is in passive storage. Working memory, as the name implies, is actively manipulated or worked with, including the retrieval of some information from long-term memory. In processing, a memory is retrieved from storage and then actively thought about or manipulated. That's what happens when we reminisce. For example, "Do you remember when you went to the beach in June and the water was so cold?" The memory is retrieved and becomes actively processed. Simultaneously it is being actively linked to other memories as well. In teaching, being able to retrieve the memory is essential for student performance. A student's working memory also functions something like a computer's search engine. We type in one name and the search engine finds all the files with that name. But our brain takes a couple of more steps as well and activates or "opens" one of those memory files. Continuing with a rough computer analogy, random access memory (RAM) measures how many bytes of information can be opened on the computer desktop and processed at one time. With a computer, we can buy more RAM to handle more files, but the brain does not allow that. The capacity of a student's working memory is limited and for the most part, it cannot change very

Table 7.2. SUMMARY OF SIGNIFICANT DIFFERENCES IN SHORT-TERM MEMORY AND WORKING MEMORY

Short-Term Memory	Working Memory
Passive storage	Actively processes information
Independent function	Closely functions with long-term memory
Lower correlation with academic performance	Higher correlation with academic performance and *g* intelligence
Specific domains of verbal and visual information and limited capacity	Capacity is less specific*
Activates information in long-term memory	Consciously directs information retrieval ("hosts the search engine")

*Working memory capacity is still being debated. Generally it increases slightly with age through adolescence (see Table 7.3). However, working memory appears to only be able to focus on about one item at a time, though it can hold more items in a ready state. How much working memory appears to hold depends on the method used to measure it; thus, we can't be specific. It is possible to increase working memory slightly through the CogMed process (see Resources at the end of this chapter).

much if at all. The student is able to retrieve and open only a few memory files. By comparison, short-term memory does not directly process information, and it can function independently from long-term memory. The information is passively stored, and its capacity depends on whether the information being stored is verbal or visual. Short-term memory may also simply be a portion of activated long-term memory, although it functions independently (Atkinson & Shiffrin, 1971).

Models of Working Memory Processing

For most mind/brain processes there are competing explanations, and working memory is no different. Three models will be presented here: the Atkinson-Shiffrin model, the Baddeley-Hitch model, and the Cowan model. I will concentrate on the Baddeley-Hitch model and Cowan's embedded model because of the robustness of the research and educational applications supporting them.

One of the first models to explain differences in memory was proposed by Atkinson and Shiffrin (1968). This simple model proposed a succession of three divisions of information processing, with different time frames as information was successfully processed into memory (see Figure 7.2) (Baddeley, 1966b). In the Atkinson-Shiffrin model, information is first perceived by the different senses. Most information is visual and auditory and is stored for a few milliseconds in a *sensory store*,

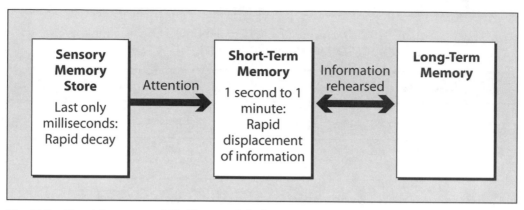

Fig. 7.2. The Atkinson and Shiffrin model of memory.

long enough to activate neurons. If the information is attended to, such as a student noticing a red jacket, then the information is passed to a *short-term memory store*. The short-term memory store has a limited storage capacity and can hold on to the information for about a minute. As newer information arrives, it shoves out the information that was already there, and if it is not reprocessed, the information is lost. Information that is processed sufficiently may be moved into the more permanent *long-term memory*. The model represented a fair start in tackling the problem of how memory works but it was found to be inadequate. Memory, especially the brief short-term store and the long-term memory, appeared to have a number of very different properties. Baddeley and Hitch (1974) developed a more thorough model of working memory that was able to predict a wider range of what happens in this brief transition period of memory.

The Baddeley-Hitch working memory model

This model has several components, and their properties have significant implications for educational practices. To direct students' attention there is a *central executive,* which inhibits attention toward some items while focusing on others. The central executive decides what to pay attention to; it further manipulates information by updating it with new incoming information or by comparing it with information stored away in long-term memory. There are two subsystems to aid these processes: the *phonological loop* for auditory information, and the *visuospatial sketchpad* for handling objects and their locations (see Figure 7.3).

The Phonological loop. The phonological loop holds auditory information, and if the information is rehearsed it can maintain it for a short period. At the beginning of the chapter we did a mind experiment with a series of numbers to be recalled in sequence. That involved the phonological loop. Listening to a voice mail and recalling a phone number is a familiar problem for most of us. Recalling the numbers is especially difficult if a caller rattles off the numbers in rapid succession. We can't remember them all. If it weren't for the ability to save voice mail on most phone systems, a lot of phone numbers would be lost. The properties of sounds in the words affect phonological memory store. If words sound similar, such as *hat mat cap cat ran man*, it is difficult to recall them in sequence (Baddeley, 1966a). (Try it for yourself!). Words that sound differently are much easier to retrieve, such as *cow day man tall wide swim*. When there are more words, meanings become important, and the central executive directs access to other systems by continuing to process the information. The length of the word also affects whether it can be recalled (Baddeley, Thomson, & Buchanan, 1975). The longer a word is, the more cognitive resources are called into play. The resources that the mind can draw on are limited. The amount of time to say the word is one pivotal factor. Let me illustrate. Saying words in Chinese takes less time than saying the same words in English. More words can be recalled in Chinese than English, because English words have more syllables and require more time to pronounce. *The more time it takes to pronounce the word, the fewer the number of words that can be recalled* (Baddeley, 2007). Think about complex, difficult sentences with unfamiliar words. It is not unusual for a reader to go back through the sentence in order to remember what was said.

In this next example, the same number of words is used as in the earlier example (there were six words: *cow day man tall wide swim*). Say the following words and then cover them up and try to repeat the entire sequence:

pneumonia, electroencephalograph, platypus, refrigerator, automobile, presidential

How many did you recall? Even though the words were different sounding, and thus easier to access, they took so long to say there was insufficient time to rehearse the words before they faded. Disruptions may also interfere in the rehearsal and recall (Klauer & Zhao, 2004), and for students with poor working memory this can easily be catastrophic to their recall.

Visuospatial sketchpad. The set of neural networks that make up the visuospatial sketchpad seems to be distributed across the right hemisphere, with some networks found in the occipital lobes, another in the parietal, and others in the frontal lobes, which are presumed to involve control. The visuospatial sketchpad system within working memory appears to have two functions: (1) to create and maintain images so they persist seamlessly from one set of information to another as our eyes move (this is essentially about information about objects in space); and (2) to handle visual characteristics of the objects by creating and maintaining information retrieved from memory. For example, if we want to describe how to get to a particular store, the mind retrieves the spatial information (where it is), along with information about the appearance of different road markers (what it looks like). The capacity of working memory to maintain the spatial information is limited. *The highly limited capacity of working memory, combined with the tendency for spatial tasks and skills to interfere with each other, strongly suggests that attempts at multitasking are likely to have failures in one or more of the tasks due to overload.* If multiple tasks are involved, and the failure of any could be potentially fatal, then very careful consideration

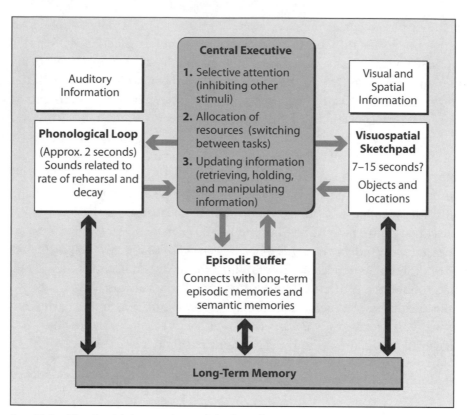

Fig. 7.3. The Baddeley-Hitch model of working memory.

needs to be made about how the tasks are designed. This property has created the impetus for the development of automated braking systems in vehicles. It suggests that a teacher's design of a lesson, and his or her delivery of instructions, should carefully consider how easy it is to overload working memory. Fatal car accidents sadly demonstrate the limitations of working memory in combining spatial skills (driving a car) and spatial tasks (sending a text message). They interfere with each other (Shallice, 2002) and avoidable crashes happen. There was not enough cognitive reserve for the working memory system to handle the attempt at multitasking. The *central executive* chooses which task to focus on.

Central executive. A major role of the central executive is to select what to give attention to and what to ignore or inhibit. Imagine a noisy house with a lot of young children yelling and playing. A couple is having a conversation with each other. While they hear the words of the children, they selectively inhibit focusing on all the noise and yelling that make up the details of the children's talking. Their mind/brain systems are still monitoring the children, but not closely. The adults' cognitive resources are directed to their own conversation. Simultaneously, the working memory is updating and comparing information both in their conversation and in the children's noisy actions. However, the central executive can malfunction at times, too.

Many of the central executive's working memory functions are carried out by the frontal lobes, which are among the last areas of the brain to mature. Errors in attention and maintenance can occur. For instance, a person repeatedly concentrates on a single action, while at other times the same person's inhibition networks fail to suppress distractions: This is a common scenario for students who have ADHD. In some circumstances with memory retrieval, incorrect associations are not inhibited. This may result in a false memory where the person produces a false explanation (confabulation). Central executive malfunctions can have enormous impact on a student's academic performance.

Episodic buffer. The episodic buffer has a limited capacity, and it appears to be a passive store where information from the phonological loop, visuospatial sketchpad, and long-term memory are collated, or associated, with each other. The binding of sensory information to objects happens when sensory information organizes into something we recognize. This is thought to be an important part of consciousness, but how an active binding process and a passive collating process actually work is not understood at this time.

A new form of visual working memory?

Another form of working memory associated with the visuospatial sketchpad was recently proposed by Wood (2007). It was discovered that *working memory for actions is stored separately* and has a different capacity than information for what and where objects are. This is potentially significant, because actions are key components of one of the most robust forms of memory—procedural memory, or how to do something. Although actions or procedures have been largely overlooked by educators, they provide a particularly powerful vehicle for instruction and building a more stable, verbal long-term memory (this will be examined in depth in Chapter 8). This form of visual working memory allows the moment-by-moment storage of information concerning where objects are at different points in time. For example, as I type this, I need to know not just where the keyboard and keys are (object working memory and spatial working memory) but also what each finger is doing in a time sequence so that I may type with fewer errors.

The Cowan embedded model of working memory

Nelson Cowan (2005) found considerable evidence for a very close relationship between working memory and long-term memory. His model emphasized the level of activation for information. The information that rises to consciousness and receives the most attention becomes the focus of attention (see Figure 7.4). In this working memory model only, the focus of attention is limited in capacity. In the classic view the capacity of short-term memory was believed to be a "magical number" of about seven pieces of information before a person generally overloaded (Miller, 1956). Cowan (2005) found evidence that the capacity was smaller, at about four items (Oberauer, 2002). However, recent evidence more strongly suggests that the mind is able to really focus on only one item at a time, while the three other or so items may be rapidly brought into focus and attended to (Baars, 1988; Verhaegben, Cerella, & Basak, 2004).

Unlike the Baddeley-Hitch model, with its attendant buffers and memory stores, the Cowan model suggests there is only a single memory storage system: *long-term memory. Working memory is highly integrated with long-term memory and is a portion of long-term information that has become activated.* Working memory functions something like a roving spotlight. The center of the spotlight is very bright. This would be information that the student mind would be very aware of and can actively manipulate. However, the illumination rapidly drops off in all directions away from the center, and the mind is progressively less aware of this less active information. Long-term memory has different levels of activation; much of the large storage capacity is passive. Information that is in the beam of focus is more active, and it also raises the levels of activity of closely associated networks. A portion of memory that has networks that reach a critical threshold of activity also becomes highly accessible. Information at the highest level of activity is in the center of the focused attention. This information is being actively manipulated. Only this single item of information, momentarily at the center of the spotlight of attention, is focused on, accessible, and manipulated. However, perhaps up to about four additional items may also be highly active, forming a networked chunk. If the focus shifts, this other information that is already in a high state of readiness can easily move into active processing. There is no apparent limitation to the amount of information that can be elevated from long-term memory past a threshold to become activated. The information brought into an active state may be done so through conscious processing or nonconsciously. Related schemas are placed "on alert" so to speak, but the student is unaware of it. As the beam of focused attention shifts, new neural network links with long-term memory form. These episodes of new linkages may form chunks of information, consisting perhaps of four items. However, activated networks forming the chunks may be linked with other networks, forming superchunks of active memory and thereby allowing rapid access to still more information (Cowan, 2001). Accessing the activated information is another step requiring a little more time, which also affects capacity. Thus, the capacity of working memory is how much information is currently being focused on, plus what a person can actively hold in his or her mind and manipulate. That capacity (or span) varies from teen to teen, affecting academic performance. Additionally, the capacity varies with age, with younger children having a lower capacity. These differences and their significance to teaching and learning will be explored more thoroughly in "The Educational Connection."

Developmental Differences in Working Memory

The span of working memory increases steadily in a near linear fashion from around age 5 to 15. As children become adolescents, they are able to hold and manipulate more information steadily in their minds and are able to refresh those memories by re-activating them (Gathercole, Pickering, Ambridge, & Wearing, 2004). However,

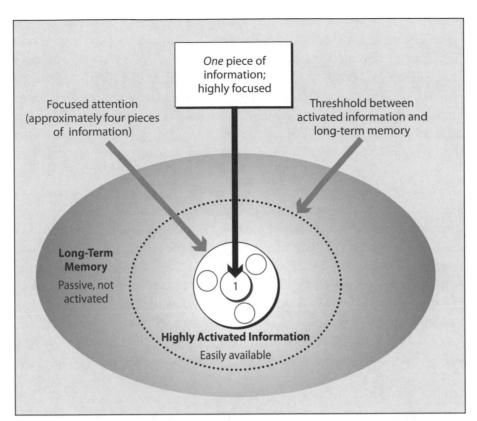

Fig. 7.4. The Cowan model of working memory. Only one piece of inform-ation is highly focused upon at a time, but several items of information are in a highly activated state and are easily accessible. Working memory is con-sidered as a portion of activated long-term memory.

children's minds appear to change their processing between about 5 to 7 years of age. It is difficult for younger children to automatically (and nonconsciously) switch their attention during brief pauses in order to refresh their memory (Barrouillet, Gavens, Vergauwe, Gaillard, & Camos, 2009).

Both the difficulty of the tasks and the age of the student affect the working mem-ory span. The difficulty of the task or cognitive load, whether verbal or visuospatial, creates different demands, making it easier or harder for the student to maintain information. At any rate, the spans are relatively small, and clear, simple tasks, with frequent pauses in lessons, will allow the adolescents to reduce their overload. Students do not all have the same working memory span; there is a considerable range. For example, a 7-year-old may have a working memory range around that of a 4-year-old, or perhaps as high as 10-year-old, a 6-year range. A student who is 14 or 15 years old may have a working memory span of a 10-year-old; a 12-year-old may have a range from that of a 7-year-old to an adult. Around age 14, the working mem-ory span levels off to the adult range (Gathercole, Lamont, & Alloway, 2006). The significance lies in the range. In a given class there will be some students who are easily overloaded, while others can juggle considerably more information. Consider for a moment. In a class of 30 sophomores, there would be about three students with a working memory span functioning at the level of an average fifth grader. Knowing students' working memory spans ahead of time can help teachers to make adjustments in instruction, and alert them to which students may need more assistance or revised tasks. Working memory information can be obtained from IQ tests, assuming there are data on all the students, but it may also be obtained using the AWMA in a short 10-minute computer-driven assessment.

Working Memory Capacity

One question about working memory that comes up constantly is whether there is a way to cram more information into memory since the number of items that working memory can hold is limited. The tests used to measure capacity, such as recalling numbers in a backwards sequence, are difficult to use in everyday teaching. Again the method of measurement suggests different capacities. One idea is chunking, in which a chunk may vary in the quantity of information. While the number of chunks that can be processed may range from 2 to 5, the amount of information within the chunk is variable. What it all means is that research doesn't have a good answer yet.

The Educational Connection

General Classroom Interventions for Working Memory

There is a strong relationship between students' working memory spans and the rates at which they can learn. The greater the working memory span the faster a student can learn (Radvansky & Copland, 2006), probably because he or she has more information readily accessible to his or her mind. That also implies that students with smaller working memory spans learn more slowly, and their minds are

Table 7.3. APPROXIMATE RANGES* OF WORKING MEMORY SPAN IN YOUTH

Age	Approximate Range of Working Memory
7	4-year-old to 10-year-old
9	6-year-old to 12-year-old
11	7-year-old to near adult
13	>10-year-old to adult
15	10-year-old to adult

*The ranges are represented from the 10th to 90th percentiles for each age. From Pickering & Gathercole, 2001.

more easily overloaded. To help keep the students from being rapidly overloaded and falling further and further behind, *information in lessons needs to be presented in smaller bites, with frequent pauses to permit review and strengthening of the just-acquired information as well as to fill in any gaps that may have occurred.* Ideally, a teacher *knows the working memory span for each student* through testing or more rapid assessments such as the AWMA, which makes it easier to accommodate and monitor those students as well as to make appropriate instructional adjustments.

Recently I taught my high school biology students about the brain and neurons and what a synapse was and why it was so important. The students ranged in age from 15 to 16. Two students had autism and two had ADHD: of the students with ADHD, one of them sat on an exercise ball while balancing a laptop. There were also a scattering of students with various learning disabilities and who had a full range of academic abilities from the highest to the lowest in the school for their age ranges. I happened to be explaining the roles of axons, dendrites, and synapses, and I started off with a simple drawing, followed by the students labeling the parts on handouts. I would pause frequently, mindful of the problem of easily overloading their working memory when there was so much information to work through. To slow down and review I would ask, "Now what is this part? What does it do?" Simple rote answers so far. When we focused on the synapse and neurotransmitters, I stopped and traced the signal from where it was picked up, how it was transmitted, and focused again on how the signal crossed the synapse to the next neuron. I thought I had done a pretty good job. I used frequent pauses, giving time for students to take notes; I even asked students to check each other's written notes and I gave the students brain breaks with short probing questions to review the information I had just presented in either visual, written, auditory, or hands-on/tactile formats. It was still a lot of information. About 20 minutes into class, after all the pauses and short reviews, I had the students individually paraphrase how a neuron worked. In the process of sharing and discussing it, many little gaps in their information were found. They had simply missed a piece here or there, and virtually none of the gaps were the same. Rather than go on, we stopped and reviewed the entire process once again, with each of the students actively explaining a portion. They corrected their notes, reworked their paraphrasing, and reviewed each other's works: all of this took about 10 more minutes. The scattering of errors suggested the students' working memory was being overwhelmed at different times. It is very important for me to do more than carefully pace, and pause using the brain breaks. Working memory will be overwhelmed at different times for different students, and without periodically checking within a class period, the teacher won't know what is being missed. The little gaps may be just enough to create misunderstandings and confusion. By using the combinations of a quick guided review, corrections, and peer review, the students came back up to speed and made the necessary adjustments in notes and explanations. *Teachers can't assume that by using short breaks, many pauses, and probing questions that they will automatically avoid overload.* Every student experienced at least one time when he or she missed some information that was important.

Verbal working memory is especially important in education because the vast majority of information is given in a verbal or phonological format, and it is more stable than visual information. Students soon convert visual information into phonological information as well. During the early stages of any new lesson the incoming information is not well established in the mind/brain systems. In the early stages of learning something new, the demand on working memory is heavy because the students are unable to rely on established memories to help them get through. The demand on working memory diminishes once the critical information becomes stable in long-term memory and the student can perform the tasks with greater automaticity and virtually without effort (Geary, Hoard, & Byrd-Craven, 2004). How well the working memory functions during the early stages of learning has a significant bearing upon the lesson as illustrated above by the biology lesson on neurons. It is imperative that the working memory load is manageable for the wide range of students we find in a classroom. In subjects like math, a student must hold instructions in the mind while simultaneously learning the procedures and performing calculations. Working memory load is particularly heavy in the initial phases of math problems. The recommendation is to *keep verbal information well structured but simple and frequently review the procedures*, especially when new material is not well established in memory.

Students with smaller working memory spans are more easily overloaded; *keep potential distractions to a minimum.* Several of the students in the biology lesson had more significant gaps in their notes and recall than other students, because they were easily distracted. The student on the exercise ball still had many errors, but he was happy because he was experiencing more success. He missed far less information than he usually did.

Students with smaller working memory spans quickly reached or nearly reached their working memory capacity, but their problems are further compounded by also having a lower capability to ignore new distractions (Kane & Engle, 2000), making the tasks at hand even more difficult to follow. That combination of smaller working memory spans and being easily distracted also makes it difficult for these students to recall recently presented information even a few minutes afterward because much of it was not encoded to begin with. This problem of information not being encoded was originally described in Chapter 3 on attention. *Classroom or lesson information that is not actively focused upon by the adolescent has almost no chance of becoming encoded into memory.* This may sound very similar to having ADHD, but it is not exactly the same. The difference is that these students have much lower working memory capacity. Those students with larger working memory spans have a greater ability to regulate their attention at both the encoding of information and retrieval of memory, and thus are better able to ignore distractions. Avoid interruptions and noises from the hallways. If a lesson involves a series of group activities where many distractions abound, consider having the short-span working memory students away from the visual and sound distractions. If they cannot physically work in an area with lower distractions, try having them work with their backs to the major sources of distraction. Sometimes music playing over the classroom noise helps, although that may be counterproductive for the ADHD students. It will be probably be necessary to try several strategies.

The span of working memory also significantly affects the pace at which academic knowledge and skills are acquired. In other words, *working memory may inadvertently function like a brake on classroom instruction, because of the necessity to slow down to allow the overcall encoding and avoid the overloading and dropping of some information. Thus some repetition of some information is frequently necessary* (Henry & Millar, 1993; Van Der Sluis, VanDer Leij, & De Jon, 2005). If the teacher goes too fast for the working memory spans of some students, the students may get lost and become frustrated. However, the faster the skills and knowledge build up, the less demand there is upon working memory (see Figure 7.5). The teacher faces several potentially conflicting tasks: (1) avoiding overloading working memory for those students whose spans are smaller; (2) building up the skills and knowledge as rapidly as possible in order to reduce working memory loads; and (3) allowing the students who have larger memory spans and have nearly mastered the material to perform meaningful tasks while the remainder of the students build their knowledge. Here is an opportunity to help both the slower and faster students simultaneously. The students who have command of the material may function as student assistants and could help the other students. We did that in the biology lesson described earlier by using peer reviews. That permits their skills to become more consolidated, and allows the other students to catch up and establish their own skills.

The next sections focus more on how a teacher might incorporate strategies into lessons to help reduce the working memory load on students. The focus then becomes even more specific, with ideas for working memory reduction in reading and math because those two subjects are particularly vulnerable to overloading students. The chapter concludes with a table of strategies that students may use to reduce overloading as they begin to develop metacognitive skills.

Avoid Disaster: Identify Students With Low Working Memory

It would be of enormous help for both the student and teacher to know if there is a problem with the student's working memory. Some students have a low working memory capacity and are easily overwhelmed. They may not qualify for special services, but ignoring their very real limitations can easily lead to their poor performance and frustration. The AWMA is a validated assessment that uses a computer to identify whether a student has a particular problem in either verbal or visual working memory. It has only been recently been available to educators in the United States. I've found the AWMA to be a valuable tool in helping students know where they are having processing problems and in helping the teachers to be alerted to students' deficits, along with strategies to compensate. I recommend screening the entire grade level just as we would administer an academic assessment to avoid the time-consuming requirements of obtaining individual permission. It is important to

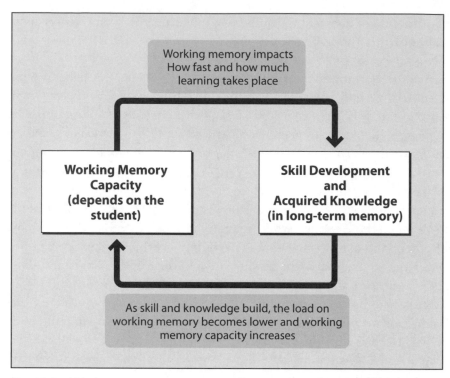

Fig. 7.5. Working memory capacity influences how fast a student learns. The greater the working memory capacity the faster the acquisition of knowledge/skills, which in turn reduces the load on working memory.

note that *students do not outgrow the problem*, and despite the plethora of Internet claims and websites that will supposedly help, none of these have been validated and they are not helpful in the crucial areas. Only a single research-based program has been found to improve working memory, and that is CogMed, as discussed in Chapter 6. CogMed is a training program that progressively builds up working memory. It has been found to increase working memory by about 8–18%, which is actually a significant amount, and these benefits do translate into higher academic performance. A teacher, armed with this information, and the student, made aware of his or her processing deficits, who work together can improve the student's performance. Additionally, such an awareness makes a potentially excellent opening for developing metacognitive skills.

Lesson preparation

Before lessons are taught, identify both the lesson and components that place heavy demands on working memory. Simplify those areas to the essentials and restructure the lesson. Select no more than a couple of upcoming lessons to start simplifying so as not to overload yourself!

Lessons should be clearly organized so the students can easily follow where they are going, but that doesn't mean the lessons should be dull. Incorporate new information in a manner that is *logical to the students*, follow it up shortly with a brief rehearsal in order to check the students' understanding of the relationship with the previously taught material. This break from notes or other work is a built in review, something we'll call a "brain break." Brain breaks are very practical ways to reduce overload. They allows the teacher to quickly spot where students have overloaded and missed information and re-teach it then rather than discovering the problem days later. Try to anticipate where in a lesson these brain breaks might be needed, and plan a review activity (see the next section for more details). As the new information is woven in, reach for higher levels of reflective thought by using questions that reveal relationships. For example, in studying Napoleon's march on Russia, the time of year for the military campaign is brought up. The teacher could probe further by asking about how this might affect the health, movement of the military, and availability of food, and then challenging students to find evidence that those factors did or did not affect the campaign (What will make the claims false?). This allows the students' working memory to stay focused and to incrementally add new information or to retrieve other information from memory.

Many teachers believe that not paying attention is the source of much student confusion. Working memory failure is a more likely cause. Some students will get the instructions or information but a number of others won't. Remember 11-year-olds could have a working memory span anywhere from the level of a second grader to almost an adult (see Table 7.3). Students will have a vast range of working memory capacity, and it is easy to overload some students in most lessons. Preventative strategies that teachers use can reduce the problems. There are also a few strategies that students can use as well.

Delivering the lesson

The following list contains strategies that educators may use while teaching their lessons that work for most adolescents, and these help to reduce the working memory load.

- Tape an unobtrusive reminder of methods or teaching strategies on your own desk to reduce working memory overload. Just glancing at this from time to time can jolt a teacher's memory back into active processing so he or she can initiate or change a classroom tactic.
- Less is more. Focus on the most significant principles and worry about the details later. Trying to cover every last detail is often a frustrating exercise for everyone. A teacher can certainly go faster, using the old sink-or-swim strategy. But if students are missing large portions of the lesson and they end up either failing or have to be retaught, an enormous amount of resources have been wasted, including both the teacher's and student's time, and taxpayer or patron dollars, let alone the potential determent to keeping students motivated.
- Use brain breaks for quick assessments of whether students have been

overloaded and missed key elements. Before the lesson, the most significant concepts and supporting ideas or processes should be clearly identified. The sections that potentially place heavy demands upon working memory should be simplified. Restructure those portions of the lesson down to the essentials. And build in some reviews to allow students to fill in gaps in their notes or understanding. Quick assessments during a brain break can make up the core of the break. As noted earlier in the description of the biology lesson, simple reviews such as paraphrasing relationships and applications can be used to reveal misunderstandings or gaps in student process. In this manner, the brain breaks allow a rapid assessment on whether re-teaching is necessary.

- Make routine use of the brain breaks! This is an important tactic to use not only for the entire period of adolescence but throughout education. The brain gets overloaded no matter what grade level is being taught. There is no precise time on when to do brain break, but after 20 years of practice, a rule of thumb for middle school and high school students is to have a break about every 15–20 minutes. In addition to the assessment strategies noted above, also change the type of mental and physical activity. Whatever method used, spend only 2–4 minutes on the refresher. Occasionally it is necessary to go to a completely different activity because the students have processed so much information. This should reduce working memory load.

- You can use instrumental music as an audio wall to help keep out other distracting sounds to keep students focused and to create a mood. Keep you volume low. When students are talking, or there is music with vocals, it may interfere with the phonological working memory because of the similarity of the sounds to their verbal thinking (Gathercole & Baddeley, 1993).

- Use simple instructional strategies. Instructions that are complex or convoluted can be inappropriate, considering the students' working memory spans. Instructions that involve too many steps may cause confusion. Certain topics, such as the social studies, the sciences, and math, are very complex. To reduce the overload problem consider advanced organizers, or skeletal outlines, to help the students. Lessons that require detailed exploration can be built later on top of the original teaching, if the foundation is clear and solid. Simple, personal elaborations made by the students might be considered in order to explore their depth of understanding. However, with too much complexity, the students can get lost in their explanations.

- Avoid excessively long instructions, such as will typically be involved with projects, experiments, or research assignments. Break the task and related instructions into smaller, rapidly achievable steps where the students can use self-talk to repeat back the instructions. An indication that instructions are too long is when they cannot repeat them all back, not necessarily inattention.

- Stay focused on the classroom lesson. Avoid rapid shifting of instructional modalities if the students are required to take notes. Guide them as you transition from one instructional method to another so they are not being left behind. Teens get lost and confused, and many will not ask for help or signal any indication that they are lost. For example, abrupt changes in instructional methods can easily leave some students behind if a teacher is explaining something on the board, then jumps to a hard-copy exercise, and then moves yet again to more lecture instructions. The rapid changes or disruptions of students' attention can result in the students missing critical information (Levin, Simons, Angelone, & Chabris, 2002). This is not the same as a fast-paced presentation that clearly follows a single theme. A characteristic of the most successful presentations is that each new piece of information is clearly and frequently connected back to the theme.

- Allow time for processing *during* the lesson and guided practice. If a student doesn't get it now because the teacher plowed right along with the lesson, is there time to reteach it later? That point has been brought up before. It is an uncomfortable question. Standards and goals often require that students reach a particular level of performance by a specific time. However, if our adolescents are not paying attention, or there was too much too fast, and the lesson fails to become a memory, then there is nothing the student can draw upon. There was no learning. It is absolutely essential that the students, especially those whose working memory can be easily overwhelmed, have a realistic opportunity for sufficiently processing the skills, strategies, and knowledge into memory (Banikowski & Mehring, 1999).

- Use mnemonics, in which a sequence of letters represents different pieces of information, as memory aids to quickly reduce the working memory load. They can be very helpful in the short run, but there is also a hidden danger with their use. If the specific mnemonic is not continuously used, or the student forgets the meaning for the cues, the information becomes inaccessible because the tenuous, single linkage to the memory has been lost. It is imperative that the student move beyond the mnemonic to understanding the information so he or she does not have to rely on it. Mnemonics are Band-Aids to reduce overloading the memory, and they are almost never sufficient in the long term for a significant memory problem.

- Because the differences in students' working memory spans are not going to change during class, there will always be both faster and slower students. Brain breaks allow some of the slower students to catch up. Additionally, peer teaching can facilitate this. It can be both powerful and helpful. However, having the faster students function as teaching assistants may become tiresome for some of them after a few times. *Build up a store of differentiated lessons, which might include a variety of enrichments to engage the faster moving students with a larger working memory. It also suggests that the enrichment might be more complex or challenging for those students.* Lack of time is still very much an issue here. This is where collaborative efforts of teacher teams, or the help of instructional facilitators, can more rapidly develop the enrichments than teachers working alone.

- Managing attention on relevant information and ignoring the irrelevant information are problems of working memory's central executive. To compensate for the faulty processing, review and rehearse strategies that should explicitly be taught to students, and consistently practice them, which improves the efficiency of working memory. Students also need to learn and practice inhibiting irrelevant information and maintaining task-relevant information (Deshler & Schumaker, 1993; Swanson & Siegel, 2001). The general review and rehearsal strategies are covered in Chapter 9. Students with learning disabilities are frequently poor at using strategies, and they commonly have difficulty generalizing the strategy use to other problems. It is important that the strategies are appropriate for their learning disability needs.

The majority of the instructional strategies discussed so far are for the teacher to use as interventions. Table 7.4 lists some strategies that students can employ (with teachers' support) as they learn to self-monitor and learn how to avoid or reduce working memory overload that originates from a variety of sources (Dehn, 2008; Gathercole & Alloway, 2008; Pickering, 2006; Mastropieri & Scruggs, 1998; Pressley & Woloshyn, 1995; Yuill, Oakhill, & Parkin, 1989). Table 7.5 contains suggestions for teaching the students how to use the strategies.

Working Memory in Reading and Math

Reading and mathematics are involved in more content areas than most other skills. A deficit in either has the potential to create a devastating domino effect through other content areas and create serious learning problems for the student. Because of their great significance to learning, the relationships to working memory for these two areas will be addressed next.

Reading

Students with working memory deficits frequently have difficulty with reading comprehension (Yuill et al., 1989), although a poor working memory is not the sole contributor. To understand the text, the mind must not only derive the meaning of the word, but it must also simultaneously build a mental model of the material just read. The mind must maintain the mental model while processing additional phrases from around the word, then retrieve relevant information from memory in

> **Table 7.4. STUDENT-EMPLOYED STRATEGIES TO REDUCE WORKING MEMORY SPAN OVERLOAD**

- Sit away from things or people that cause distractions, such as open doors or windows.
- Get organized immediately. Have all your class materials ready. Looking for them during a lesson means more of the lesson will be missed.
- For similar-sounding words, focus on the differences in the words.
- Listen to nonvocal music (have the teacher okay it).
- With note taking, don't write the teacher's words verbatim (word for word). Use phrases and draw stick figures with labels.
- Become aware of when you get confused and ask for help at that moment.
- Practice identifying what is important and what is relevant. Using a pencil, cross out what is unimportant and irrelevant.
- Write a few strategy cues on cards or tape them to a notebook as a simple visual reminder (memory aid) about ways to reduce working memory load. If no other students use your desk, tape the cues on the desk.
- Repeat the instructions. Use self-talk and say the instructions over again (quietly).
- Practice with cue cards for math steps. Have the cards face down. Start with self-talk, saying the steps for doing the problem. Check the cue card when it is needed, but gradually work (with teacher direction) to mastering the steps so they become automatic. It is a form of self-testing. Practice.
- With longer math problems that have multiple steps, don't do them in your head, because this will cause working memory failure. Write the steps out.

order to understand the word in context. That is a lot of work, and working memory is where this processing occurs. Working memory is a major predictor of reading comprehension in adults, though not necessarily in younger children. *Students with poor working memory frequently have difficulty during reading because of their problems in suppressing irrelevant information. It is important for them to increase their speed of word attack skills and fluency in order to improve their reading comprehension.* Those with poor reading comprehension are slower to suppress ambiguous words and other irrelevant information (Barnes, Faulkner, Wilkinson, & Dennis, 2004). Their central executive's ability to weed out and ignore extraneous information is limited, and subsequently irrelevant information may creep into their memory (De Beni & Palladino, 2000). Readers who spend a lot of effort decoding words use a large portion of their working memory capacity. Thus by the time they finish the sentence, information from the beginning may already be lost. Reading programs that increase word attack skills, vocabulary, fluency, and especially skills in the sounds

Table 7.5. TEACHING STRATEGIES TO REDUCE WORKING MEMORY OVERLOAD

- Explain the rationale to the student for focusing on the particular strategies that are targeted. As in the chapter on motivation, this sets the goal. Outline the small, achievable steps, it also addresses the motivational needs of the student. Explain how the strategy will help the student's memory, reduce overload and help in all areas of learning. This will facilitate the development of the student's metacognitive abilities.
- The student must be serious about the training. If the student experiences some initial quick successes with simple problems, it may help to motivate the student.
- For many students with smaller working memory spans, one-on-one instruction on using one of the learning strategies is usually more desirable. Brief sessions several times a week are more helpful than once a week, and each session should focus on using only a single instructional strategy because the students' working memory is easily overloaded. Don't move on to another strategy until the first is solidly learned and repeatedly demonstrated by the students.
- Review with the student his or her memory strengths and weaknesses.
- The intervention strategy and the student's needs must match. The material, concepts, and language must also be age appropriate.
- Have the students practice crossing out irrelevant material and underlining or highlighting relevant information, along with identifying the correct procedures to use on a task. This can be conducted individually, or classwide, with more one-on-one practice at a later time for the students who need it. Keep in mind that highlighting alone doesn't help produce memory; it simply identifies what needs further practice or reflection.
- Model the new learning strategy step by step, using only small amounts of information punctuated with frequent reviews. Demonstrate and practice each strategy with different examples.
- During the practice, or modeling, explain each step with simple examples and explain the details. Again, present information in small amounts with plenty of guided practice until the student can perform several steps of the strategy automatically. Then add another step. In motivation, the goals should appear to be attainable and not too distant.
- Develop cues or acronyms to reduce the working memory load. Practice identifying what the problem or task is asking for. Using a default approach with lower ability students, "If this . . . then do this . . . ," will help initially; however, the students will need to practice recognizing increasingly complex combinations as they mature.
- Have the student practice generalizing the strategies to other problems. Check that the student can periodically practice generalizing after the strategies have been learned.
- With guidance, all students should develop the metacognitive skills of knowing why, when, and how to use a given strategy. Even top adolescent and young college students will not necessarily initiate the use of a strategy without a reminder. Their still-developing frontal lobes may be the reason why students don't initiate the helpful strategies.

of speech (phonological processing) are very helpful. They reduce the load upon working memory. Additionally, increasing an awareness of the syllables' sounds (phonemic awareness) demonstrates greater benefit in helping the reader with poor phonological working memory (Hurford et al., 1994). Increasing both phonemic awareness and the skills to process and blend those sounds (phonological processing) are excellent for spelling and reading fluency (Bus & Van Ijzendoorn, 1999). There are commercial, solidly researched programs, such as RAVE-O, that have successfully addressed these problems.

Most teachers do not have training as reading instructors. However, a greater awareness of the reading skills the adolescent needs to have may help educators in developing more sensitivity to the sounds and reading difficulties as they design lessons. For example, fusion and fission are very similar-sounding words. Students must focus their attention on the "fu" and the "fi" sounds to distinguish the words. Failure to do so may result in retrieval of the wrong long-term memory.

Phonemic awareness interventions that can reduce working memory load can include

- Rhyming, starting with familiar words to increase awareness of sounds;
- Using alliteration to further increase awareness (e.g., Peter picked a pound . . .);
- Identifying phonemes in the words, such as the three phonemes in hat;
- Practicing blending syllables;
- Practicing blending phonemes until a word is smoothly pronounced;
- Practicing segmenting words into syllables before saying them as individual phonemes;
- Combining segmenting and blending tasks (the key phonemic awareness skill); and
- Manipulating phonemes by adding or deleting them from the end or middle of the words.

Math

Math places a considerable demand on working memory. Many students are easily overloaded because they must perform three demanding tasks. They must hold in mind the sequence of the procedures while performing the calculations, then shift their focus to the appropriate new strategies. Since working memory capacity may be rapidly exceeded, especially for students with a smaller working memory span, extraneous information or unrelated demands should be eliminated, or considerably reduced at the very least. Teachers should trim the problem to the essentials when initially teaching the procedures and principles. It may be helpful for the teacher to *identify the parts of problems that produce a heavy working memory load*. Then carefully break those parts down into smaller parts, with built-in reviews. This may reduce not only the overload, but also serve to reduce the accompanying frustration and motivation problems found in mathematics. Also, have students explicitly demonstrate, model, and practice how to identify irrelevant information from the relevant, especially if similar foils are used in assessments.

In many math problems, the visual representation of numbers is shifted by the mind to verbal representations, but these quickly overwhelm working memory. *Occasionally, it is more helpful to switch from a verbal presentation of information back to a visual one in the form of a drawing, then figure out the necessary steps ("tools") to use for each operation. With the lesson back in a visual mode, break it down into steps that are simple from the students' perspectives, and use probing questions to help them figure out the procedures they need to use* (Riding, Grimley, Dahraei, & Banner, 2003). Let me elaborate. I start with visual, and then use verbal probes to guide what we are trying to accomplish. By using pictures to illustrate what happens when a math function is applied, the function becomes a mental "tool" and the students develop an understanding of why that particular tool was used, versus a plug–in-the-numbers-and-chug-through-the-calculations approach. I've found combining the visual and verbal often works well such as in introductory statistics. In statistics, we might examine a drawing of a shape or curve, and determine what we wanted to do to the drawing, such as removing a portion or finding the area. Then we would verbalize the operations and match it a step at a time with a mathematical operation that would do what we wanted. We worked out the entire problem visually first, then identified the appropriate mathematical "tools" before commencing on any calculations Of course, this wasn't necessary for everyone, but it certainly allowed a number of students to grasp what was going on and how to proceed. A similar verbal to visual strategy can be used for many of the abstract concepts in the sciences.

When any new procedure, knowledge, or skill set is first taught, adolescents with a small working memory span are especially prone to being distracted by extraneous information. It is difficult for them to stay focused on the task and inhibit other information. Keep it simple, keep it focused, and frequently check for understanding. When a teacher asks, "Do you understand?" and the student replies, "Uh huh," the teacher should then have the student demonstrate his understanding, rather than accepting his answer. However, students can also help the teacher identify where working memory problems occur when they comment, "I can't remember the number" or "I forgot what to do" (Gathercole et al., 2006). Somewhere just before that point of the procedure their working memory overloaded. Go back with the students and examine where the load became too great and they forgot.

If a teacher thoroughly examines the steps for solving a math problem, he or she will find the student must employ a multitude of decisions and strategies. Knowing where key decisions must be made, or a change in strategies takes place, is quite important in helping students who are poor in math or who have a shorter working memory span. What is being suggested is a different approach to the math, concentrating on the points that are likely to cause overload and the places of key decisions. Such an examination of the problem's details may be necessary in order to identify where working memory overload may potentially occur.

Summary

Working memory appears to process information both visually-spatially and auditorially, each with slightly different capacities. A student's working memory is easily overloaded when newer information is constantly replacing or shoving out older information unless the information is actively reviewed or thought about. In the Cowan model, working memory appears to focus attention on only one item at a time, while the mind keeps several pieces of related information in a highly active and accessible state. This allows the working memory to rapidly shift to other information. Working memory capacity increases with age, but with adolescents there may be some students in a classroom who are functioning at a low elementary level and others who are near adult levels. Students with low working memory capacity do not outgrow it, which can create continuous learning problems. Because of the enormous range in capacity, and the tendency for easily overloading the mind, leading to working memory failure, it is better to take preventative interventions. One promising assessment is the AWMA. This would help teachers to objectively identify students with working memory problems and who might not qualify for special services. Identification of these students also presents an opportunity to help them develop metacognitive skills, such as how to ignore irrelevant information. The students need to develop an awareness of when they are lost because of too much information and they need to employ strategies to keep them on track. Another intervention might be accomplished by pre-identifying complex information and breaking it into steps that all students can process, along with frequent reviews using different modalities to allow students to catch up. Many problems of missed information or gaps in understanding of just-presented information may have less to do with inattention than with working memory failure in which the students' systems were overwhelmed. While there are limited strategies that students may learn to help themselves, it is perhaps a better approach to first change the working memory load, with teachers carefully critiquing their lessons and simplifying or reducing the load.

Key Points and Recommendations

- *Words that have similar sounds are difficult to recall, especially in sequence.* Sounds of words that are different are much easier to retrieve, such as *cow day man tall wide swim.* Provide the students with additional search cues or key words for the mind to use when asking for words that are similar. When teaching words with similar sounds, focus on the differences in the sound or spelling or on other cues that will help to distinguish them when they need to be recalled. Practice recalling them, using those distinctions.
- *The longer it takes to pronounce the word, the fewer the number of words that can be recalled.* Long words overload the working memory more quickly, leading to working memory failure. As students encounter more challeng-

ing texts, allow more time and use questions for each paragraph as they read. Don't wait until the end of the section, because working memory failure may have already occurred. The questions can guide the students and help them process the information before going on to the next paragraph.

- *Working memory has a highly limited capacity and, when combined with the tendency for spatial tasks and skills to interfere with each other, it strongly suggests that multitasking is likely to have failures in one or more of the tasks because of overload.* If multiple tasks are involved, and the failure of any could be potentially fatal, then very careful consideration needs to be made about how the tasks are designed. This property has created the impetus for the development of automated braking systems in vehicles. It suggests that when a teacher designs a lesson and its instructions, he or she should carefully consider how easy it is to overload the working memory. A student with limited working memory capacity does not outgrow the problem. It can be increased slightly (8–18%) with CogMed.

- *Working memory is highly integrated with long-term memory*, and is a portion of long-term information that has become activated. Working memory is constantly retrieving information stored in long-term memory.

- *There are different levels of activation for working memory.* There is a large and passive long-term memory and more activated levels that are more closely networked with the information that is being focused upon. A portion of memory whose networks have reached a threshold becomes active, and thus becomes highly accessible. A highly active level where the attention is focused upon is where the information is also actively manipulated. The roving focus of attention typically has only a single item being manipulated at one time, although perhaps up to about four items may be highly active and form a networked chunk.

- *Activated networks forming chunks may be linked with other networks, forming superchunks of active memory that allow rapid access to more information.* The key words or search cues that are currently being used in the instruction will facilitate linking to other networks of information. However, for the cues to work well, they must also have been practiced, too.

- *Keep verbal information well structured and simple, and make sure to frequently review procedures.* Inattention is more likely less of a problem than working memory failure because there was too much information presented too fast. Have students use quiet self-talk, or restate the entire set of instructions to each other, before proceeding. Encourage students to ask for the procedure again if they missed some information. Belittling them for not paying attention solves nothing if their working memory failed due to being overloaded.

- *Students with smaller working memory spans are more easily distracted;* keep potential distractions to a minimum. Keep these students away from windows, open doors, or other students who tend to be loud or disruptive.

- *Working memory may work like a brake on instruction, slowing down the overall encoding by overloading, and dropping some information, necessitating the repetition of some information.* The lack of time is a constant problem. Focus on the most salient information and use the rest of the lesson to elaborate as time allows. Students with shorter working memory spans may need greater assistance in the form of advance organizers, or skeletal notes, so they are not left behind. Using brain breaks helps these students to catch up and also reinforces the information for other students.

- *Students with poor working memory frequently have difficulty during reading because of their problems in suppressing irrelevant information.* It is important for them to increase their speed of word attack skills and fluency in order to improve their reading comprehension. Reading programs, such as RAVE-O, can help students develop word attack skills.

- *Many missed pieces of information, missed instructions, and gaps in understanding lessons are more likely due to working memory failures because of overload than to inattention.* Be alert to the fact that a given class will have a large range in working memory, with some students at a second- or third-grade level and others at nearly an adult level for working memory. Identifying the working memory range beforehand and making it part of the students' learning profiles can be of immense help. This allows teachers to know those who are at most risk for missing information. The AWMA is especially helpful in diagnosing these problems.

- *Identify the parts of problems that require a heavy working memory load.* These are the sections of the lesson that need to be broken into smaller steps, or simplified, and then followed by a brain break or some type of review to ensure the students didn't lose information.

- *Occasionally, it is more helpful to switch from a verbal presentation of information back to a visual one in the form of a drawing, and figure out the necessary steps ("tools") to use for each operation.* Once the entire procedure is planned out visually with the accompanying steps, switch back to doing the problem with the numbers.

- *Students with smaller working memory spans are especially prone to being distracted by extraneous information when any new procedure, knowledge, or skill set is first taught.* The presentation of the information is often very critical. Missing fundamental information places the rest of their comprehension in jeopardy. Make certain there are no distractions and that their working memory is not overwhelmed. Shortly after presenting a major new concept or skill, pause and have the students review it, perhaps by explaining or demonstrating it to each other. Follow with the smaller differences or nuances of the lesson that fine-tune the concept.

RESOURCES

Alloway, T. P. (2007). *Automated Working Memory Assessment (AWMA)*. Oxford, UK: Pearson Education. http://psychcorp.co.uk

Alloway, S., & Gathercole, S. (2008). *Working memory and learning*. Los Angeles, CA: Sage.

Dehn, M. (2008). *Working memory and academic learning: Assessment and intervention*. New York, NY: Wiley.

Pickering, S. (2006). *Working memory and education*. New York, NY: Academic Press.

CHAPTER EIGHT

Long Term Memory

Memory is simultaneously fragile and powerful:
Memories are often ephemeral and distorted . . .
yet subjectively compelling and influential.
—Daniel Schacter (1995)

The college amphitheater classroom was silent as nearly 200 students bent over their exams, working through the questions. The professor and teaching assistance proctors roamed up and down the aisles. Then, in the silence one student closed her eyes, her arms thrust upward in the air, but moving around very precisely as if she were plucking invisible items from the air. A few startled students looked at her as the professor and a proctor converged on the scene of the silent actions. In a quiet, but very firm, voice the professor asked what was going on, why all the arm "waving"? The student replied that for one of the essay questions she was recalling the details of a complex process that was part of photosynthesis by visualizing a mind map that she used 2 years earlier. Each part of the process had a specific shape she could remember and a specific location. She was recalling all the information by visualizing information and remembering the shapes, positions, and movements of the different components. The shapes told her the names, and the positions cued her to the when and where in the photosynthetic process they occurred. The information was still largely intact in her memory and in her studies she needed to only briefly review and practice moving the imaginary items through the process to recall it in detail. It was like recalling a familiar dance step. She earned an A on her test and essay that required the information, and she continued to use the same technique successfully on other tests.

Long-Term Memory

Memories that are maintained for minutes to days or years are generally considered to be long-term memory. Most of what education attempts to build and later measure is some form of long-term memory. These memories also exist in different forms, such as how things are done, or verbal memories for the meanings of words and names, and they are stored in different locations. The memories are distributed across the thin cortex of the brain, but not evenly. Information is broken up and distributed in different regions that are all networked together. Additionally, some regions or types of memories also have different potential for establishing a memory. As we will see, long-term memories exist in different forms, with some more readily stored than others. Newly arrived information appears to be organized and consolidated through structures in the temporal lobe but is not permanently stored there. The information is moved to different areas, and when it is retrieved, those areas that were originally active during the storing process are reactivated. The different regions of the brain cooperate with each other through neural networks; all are connected with each other by the long axons of their neurons.

The Significance of Long-Term Memory

Memory is the bedrock of learning. If information fails to be encoded and does not become established in long-term memory, essentially no learning has occurred. However, for practical purposes, learning has probably failed when the student successfully encoded information into memory but cannot consciously retrieve it, or there is no memory to influence actions in a nonconscious processing. For most students, the memory must be retrievable when they need it. Memory can be established through a variety of routes, some more reliably than others. Other forms of long-term memory, such as word-based or semantic information, often required repeated exposures to become established and are heavily influenced by outside instructional methods. Many of these recalcitrant memories can also be networked to create even stronger memories if the teacher designs his or her instruction appropriately. By intentionally combining some forms of memory, educators can substantially boost an adolescent's performance, sometimes dramatically. The potential for great performances of the mind appears to be present in most students' brains, but for many, educators do not know how to tap into these capabilities. This chapter lays out the types of memory educators can make use of and provides strategies to network several forms in order to improve the adolescent's performance.

No brain is perfect, and those extremely rare individuals with an apparently "photographic memory" do not necessarily lead a charmed life (Luaria, 1973). The brain normally sheds information, a lot of which is actually unimportant; however, occasionally, the brain miscalculates in what it deems as unimportant. Everyone experiences memory errors. While some errors are inconsequential, others memories carry greater significance even though our brain may not consider them to be significant. This is where the actions of the teacher make a difference. In the opening example of a college test, the student's high school teacher some years earlier made a significant difference by helping the student create several different types of accessible memory for a single topic. *If a teacher is able to help the student in making multiple memories that all network to the same topic, there is a greater chance that the specific memory can be found at a later time.* We will extensively explore that concept in "The Educational Connection" in this chapter. One problem educators face is how to have the mind direct the brain to save information it naturally finds of little importance because it has either little salience or valence to the person. To understand how to build better and more retrievable memories, it is first necessary to explore the types of memory known to play major roles in education.

Types of Long-Term Memory

A student's everyday performance depends on the buildup of a store of information. As we noted earlier, information lasting for minutes or longer is known as *long-term memory*. Ideally, the information is readily available for years to come, but, as too often happens, a memory may not be available even minutes, let alone hours, later. Memory is broadly divided into information that is consciously available, known as *declarative memory*, and information that cannot be consciously described, such as motor actions or procedures, which are known as implicit or *nondeclarative memory* (see Figure 8.1). Much of traditional academic teaching is in the realm of declarative memory, and lapses in that form can be devastating. Nondeclarative memory is used in shop classes and courses that teach consumer science, physical education,

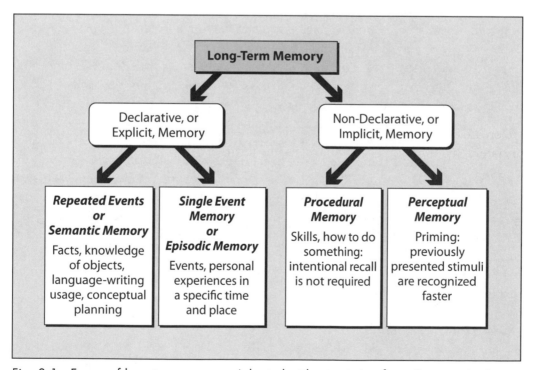

Fig. 8.1. Forms of long term-memory. Adapted with permission from Gazzangia, Ivry, & Magnum, (2009), *Cognitive Neuroscience*, 3rd Ed.

art, and other areas where procedures and executing precise physical movements are more common. Both forms of long-term memory have fairly distinct subtypes, which will be described below and can significantly impact adolescents' performances. Although more than 40 other types of memories are described in the literature, most of these are not helpful because they overlap or seem to be the same types of memory but with different names.

Declarative memory

Memory for repeated events (semantic memory). If a person can describe an object, task, or concept, either verbally or in writing, *semantic memory* is being used. *Semantic memory lies at the heart of most traditional education, and it is here that a student's academic fortunes often rise or fall because so many lessons are presented in a semantic form.* Semantic memories are the fact files of stored knowledge. It may include such things as your street address, the capitals of the states, how to multiply, or the meaning of a word. Semantic memory also holds knowledge of *concepts,* such as "dog," though not of any particular dog but simply what is considered to be a dog. Concepts such as democracy, religion, school and vacation are part of semantic memory. These memories store both specific and general knowledge, but they are separate from the knowledge of *when* they were acquired. Memories based on when particular information was acquired are *episodic memories.* As we read in Chapter 6, Gardner observed that a person can be smart in ways other than in traditional semantic-based memory of concepts, which depend on words and number usage. By incorporating different forms of "intelligences," memories other than those that are semantically based may be accessed, changing the adolescent's performance.

Memory for single events (episodic memory). When a teenager goes on a trip or attends a rock concert, whenever he or she has personally experienced something, just a single exposure creates an *episodic memory* of the event. *Episodic memories are memories of our personal histories.* When a student recalls a ball game, or what he did with a friend, episodic memories are tapped. These memories are personal stories, and they often have considerably more emotional significance than other memories. The emotional component enhances their recall. *Episodic memories, properly used, can provide a powerful linkage to semantic information.* Conversely, semantic memories are typically created through multiple exposures to information. For example, lessons that require multiple exposures are sometimes referred to as "drill and kill" routines. The skill teachers need to develop is how to create solid semantic memories in the students' minds without destroying their natural inquisitiveness, while concurrently keeping the students alert and involved. Those strategies will be explored later in this chapter.

Nondeclarative memory

There are also memories that are not made of words. These are memories of earlier experiences, such as how to do something like balancing a bicycle as you ride, walking, or throwing or catching a ball. Such memories are retrieved without willful effort and are closely linked with the cerebellum for fine-tuning the movement commands, as well as some emotional processing. There at least four types of non-declarative memories, including the classical stimulus-response, such as ducking when a ball is thrown at you, and habits in which a process has become so automatic no conscious effort is needed. Nondeclarative memories also include *procedural memories* and *perceptual memories*, which may be used to network with semantic memories of general knowledge, creating powerful memories that can be used in traditional academics. The latter two are described here.

Perceptual memory

Perceptual memory can get the brain ready or primed to recognize words or objects that have been previously learned. When the brain is primed, it recognizes stimuli more quickly. For example, words that are linked in the same network can be picked out more quickly. To illustrate this, read the following sets of words:

tulip, rose, daisy

In the next set of words, which word does not belong?

carnation, orchid, hammer

The brain is primed to the category of flowers and can make a decision faster about what does not belong with the flowers. Teachers often use a form of priming as hints to get students thinking about their lesson by using words of the same category. However, the brain can be fooled in the priming. In the following classic example, try this simple experiment with your students. Have students shout out their answers as rapidly as they can.

"We are going to conduct a little experiment. It is simple and should be fun."
Ask the students, "Are you ready? When I ask a question shout your answer as fast as you can."
Hold up a white sheet of paper and ask, "What color is this?"
They shout, "White!"
Next ask, "What do cows drink?"
A number will shout, "Milk!"

Milk, of course, is the wrong answer, but the cues "white" and "cows" primed the brain and formed a natural linkage to "milk." As we see, linkages do not always help produce the right information; sometimes the way teachers set up the problem or ask questions will encourage the brain to search down the wrong path. For example, trying to capture fish in a pond with a bucket and not succeeding doesn't mean there aren't fish, just that a poor choice in tools was used. The questions are tools of the teacher, but she must carefully choose the right tool.

Procedural memory

Memories for how to do things such as tying shoelaces, riding a bicycle, or skiing, which all involve a series of motor skills and cognitive skills, are *procedural memories*. In many traditional academic lessons, procedural memory receives only a cursory use, while in the vocational classes, which may teach woodworking, computer skills, metalworking, sewing, and cooking, it is the major way for the lesson to be learned. *Combining procedural memory with semantic and episodic memories can create very robust memories for abstract concepts* because students are also creating personal (episodic) memories for actions (procedural) they took while describing what they are doing (semantic). This powerful technique will also be explored in some depth in "The Educational Connection."

The Learning Curve: The Shape of Memory

When an adolescent is suddenly thrust into a new situation, such as learning a brand-new type of software, or a completely different way of solving a math problem, there is a lot to learn and the learning curve is steep. There are several reasons the shape of learning is important to teaching. With practice, the rate at which students learn more new material slows but never stops (Newell & Rosenbloom, 1981). Many of these diminishing returns are described mathematically as a power function, similar to a logarithmic graph. How the learning slows, as described by one end of the graph, is one of the key problems in keeping a struggling student going, whether as a freshman in high school or as a graduate school student. The tremendous effort required as learning slows is very hard to sustain without support and encouragement. Learning gains in these circumstances have become a motivational issue. How those various forms of long-term memory are progressively built upon and maintained is considered next.

The Educational Connection

General Strategies for Increasing Long-Term Memory

Most of the successful strategies that affect long-term memory have already been introduced in the previous chapters on attention, emotion, and working memory. Other strategies were described in the chapters on motivation and intelligence. To reinforce the reader's memory, these strategies will be briefly reviewed, along with more specific memory applications.

Emotion

Lessons that have significant personal meaning may also become episodic memories. Sometimes a single lesson will stick in the memory. *If a student is directly involved throughout the lesson, and she is describing what she is doing, she is producing more personally significant details that can be retrieved later.* Details can still fade, but a number of connections remain, linking back to the desired memory. The variety of details can function as cues to help the student's mind in its search for the appropriate memory.

For example, "Megan, do you remember when you picked up the lizard at the zoo? What color was it? Did it have any stripes?" These questions are loaded with search cues. For instance, *when you picked* tells the mind this is personally experienced information; *at the zoo* directs to search in the mind's "where" in the "zoo" files; *What color was it?* specifically asks for details related to personal experience; *have any stripes?* helps the mind to think about the surface of the lizard. Simply saying "Megan, please describe the lizard" provides context but almost no cues for the brain. Framing a question that includes the context is often essential for many students in directing their search.

A personal event, especially one coupled with personal action, creates a context that helps to create a very solid memory. Using personal connections aids the adolescent in retrieving a memory when he reflects back to an action in which he participated. Of all the forms of memory, personal memories are considerably easier to retrieve. Even years later, when an event seems to be entirely lost, if sufficient details or cues are present, the person can usually retrieve the memory (Schacter, 2001b). Although the connections have lain dormant and were unreinforced, a path can still be found through the cobwebs of the mind.

Attention-working memory

In the creation of a robust memory, attention goes hand in hand with emotion and action. A student must use her attention systems when she is personally involved and taking actions. Recall that the mind generally focuses on only a single item at a time. While the adolescent is performing the action, her working memory is processing information about what she is paying attention to. If a middle school student is describing her actions to someone, jotting notes down on what she just did a moment before, or if she got involved in a discussion about the lesson immediately following the lesson, then more connections are networked. *The personal elaboration about her own actions creates semantic links with the episodic memory.* Because most lessons are still assessed traditionally by writing or talking, reinforcing networks to the semantic memories is very important.

Intelligence-personal elaboration

In the chapter on intelligence, I noted that Keith Stanovich suggested reflective thinking was a missing component in measuring intelligence. Active reflection in the form of personal elaborations allows the student to discover and establish further connections in the problem. The reflection sets the stage for the treasured "a-ha" moments, when critical details are still readily available where the student personally and actively makes the links. If this is followed by the adolescent taking overt actions such as describing or writing about the problem, the personal elaboration can further strengthen the memory (Rogers, Kuiper, & Kirker, 1977).

Experiential learning

Well-structured lessons, where the student is physically immersed in a task for a longer period of time, perhaps over the course of a half hour to a month, bring together all the key elements for making stable, accessible long-term memories. The adolescent becomes emotionally invested. He is the one taking a series of actions. The actions provide immediate feedback, affecting both motivation and his emotional state. Because he performs the actions personally, a series of episodic memories are also created. If the student has several break-outs (or feedback) where he discusses what he did in problem solving, his elaborations create multiple semantic memory networks, any of which might be used later to locate a particular memory. *Experiential learning is something like a natural series of discovery learning lessons.* A set of tasks or challenges is designed, usually with obvious linkages created by the circumstances the student finds himself in. Built-in discussions about the immediate activity can function as natural brain breaks, reducing overload and permitting the memory networks to be strengthened. Sometimes the experiences are so profound that they are life-changing and create powerful memories. Additional practices reinforce the new memory network for the knowledge or skill. However, educators must be alert to working memory overload. Confusion in a task that immediately follows may be an indication of overload. The amount of information may be too much for students with smaller working memory spans, unless the emotional connections are significant. It will take practice on the teacher's part to establish how much information the students can handle at a given moment.

Memory errors

It is rather remarkable that the brain functions so well and that more errors don't occur in its trillions of possible neuron connections. For adolescents, errors in reasoning and memory are frequent sources for problems in academic performance. How the student processes new information can contribute to the errors if she has learned inefficient habits or biases that interfere with future learning. Conversely, other learning habits may propel the student rapidly forward.

Inefficient learning strategies that have been repeatedly used may lead to failures in retrieving appropriate information, which is often frustrating to adolescents. They don't understand why they can't do well. Essentially they are using the wrong mental "tools" for the job but don't realize it. If errors occur too frequently they may give up, potentially becoming at risk for dropping out of school. The fundamental question here is why failures occur and if there is anything that can be done about them. One of the first problem areas that we will examine concerns misconceptions.

False beliefs and changing misconceptions

Adolescents, like adults, frequently develop misconceptions or false beliefs. These may stem from childhood, their upbringings, or misunderstandings of information presented in school. Whatever the source, they are serious problems, because misconceptions or false beliefs interfere with solving both personal and societal problems.

Researchers are beginning to understand why it is so difficult to change a false idea, or a firmly held but false belief. This difficulty seems to occur in many controversial topics, such as conspiracies, alien abductions, or many classic social, religious, and science conflicts (including racial and sexual bias, intelligent design versus evolution, and arguments about health care). It appears that how the brain processes information is at the heart of many of these conflicts. For educators, our understanding about the brain's processing is a good news–bad news situation. The model in Figure 8.2 represents one hypothesis of how information is processed in respect to maintaining misconceptions or false beliefs in the face of clear evidence to the contrary. It also suggests why it is so difficult to overcome conceptions that are based on errors and to shift to an alternative explanation.

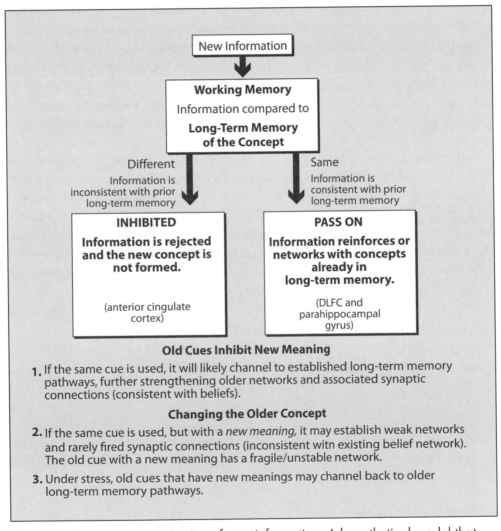

Fig. 8.2. Acceptance or rejection of new information. A hypothetical model that suggests why some information is accepted or maintained and other information rejected regardless of the evidence.

Long-term memory is intricately involved with false beliefs and the maintenance of misconceptions. When information first arrives, it is focused upon in working memory and compared to information in long-term memory. If the information is consistent with both old cues and prior information, it is passed on, further reinforcing the concept and creating an ever-widening network. For instance, *if the information is similar or matches with one's beliefs, there is no reason to ignore the information, and very little reflective thought is necessary*. Often all that is necessary for acceptance is that the information comes from a trusted source; the person does not engage in critical evaluation and the information is not questioned. However, if the accepted information happens to be false, biased, or is a misconception, the error is further reinforced, making it even more difficult to overcome.

If the new information has cues that don't match with stored information, more effort or reflective thinking is needed to process the information to avoid being immediately rejected. When cues fail to agree with prior information, a different brain structure handles the processing, making the information significantly more difficult to reconsider. Effortful reflective thinking is needed (Stanovich, 2009). In a sad, but true, example, a politician reviewed a proposal and thought its argument was pretty good. Upon learning that it originated from the opposite political party, he then ridiculed the idea and gave it no further consideration. Overcoming the nearly automatic rejection by the brain is a difficult task.

In making any conceptual change, and especially ideas that are erroneous but firmly held, it is first necessary to precisely identify the beliefs that are based on misunderstandings or biases, which abound in our youth. Every now and then parents are in for a rude shock about their children's understanding of some concept. To illustrate this, consider two parents, both biologists, who were watching their children play in the pool. The older child was 7 and was in a discussion with a mutual adult friend when this exchange occurred about things that are alive (Schenck, 2003):

"Is your sister alive?"	"Yes."
"Is your dog alive?"	"Yes."
"Are clouds alive?"	"Yes."
"Is the sun alive?"	"No."
"Is the water alive?"	"Yes."
"Is a rock alive?"	"No."

The parents were in shock. Despite their efforts to teach their child, he held common misconceptions about what makes things alive. The 7-year-old believed that if something moved, it was probably alive.

The Conceptual Change Model

One promising method to change concepts is called the Conceptual Change Model (CCM), developed by Stepans, Saigo, and Ebert (1999). If misconceptions, or false ideas, are routinely reinforced, the supporting neural networks are woven into so many other areas that they are very difficult to change. The CCM provides a more accurate alternative to confront the misconceptions that the students hold. The CCM begins with the teacher clearly identifying the misconception because the lesson must start where the students are in terms of their knowledge and comprehension, as well as level of cognitive development. To discover this place of understanding and development, a dialogue with the student is necessary, usually conducted in the form of an interview. *Most pretests are inadequate if they are in a multiple-choice format because they miss the nuances and level of comprehension while providing only a crude idea of the student's conception.* Like a detective, a skilled interviewer will work around the topic, probing in order to learn the nature of the student's misconception. Do not rush the questions, and ask them in an open-ended manner. The student reveals more facets of his understanding when he explains his reasoning. By interviewing several students of high, middle, and lower abilities, the educator will gain an idea of the range in their conceptions. Ideally this is accomplished privately, several weeks before the topic to be studied. If the topic is one that other teachers will also be presenting, share your findings so that the lessons start where the students are conceptually.

Although the CCM model was originally developed to address many science and math misconceptions, it works reasonably well with other concepts. In general, the model asks the student to state her belief about the topic, usually in writing because the statement will be examined later on. Using her own conception, the student makes a prediction about how some situation should turn out, again writing down her prediction or expectations. This is followed by testing or checking her predictions several times. Once is probably not enough. With the guidance of the teacher, the inconsistencies are pointed out, discussed, and reflected on.

After discussion and reflection, *the student proposes an alternative explanation*, and that is checked out. In all cases, it is the student doing the predicting and checking, with guidance. The teacher does not provide the answer, because the misconception and the new information must be owned by the student. It is her new idea, and her "a-ha!" moment. Remember that it is easier for the mind to default and do little or no reflecting. Also be aware that some concepts are more difficult developmentally to process compared to the much easier option of simply accepting what a trusted person has said. For example, many science concepts require abstract thinking and the linking of several abstract thoughts. *It doesn't matter how much evidence is presented if the student can't or chooses not to think at that level. Simply defaulting to "Because _____ said so" is much easier for the mind because the effort of thinking is not required.* Additionally, the student may not be building up any cognitive reserve that will be helpful in her older adult years.

If the CCM model sounds a bit like the scientific method and reflective learning cycle, you're right except that it is placed in a realistic social context.

Summary of procedures to change concepts by using "wrong answers"
- Identify the misconception precisely. This is often best approached

through detailed interviewing of several students with different abilities, with the individual interviews conducted away from the class. Generally, it is ideal to conduct the interviews several weeks before the lesson in question is to be studied. Multiple-choice instruments that are focused especially on the conceptual issue and use the alternative concepts as distracters may be a faster method of assessing more of the students. In this approach a series of questions are posed that explore different aspects of the concept. The multiple-choice items have the explanations as well as the more common alternative, but incorrect, explanations. Such instruments provide information on who has a better understanding of the concept and what are the most prevalent incorrect answers (Tanner & Allen, 2005). When there are very large numbers of students, such as in college classes, and now many elementary classes through high school classes, the use of clickers provides the instructor and student with nearly instant feedback. For example, during a brain break, questions on key pieces of information can be posed and the anonymous clicker response is projected on the screen, which can alert the teacher to misconceptions. Carefully worded questions permit the students to identify their misconceptions and help point them in the appropriate direction (Wood, 2004).

- An explicit confrontation between the new knowledge and the students' preexisting knowledge is essential (Posner, Strike, Hewson, & Gertzog, 1982).

- The activity starts at the level of the students' understandings. Meet and begin the lesson at where the students are, rather than where we think they are. In experiential classes, have the students individually explain their approach to the problem and have students also write their ideas down for later reference and discussion.

- Students use their alternative conception (or misconception) to make a prediction.

- Students explain (in writing) why their view of the concept will create the predicted results. The written statements make the students commit to their positions.

- The students test the claims to produce dissatisfaction with their own explanations (Posner et al., 1982).

- With guidance, have the students explore and explain why their alternative concepts failed to explain what happened.

- Explore other plausible alternative concepts that might offer an explanation that works. Students will examine these predictions and see if they intelligently explain why a claim is true, or if it can or can't be falsified. This approach is generally more successful than traditional approaches (Duit & Treagust, 1998, 2003).

- Apply the new concepts repeatedly to new situations. With each trial application, students explain (demonstrate, write essays or debate) how the new concept works better at explaining the situations. Recall that new memory networks are fragile until used for a while in a variety of situations. It will take repeated efforts to consolidate the changes, which are tentative at first, and students are prone to default back to older concepts, especially under stress.

- Have the students discuss and explore how the new concept will also provide new insights or possibly show new relationships. For example, in discussing climate change, students learn that as more sunlight energy is absorbed by the oceans, the temperature of the water rises. That leads to insights on weather change, not only for the local area but thousands of miles away, such as how the Gulf Stream affects weather for the British Isles and Scandinavian countries.

Conceptual change activities are student-centered rather than teacher-centered. The new concepts and the discovery of new explanations are the student's experiences, creating emotional connections with the lesson. For those students not trained to routinely use critical thinking, the brain's processing is nearly automatic in rejecting information that fails to match with its stored prior knowledge. Building a new concept will likely be a slow process, with the connections being initially unstable and more easily disrupted.

A couple of caveats are in order. In looking at the model for accepting or rejecting new information, which may lead to a new conception, older learning is not erased or lost from memory. I've repeatedly found that the older concept remains. When the student (or even adult) is under stress, I've observed that information or stimuli originally associated with other meanings, but now linked with an unfamiliar meaning, may default and link back to old associations. Two examples will illustrate this. A young man learned that swearing is unacceptable in most of society. He does well for years. Then one day he smacks his thumb with a hammer and lets off a stream of profanity. The old network (a habit), though little used, still exists. The same default processing might be used when new cues are presented. In another example, a student got mixed up when learning how to divide fractions and he constantly set them up backward. Eventually, he learned to perform the operation correctly, but whenever he was under stress and had to do a calculation quickly, he still starts to set the problem backward. The adage "old habits die hard" describes it well.

Broadly speaking, memory errors take two forms. There are errors of *omission*, the failure to recall an event or information, when students try to remember something, which most students are painfully aware of, and *commission*, where a student remembers an event quite differently from what actually happened or he or she remembers something that never even happened, such as an alien abduction. These are serious distortions of memory. In the following section I will explore an important type of commission error, the creation of a false memory.

False memory: The questions change the memory

False memories are memories of events or experiences that never happened but that a person believes to be true. These are more than just inaccurate memories, and false memories can be insidious because of the potential damage they can do to the adolescents harboring them and to everyone around them. False memories may occur at any age and may linger from childhood experiences.

False memories can be created in both children and adults, although children appear to be more susceptible by outside events or actions of other people (Poole & Lindsay, 1995). The susceptibility of children to the creation of false memories led to a rash of criminal cases of child abuse based on "recovered memories" in the 1980s to 1990s. To be certain, there were cases of actual child abuse. However, thousands of cases of "recovered memories" of abuse were memories created by the methods of questioning used by therapists or police officers (Loftus & Ketcham, 1994). As a result of the false memories created by therapists and others, families were broken up, children lost their parents, divorces occurred, and the falsely accused were no longer trusted. The false memories created a "lose, lose" situation. Nobody benefited from the sensational creations of such memories. When asking questions of a student who may have been in some kind of serious conflict, or when debriefing situation with staff, avoid leading questions that make or hint that certain actions might have happened (Clancy, Schacter, McNally, & Pitman, 2000; Winograd, 1988). A link to a tested, validated protocol for interviewing potentially sex-abused persons is listed in the resources at the end of the chapter. It is absolutely imperative in sorting through the allegations that the protocol be followed, no matter whether the case is about sexual abuse or a student fight. Unskilled questioning can alter a student's or staff member's memory.

False memories also have implications for the student's memory in test situations. To illustrate how memory can be changed by the mere asking of a question, consider the classic set often used by trial lawyers.

A witness is being asked about a car accident (Loftus & Palmer, 1974).

Any of the following initial questions might be asked: "Did you see the car bump the other car?"; "Did you see the car hit the other car?"; "Did you see the car slam into the other car?"; "Did you see the car crush the other car?" The words used in each question may permanently alter the memory of the witness. *How teachers frame a question may alter how the student remembers*. The differences in the cues change the memory, which has implications for the way a teacher asks questions. For example, many teachers make up their own multiple-choice questions. Typically, a question has four choices, with two being more obviously incorrect. There may be only a slight difference in the remaining two choices. What appears to be happening with some students is that during the process of shifting through the nuances of the question and trying to determine which selection is correct, they start making associations or linkages in their minds to information that was never originally connected. Now the problem for the mind becomes trying to determine whether this new linkage is a true memory or a false one. The brain doesn't have a conscious way of letting the student know if the memory is true or not. Some students will select a wrong answer possibly as a result of having created a false memory by the way the question was posed. There appears to be some evidence that the brain changes levels of activity for true information compared to false information. However, it is still unclear how the brain sorts out true and false information.

To address the problem of creating false memories by multiple-choice questions, a class of my graduate students, virtually all practicing teachers, attempted to write a multiple-choice question that would avoid creating false linkages. After 2 hours of effort by more than 25 people, they gave up. Everything they tried had the potential to make inappropriate linkages. They generated two questions for high school level students. One was absurdly simple, and the other appeared to be similar in style to a difficult IQ test question. Both were deemed worthless for the classroom. The effort expended strongly suggested that it would be unrealistic to expect teachers to devise an exam that could avoid the potential for creating false memories. If multiple-choice questions are used, it may also measure the susceptibility to creating a false memory and not be a measure of what the student knows. Avoid such questions when possible. However, high-quality multiple-choice tests can be constructed, but even for those with considerable test design experience, these are difficult to write and it takes a considerable of time.

Absentmindedness

Where I teach, I am, unfortunately, well known for forgetting any manner of things, from meetings to papers. These memory errors are not "senior moments" but are likely errors of encoding and retrieval problems. Students have these problems, too; they misplace things such as their assignments or books. These are errors of omission where the memory failures involve inattention (Schacter, 2001a). It often happens when the student moves about and sets something down; it may be her pencil, a piece of paper, or something generally smaller than a heavy suitcase. Why 'wouldn't a heavy suitcase be forgotten? The personal involvement, the level of focus in moving an object like a heavy suitcase requires considerable attention for several minutes; moving books, pencils, or paper requires much less mental effort and very little attention. Shortly afterward, if a student can't find the item she may spend countless frustrating minutes trying to locate it. When the missing item is eventually found, she will usually have no memory of having set the object in that particular spot.

A second type of inattention memory error occurs when attention is disrupted because of another action. For example, the student is performing a task but he is distracted, perhaps by an announcement over the PA or by a change of instructions. He loses track of where he was in a procedure or what he was doing. The underlying memory problem is, "Why didn't the student remember?"

There are a couple of possible explanations for such attention/memory errors. Fortunately, such errors are preventable, and sticky-note reminders may not be needed as a coping strategy. In the cases of students misplacing homework, the information was probably either poorly encoded or never encoded into memory.

There was an omission. The previous chapter on working memory noted that the brain only really appears to *focus* on one thing at a time, while it possibly juggles up to three or four pieces of information. The student whose attention is divided during the initial encoding of the information memory is particularly susceptible to errors. Think of the disruptions that routinely happen during the course of any instructional activity. All of these are potential problems for some students. If the student's attention is disrupted and shifted by some distraction as he was setting down a piece of paper, the encoding of the memory for where that paper is located may be very poor. He might recall something to the effect of "I remember I was in this room, and I still had my papers with me." *The key to solving this problem is to intentionally give thought to where you are in a task or to the object while it was being placed.* For example, if a person consciously says to himself as he is performing an action, "I'm placing my keys here, because I'd more likely look in this place for my keys," he will rarely forget where his keys are located. This type of effortful attention takes practice. It is not always successful, but a student is more likely to remember; however, initiating the action is a developmental problem for many adolescents. For adolescents with this problem, a routine or a checklist that is rigorously followed, at least while they are at school, may help. Outside of school it is ostensibly more difficult. Parental assistance would be great, but sadly that is often unrealistic. Teachers can set out a checklist and even make sure it is taped to a usable location that can't be missed, like a student's notebook cover, but once at home it is a different story. Something that might be tried (this is merely an untested suggestion) is to get the student's e-mail address or phone number and to send them an e-mail or text message to remind her about an assignment. I've done this several times with excellent results. (However, be alert to the problems of potential inappropriate contact with students—check your school policy.) Another idea is to coax students to leave two reminders for themselves: one taped to the computer and another on the refrigerator or in some location that they *always* see before they leave for school.

"Out of sight, out of mind" is a second inattention/memory error where a retrieval cue that was needed is missing. With students, this type of error is more likely to happen when they didn't have the reminder when they needed it. *The solution to the problem is to have a reminder or cue already in place so that when the student sees it, he or she is prompted to attend to schoolwork or take another appropriate action.*

Student memory errors also include forgetting they even have assignments to do, let alone forgetting to take their books home or to return with their assignments. These are problems of *prospective memory.* A student who remembers that she must do her assignment is using prospective memory. A number of partial solutions for creative prospective memory have been around a long time, from student planners and sticky notes to writing notes on their hands, which, though messy, can be reminders that are hard to miss. I've even seen doctors do this. All are memory aids. Schacter (2001a) observed that reminding students during their practice sessions is insufficient and doesn't produce much benefit in getting them to remember what they are supposed to do. Remembering to do something improves *only* when the cue or reminder is presented at the time when the person could do something. *No cue at the right time can mean no cue in mind.* Alarm clocksand automated computer reminders to renew programs within 15 days all function as cues for prospective memory.

When reminders are presented, they appear to have a pivotal role in assisting students to initiate desired actions. Teachers do this all the time by reminding students to take out their papers and to take the necessary books home. What becomes necessary is to arrange to have those reminders visible at the places where they will be needed at crucial times, such as placing a note that can't be overlooked. There are a lot of strategies to help students. Many are visual reminders, with pictures showing exactly what they should be doing at that time.

Sleep deprivation and memory consolidation

Pulling an all-nighter to prepare for a test in the hopes of achieving a better grade is a lousy bet. Students who don't get enough sleep do worse than those who do (Thatcher, 2008). Even students who load up on caffeine (through coffee, tea, or soft drinks) don't do better than students who get more sleep (Harrison & Horne, 2000). Caffeinated students will be more alert, but improvement in learning isn't taking place. Researchers are not exactly sure what sleep does. What is happening is still largely unknown. However, the lack of sleep clearly reverberates through the different forms of memory, increasing the levels of errors in recognition and seriously interfering with any new learning (Walker, 2008).

The brain does not have a single, homogenous level of metabolic processing through the 24-hour cycle; its processing changes. During sleep, the brain undergoes cycles of roughly 90 minutes, which include REM (Rapid Eye Movement) and NREM (non-REM) cycles. It is during these cycles that memories appear to be reactivated, reorganized, enhanced, and consolidated into more stable forms (Rasch & Born, 2008). The process of consolidating memories with emotional information appears to be particularly sensitive during the REM cycle. If the person is able to sleep, memories with emotional information become fairly resistant to interference for up to 4 years.

During a night's sleep, there is a later period of processing when memories become unstable again and are reconsolidated, allowing restoration of lost memories or generating new learning even without further practice. One stage of processing for procedural memories doesn't take place until roughly 5:30 A.M. to 7 A.M. A person's performance on a task that requires a physical sequence improves if he or she has that last critical period of sleep. However, this is a time when many adolescents have to wake up and be at school for early sports practices (Walker et al., 2003).

For educators, two major factors of sleep deprivation that concern adolescent performance stand out. First, *the lack of sleep makes it harder to recall previously learned information.* There are significant differences in recalling emotionally tagged information, and in procedural memory for skills where tasks must be done in the ap-

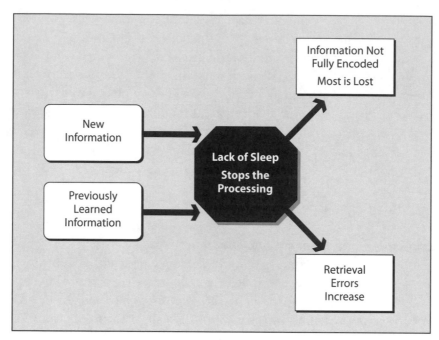

Fig. 8.3. Impact of Sleep Deprivation.

propriate physical sequence. Having a good night's sleep improves recall for both areas. Lack of sleep creates more retrieval errors (Fenn, Gallo, Margoliash, Roediger, & Nusbaum, 2009). Second, *the lack of sleep also impinges upon a student's ability to acquire new information*. That is readily apparent if you've ever had a student stagger into class after being up all night. His ability to pick up new information, process it, and comprehend it is very poor. The lack of sleep interferes with long-term potentiation in the hippocampus while the mind is trying to encode new information (Yoo, Hu, Gujar, Jolesz, & Walker, 2007). During sleep, memories that have been temporarily stored in the hippocampus are transferred to other areas for storage. The lack of sleep interferes with this transfer processes. Therefore, the student can't recall much of what happened, let alone create new linkages and stabilize his memory because there is not much information to work with.

To summarize, sleep deprivation interferes with the creation and retrieval of long-term memory. Some cognitive skills are more affected than others, and a person's age affects the degree of interference. Older adults have fewer problems than older adolescents and young adults do.

Cramming

Many of us know adolescents who cram before tests, and we probably did it ourselves, only to experience the well-known phenomenon of shortly afterward forgetting vast amounts of material. Figure 8.3 shows some of the problems that cramming poses. Often the student is trying to take new information that she hasn't learned earlier and get it into long-term memory. If she pulls an all-nighter, the newly acquired information doesn't have much, if any chance, to go through the consolidation process, let alone the transfer necessary to develop a stable long-term memory. As many students have experienced, there might have been just enough memory to answer some questions, but information learned earlier was also being compromised during their test, and the retrieval is more prone to errors because of lack of sleep.

A similar consolidation problem occurs with cramming right before a quiz or test, even when students have slept well. If students cram right before a quiz, as many do, the new fragile memories have had no time to consolidate because the students haven't slept yet in order to process them. Consequently, much of that new information is lost as well. Students survive the quiz but little information gets into long-term memory. When cramming is allowed before a quiz, the quiz does not measure what is available from a stable long-term memory; rather it is a measure of the very unstable early stage of long-term memory. Quizzes or tests that have been crammed for shortly before (and the information was not slept upon) are a lousy indication of what students know. Assessments that are delayed give a much more realistic idea of what is still in their memories. Unfortunately, virtually all public schools are focused on test scores and not what is truly stable and accessible in students' memories. Test scores are mistakenly believed by many in education and by the public to accurately demonstrate learning, but they are a poor representation of learning. We're attempting to assign one or two numbers to represent how much a brain knows, the most complex system in the universe, but the methods in use are only crude guesses. This will be explored in detail in the next chapter.

Building a Better Memory

Mnemonics

Mnemonics are powerful memory strategies for handling large amounts of information, and in the days before printing presses operated, when oral tradition depended on memory, whole books of knowledge were organized and stored in memory for later retrieval (Boorstin, 1983). Acronyms are a familiar form of mnemonics in which the first letters of the acronym represents the first letters of the concept. For example, there are ROY G BIV (for the order of the colors of the rainbow, red, orange, yellow, green, blue, indigo, and violet) and HOMES (for the names of the Great Lakes, Huron, Ontario, Michigan, Erie, and Superior). The more distinctive, bizarre, or personally meaningful the name is, the easier it is to recall. Countless variations may be used. In one, each letter of a bizarre name represents yet another whole mnemonic, which organizes information and provides access to still more details. Here is an example:

LTMIE = **L**ong **T**erm **M**emory **I**mplicit **E**xplicit

You can add another layer of depth under the letters **I** and **E**:

Mnemonic Example With Additional Mnemonic Under **I** and **E**

L T M	**I**	**E**	**I** (implicit)	**E** (Explicit)
	PRO	R	**Pro**cedural	**R**epeated Events
	PER	S	**Per**ceptual	**S**ingle events

LTMIE also demonstrates one of the inherent problems with this form of mnemonic. Many mnemonics are only helpful as long as they are used with sufficient frequency to maintain access to the information. Another problem is that when the information is memorized, the student must know exactly what each letter represents. *If, for any reason, the student forgets a letter, or what the acronym stands for, the information in memory is effectively lost, leaving it inaccessible.* For example, hospital emergency room staff use a series of acronyms to help them recall vital steps to a number of different procedures, but the acronyms are used frequently enough to be maintained. In the classroom, the use of mnemonics often ceases when the class is over. Many students have survived a course by using the acronyms, but within weeks after the course they were unable to recall the information. Looking back at the acronym LTMIE, several problems should become apparent. LTMIE is not particularly distinctive and what "I" and "E" stand for must be used frequently if the connections to information are to be maintained. This represents an excellent example of the "use it or lose it" principle. Using acronyms is frequently a short-term memory skill for classroom survival but is not especially helpful for adolescents wanting to build a stable, accessible memory.

Key Words

Key word mnemonics work well for students when learning the meanings of words in a different language (Atkinson & Raugh, 1975). For example, *el tiempo* is paired with *tempo*, a word that sounds similar. Tempo means speed or time, which is then paired with an image, such as a conductor marking out the time. Tempo provides the linkage for tiempo and time. Tiempo > tempo > (visual image/action: *music conductor*) > time. The image of the music conductor and the action of marking the time are paired, and then associated with the key word. This technique can be useful in math, if practiced to automaticity. For example, when the student sees a particular operation symbol, such as $\sum$, it is pointed out that it resembles a modified S. S is the visual cue for sum; $\sum$ is associated with summing up. If the image (or symbol in this case) is forgotten, then the meaning for the entire sequence is likely to fail. To strengthen the connections, the network must be used repeatedly, and the associated image should be *intentionally visualized*. This same technique is useful when recalling names by making associations with faces. For example, there is a brilliant neuroscientist whose name reminds me of a Russian Cossack, which provides links to his name Kosik, Dr. Ken Kosik. The association sequence is then face > Cossack > Kosik > Dr. Ken Kosik. *Adolescent students often need to be provided the key word* (tempo, Cossack), then they are able to create their own mental images for the links. Reversing the sequence to remember is not necessarily helpful. Backward recall tends to work poorly (for example, when first learning English to Spanish, it does not work well to try to remember the Spanish word first and then translate back to English; Pressley & Dennis-Rounds, 1980).

Narrative Story

Another method that is relatively effective for learning lists (such as a grocery list), or vocabulary, is the *narrative story*. This strategy uses a short one- or two-sentence story that incorporates all the words of the list to be recalled. It might be a grocery list such as *carrots, cabbage, pie, milk, salsa, cookies*. The one-line story to help recall the list could be "Dip the cookies in milk while eating the carrot with salsa poured over the cabbage pie." One study found that after a lapse of several days the group that used a narrative story method was able to recall 93% of the words compared to 13% in the control group (Bower & Clark, 1969).

Imagery/Method of Loci

The method of loci mnemonic, which uses imagery, is one of the oldest memory strategies. It has been around since ancient times. Fixed locations, or loci, are associated with specific stored information. A person imagines a walk he has taken, with a series of fixed locations that he can readily visualize every time and always in the same sequence. Each location is associated with a specific thing to remember, as he mentally "walks" from one location to another. At each location is the stored information that needs to be recalled. The technique was well known even by medieval times, and *thousands* of items or facts could be retrieved. Around 1596, a Jesuit priest named Matteo Ricci was noted for teaching the Chinese the techniques of the "memory walk" (Spence, 1984).

Mnemonic Caveats

Using mnemonics increases the speed of learning in simple recall items. It tends to work better if students can generate the key words, but that is difficult for younger adolescents, and teachers may need to help. Mnemonics do not help with comprehension. They merely allow rapid access to large volumes of facts or information. However, the access to the information is easily broken if a mnemonic is not routinely used. Research is divided about how effective mnemonics are in the long term; some researchers indicate this method is not better than rote memorization. I would recommend judicial use of mnemonics for some problematic lessons, but not routine use in everything, because students' long-term memory needs to rise above regurgitation.

Elaborative Rehearsal and Depth of Processing

Craik and Lockhart (1972) found that a person could increase her recall if she processed the information more thoroughly, and thought about it to a greater depth rather than just giving the information fleeting consideration. This is known as a deeper *level of processing* or *elaborative rehearsal*. When information is in working memory, most of it is given very little attention. It is not mulled over and really considered. That shallow processing usually leads to very poor recall. Deeper, more thorough processing requires more deliberate cognitive effort, and the intentional action may be creating more of an episodic, hence personal, memory (Terry, 2009). A student's elaboration expands the network connections to other related facts and skills stored in long-term memory. The wider network also suggests that a wider range of retrieval cues will succeed at locating the specific memory at a later time. This property also appears to apply to pronouncing names. *A name that a student can't pronounce is one that isn't available in memory for recall.* When the name is pronounceable for a student, the student can gain meaning, make associations, and visualize an image with the name even if it is about an abstract concept (ibid.). To help the students with pronouncing names and to avoid embarrassment, the teacher should point out the problem word and have the entire class, as a group, say it several times. This reduces potential stumbles over the words.

Elaboration

Information that is not elaborated upon probably has only a small network of connections and is more likely to have fewer specific cues available for the mind to locate the information. In a general way, this search is similar to Googling a term on the Internet. If a general term is entered, thousands of potential hits are made. If very specific terms are used, a smaller number of potential items are located. The elaboration creates a wider network, increasing the chances that the student's brain will respond to a cue and make later retrieval easier. As more details are transferred into memory, each detail creates potentially more links that may assist future recall (Schacter, 2001b). When students are more active in the learning, the memory network is strengthened. Students actively transfer more detailed semantic information by taking notes, writing their own examples, drawing and labeling pictures, demonstrating, or peer teaching.

Research evidence suggests three ways in which elaboration may function. First, the information becomes more meaningful when it is thoroughly processed. Second, elaboration can make the information more distinctive. Through elaboration the student becomes aware of, describes, or is able to identify how the information is different from other memories. The more distinctions an adolescent is aware of and able to comment on, the easier it is to find in memory. For example, a student thinks about and lists some characteristics of an elephant, then of a bird. The student can point out many easy distinctions, from size to having hair or feathers. Compare this to having the student describe the differences between the processes of *transmuting* and *transforming*. There are differences, but the effort to distinguish these requires considerably more effort. One problem is when the student searches his memory he is stuck with very similar sounds because both start with "trans." The mind may accidentally pull the wrong file. A similar problem is illustrated when a student is given a definition and recovers an incorrect but similar-sounding term, such as with the bone names metatarsal and metacarpal. Science has hundreds of very similar-sounding words and it is confusing for many students. Nuances in the sounds are particularly difficult because they are even harder for the mind to distinguish in its search for the correct memory.

A third aspect of elaboration also facilitates building a stronger memory: The amount of cognitive effort also influences the memory. It is not necessarily how hard the information is, but how deeply the students explore and probe the concept. Deep judgments require more time to process than simple, shallow judgments (Eysenck & Eysenck, 1979). If the student makes more cognitive effort *during* the period of encoding, and students focus and expand on the meaning or implications of the information, sooner rather than later, they would probably learn more (Kulhavy, Schwartz, & Peterson, 1986). This is *if,* and it is a very big if, the teachers don't make the mistake of making the elaboration tasks so difficult that students become discouraged and demotivated. Combining the appropriate motivational tenets within the properties of working memory is still very much an art.

All three aspects of elaboration—*(1) being meaningful, (2) being distinctive rather than similar, and (3) needing conscious effort*—suggest that mnemonics can be effective. The information is meaningful to the person, the mnemonic is often chosen for its distinctive properties, and conscious effort is needed to remember its meaning. However, the comprehension and understanding that a great depth of processing brings is generally not found with mnemonics. *Lessons that are made meaningful and distinctive and that the students must actively process or make some effort to explore below the surface can create a better chance of moving more information into long-term memory.*

A Sampling of Instructional Strategies for Elaboration
- Describe why the concept, process, person, or object is important.
- Restate the ideas in your own words.
- Connect the reading with things you already know by describing your own personal example.
- Describe or explain the effect of the concept on something.
- Draw your own mind map of the concept with its relationships to others.
- Describe, draw, or explain how the concept is different.
- Describe, illustrate, show, and explain the major characteristics of the concept.

I will often use at least three or four of the above strategies in the same lesson, all targeting the same concept. The students quickly become more astute about the concept. They'll ask, "Dr. S, isn't the same thing as in question 12?" I'll respond, by saying, "What do you think? What is this question referring to? Is that similar to

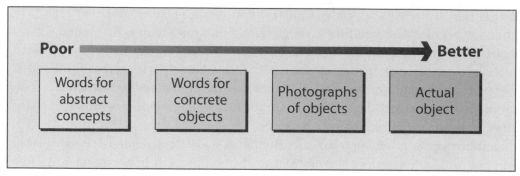

Fig. 8.4. Type of information influences ease of recall.

what was asked in number 12? Tell me how it's similar [or different]." By having the students explore the idea from different angles I intentionally try to build multiple pathways to the same concept as well as build their store of cues to help them at a later time to find the concept.

Limits on Elaboration

On the TV show *Wheel of Fortune* contestants use only a few letters as cues and try to complete a word or phrase in the word puzzle. Word fragment games used in research tests are similar. However, even though a person might have employed the deeper processing elaboration techniques to create the original memory, the practice elaboration does not appear to help them to complete the fragmented word (Bowers & Schacter, 1990). I've seen numerous commercial worksheets that use word completion activities. Although convenient for the teacher, these worksheets may be a waste of time in helping the students to develop a deeper understanding.

Verbal elaboration may also limit memory for pictures or drawing. Using words to describe pictures or other nonverbal information inhibits the recall of the image itself. Less accurate recall of the images may result because the words are encoded rather than the image or the visual event (Schooler, Ryan, & Reder, 1996). Many textbooks for all ages incorporate diagrams and photographs that illustrate important concepts. *Actual objects are better recalled than photographic images, but photographic images in general are usually easier to recall than words* (Nelson & Schreiber, 1992; Standing, Conezio, & Haber, 1970). *In terms of recall, words for concrete things that can be visualized by the student are easier to recall, while words for abstractions are the most difficult to recall* (see Figure 8.4). Have the students draw the essentials of the illustration and add their own descriptions rather than just describing the supplied image. Practice a few repetitions of the drawing and use simple explanations. Words are usually encoded with one system in the brain while pictures are encoded through two: a visual translation and a verbal translation of the image that create a semantic memory. This is known as *dual processing*. Additionally, visual images are usually more distinctive than words (Paivio, 1969).

Didn't They Learn Anything?

After teaching a while, many educators will have witnessed spectacular crashes in student memory, sometimes on topics in which the teachers have worked diligently over days or weeks with the students. My own experience came early in my teaching career. I was sitting in the back of a colleague's room grading papers while he lectured. The teacher asked about something related to a topic I had taught to the students the year before. In fact, when they were freshman, I had spent a week of class time on the problem, carefully having each student calibrate, calculate, and plot information. When the present class, now sophomores, moved on to discuss the same topic 1 year later, no one appeared to even recognize it, let alone recall anything about it. Their silence was deafening. Horrified, I joined in and started to ask the students some probing questions. Still nothing. I felt chastened in front of my fellow teacher. Questions ripped through my mind. Had they learned nothing? Had the time been a total waste? Had I done that lousy of a job? What had happened that even the best performing students couldn't recall anything? I'm still working on the answers, but research has begun to get a handle on the problem of how long memories last.

Countless educators have had similar disquieting experiences and have questioned what their colleagues were doing in the classes before them, and whether they were teaching anything at all. That was the old blame game. While I've not heard such accusations recently, all educators are very dependent on what our fellow professionals are able to accomplish before them. Like Isaac Newton, we "stand on the shoulders of giants"; educators build on the earlier successes or failures of others (Newton, 1675). Each educator is part of the foundation for those who follow. In fact, even when it seems that students haven't retained anything that they can either recognize or recall, the earlier efforts still make a difference. Re-learning is accomplished at a much faster rate (MacLeod, 1988). Neural traces were established, and although the paths are weak, they form a foundation to build upon. Our expectations of students and fellow staff need to be grounded not only on how we establish a memory, but also on the rate at which that memory fades or decays.

The rate of forgetting

Hermann Ebbinghaus in 1885 was one of the first to study the rate of forgetting by using three-letter nonsense syllables (Ebbinghaus, 1913). Using himself as his entire sample in a carefully designed experiment, he found that his memory rapidly plummeted. Gradually his memory for the syllables stabilized, not dropping to zero (see Figure 8.5). Although the pattern does not directly apply to all learning situations, the pattern of forgetting is still quite significant to educators because the decline in memory affects a student's test performance. It hints at how much memory may be left long after the lesson; additionally, the timing for when an assessment is conducted after the lesson will also have considerable effect on the results. Further, the methods of instruction, the age of the student, and the type of memory be-

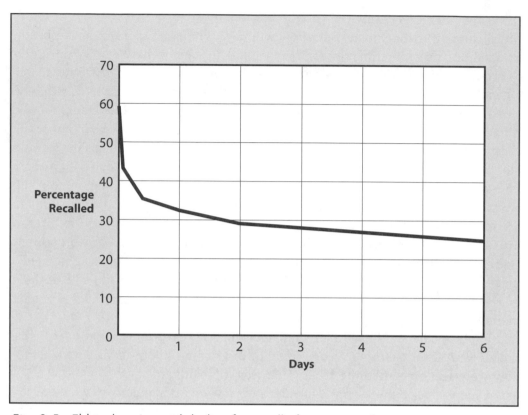

Fig. 8.5. Ebbinghaus's rapid decline for recall of nonsense information.

ing assessed all have a significant bearing on how rapidly memory decays. *Because memories are not created equally, not all will fade in the same pattern as Ebbinghaus showed.* Memories for significant personal events seem to stay quite vivid, such as the day a person witnesses or experiences a major celebration or tragedy. These are known as flashbulb memories.

Flashbulb memories

The flashbulb memories record events that are personally very important. The idea is that a memory for some dramatic, emotional event is frozen in memory, like an image is frozen in time with a camera's flash. For example, do you recall where you were when you learned of the terrorist attacks on 9/11? Most of us can. But can you also recall what you were wearing? Most of us can't. It is the same time, same event, with two profoundly different memory strengths. The attack created a very stable episodic memory. However, the other memory for the clothing, a semantic memory, was no better than other semantic memories whose details have long since faded. *In education, most lessons are semantically based, and teachers need to be very aware of how naturally unstable their students' semantic memories are.*

A further examination of Ebbinghaus's data in Figure 8.5 provokes several questions. Does semantic memory always decline in this pattern? What if an adolescent recalls only part of the information but recognizes other portions? There are vast differences between recalling information and recognizing it.

Recognition and recall

In recognition, the memory is fragmentary. With only a few bits of information the students can tell if they've seen the information before, but they can't recall the missing details. The capacity for recognition is huge; no one is quite sure how many thousands of items can be recognized within a single category, such as houses (Standing, 1973). The problem is the lack of details. Recognition produces only weak connections and it is unable to retrieve details necessary for an adequate student performance. Students will sometimes mistakenly believe that they have studied sufficiently when they are able to recognize names and other information. Indeed they may have *looked* at it or heard it, but they are unable to provide details or explanations because there has been virtually no elaboration. Our tests frequently don't help either. Multiple-choice tests made by teachers often depend heavily on recognition, which may require recall of only shallow detail and possibly simple, if any, problem solving. Assessments should probe below the shallow level of recognition and simple recall. Let's look at an example involving recognition memory.

In a social studies class students were required to "know who the following people were: Thomas Jefferson, Richard Nixon, Mao Tse Tung." That requires only minimal recognition and by itself is probably not significant in education because it doesn't create any understanding. Expanding the question to knowing *what they did* rises ever so slightly to a level of shallow recall and might be useful in creating some mediocre understanding. *Explaining why they took certain actions* starts requiring some elaboration and finding connections. That can lead to useful learning.

During recall, a student can retrieve considerably more details but only for a much smaller number of items. Knowing how detailed recall is created for a few items is important to educators because how the lesson was originally taught and the age of the student make a difference in how much can be successfully recalled by the student. As a result, there is a wide variance in the recall pattern of memory decay. The next section will explore how differences in the instructional method (or encoding) can affect recall in long-term memory over a period of days or even months.

Long-Term Memory in the Classroom

In a series of long-term memory developmental studies that I conducted, which involved more than 300 second graders to 12th graders, a series of memory patterns emerged. These generally resembled Ebbinghaus's sample of one, but with important distinctions, which are summarized in Table 8.1. As the student's age increased, the number of common items that could be recalled also increased except for seventh graders, aged 12 to 13, which may be a sign of a developmental issue.

Table 8.1. DEVELOPMENTAL DIFFERENCES IN SIMPLE RECALL FOR STUDENTS, AGED 7 TO 18, FOR 24 COMMON OBJECTS		
Grade	**Age**	**Mean Items Recalled**
2nd	7–8	4.9
4th	9–10	5.9
5th	10–11	8.7
6th	11–12	10.4
7th	12–13	9.4
10th	15–16	12.1
12th	17–18	3.1

Figures 8.6 and 8.7 illustrate the different effects of personal elaboration and significance. Personal elaboration in which students provide their own examples, paraphrase a concept, or use the information to make decisions or applications, creates information that is personally more meaningful, which generates stronger links to memory (Rogers et al., 1977). Typically, that will lead to a higher level of lasting recall for most students.

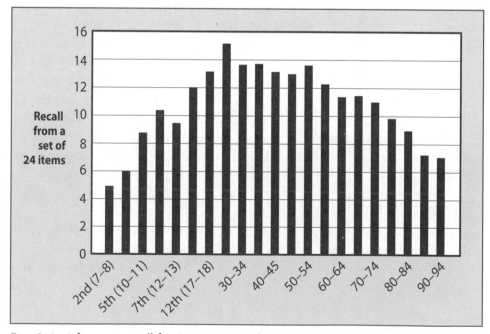

Fig. 8.6. Life-span recall for 24 common objects.

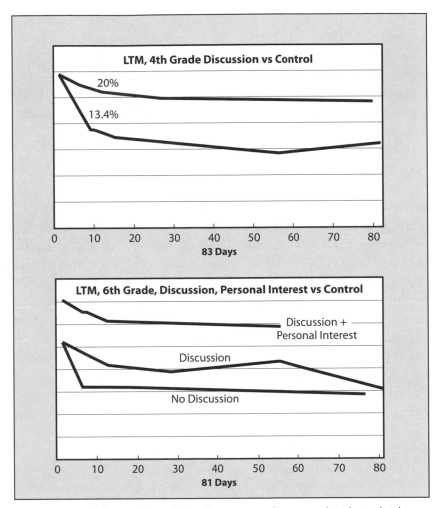

Fig. 8.7. Memory decline for 24 common objects with 4th and 6th grade students. When students had a single discussion of the items, recall remained higher, except in 6th graders. When there was personal interest in the task and a single discussion, recall remained considerably higher.

A Summary of Long-Term Memory Patterns

- In the life-span recall pattern, the maximum initial recall of visual information appears to be after adolescence in the late twenties, with a slow tapering until the seventies, where the rate of memory decay accelerates.
- As students become older their long-term memory recall progressively increases. In Table 8.1 and Figure 8.4 there is a steady increase through age 18, except for 12- to 13-year-olds, which may be part of a development cycle. Educators can expect students to recall more each year except possibly for a period during middle school. A drop in recall performance at this age may not be due to poor teaching.

- Long-term memory typically stabilizes after about 2 weeks. Educators can expect a large initial drop, but the method of instruction will make a difference in the initial drop and eventual level of recall. Hands-on activities without personal significance produced no real lasting gains.
- When middle school students (sixth graders) were personally interested, the recall was nearly twice the level of students passively processing information and still considerably higher even for those students who discussed the information.
- When students personally elaborate, the recall levels are much higher.

Producing Robust Long-Term Memory From Physical Actions

An enduring educational problem is what accessible memory is left long after the lesson. What have the students really taken away from the lessons? Considering how working memory rapidly sheds information, and still more information fades shortly after a lesson, I believe *it is imperative to identify the most significant information that still needs to be available after most everything else is forgotten, and to know what instructional method will make the longest lasting and accessible memory for that crucial information.* This goes past the politicization of standards by special interests; educators should know what students most urgently need that will be useful for life. As for the instructional methods that produce long-lasting and accessible memory, we have precious little information available.

Long-term memory for actions provides a hint that some teaching strategies create more stable long-term memory. Teaching strategies that use physical action when combined with a procedure create episodic memories. It usually takes only a few trials to stabilize the memory. Semantic information is layered on top of episodic memories as the student elaborates on the actions they are performing. These combined strategies work well with complex or abstract material, but they are not equally effective for every subject. I have repeatedly used these methods for the past decade with the most complicated and abstract material. Not only has student memory remained stable, but the students find the strategies a relief when tackling difficult material.

Before strategies are presented, a bit of background is necessary to understand what is happening in Figures 8.8 and 8.9. Students performed a learning task as part of regular classwork, where they had to recall the names of proteins and their complex movements, positions, and sequence of actions in describing how a gene is turned on. There was a lot of information to master; 10 *sets* of information were divided into 7 steps. A thorough written explanation of the process required more than a full single-spaced page. The original experiment was conducted with both 17- to 18-year-olds (n = 24) and 15- to 16-year-olds (n = 31). As expected, the older adolescent had greater lasting recall than the younger sophomores. I call the learning process Complex Subject Performed Tasks (SPTc) because it will involve the student physically manipulating paper models and verbally reviewing the names

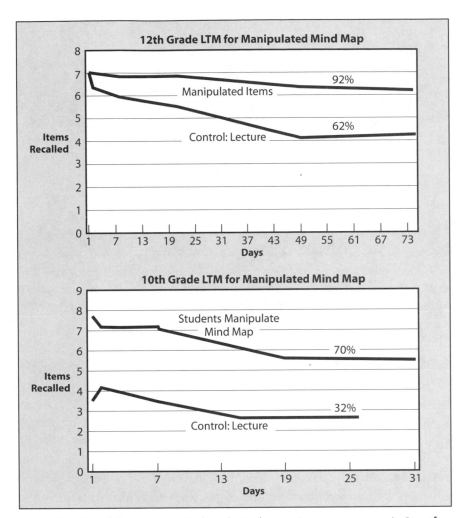

Fig. 8.8. Recall from a manipulated mind map (or concept map). Significantly greater recall resulted by manipulation and elaboration on items. Developmental differences are also evident.

of the parts and their respective functions and movements. The lesson was presented only once, with a review in the same class period. It was never reviewed after that day. Multiple forms of memory are involved, including episodic, spatial, tactile, semantic, and procedural, any of which may become cues to enhance later recall. The precipitous decline that classically marks other forms of instruction (see Figure 8.7) is greatly diminished, producing a higher, stable level of recall after the initial 2 weeks. In Figure 8.8, the 10th-grade sample, the younger adolescents' recall is lower, and it still takes approximately 2 weeks before memory tends to stabilize. However, when students personally perform a physical task, and simultaneously explain what they are doing, there is considerably greater initial and later recall.

In the following section I will describe how to implement the combined instruc-

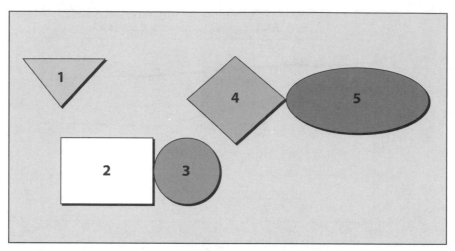

Fig. 8.9. Mind map or concept map with a sequence. Each piece of information has its own unique shape, color and position. Students practice manipulating the parts and explaining to mastery or slightly beyond what each one represents and its relationship to the next object.

tional strategies. All students practiced (in a single class period) until mastery was reached (85%) for either the traditional lecture mode or the SPTc mode. With the paper model functioning like a mind map that can be manipulated, it is not unusual to have students reach 95–100%. A detailed recall was produced by 12th graders who actively performed tasks to mastery and explained what they were doing as they manipulated objects. The retention level stabilized near 90% after only a single lesson. Assessments were written. Teaching the lesson by SPTc took about 8 minutes, and the lecture for identical material required 15 minutes. When the lecture was used as a control, the seniors needed 15 minutes and the sophomores took 40 minutes. The instructor modeled the process, with students following along with their own paper models. Presentation by SPTc was considerably faster. Although the students were exposed to the material only once in all cases, there may be a test effect because of the repeated assessments.

Overview for Building a Robust Memory

In the opening of this chapter, I described a student in a college class recalling in a test situation a mind map that she had physically manipulated in practice and which had created an accessible and fairly accurate memory. This teaching strategy (SPTc) will be described next. Although it may seem complicated, the actual process for building the memory is fairly simple because it uses a variation of the concept or mind map.

Using shapes as a mind map

In a concept map or mind map each shape represents something with significant differences (see Figure 8.9). First, each object will have its own unique shape and color. Second, instead of the student filling out labels on a sheet, all the objects are cut out (it is best to have the students do this to save you time) and a complete set of objects is then placed into an envelope for each student. The idea is to *make a mind map that can be physically manipulated by shape, color, and position.* The students will explain or elaborate upon how the shapes relate to each other. One side of each object can have the label (so it can also function like a flash card).

Creating the memory

The shapes may be used either in a specific sequence like a flowchart if needed or like a standard mind map; the parts are clustered around key items in dynamic relationships as in Figure 8.10. In the memory experiment on how a gene switches on, a sequential process was used with a distinct start and finish. In actual teaching practices for both methods, *the principle of practice past perfection is used. Mastery performance merely suggests that most, but not all, of the memory network has fired correctly at least once.* However, as the data have repeatedly demonstrated, long-term memory is initially unstable. Stopping with a single correct, physically practiced performance is inadequate for complex tasks. Consider an athletic, music, or drama performance. Any coach, band instructor, or drama teacher can tell you one correct practice run is not enough. The student performance is not yet stabilized. *Practicing past perfection* permits repeated correct firing of the network to facilitate the stability of the memory. In order to avoid a cramming effect, ask the students to have an initial mass practice, then space out subsequent practices.

Method for sequential events

Each item, or "player," has its own name, unique color, and unique shape. It is possible that each may be textured as well. Students may identify players by color alone, or even by shape. They are also creating a mental spatial map if they practice blindfolded. (Using both methods is helpful.) As the student picks up the player, they name it, state what it does, why it is significant, and where it goes in relationship to the others. This provides both spatial and semantic information. Each player or object is identified in turn, and its function and relationships to other objects or processes is elaborated upon (this creates deeper personal elaboration). Each player is physically picked up and moved to its appropriate position (this forms spatial / kinesthetic memory). If a student has a leftover part and can't recall a player's function or relationship, they have gained immediate feedback that they are missing that portion of the memory. The process allows self-monitoring. No one has to tell him or her that not all of the processes and relationships are correct. The goal is to have all the players in sequence, correctly elaborated upon, and relationships explained. The process is repeated, but identification is accomplished tactilely by feeling the shapes in order to create a mental visual image of the item and its spatial relationships.

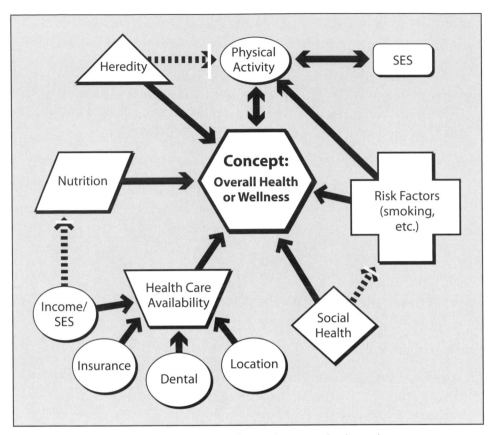

Fig. 8.10. Mind map with dynamic relationships. Each object has a representative shape and relationship with other information. As the students moves each item into place, they explain what it is and its relationship, but they may start at any point. Also the removal of an item may change relationships, so multiple forms of the model may exist, allowing deeper levels of understanding to be demonstrated.

The entire process is *practiced past perfection* about 7–10 times with no errors. Practice the assessment, too. If the student is required to write out the process or relationships, practice that right after the physical manipulation. Repeat the process 2–3 days later, followed by brief random practices across several weeks or months. The delay forces the mind to work harder, and though it is initially more difficult, the memory performance is higher and produces longer-lasting learning.

Circular or dynamic relationships

The overall process is the same, except that there is no specific starting or stopping point. Each player has its own distinct shape, which serves as a tactile cue, and its physical relationship or proximity to other cues. The student may also elaborate on each player's relationships in such a way so that if one or two items are removed, the student can elaborate on the new resulting dynamics or relationships (see Figure 8.10).

Developing Specific Teaching Strategies for Increasing Student Long-Term Memory

Focus on the Long-Term Goal

For each unit or major lesson, what should the students really take with them after everything else is forgotten? It may be one or two items of knowledge, principles, or skills. We do know that much of the knowledge or facts we teach will soon be out of date except for some fundamental information. Although the most essential principles or items of knowledge should have been identified and established earlier, they may not have been. For these memory strategies to work, the learning goal of principle or knowledge needs to be written, along with several supporting goals. Make sure you also know whether the student should eventually be able to demonstrate those goals or articulate them by explanation, writing, or some combination. *The student's performance after your class is over represents the long-term memory goal.*

With the eventual goal in mind select specific methods of instruction to build a retrievable memory. Don't limit the initial instruction to a single method, but keep all strategies focused on the same goal. Additional methods of instruction and earning modalities can be added later during the review processes. Plan the lesson, re-inforcement around the goal, with other knowledge and skills playing a supporting role. Emphasize the goal to the students. However, don't assume the students know the goal. They should be able to state and explain the long-term goal, not just recognize it. For example, the long-term goal or principle that the students really need to learn is "Key supporting skills, knowledge, and principles." Going deeper, should the student be able to use the principle, knowledge, or skill in multiple ways? Is the goal mere recognition, or a deeper use of the information that perhaps requires some reflective thinking?

Summary

Long-term memory is the bedrock of learning and exists in multiple forms, most notably one that is consciously available and can be expressed in language, or in a nonverbal form for actions and procedures. Memory for repeated events is known as semantic memory, and it requires multiple practices to become stable, while single episodic events are memories from our personal history, which is often coupled with emotional information and is more stable. Nonverbal procedural memory is taking an action, like riding a bicycle. The more personally involved adolescents are with the learning process, the more their attention, emotional systems, and working memory are involved. Instructional methods to build stronger long-term memory include experiential learning and the use of mnemonics for lists of information. Confronting and changing misconceptions (alternative conceptions) is at best difficult because of the default processing by the brain. One method to address the false ideas or misconceptions is the Conceptual Change Model. False memories are of events that never happened; however, these can be accidentally created by children, adolescents, or adults. False memories are especially tragic in sexual abuse allegations. It is essential that the persons doing the debriefings be thoroughly trained.

Absentmindedness is common to many students and adults alike. One of the keys to reducing absentmindedness is to actively note the actions being taken with small items so that the items are not misplaced. To make long-term memory more stable another major technique is the use of elaboration in which the students actively expand upon the concepts or information. The stability of a memory is significantly influenced by sleep, or the lack of it. Sleep deprivation may interfere both with recall of information learned earlier, but also with the laying down of new memories, such as in cramming for an exam. A common experience among educators is to witness the apparent loss of memory of earlier lessons. One of the goals of education should be to establish stable and accessible memories for essential information long after the lessons cease. One method is to combine the students' physical actions, while they elaborate on the components of the lesson. Such a task creates episodic/personal memories for the lesson, as well as greater semantic memory, all coupled with spatial, tactile, and kinesthetic memories, resulting in robust memories for complex and abstract actions. Long-term memory is not a simple storage system of knowledge and skills but is a complex, variegated series of networks that can be greatly influenced by the instructional methods.

Key Points and Recommendations

- *If a teacher is able to help students in making multiple memories where each networks to the same topic, there is a greater chance that the specific memory can be found at a later time.* A larger network for a memory is like a larger target: It is easier to get a hit on some aspect of it and then use that to connect more detail. One way to do this is to use several teaching strategies that incorporate different forms of memory for the same concept. For example, consider using multiple intelligences and different sensory modalities.

- *Semantic memory lies at the heart of most traditional education, and it is there that a student's academic fortunes often rise or fall because so many lessons are presented in this restricted form.* Most assessments use verbal or written language. Teachers can assist students' performances by giving lessons in which the students take personal actions that they can describe or more easily recall.

- *Episodic memories are memories from our personal history and, when properly used, they can provide powerful linkages to semantic information.* As noted above, a personal action is easier to recall, especially if the students are physically active and elaborating on what they are doing and why they are doing it. Physical actions that can be elaborated upon include playing pantomime or charades, role playing, constructing models and projects and posters, making public service announcements, and developing a Power-Point presentation.

- *Combining procedural memory with semantic and episodic memories can create very robust memories for abstract concepts because students are also creating personal memories (episodic memory) for actions they took (procedural memory), while describing what they are doing (semantic memory).* Personal memories are the easiest to recall because the student is the star in his or her memory. If he or she is sitting passively and doing nothing there is nothing to distinguish the memory from thousands of others. The more distinctive the memory is, the easier it is to locate at a later time.

- *Experiential learning is something like a natural series of discovery learning lessons.* It is essentially one distinctive memory after another, often with personal action and emotional significance. The stage is set or framed by the teacher so the student is primed in how he or she will view the learning activity. This is followed by a direct debriefing, which is used to bridge to an application and possibly an activity. The learning continuously builds on prior experiences. It is thoroughly student-centered. Experiential learning is probably one of the most powerful ways to teach multiple lessons and link them in a natural manner. When the opportunity arises, carefully plan out a number of lessons that will generate these powerful episodic memories. For example, students research, prepare, and present a proposal to a community group. It is important that members of the community interact and actually discuss the proposal with the students, rather than merely thanking the students and accepting their proposal for consideration. The presentation and subsequent discussion is followed up back in class (the debriefing). Students make adjustments and use it to revisit the community group or to take a different path of action. The point is that the students apply what they have learned from the debriefing. Good experiential lessons take planning and coordination.

- *Incidental learning for important concepts, attitudes, and skills can be woven into experiential learning or regular classroom activities.* Rather than have such "accidental" opportunities, plan the little hidden lessons. They are often picked up by the students without the teacher having to be overt about them. Incidental learning can be used to accelerate lessons because the students will have already learned key information in earlier "incidental" activities (i.e., hidden academic agendas).

- *Mnemonics are powerful ways to retrieve large lists of information. However, if for any reason, the student forgets a letter, or what the acronym stands for, the information in memory is effectively lost, leaving it inaccessible.* If there are a multitude of items to memorize, and elaboration is not necessary at this stage, mnemonics can be a powerful tool. It is important to realize that most students will probably forget most of the mnemonics fairly soon, and the mnemonics should probably be considered as a temporary aid to survive some assessment. Information that is critical in the long run should be taught with other methods in order to create a lasting network. Mnemonics don't build a wide network base; hence a search in memory will usually turn up empty if the single connection is lost.

- *Acceptance or rejection of a concept: New information will further reinforce the concept if it is consistent with both old cues and prior information is passed on to further reinforce the concept. The result is the creation of an ever-widening network.* The mind does not ignore information that is similar or matches with one's beliefs; however, there is very little reflective thought given to information that agrees with prior concepts. A thoughtful challenge to deepen students' understanding is often absent. Meanwhile, information that does not match with prior concepts may be automatically dismissed and given no further thought, perpetuating the problem of still maintaining the misconception. Once a new conception is established, it is likely to be fragile for a while until well used. Back sliding should be expected.

- *It doesn't matter how much evidence is presented if the student can't or chooses not to think at a more reflective level. Simply defaulting to "Because _____ said so" is much easier for the mind because the effort involved in thinking is not required.* When presenting a logical argument and showing a mountain of data, graphs are unconvincing. Many people have difficulty processing numbers or abstract representations that explain or "prove" some idea, but they can more readily see the relationships when they are presented as a simple, unambiguous image. A bit of Zen is used in the approach. This is what the best presentations, sales pitches, and advertisements do. Numbers and charts are very convincing for many people, but pictures, especially emotionally laden ones, can be. The groundwork for building a conceptual shift is established with their predictions and experiencing the result along with visuals (pictures) and emotional responses. For example, if social issues were being addressed in class, and statistics, graphs, and charts were being used to make the case, what is there to hold the students' attention? How do they emotionally connect with a number? Then a few supporting numbers and simple graphs can be used in the exploration and elaboration of the topic. When it comes to working bias and rigidly held concepts, the teacher has to open the door to his or her mind first, before the supporting ideas can be effective.

- *Conceptual change activities are student-centered rather than teacher-centered. The new concepts and the discovery of new explanations are the students' experiences, and thus emotionally connected.* By having the students accumulate a series of experiences as a result of their own predictions, the students will personalize the new concept.

- *False memories are memories for events or experiences that never happened but that a person believes to be true. False memories can be created by children, adolescents, and adults, although children appear to be more susceptible.* Educators and others must be careful in how they frame their questions because the questions may create linkages that gradually build up a memory for something that never happened. If the false concept is repeated enough, it may become well established in the memory.

- *How teachers frame a question may alter how the student remembers.* Even on tests and review items, the way that teachers word questions can make it easier or more difficult to recall. If the object is to find out what the student knows as opposed to his or her ability to wade through the language of a question, then reconsider the intent of the assessment. Questions that weave and contort information may also inadvertently create false ideas or concepts that the student can't distinguish from true facts.

- *A key to solving the problem of absentmindedness is that thought should be given to an object while it was being placed.* It takes practice, but the act of subvocalizing (saying to yourself), "I'm placing the assignment here on the . . ." usually provides sufficient attention to recall the item. Merely looking at the item as it is placed is not enough.

- *The solution to the problem of forgetting assignments is having a reminder or cue already in place so that when students see it, they are prompted to attend to their schoolwork.* The reminder needs to be placed in such a manner that it is impossible for the student to ignore. Several strategically placed reminders may help, such as on the notebook, inside a locker door, on the refrigerator, or inside of the door, all at eye level.

- *No cue at the right time can mean no cue in mind.* The cue or reminder must be present at the right time and place. Telling students at the end of the class to remember to do their homework is not as effective as a reminder later that is presented where they can't avoid it.

- *A name or word that a student can't pronounce is one that isn't available in memory for recall.* Students may recognize the name, but they can't recall it for use unless they can pronounce it because a memory will not have been created.

- *Elaboration has three properties. The information (1) is being meaningful, (2) is distinctive rather than similar, and (3) can be moved more into long-term memory, when generalized to other lessons.* If the student practices have these qualities, there is a greater likelihood they will be able to recall more information about the topic.

- *Actual objects are better recalled than photographic images, but photographic images in general are usually easier to recall than words. And words for concrete things that can be visualized are easier to recall than words for abstractions.* The more real the object or concept is, the more easily it will be recalled. Subjects with abstract concepts, such as math and science, need to make the concepts as concrete as possible to help the students visualize what is happening. When they can see concepts as images in their mind, they can start to manipulate them and describe what is happening.

- *Pulling all-nighters to prepare for tests in hopes of a better grade is a lousy bet. The lack of asleep affects cognitive performance for retrieving previously learned material. The lack of sleep also impinges upon the student's ability to acquire new information.* Trying to build a retrievable memory at the last moment goes against how most memories are formed. Because adolescents (even through college) will often not initiate good study practices to build up the memory, it is important that the initial instruction be conducted to build up a number of networks to the memory. That means teaching in a variety of modalities and having the students be personally active and providing their own elaborations over multiple practices.

- *Memories are not created equally; not all will fade in the same manner.* Each type of memory has its own properties. Educators should not expect all concepts to be equally recalled if they were taught in different manners creating different memory strengths.

- *In education, most lessons are semantically based, and teachers need to be very aware of how naturally unstable their students' semantic memories are.* Assessments are frequently conducted within a day or two of a review. If the lesson is largely based in language (written or verbal), much of the memory is still unstable and will rapidly decrease, depending on how the lesson was taught (semantic versus elaboration with actions, building episodic memories).

- *Recognition memory works with fragmented information.* Recognition is one of the "lowest forms" of memory and provides almost no detail. Students who operate at this level can tell if they've seen the information before; however, they can't recall the missing details. Make certain the lesson targets higher levels of thinking if you're going to spend the time to teach it.

- *In long-term memory there is a period of rapid memory decline and then it stabilizes. Additionally, the more personally involved the students are with the lesson, the greater the recall will be.* Around 2 weeks many forms of long-term memory start to stabilize. If the educator really wants to know what is retained, delay the assessment for at least 2 weeks. Otherwise, the assessment is probably measuring how much is in the unstable portion of memory.

- *It is imperative to identify the most significant information that still needs to be available after most everything else is forgotten, and to know what instructional method will make the longest-lasting memory for that crucial information.* It is not a one-size-fits-all style of assessment. Lesson instruction should be tailored for the type of memory that the students will most likely need. If there is any overriding goal for directing instruction on any unit in any class, this is it. It should drive most of what education does, yet most teachers don't have the tools for achieving this goal.

- *The principle of "practice past perfection" should be used. Mastery performance merely suggests that most but not all of the memory network has fired correctly at least once.* Too often students and teachers cease to practice once the students have gotten everything correct. That simply means the appropriate network finally connected properly just once. The connections are not stable. Practice past perfection in order to stabilize the networks, and do it within assessment-like conditions to achieve better performances.

RESOURCES

Interview protocol (full version, background is given first, protocol is further down in the document): http://www.ncbi.nlm.nih.gov/pmc/articles/PMC2180422/

Simpler 10-step interview protocol: http://works.bepress.com/cgi/viewcontent .cgi?article = 1004&context = thomaslyon

Engelkamp, J. (Ed.). (2001). *Memory for action: Essays in cognitive psychology.* New York: Oxford University Press.

Loftus, E., & Ketcham, K. (1994). *The myth of repressed memory: False memories and allegations of sexual abuse.* New York: St. Martin's.

Schacter, D. (1996). *Searching for memory: The brain, the mind, and the past.* New York: Basic Books.

Terry, W. S. (2008). *Learning and Memory, basic principles, and procedures* (4th ed.). New York: Allyn & Bacon.

CHAPTER NINE
Review, Studying, and Assessment

I didn't fail the test,
I just found 100 ways to do it wrong.
—Benjamin Franklin

During the class review held earlier that week it was evident that Will clearly knew the material. He could explain the concepts and perform the calculations. When the test was set out, it was just as obvious that Will was a wreck, jittery, with a frightened look in his eyes like a prisoner facing certain execution. The teacher saw at once that this was not normal behavior for Will. A number of other students were displaying similar nervous behaviors, because the test was very high stakes, one that determined their future directions. The teacher stopped the class, not allowing the test to start. He began talking, slowly, reassuringly, reminding them of how they had attacked many of the math problems in previous days. Gradually the class members relaxed. Finally, the teacher said, "Okay, you know how to do the problems, you've done them before, it's the same stuff, just like class, another day of practice." Because it was a blocked class, there were 2 hours available, even though the exam required barely an hour. Will relaxed, as did the rest of the class members. Everyone not only passed, but the lowest score was a B. The teacher had done an extraordinary job of not only preparing the students, but also intervening to build their confidence in what they rightfully perceived as a very important exam.

The learning process extends naturally through review and rehearsal techniques, bringing both the student and teacher full circle to assessments. It is in the assessments that the students demonstrate their success in being able to retrieve, on demand, the memories representing various skills and knowledge and to show what has been learned. *Although the review and rehearsals are the last preparations before the assessment, new learning is still taking place.* During the review processes new material, new insights, and relationships are still connecting with older memories. Think of rehearsals as a slightly different form of review, like a dress rehearsal for a play. In rehearsal, the skills are polished and the existing connections are strengthened with an assortment of techniques.

Throughout the earlier chapters I assembled a larger and more diverse toolbox of cognitive skills that will allow educators to address a wider range of learning problems. With these cognitive tools in hand, we will examine methods of review, then finally assessments.

The Process of Reviewing

The word "review" itself suggests that the student is looking at or considering information or skills again. Certainly, that is still the case in most learning situations, but research on studying has grown extensively beyond just looking back over the materials, as we will see.

Considering all the information and strategies presented so far, there is a substantial amount of information to keep in mind because it has a culminating effect on study and assessment. With that in mind, educators must also be very aware of what they are asking the student's mind/brain systems to do as they study. To avoid overloading working memory, a quick checklist at the end of this section may be easily copied and used if needed.

In-Class Note Taking

For almost everyone, simply looking over something doesn't give a sufficient boost to memory, so memory aids were developed. If we were to visit with our students, their metacognitive view of note taking would probably be something like, "I'm told I have to do it. It's boring." I've almost never encountered young students who really grasped the concept that note taking was a memory aid to assist them. They were just required to do it, without understanding why.

However, note taking is also more than a memory aid: *It can increase learning if certain strategies are used.* Learning to take notes that are useful, however, is a challenge, especially for students who are just beginning or still learning how to do it. These skills in development will probably encompass a student's entire school career, even into the college years. Hence, the ideas throughout this chapter may be applicable to learners across many age groups.

Students' note-taking skills progressively mature as they learn during reading or a lecture to identify what is important by abbreviating, paraphrasing, and stating concepts in their own words as they build their comprehension (Van Dijk & Kintsch, 1983). Note-taking skills are just that: skills that must be taught and nurtured. Yet, too often teachers merely assume that the students have learned these and the skills are in place, leaving their meager directions to only "all right, get out your notes." Then students are left to their own devices. Students need to be taught what is important, how to recognize it, along with several methods of note taking; all of this should be initially directed by their teacher.

When students from middle school and high school are left on their own, their notes are frequently a hash of words, is disorganized, and has illegible key words. When students go back to study or find something in their notes, it is an arduous task for many to even locate the material, let alone make any sense of it. I can recall a number of times where a student's notes looked as if they had gone through a blender. There were fragments of words and phrases all in a spectacular jumble. Although I knew what I was looking for in trying to help the student, I still had considerable difficulty even finding a section in the notes that might be distantly related to what was presented. If I had trouble, how on earth was the student going to find anything, let alone comprehend it? Note taking is a skill, but some forms lend themselves far more readily to student improvement than others.

Styles of Note Taking

Working memory is rapidly overloaded because it can't sustain a large cognitive load (Baddeley, 2007). When the cognitive load is paired with its other property of tight focus on just one thing at a time, taking usable notes is going to be a challenge. One of education's dilemmas is how to reduce this continuously overwhelming load and still improve long-term retention. *Note taking as a memory aid works only if the proper notes are acquired first.*

When students begin to take notes, it often happens that they laboriously try to write down everything that they hear and to spell all words correctly. By the time they finish a sentence, the teacher may have spoken another dozen or more sentences. Note taking is more than transcribing what is heard; it goes beyond even just writing observations and thoughts. It also *implies comprehension* of the material (Van Dijk & Kintsch, 1983). In the face of unrelenting pressure to keep up, students need to learn to abbreviate, use short cuts, reflect, and paraphrase (Piolat, Olive, & Kellogg, 2005). In older adolescents, *effective note taking can reduce the cognitive load so that the student is able to listen, briefly reflect on what he has heard, and still record pertinent information along with personal comments.* All of these actions potentially interfere with timely note taking, making both comprehension and learning even more deficient (ibid.).

Younger students also need to learn to do more than transcribe what is said. Cognitive overload is the principal obstacle to doing more than simple note taking, and much of that overload is caused by the differences in speaking and writing (Yeung, Jin, & Sweller, 1997). *A person can speak about 2 to 3 words a second but can only write 1/10 as fast, about 0.2 to 0.3 word a second* (Piolat et al., 2005). The brain does not process written language as fast as it does spoken language. Almost immediately, the student is inundated with too many words for working memory to hold. The cognitive load on the student's working memory is tremendous.

At first, the student is faced with three options when they must take notes. One is to just listen. A second option is to read the material written on the board or in a PowerPoint, which leaves few if any notes to work with in order to reduce the cognitive load. A third option is to transcribe what is heard or read, but not have time to think about it. The problem is to create a viable fourth option, where a student can listen or read and take usable notes at a rapid pace without overloading. It is the teacher who will need to provide guidance and the means for students to accomplish this. The teacher must provide effective options for note taking.

Writing Their Own Notes

In traditional note taking, students write all their own notes, such as outlining, or recording information in a linear, sequential fashion. But that method is not as effective as using nonlinear, graphic organizers where students fill in tables, figures, columns, and mind maps, when it comes to helping students comprehend and remember. In a comparison of traditional and nonlinear forms of note taking for classroom lectures, the nonlinear style produced 20% greater comprehension (Makany, Kemp, & Dror, 2009). In traditional note taking, even with an outline to guide students, the working memory is rapidly overloaded because of the amount of transcribing going on. Many key pieces of information go missing, making later study even more difficult.

Outlining

Although not ideal, the traditional format of outlining is better than much of the disorganized jumble that constitutes many students' transcribing. However, the teacher must supply the basic outline for students. Provide younger students with directions both before and during the lesson when they are taking notes. Remember, their working memory is easily overwhelmed, especially during note taking, and younger students have an even lower capacity than older students.

Student-generated notes are the least effective for better retention, so an advanced organizer provided by the teacher as either a handout or presented on the board for reference can greatly facilitate the students in keeping their information organized. In upper high school and college classes some instructors opt to provide their entire sets of notes, or PowerPoints, to the students. While this produces better retention, even if the student is annotating the slides, it is still not the most effective form of note taking (Kiewra, 1985a, 1985b; Larson, 2009). One strategy that organizes the information as the students take notes is presented in Figure 9.1. As the teacher gives notes, *he or she also directs the students to the section the notes are to be placed in,* thus automatically organizing the students' notes. This graphic organizer template attempts to parallel what the brain pays attention to, what it finds important, and what is easier to recall. These are represented as different boxes, labeled as *major differences*, *per-*

Topic	Processes
Key Knowledge/Facts	Why It's Important—**How It Affects ME**
Important Processes or Principles	Examples
How It Is Different From:	
Textbook or Partner's Example:	
My Example:	
What I Did to Show This Topic/Process, or Skill:	
My Drawing and Explanation of Drawing	

Fig. 9.1. Note-taking template. This template emphasizes aspects of information that will make information easier to recall. It also helps students to organize information quickly. When used as a word document and posted on school network, different areas can be changed or emphasized as teachers need.

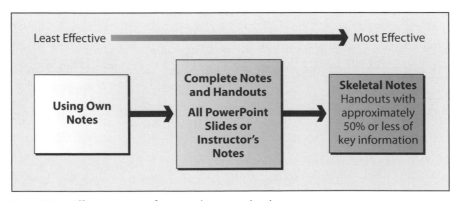

Fig. 9.2. Effectiveness of note-taking methods.

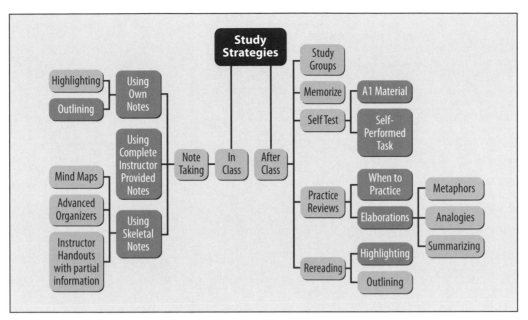

Fig. 9.3. Non-linear note-taking as a mind-map. This is a mind-map on study strategies to illustrate non-linear formats. Skeletal notes would already have some information present in the blocks.

sonal connections, and their *own examples and drawings*. The template is organized in a fashion that makes it easier (when compared to traditional note taking) to find information and to review later. A more successful method of note taking for long-term retention is to write skeletal notes, which is described in the next section.

Skeletal notes

These are *partial* notes, where the students are provided with some of the organizing information, along with some key ideas, but they must actively write in other pertinent information. *For lectures, note taking in a nonlinear format such as with concept or mind maps or advanced organizers produces the most effective recall* (Titsworth & Kiewra, 2004; see Figure 9.3). Older students who are able to spontaneously generate their own concept maps also produce better recall than with just written notes (Slotte & Lonka, 2000). Generally, skeletal notes are most effective when less than 50% of the information is provided by the teacher, and the student must take notes on the remainder. In practice with skeletal notes, I find younger students need more information to be provided, perhaps as much as two thirds of the notes, so they pay better attention to what is said and jot down the elaborations or examples more effectively. When the teacher uses handouts it also frees up time for him or her to give more examples and cover more topics (Larson, 2009). Skeletal notes are also known by a variety of other names, such as advanced organizers, guided notes, note-taking guides, partial handouts, and mind or concept maps.

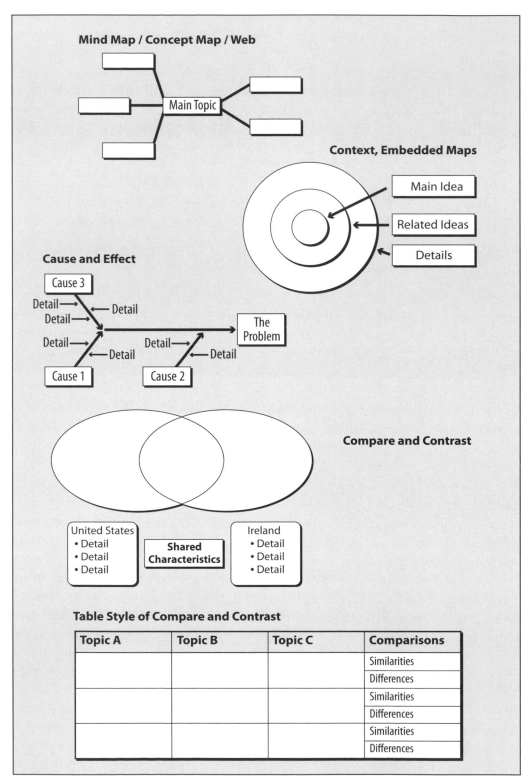

Mind Map / Concept Map / Web

Main Topic

Context, Embedded Maps

Main Idea

Related Ideas

Details

Cause and Effect

Cause 3

Detail→   ←Detail
Detail→

Detail→   The
Problem
Detail→   ←Detail
Detail→ ←Detail

Cause 1   Cause 2

Compare and Contrast

United States
• Detail
• Detail
• Detail

Shared Characteristics

Ireland
• Detail
• Detail
• Detail

Table Style of Compare and Contrast

Topic A	Topic B	Topic C	Comparisons
			Similarities
			Differences
			Similarities
			Differences
			Similarities
			Differences

Fig. 9.4. Other forms of non-linear note-taking. Non-linear notes show relationships and tend to result in better performance than traditional sequential notes.

An example of a mind map on study strategies is presented in Figure 9.3, and Figure 9.4 provides a sampling of other nonlinear styles.

Digital note-taking adjustments

Figuring out how to have students use computers to take notes is a work in progress because technology changes so rapidly. Consequently, the information here is largely the result of action research, not the results of clinical studies, and is hard won in the trenches of daily instruction where students have their own laptops or computer notebooks.

Students with computers still benefit from having an outline form to guide their organization. If the school should be fortunate enough to be wirelessly networked, have a note-taking template available that all the teachers and students can download (see Figure 9.1). Our school has also made it available in hard copy for students not using laptops. Make sure the template is still modifiable (keep it saved as a Word document rather than as a PDF.).

With computers, the presentation of notes and lectures takes on a totally different style. Rather than the teacher being in front and moving around among the students, *it is almost always necessary to be behind the students in order to monitor their screens.* So far, it doesn't matter if the school has blocked sites or has monitoring software such as SynchronEyes, because the monitoring software often doesn't work consistently, and students will have numerous back-door methods to get around the school's blocking. Teachers have found up to half or more of the laptops could not be monitored despite repeated efforts by highly skilled technical staff. Consequently, teachers needed to use a lot of proximity with the students as they had done before the use of laptops, but now teachers had to point out things students missed from the PowerPoint or to be aware of information that they need to add in a particular section of the note-taking template. In respect to the presentation material, much of it has to be prepared well so the PowerPoint slides are lively, and teachers should integrate photos, videos, or sound clips. It is imperative that teachers don't simply go from lecturing the kids to "Death by PowerPoint." There are excellent guidebooks available for effective PowerPoint design listed at the end of the chapter. To run programs from the rear of the room, it is also usually necessary to have a wireless remote to advance the slides. Many remotes have built-in laser pointers, and some have features that allow you to highlight or underline with the pointer. As with any new instructional skill and technology it takes a little getting used to. This allows the teacher to move around constantly, attending to the program and students while not having to be physically beside the computer to run the program.

Note taking with computers is still an emerging art form. In addition to providing students with skeletal notes, *students need to learn that they do not have to write or transcribe verbatim.* A number of teachers have found that the students not only try to be more careful with what is being said, but they also try to spell everything correctly. Normally, careful writing would be a good thing. But I've repeatedly observed in my classes that presentations can't go any faster and the teacher can't incorporate any more examples or explanations when students are laboriously transcribing everything. A major advantage of having a computer for each student in school is lost. What we are attempting to do (this is in-progress action research) is have the students type as fast as they can . . . sloppily, using phrases alone, with little or no sentence structure. To help them speed up, I have the students turn down the computer screen so they can't look at it as they type. This helps them concentrate on the lecture material rather than looking at the screen. The problem with all of this is that it is very fast-paced, and most students don't have time to reflect or think about the material and ask questions. Pauses or brain breaks are essential. A paper note-book is still necessary for drawing pictures. Afterward, *students can go back, clean up, and retype the notes, which provides them with an automatic review.* This is not a rereading. Students go through the material only once if they comprehend what they are reading, because, as Callender and McDaniel (2008) found, *rereading material produces virtually no gain in learning if the material was originally comprehended.* That will be explored further in preparation for assessments.

After the Class: Studying the Notes and Text

After the initial reading when students have comprehend the material, many students will go back later to reread the material. *One of the classic, seemingly obvious but highly inefficient ways to study for a test is to reread the material or to highlight and read that material over again* (McDaniel, Howard, & Einstein, 2009). Ask most teachers from elementary school through graduate school, and it is likely you'll find that rereading and going back over the material has been recommended as a study strategy at some time. With older adolescents in college, rereading is the most common technique used (Karpicke, Butler, & Roediger, 2009). As noted ear-

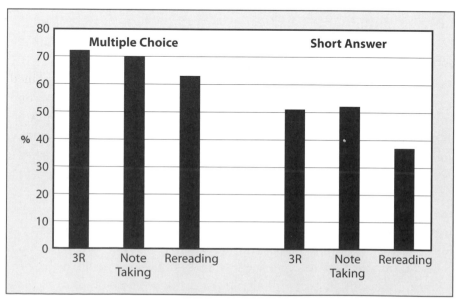

Fig. 9.5. Effect of study methods on different types of assessment.

Table 9.1. MOST COMMON STUDY STRATEGIES*	
Rereading	84%
Practice problems	43%
Rewriting notes	30%
Study groups	26%
Memorizing	18%
Mnemonics	13%
Self-testing	11%
Highlighting	6%

*Students tend to employ several strategies and do not use one exclusively.

Adapted with permission from Karpicke, Butler, and Roediger (2009).

lier, in respect to using time efficiently to study, rereading is probably one of the most wasteful because the performance gains are minimal (see Figure 9.5). With reading, a study form known as 3R for read-recite (self-test)-review produces greater gains on later tests than most other study methods (McDaniel et al., 2009). Note taking during reading produces almost the same level of gains. In dense, difficult text, it may help if the student also constructs a web or mind map as she goes along during the initial reading, but later rereading of the original text does not appear to help. Indeed, I've used just such a technique of drawing relationships as a web drawing in order to figure out new relationships that weren't obvious from the reading, However, that was an aid in comprehension and not necessarily always used for preparing for a test.

Metacognitive Awareness

Metacognition refers to our students' awareness of how they learn, combined with their active control of when and where to use strategies that actually work for them, while *metamemory* refers to their knowledge about their memory, and how to use it effectively. Both are important to facilitate their studying because such skills generally work across many content areas (Schraw, 1998). Indeed, I consider *metacognitive skills among the most important skills for developing a lifelong learner.* As I said in the introduction, in one respect this entire book may be viewed as an exercise in metacognition for teachers as well. Students need to develop such skills right along with learning their times tables in elementary school. However, neither younger nor older students appear to be in the habit of actively monitoring how they learn. There are a number of studies that suggest that when metacognitive skills are part of classroom instruction, there are significant gains in learning results (Brown & Palincsar, 1989; Cross & Paris, 1988; Schraw, 1994; Swanson, 1990).

There are three broad elements in metacognitive skills that students need to develop:

- Planning how they are going to go about studying;
- Learning to self-check; and
- Discovering which strategies work best.

In helping students develop metacognitive skills, educators should be alert to some striking facets. The skills need to be actively taught and repeatedly reinforced. Some studies suggest that the acquisition of metacognitive skills is not dependent upon the IQ. This implies that all students, not just the "bright" ones will benefit (Alexander, Carr, & Schwanenflugel, 1995). There is also, however, the tendency for students to significantly overestimate what they think they know (knowing what they know), indicating they don't have a very good grasp of how well they are studying. Additionally, students also need to have a working understanding of how their memory functions, and when to use different memory strategies (metamemory). Self-regulation is the key to their use of their metacognitive skills. A student's monitoring of how well she is learning, recognizing when she is not learning, and whether the method she is using is working contribute significantly to her success in employing the appropriate strategy (Harris & Graham, 1992; Reid & Harris, 1993). As students reach middle school and higher, they may need to be taught a generalized list of knowledge and skills such as in the following list:

Knowledge and Awareness of:
Attention
How emotional information affects processing
Properties of working memory
Properties of long-term memory
Conditions for initial intake of information versus test study conditions
How well they are self-regulating

Skills Pertaining to:
In-class note taking
Computer-aided note taking
Initial reading comprehension
Summarizing
Using metaphors and analogies
Elaborations
Self-testing strategies (both sequence and spacing of the self-tests)

One way to develop metacognitive skills is to use a strategy evaluation matrix (SEM). The SEM is a user-friendly method that has been demonstrated to create significant gains in learning, and it can be taught to students (Jonassen, Beissner,

Table 9.2. LEARNING TASKS AND STUDY STRATEGIES FOR READING			
Learning Task	**Study Strategy**	**Using the Strategy**	**Why It Works**
Starting new task or new section of reading	Reflection: What do I know about this?	Stop and elaborate: What do I know? What else do I need to know about this?	Activates older schemas. Working memory is focused and activates related areas in long-term memory, placing new material in context.
Extensive reading	Skimming	Read previews and summaries, headings, and bold print, highlighted words.	Focuses attention on major concepts; recreates a rapid overview of content; reduces working memory overload.
Reading important information	Go slower	Read, pause, reflect on what it means; jot notes on meaning.	Focuses on specific information; elaboration creates more memory.
Comprehension, achieving a deeper understanding of complicated reading	Reflective thought	Identify main ideas and relate them to a conclusion. Paraphrase main ideas. Do ideas support the conclusion? What will falsify the conclusion?	Personal elaboration reduces cognitive load; creates deeper level of understanding and makes it easier to retrieve memory.
Large amount of information or facts to be read and organized	Concept maps or mind maps, webs, diagrams	Identify and link major ideas; list or link supporting ideas and details.	Shows relationships, organizes information, creates spatial memory, and reduces cognitive load. Personal elaborations create deeper understanding and more retrievable memory.

& Yacci, 1993; Schraw, 1998). When students are formally taught to examine their learning tasks, and to evaluate them in respect to selecting appropriate study strategies, it may be helpful for high school students and older adolescents. I use an evolved form of the SEM concept, presented in Table 9.2, to help high school students evaluate a reading task and to select the appropriate study strategy.

While the focus in this book is on the adolescent, metacognitive skills that have already been learned by younger students can be very important. With those students, including those in middle school, a checklist similar to Table 9.3 may be used. It is a form of a learning cycle to develop metacognitive skills. Younger students can probably be introduced to metacognition without needing to be aware of the skills and knowledge areas that are listed above. Guide the students formally through the actual use of the charts, and periodically reinforce their use. Students who have these charts or procedures to assist their development of metacognitive skills perform considerably better than students without such metacognitive skills (King, 1991). Many teachers have frequently observed that students do know the strategies but will not initiate them, even if they are in the top of their classes academically. A contributing reason may be that they fail to persist and give up quickly (Schraw, 1998). This is where either teacher or parental guidance is often necessary. Such guidance provides the structure and discipline (self-regulation) that students have

Table 9.3. A YOUNGER STUDENT'S METACOGNITIVE CHECKLIST

My Study Plan
- ☐ What am I supposed to do?
- ☐ My goal is . . .
- ☐ To get started, the information I need is . . .
- ☐ To reach the goal, the strategies that will help me are . . .

My Self-Check Plan
- ☐ Do I know what I am doing? (Can I explain it to another student?)
- ☐ The strategies I am going to use are . . .
- ☐ Do I understand why I am using these strategies?
- ☐ Am I getting closer to my goal?
- ☐ What do I still need to do?
- ☐ What changes do I need to make with my strategies?

Evaluating the Plan
- ☐ Am I there yet? Did I reach the goal with those strategies?
- ☐ Which strategies helped me?
- ☐ What did I do that didn't help me, or what slowed me down in reaching the goal?
- ☐ Changes I need to make are . . .

not yet mastered. Recall that their frontal lobe is still immature. If students learn to achieve mastery on the strategies, they may be more likely to initiate them.

Specific Review Techniques

In the previous section on metacognition, broad approaches to study were generally outlined. In this section I will survey specific techniques or strategies that are part of the metacognitive skills.

Metaphors, analogies, and summarizations are forms of personal elaboration that work because the students generate their own examples and restate the lesson principles in their own words (Marzano, Norford, Paynter, Pickering, & Gaddy, 2001). These are not simple tasks but are skills that need to be developed by the students. The educator will need to provide close guidance and encouragement in the student's early attempts to learn these skills.

Metaphors, Analogies, and Summarizations

In creating their own metaphors, the student will make a comparison between one object or concept with another object or concept, but first he must be able to identify the basic pattern or principle involved in the topic. The comparison of the key patterns to an apparently different topic helps him create a mental image that might be easier to grasp. For example, "His hair was white as snow." However, students will need guidance and practice in writing metaphors. *Help them make comparisons by using several examples as models, as well as providing some graphic organizers to facilitate the process.*

Something With the Same
General Pattern

Abstract Relationship or
Fundamental Principle
Identify Basic Pattern
+ Important Details

Example: Fingernails
Fingernails scratch, scrape, claws
"Her fingernails were like claws."

Analogies are another type of elaboration, but they make comparisons between two groupings of concepts. In an analogy, a student compares the similarities between two different things, often by using something common paired with something unfamiliar. This requires the student to correctly identify the relationships between the objects. Finding the relationships is definitely an exercise that can involve higher levels of thinking. Some analogies are easier to understand, that is, the relationships are more accessible, while others may be more difficult. In fact, the Miller Analogies Test is used to estimate the traditional IQ. Two examples of analogies are:

A lens is to a photograph as the eye is to a memory.

Working memory is to the brain like RAM is your computer. It's what is being processed in your mind right at this moment, or what computer files you have open and are working on. Shut off the computer and it's gone. Stop thinking about the object and it's gone, too.

This last analogy is hardly perfect. As we have learned, the memory may not completely disappear, so an exact comparison is flawed. When you are first introducing a concept, analogies may help the students to understand, although as in the example with the computer, the analogy may require fine-tuning because it may not precisely capture the point you want to make.

For teaching analogies to students, one format is,

_____ is to _____,

as _____ is to _____.

(or, like a . . .)

Identifying why the relationship may be flawed also demonstrates a deeper understanding of the concept. It requires more analyzing of the problem but at several levels.

With summarizing, less is more. While this may be a personal elaboration for the student on a succinct scale, it is another skill that must be taught or checked to see if he or she knows how to summarize, rather than assuming they know how. As with other skills, summarizing takes practice and a lot of cognitive effort on the part of the student. There are many excellent books and online sources for sample strategies and activities. The recommendations listed here represent a simplified set of directions for students to help them get started in learning how to summarize, and it is by no means comprehensive. Summarizing is not a comprehensive note-taking skill; it is a concise description of a number of general points. If a teacher emphasizes nuances to see if a student understands details, or asks vague or broad questions, the broad sweeps of summarizing strategies will not be sufficient. To address that level of understanding, the student will need to elaborate deeply on each of the 5W's + H listed below.

The following list is an example of instructions to a student about learning how to summarize:

Include only the important stuff
If it doesn't matter, don't include it. Find the important points. Use the 5W's + H listed below.

Who
What
Where
When
Why
How

You can lightly draw a line through the unimportant material as you find the 5W's. Or use a highlighter in the material you're reading to identify only the most important things. If you realize it is something that you won't remember, or can't make sense of, don't include it.

State it *only* once. All the important information must be there in that sentence. (However, you will need to use full sentences and proper spelling, not cyber short cuts!)

Don't say the same thing in a different way. Your time is valuable, Don't repeat the same idea or phrase in your writing, even if it is stated slightly differently.

Use general terms or categories to represent specific things: for example, use birds for finch, jay, crow, ducks, and eagles.

Get to the point. What is the whole thing about? State this as your topic sentence. Everything else you say will need to relate directly back to the topic sentence. It is something like tweeting. Imagine you are logging on to Twitter, but you can send only a single message. The most significant information must be in the single tweet.

Other summarizing techniques

One-sentence summary: Have the students practice taking a paragraph and summarizing it in a single sentence. Use a movie review or a listing from the newspaper as a model where a single sentence is used to describe a film. This may be initially done as a small group exercise, where the group marks the sentence or phrase that they found meaningful and share it. Discuss the statements and paraphrase. Then, individually, have the students focus their sentence on the main idea and what happens.

The business card: Students combine creative skills with images (drawing or photograph) along with a few key words describing the topic. Have students share their business card designs.

Vanity plates: Similar to the business card, this fun summary activity is where the students take a selected topic that must be represented on a license vanity plate using 8 to 10 characters. Students present or post their ideas so everyone can see them.

Summary frames: This utilizes a series of questions that emphasize the most important patterns found in reading materials. For example, the student addresses each of the who, what, when where, and how questions and then shifts his or her focus to significant details of each component.

Four box synetics: This activity promotes creative thinking as the students figure out the essential characteristics. Students work in small groups of four. Using an assigned category, such as a beach, house, forest, or city, have the students in each group list four common objects that could be found in the assigned category. These names or objects are listed in the four boxes. Then the teacher, using the topic that is being reviewed, such as the ocean, presents a question using one of the four items in the box. For example, "How is the ocean like a mall?" "How is the ocean like a freeway?" Students are given 3 minutes or so to brainstorm all 4 items, and use each one in a sentence. For example, "A mall is like an ocean because . . ." Continue with each box: "A theater is like an ocean because . . ." Finally, share all answers in a classwide activity.

Category: City

| Taxi | Mall |
| Theater | Freeway |

Challenge envelope (Rogers, Ludington, & Graham, 1999): The class is divided into small groups, and each group receives an envelope. On the front of the envelope each group writes a question that is a challenge. For example:

What has . . . ?
How would . . . ?
What is a difference between . . . ?
What would happen if . . . ?

The group writes their criteria for the correct answer and places it inside the envelope. Shuffle all the envelopes. Each group now has a new envelope that some other group wrote. They read the challenge question, write their answer, and then check against what was inside the envelope. They place their own answer in with the original answer. Shuffle again, until every group has had the opportunity to do all the envelopes. Each time they get to compare their answers with the other groups' previous answers already in the envelope.

Feedback and Self-Testing

In this section, I explore important aspects of feedback that contribute to student performance. Feedback is inherently part of the metacognitive skills of monitoring, self-regulation, and the various forms of review discussed earlier. Feedback is also crucial to the success of one of the most powerful forms of study, self-testing. Of all the types of instructional inventions, Hattie observed that *feedback is "the most powerful single modification that enhances achievement"* (1992, p. 9). The manner in which feedback is provided is significant; not all forms have equal impact. Feedback is an opportunity for individualized re-teaching.

Be Specific

Vague or generalized feedback is of little help to the student. It gives no cues to act as guideposts. All students, from those with top performances to those who are struggling, benefit from specific feedback. For example, feedback that is entirely too vague to provide helpful direction to the student might sound like, "You did a nice job" or "That wasn't too bad, but you can do better." There are no useful cues for the mind to work with.

Specific feedback that is more helpful might sound like "Kasandra, you started off well. Those answers were thoroughly explained, but questions four through six need to be in sentences with proper grammar." Another example might be "Number six is confusing. You seem to have the idea of what happens, but it is not clearly stated. Restate this so it shows how the idea of . . ."

The feedback tells the student what he has done well, and where he needs to improve. The cues he needs to guide him are present in the comments. Unquestionably, such direct feedback takes time, but the dividends to the student are worth it.

My personal experience (with middle school students through graduate students) has been that significant feedback on several of the initial assignments produces consistently higher quality in later assignments, and it especially encourages the students in their efforts. After the students are achieving to the standards of the rubric, such detailed feedback can be scaled back, though it might be wise to keep encouraging the students. In short, the feedback helps to motivate the student in that he is not only capable, but the tasks or improvements before him are reachable, and the actions are within his power to take. The student has the control. Feedback connects with fundamental motivation strategies.

Be Prompt With Feedback

If feedback is to be helpful, it must also arrive in a timely manner so that students can make use of it (Marzano et al., 2001). Usable and timely feedback is significant for improvement. Late feedback, when papers are returned a week or even a month later, appears to be of almost no help to the students. Their efforts are not reinforced; there are few if any motivational needs that are met. Providing prompt feedback takes considerable effort by the educator, but his or her job is to help improve student performance. When I interviewed my students over the years they've volunteered that my comments gave them encouragement and direction. They felt emotionally supported in their efforts. Occasionally, I'll draw a little smiley face when I suggest a correction. In several different classes students who had difficulties actually beamed when they saw the smiley face.

Convenience may be important to the person who views teaching from a clock-punching perspective; however, it can be the educator's effort outside of class that distinguishes the professional educator from the rest. Another way to look at student feedback is to think about how teachers feel when they have to give standardized tests that rate their school, but they don't learn of the results until school has already started the following year. In a word: *Frustration*. Like students, educators are frustrated when they receive information so late that there is nothing they can do to make instructional corrections. To make adjustments, feedback must occur promptly.

Seek Feedback From the Students

Feedback should be a two-way street. The teacher needs it as much as the students do. I've learned a considerable amount about how my teaching was affecting the students from their comments, both formal (anonymously submitted to carefully structured questions) and informal (such as comments, asides, notes written on the board). Student comments can lead to asking for more specific feedback. Your response can heavily influence the student honesty and success of the feedback. If the students see that you are actually making changes in response to their comments, and they see you value what they say, they are often more willing to help you in order to help them. I've known many teachers who were reluctant to take the step and ask students what they thought, fearing it would turn into a gripe session.

It does take some courage. I was scared at first about what the students would say, but I thought about what they actually meant and it helped me to make changes that we all benefited from. Guide students in their feedback by asking about the lesson, not about yourself personally. Keep the feedback survey short and focused. Here is a small sampling of questions.

- What went well?
- Did you get lost? Where?
- What part went poorly?
- Were there sections that went too fast, too slow? Which ones?
- What was the most interesting part of the lesson? Why?
- What was the dullest part of the lesson?
- What was personally the most important thing that you got from the lesson?
- Were the instructions clear?
- When you first got the lesson, did you think you could do it? Why or why not?

Peer Review

This potent review process not only helps the students to identify and learn from the errors, but often creates lasting memories for the material in the lesson. When students check over other students' work, it can be a triple-win combination. It is natural for the writer to overlook grammar errors, misspellings, missing words, and confusing phrases. The peer review can reduce many of these problems. A two-stage peer review creates the triple win.

In the first review, peers (paired up by the teacher) check only for simple grammar. They identify errors such as missing punctuation or possible spelling errors. *They do not correct them.* The writer of the paper makes corrections (first win).

In the second round of review, students look over a different paper and read through the answers for selected questions, checking the content for confusing answers. Students will often go to the writer and say, "I don't understand; this is confusing." And frequently they pause to work with the writer, sometimes suggesting different wording. Additionally, in the process of checking content, students will realize some errors they made on their own papers. Remember, successful learning often doesn't occur in the first exposure to the lesson. The second win is for both students: One gets many (but not all) of the problem areas identified, and there is an opportunity to learn and then correct his or her own paper. But isn't this copying or just cheating? If the lesson is complicated for that age group, they learn from each other and expand their knowledge base. To ensure they also focus on learning, they may still be held accountable with an exam covering the same material. Remarkably, I've seen a number of students who used this peer review process, but they failed because of absenteeism or other problems; yet a year later they could often recall in great detail those lessons that were peer reviewed. Such a recall performance was not an isolated incident. I have repeatedly observed it for over a decade with very low-performing students.

The third win is for the teacher. Lessons come in with considerably fewer errors, the quality is generally much higher, and further feedback from the teacher contributes to even higher student performances.

There is a caveat to all of this. *Such an approach can't be used on every lesson because there is insufficient time. Generally, select only questions or problems that are of great importance.* Focus on the questions that you really want the students to retain. On major or extended lessons of substantial importance, the peer review works to drive home the lesson at hand. The students are being repeatedly exposed to the lesson through personal elaborations at many levels as they help each other, but they also simultaneously learn about being responsible and learn that quality counts.

Microfeedback Loops: Student-Centered Accountability

The student-centered accountability (SCA) model also emphasizes prompt feedback (Greenleaf, 2008). Developed by Robert Greenleaf with a number of educators formally associated with Brown University, this model provides a clear, focused structure for feedback. It is designed to reduce the amount of data collected (less is more), but it still zeroes in on a specific learning target, while rapidly collecting organized data that can provide information for immediate use and corrections. A significant focus is to collect information on only a few items, not mountains of material on many lessons. As with all feedback to students, it must be at their level of understanding. A similar approach is taken in the peer review process. The feedback provided by students is on selected items and communicated in language they can understand. In order not to overwhelm yourself and students, narrowly focus on only the most significant items: the crucial take-home lessons. As with peer reviews, the SCA concentrates on the student's learning and whether the current instructional strategies actually teach the needed knowledge and skills. A significant benefit is that the SCA also provides a method of consistent regular feedback, rather than a haphazard, occasional approach.

Self-Testing: Using the Test Effect to Advantage

Of the various forms of feedback, self-testing is among the most powerful. If we look at Table 9.1, self-testing ranks close to the bottom as a method used for studying, while rereading material, such as rereading highlighted items, is the most common practice. But in terms of actually knowing the material, rereading produces almost no benefit in retaining the material (Callender & McDaniel, 2009; Karpicke et al., 2009). This is not to be confused with initial reading for comprehension where passages are gone back through to improve comprehension or making illustrations, charts, and concepts to further that comprehension. Just rereading the text assumes that it will not only become more familiar, but also that the student will remember more details. However, recognition does not improve understanding.

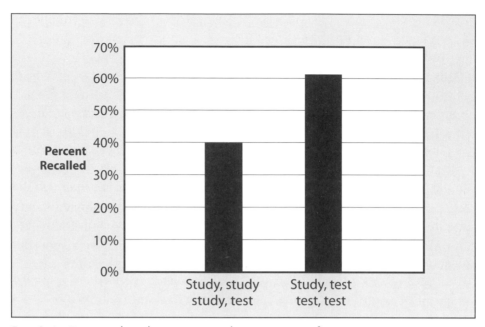

Fig. 9.6. Repeated study vs. repeated testing on performance.

Many students use some variation of the traditional method of study, study, study, test by simply going back over the material. Unfortunately, this is not only highly ineffective, but is essentially a waste of time because another method, self-testing, is substantially more powerful (see Figure 9.6; Karpicke & Roediger, 2006). Additionally, students may believe the illusion that they are competent by continually reviewing the material without testing, at least until the test occurs. It appears that many of the students (and teachers) lack the metacognitive awareness that self-testing produces greater memory retention faster.

The problem with rereading's lack of benefit still applies if it is massed into a single study lesson; it is especially poor (Rawson & Kintsch, 2005). This brings up the question of "How should study practices be conducted?" A distributed practice of equally spaced self-testing sessions generates a sizable increase in academic performance. There are two important facets to the study sessions using self-testing: (1) How far apart should they be before the test? and (2) Should all the content be studied each time? In looking at whether all the content should be studied each time, Karpicke and Roediger (2006) found that if students studied, then studied again and then tested, and retested again they did considerably *poorer* than if they simply adjusted the study procedure. By adjusting the procedure to first study everything, then test on all of it, then study the missed items only, and then delaying a week to a final test, the long-term retention was substantially larger. The practice of studying only the missed items, but testing over everything, allowed the student to practice a key skill needed on tests, that of memory retrieval. Students who prepared in the most traditional manner (studying and studying the same material again and again and then testing) did the poorest. At this time, it is not known whether a third study session on the missed items and testing would produce higher gains.

Overlearning Versus Spacing Study Sessions

Another technique that avoids the potential problem of overlearning, which may occur with the study, study, study, test strategy, is to space the study sessions apart. How far apart should study sessions be?

Consider a common study situation (assuming the student is actually studying): The student is up late with her iPod playing as she reads through the text. After a while she realizes she is seeing the words, but there is no comprehension. The words are being passed over, becoming a blur in her mind with no meaning. When she finally becomes aware of the situation, she must decide if it is time to quit. Different strategies for staying alert include changing tasks, doing a short burst of intensive exercise, or drinking yet another round of a heavily caffeinated, high-energy drink. Or she could get some rest before going back through the material one more time. Some students attempt to overlearn the material in hopes of a better performance. Overlearning is reached when the student has at least one review without errors and usually involves semantic or word-based information. This is different from learning a procedure or sequence that combines spatial positions as presented in the previous chapter in manipulating the mind maps. Although a boost to grades generally occurs with overlearning if the test is soon after the study session (Driskell, Willis, & Copper, 1992), long-term learning may suffer (Rohrer & Pashler, 2007). Once the overlearned or error-free conditions are reached, should more time be spent when it is unproductive in most academic situations? One solution that doesn't require more time but improves learning is to space the study sessions apart.

Returning to the question posed earlier, "How far apart should the study sessions be?" there is a trend emerging in the research. Most students have probably crammed for a quiz or test at some point, and it is well known that mass study practice can produce a boost in scores, though the retention is rather short-lived. If learning is the goal, and not just a test score, a different approach will be needed.

Table 9.4 RANKING OF STUDY METHODS AFTER 1–WEEK DELAY TO FINAL TEST		
Poorest	SSSST	→ Test
	STST	→ Test
Most Effective	$S_e T_a \; S_m T_a$	→ Test

S_e = Study everything, T_a = Test all, S_m = Study missed items

Having a series of practices leads to more immediate short-term improvement, but studies suggest spacing the practices out equally enhances the long-term memory (Karpicke & Roediger, 2006). Increasing the amount of study time does not facilitate the memory performance, but delaying the initial studying does (Karpicke & Roediger, 2007). If the first practice test can be delayed for more than a week, perhaps even a month, it makes the first practice more difficult, but the effort leads to more gains in long-term memory. If practices start right after the lesson, there is less time between practices and the student's long-term performance worsens. Unfortunately, close spacing between the initial lesson and the practice is endemic with mathematics textbooks. After the demonstration example, most books appear to have many practice problems of the same type. But the learning gains after just three or four problems of the same type are nil after a week or so (Rohrer & Pashler, 2007). Here is a summary of these important strategies:

Delay the initial practice: This makes it more difficult but produces greater lasting memory.

Equally space the practices.

Avoid further repetitive practice after the initial three to four problems are done where the students demonstrate understanding (close spacing of practice with no delay).

How much practice testing is really needed?

A natural question arises with the practice assessments when they are used as a major study vehicle for the final assessments, or still other mandated assessments: When is there too much practice? Both students and teachers can wilt, becoming frustrated and demotivated. There doesn't seem to be any magic formula as to how much testing is too much. If the practice assessments are woven into regular assignments and they connect the current work with lessons presented a week ago, looping back to earlier topics can seem more natural, especially if it becomes routine. This serves to constantly maintain the relevance of current lessons, as well as refresh the student's memory for older material. Although not specifically noted, I would suggest the practice assessment be highly focused and short in nature so as not to take up a lot of time. This still has the students practice the skill of accessing pertinent information. The practice assessment can be used as a point of discussion and should seem less like a standard test, possibly reducing the student feeling of being overwhelmed with so many formal tests.

Study groups

I failed to learn the value of study groups until graduate school. In the massive body of research on cooperative group learning one trend stands out clearly: Students who used group study sessions consistently performed better than students who don't make use of them (Walberg, 1999). These can be used in class, such as cooperative learning groups, or independent study groups if they are focused (no TV or ball games to distract them) (Johnson & Johnson, 1999). Even high school students can make effective use of such groups, though they will often not initiate them unless directed to do so. When some groups of students seem unable to get themselves organized, I will hold voluntary study/group tutoring sessions that I direct, before school, at lunch, evenings, on weekends, whatever time works best for most of the students. The study groups allow the students to explain, elaborate to each other, and explore in a more comfortable, noncompetitive learning environment.

Level of difficulty and ultimate learning goals

The cognitive task and the level of difficulty should be the same between the review-rehearsal sessions and the final assessment. Too often students are lulled into a false sense of competence because the study guide preparations were easier than the assessment and had simpler questions. Multiple-choice practice questions tend to have students focus on specific content rather than on principles. Short answers, while more difficult, produce greater long-term learning, though often with initially lower scores. All of this provokes a critical philosophical question about learning.

What is the school's goal? Nationwide, schools are pushing for higher test scores, yet we know that deeper and longer-lasting learning is achieved with short answer questions when compared to multiple-choice exams. But short answer questions, while producing better learning, also tend to generate lower scores. In selecting assessments, consider the style of questions and whether the goal is a score level or learning. They are not the same, and parents, politicians, and administrators need to be very aware of that. Everett Lindquist, who was instrumental in developing standardized tests, made a significant admonition about misusing tests, noting that many ". . . fail to provide an adequate basis for educational guidance and the evaluation of instruction" (Lindquist, 1951, p. 141.).

Assessments

Assessments, whether done with traditional paper and pencil, or through performance and demonstration, should have a clear purpose and actually measure what they claim they are measuring in a timely and usable fashion for educators who work directly with the students. In this section I explore a different way of looking at tests and how educators might design better assessments. Educators need to have an idea of what students have learned and can do, in order to figure out where the instruction should go next as indicated by the assessments of student performance.

Here I examine assessments on two very different levels: one is from the daily perspective of what teachers can do and the second is on a national scale. This second type of assessment is a completely different way of assessing student performance that considers not only what the brain is doing, but where the student should be headed next.

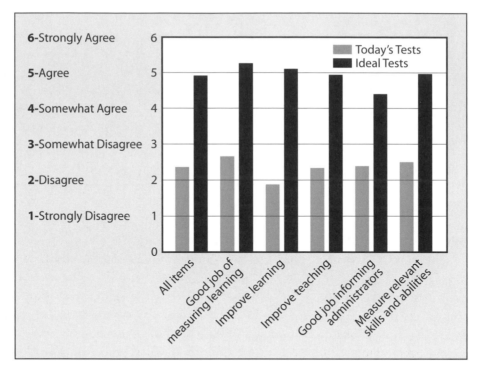

Fig. 9.7. Survey on ideal vs. today's testing.

Getting Usable Information

Do the tests do what teachers want them to do? In a national survey by Developmental Testing Service most people indicated tests were falling far short of providing the information they needed and wanted (Dawson, 2009a).

It appears to be commonly assumed that higher test scores mean greater learning, although, as we've seen for many years, that may not be the case at all. Even so, in the current atmosphere, there is enormous pressure to attain both higher scores on state standardized test scores and on ACT or SAT college entrance exams. But there is precious little public understanding of tests, and there is a great proclivity to misuse standardized tests despite a strong warning carefully given by Lindquist, one of the inventors of such tests (Lindquist, 1951). However, before exploring what teachers can do with their own tests, some cautionary notes are in order. All tests, whether they are the hundreds of thousands of teacher-designed tests or the huge nationwide assessments, face several common problems that must be addressed if the tests are to be accurate and provide anything usable. These are errors in measurement, reliability, and validity.

Measurement Errors

Imagine weighing a bag at the airport to determine if you'll be charged for excess weight. Your bag comes in 1.5 lbs too heavy, and you're charged. But you want to see exactly how much weight the scale showed. They place the same bag back on the same scales, but now it shows a different weight. The slight inconsistency is a measurement error. But in education it may create a huge difference. For example, both SAT and ACT tests have their own parallel forms, where one form is as close to the first version as possible. Students often retake one of the exams in the hopes of a higher score. If a student *scores just a little lower or higher on the second test, it can mean the difference between being admitted to college or not and it could affect the student's chances of receiving a scholarship*. Students have good and bad days like anyone else. Having a student take a test when he or she is emotionally distraught is likely to yield an inaccurate measure. In the chapter on long-term memory, we learned that staying up all night or sleep deprivation makes recall more difficult and prone to error. All of these may cause problems for accurate measures of what a student knows or can do.

Reliability

Tests that consistently measure in the same way are reliable. Let's take the airport scales example again. In this situation, the same scale measures everyone 1.5 lbs too heavy, and charges may accrue. That is one reason to check the certification tag to see how long it has been since the scale was calibrated. The same type of problem occurs in the science labs or for weighing in athletes for wrestling. Does the measuring instrument (test, scales, etc.) consistently measure the same way? My car consistently measures my speed at 3 mph too fast, so when my speedometer indicates I'm at the speed limit, I'm actually driving slower, which has probably helped me avoid some speeding tickets. However, in schools, the reliability of scores or grades can create problems for the student. For example, if a school reports a high GPA year after year, with perhaps 75% of its students receiving 3.5 or higher, but less than 25% survive their first year of college, the grades may be reliably too high. There is possibly grade inflation. *Reliability does not mean accurate estimations of student ability*. School-made assessments need to be both reliable and have as few measurement errors as possible. Errors, however, can creep in another way, too.

Validity

Teachers want their assessments to be reliable and valid. They want an accurate picture of what their students really know. If the English class learned the work of Chaucer, but were tested over Shakespeare, the test could be highly reliable if the questions remained the same from test to test but would lack validity because it measured something different from what was taught. For teachers in the classroom, there are two properties to validity over which they can exercise some control: *content, and cognitive processes* (Hopkins, Stanley, & Hopkins, 1990). Both can change validity. Testing over content that was different from what was taught is a problem with content validity. You may have heard or experienced college classes where the professor gave a test that totally ignored the required text. Or the test was over the text but ignored all those days of lecturing. Students need to know what content is being assessed. The focus here is not about the questions to be asked, but the subject matter. There was a mismatch. The assessment must measure the students' knowledge of what was actually taught if the instructor is to improve their teaching. A second aspect involves the cognitive processes that are being used. If students practice with multiple-choice tests in their study guide but are tested with short answer questions, two different cognitive processes are involved. Multiple choice relies more heavily on recognition, while the short answers require greater recall. Again, there is a mismatch. *The method of review and rehearsal should mirror the final assessment* (Baddeley, 1997). This also includes the time of day. For example, a test that is given at 8 A.M. for a course that was always held in the evening is a mismatch. Earlier in the chapter, I alluded to the use of music during study. If music was permitted during final rehearsals or study sessions, then the same conditions should be allowed during the assessment. However, I would recommend that the rehearsal *not* have music if the test conditions don't permit it. When the practice environment does not match the assessment environment, student performance will often be lower. That is why there are dress rehearsals, scrimmages, preseason games, and basic military training with live gun fire, so students can be as close as possible to the final assessment condition.

Design and Purpose

For teacher-designed tests, what should be looked for?

Is the goal of the test clearly identified so both students and teachers know what is supposed to be measured?

For the teachers, is there a plan to use the collected information?

For the school, is the test to determine if there is overall school progress, or is the test supposed to measure individuals' progress?

For the student, does the assessment give them feedback? What kind and how soon?

For the teacher, is the assessment timely enough to matter to make changes before the next school session?

Specific Characteristics

Check each test item.

Is the question parallel to what was actually taught?

If specific content was emphasized during instruction, does it have similar emphasis in the test? For example, if a few topics were given only cursory attention, but are heavily tested on, there is a mismatch.

Trivial content should be eliminated from the test. Does the test focus on the significant processes and knowledge that students should take with them after the course is over?

Are the same basic cognitive processes that were taught also tested over?

If the test requires an application, has the application of the same difficulty been practiced more than once? Questions that require transfer skills are also affected by cognitive development. For example, suppose a problem requires three different cognitive skills. To have successful transfer and solve the problem, the student will need to have developed all three cognitive skills *and* practiced all three skills. If his brain has not developed one of those skills, perhaps because it is slightly delayed, the student is short one of the necessary skills and is not likely to have successful transfer. Cognitive development has its own schedule, and a teacher can't hurry it up (See Chapter 1). The transfer problem is unlikely to be solved. The challenge for the teacher is to determine when using transfer problems what set of skills are needed, and then specifically teach *all* those skills, and practice their use in concert, not separately (Theo Dawson, personal communication, April 2009).

Short answer practice tests produce better retention than multiple-choice tests (Rohrer & Pashler, 2007).

Questions with different levels of challenge can be used to distinguish between those students who have memorized processes versus those who can think with the processes. Have some questions that are just hard enough that not everyone can get them, and some that are easy enough for all to answer. These will sort out who knows the material better than others. It does not create differences; it *reveals* differences between the students. In other words, there are no winners or losers—just an indication of who has better command of the material.

A single assessment doesn't reveal much of what a student really knows. It usually requires several assessments (or samples) of the mind. These can be built into future activities or assessments when a lesson loops back and connects with earlier lessons.

Diane Ronis (2007) developed a series of simple assessments that may help educators build their own assessments. These designs expand on the fundamental principles described above, and they make use of different learning processes such as Gardner's multiple intelligences as well as collaborative learning and metacognitive processing. The material is easy to follow and excellent for teachers just getting started.

What Tests Tell Us

A well-designed test takes a snapshot of what a student knows. It doesn't represent everything a student knows but attempts to be representative of each student's knowledge and skills (Koretz, 2008). However, there are assessments being designed today that can also measure *what the students think they know and suggests what should be taught next, based upon the students' cognitive development* (Dawson, 2009b). This is a more comprehensive view of student performance, and it can significantly help schools, business, and the military. This reduces the seat-of-the-pants approach to both assessments and standards of "we think this is developmentally or age appropriate, based upon our experiences in the tests." The newer, developmentally based assessment finds out where the student's understanding is conceptually and indicates what the student needs to learn next. This is an entirely different method, and it is based on the heavily researched brain development cycles discussed in Chapter 1 (Commons, Trudeau, Stein, Richards, & Krause, 1998; Fischer, 1980). The significance lies in the fact that the brain's cognitive development can be used as a natural ruler, and thus can be measured cross culturally. Such cognitive skill information may provide teachers with more precise instructional direction, saving time, effort, and money. As currently designed, teacher-designed tests, and virtually all commercial standardized tests and major national tests, are poor measures of how well students actually understand the concepts (Agung & Schwartz, 2007; Sadler, 2000; Schoenfeld, 2007; von Bergmann, Dalrymple, Wong, & Shuler, 2007). To get a rough idea of how the new, developmentally based assessment approach works, try the exercise below.

Arrange the statements about the process of diffusion from the simplest at the bottom, in progressive order, with the most comprehensive and inclusive statement at the top.

A Gases diffuse until they run out of room.
B Garbage stinks.
C The energy in the gases helps to disperse the gases until they are equally concentrated.
D The odor spreads out.
E The material (gas or liquid) goes from a higher concentration toward a lower concentration.
F The gas or liquid materials spread out more rapidly than others because they have greater volatility.

To gain a greater insight into students' understanding of very important concepts, have the students also explain why they arranged the answers in a particular order. This should *not* be used for a grade.

The students sort out the items according to their understanding of which represents the simplest to the most inclusive explanation. The point at which they start confusing issues and processes suggests where they are in understanding the concept, and, importantly, it infers what should be taught next. It may also suggest whether the standards students are accountable for are within their cognitive range. Standardized tests such as the ACT and SAT cannot do this. At this time Developmental Testing Service is pioneering these new methods of testing based on the brain's development of cognitive skills.

Answering such a question takes time and considerable thought on the student's part. At this time, I would suggest that this be tried only a couple times a semester in order not to frustrate the students. I also suggest they be used on only the most important principles that students need to carry with them when they leave class.

Summary

Researchers have identified techniques for note taking, study, review, and assessments that are more efficient than what is commonly practiced. The implications are also significant because they suggest that the actual delivery and textbook design for a course may take a different path from traditional practices because of the ineffective methods currently used to learn and review materials, especially in math. Assessments are also changing, going beyond only measuring what students know, to also determining their level of understanding by basing their designs on how the brain develops cognitive skills. These new assessment designs provide direction for the educators by suggesting what students need to learn next. Such assessment designs also have implications for admittance policies for schools and colleges. It can reveal to admission directors far more information about a student's capabilities than traditional standardized tests such as the ACT and SAT. As Bob Dylan said, "The times, they are a changing."

Key Points and Recommendations

In-Class Note Taking

- *Note taking can increase learning if certain strategies are used.* For example, the process of filling in skeletal notes or the various web or mind map formats help to increase learning and realize more relationships.

- *Effective note taking needs to reduce the cognitive load so the student may be able to listen, briefly reflect on what he or she heard, and record pertinent information along with personal comments.* If the students are so busy taking notes that they have no time to think, when will they have time? Overload is a constant problem, and there is no mental reserve left for reflection. If there are that many necessary notes, consider giving some of them in skeletal form to reduce students' overload problems.

- *A person speaks about 2 to 3 words a second, but they can only write $1/10$ as fast.* That suggests that the moment a person starts writing she is facing an overload problem because she is trying to follow almost everything that is said. Notes must be succinct, but should allow a student time for some reflective thought, which suggests that the time spent on taking notes needs to be brief. Using a laptop, or skeletal notes, and filling out mind maps or webs could potentially reduce the student's cognitive load.

- *Student-generated notes are the least effective for better retention, so an advanced organizer, provided by the teacher as either a handout or presented on the board for reference, can greatly facilitate the students' understanding.* Student notes tend to be organized in an inefficient manner, and they are often illegible. The advanced organizers assist in the organization and in providing direction on what kind of material needs to be noted.

- *For lectures, note taking in a nonlinear format such as drawing mind maps, or using advanced organizers, produces the most effective recall.*

Handing organizers out prior to note sessions, and gaining directed practice, is often much easier for students to develop explanations or elaborations in order to study from. Notice that just rereading notes is *not* an effective study technique. Students need to be actively summarizing and elaborating from their notes, not passively reviewing them. (See "After-Class Studying" below.)

- ***Students with computers still benefit from having an outline form to guide their organization.*** Even though computers may allow the students to write notes much faster, having a skeletal outline or template where they can rapidly find the correct section will help them organize their information or place it in proper context with other notes.

- ***When teaching with computers, it is often necessary to be behind the students in order to monitor their screens.*** Technology being what it is, instructional styles must also adapt to the evolutionary processes of electronics. Explaining from behind the students, while using a wireless pointer or presentation tool, permits much closer monitoring of what is going on, as well as if the teacher is going too fast, because the teacher can directly inspect several of the screens quickly. Further, lecturing from behind the students encourages greater proximity to all the students. It may be that technology will eventually allow highly consistent monitoring of student laptops, but at the present it still lacks reliability despite manufacturer claims. The use of "clickers" is increasing student involvement during lecture formats in addition to providing very rapid individual feedback to the students about the accuracy of their answers. Another benefit of clickers is that it avoids embarrassment because the projected responses do not identify the individual students.

- ***Students need to learn that they don't have to write or transcribe verbatim; they can go back, clean up, and retype the notes, which provides an automatic review.*** Students try to practice writing carefully in note taking with computers. Such an effort to careful detail slows the entire process so much that it can be as slow as handwriting. By typing fast, and sloppy, with lots of fragments, but cleaning up the notes at a later time, the students get a thorough review without increasing study time.

After-Class Studying

- ***One of the classic, and seemingly obvious but highly ineffective, ways to study for a test is to reread the material or to highlight and read material over again.*** Countless students highlight and believe they have studied when they recognize the material. However, recognition memory does not carry details with it. If students look at the highlighted topic and then write their own elaboration of the material, that may help because it practices retrieval (a practice assessment). After comprehension is gained, rereading wastes time in regard to improving long-term retention.

- *Metacognitive skills are among the most important skills for developing a lifelong learner.* The lifelong learner needs to know what learning strategies really work. As adolescents become adult learners they need to keep abreast of changes to function optimally in a fast-changing world. Metacognitive skills can facilitate their performance.

- *Help students make comparisons using metaphors, analogies, or summaries by presenting several examples as models, along with some graphic organizers to facilitate the process.* Models change abstract ideas into something concrete that students can see, while simultaneously illustrating relationships between the various parts of the model.

- *If feedback is to be helpful, it must also arrive in a timely manner so the student can make use of it.* Feedback should be within a day, and preferably not more than several days later, because it can provide progressively less correction and understanding the longer it is delayed. With the massive amount of paperwork that teachers face, the necessity of effective feedback suggests that teachers carefully select what will be assessed that will provide immediate help to the student. Less is more. Keep assessments succinct and focus on the principal concepts and skills.

- *Peer review is a potent review process that not only helps the students to identify and learn from errors, but often creates lasting memories of the material in the lesson.* When students peer review and work closely with fellow students, they are peer teaching. Those particular lessons often remain with them for months to even a year.

- *Peer review can't be used on every lesson because there is insufficient time.* Generally use the approach on selected questions or problems that are of great importance. There is never enough time, so focus on the pivotal items in the lesson. By doing so, teachers can also identify the fluff questions and weed them out.

- *Scores just a little lower or higher on the second test can mean the difference between being admitted to a college or not or a student's chances of receiving a scholarship may be affected.* Like it or not, such score differences do mean this. Standardized tests strive to reduce fluctuations in the parallel forms, but they normally vary slightly. However, teacher-made tests will vary even more. Excellent test design is difficult to achieve.

- *Reliability of a test does not mean it is an accurate estimation of a student's ability.* As long as the evaluation instrument produces consistent results, it is reliable, but it may not be measuring what was intended. The content must also be examined.

- *The method used to review and rehearse should be mirrored in questions or tasks in the final assessment.* If the practice retrieval assess-

Problem	Study-Review Strategy	Assessment Design
	Table 9.5. QUICK CHECKLIST FOR REVIEW AND ASSESSMENT	
Assessment Environment	Use the same room, stage, or field at the same time of day.	Use the same environment as rehearsal/study session.
Threat or Fear	Reduce or eliminate tension by relaxed deep breathing and a short relaxation activity.	Consider using the same relaxation activity just before assessment.
Music During Study or Rehearsal	Use nonvocal music as a quiet background but not in rehearsal or in assessment-like conditions unless the test conditions allow it.	No music unless permitted and it should be the same music that was used in rehearsal. Music is nonvocal and the teacher's choice.
Types of Questions (Cues)	Practice the entire variety of questions that will be used so students cue on the task being asked of them.	Use the same types of questions that were practiced and the same style of question as in the rehearsal.
Making Connections	Students elaborate with multiple personal examples that illustrate the lesson.	Students are asked to give an example and explain the lesson or principle.
Content	All critical content is actively reviewed.	Assess only the content taught, not new material; the application is a different issue (see next problem below).
Application Transfer	Make certain all necessary skills are practiced together and repeatedly in making applications transfer to new problems.	Application transfer uses the same skills or fewer skills that were practiced together.
Difficulty of Problems, Level of Cognitive Development	Finish practices at the same level of difficulty and complexity as will be on the assessment, not with easier problems. Students also need to have the level of development necessary to solve problems. Just because students are of a certain age doesn't mean they have reached a developmental level of cognitive skills that will enable them to handle the problem. That's assuming readiness by astrology and not research.	The cognitive difficulty is the same as during rehearsal.
Important Nuances	This is a combined cueing and level of difficulty problem. Practice detecting, analyzing, and answering nuances if the test will require such skills.	Avoid questions that use nuances unless the same type were practiced and at the same level of difficulty.
Tables, Graphs, and Illustrations	Practice interpreting and explaining with material similar to the assessment.	Use a similar style and content as practiced.
Deep Knowledge	Practice elaborations, writing short answers, using mind maps, and explaining relationships.	Use questions that ask for explanations and relationships.
Metacognitive Skill	Peer review. Have students use a rubric, check each other's work with study missed items, retest over all items. Become alert to what they don't know yet at the rubric level.	The assessment is parallel to review items.
Adjustment in Study Methods	Analyze performance and adjust study methods with guidance from the teacher (learning cycle).	Give prompt feedback.
Timing of Assessment	Practice at least a week or more ahead of assessment. NO CRAMMING.	Assessments should not be done the next day, with only one day of review.
Getting Practice or Review Time	Embed portions of the review throughout the lesson and link them with other prior lessons.	Select just one or two pivotal concepts or skills and include these as part of a brain break or mini review.
How to Take Tests	Practice the skill of test taking with parallel tests.	The assessment is similar in all aspects to earlier parallel tests.
Rereading Material	Reread only if the material was not initially comprehended.	

ments used to study are multiple-choice exams, then the final assessment should not be a short answer test but a multiple-choice exam. The cognitive tasks and the level of difficulty should be the same between the review sessions and the final assessment. Too often, students are lulled into a false sense of competence because the study guide preparations were easier than the assessment and simpler questions. Multiple-choice practice questions tend to have students focus on specific content rather than on principles. Short answer tests, while more difficult, produce greater long-term learning but lower scores initially.

- ***New assessment designs not only measure what a student knows, but what the student believes that he or she knows, and the assessment suggests what should be taught next, based on the student's cognitive development.*** Using brain development patterns, assessments are entering into a new era that can potentially assist the students, their instructors, and schools in achieving a better understanding of what learning is going on. Teachers and administrators need more information than just what a student knows if they are to plan effective education. They must also know the student's potential capability of learning the next level, and in what direction the instruction should guide the student. Test designs based on a student's cognitive development can possibly give that information.-

RESOURCES

Kosslyn, S. (2007). *Clear and to the point*. New York, NY: Oxford University Press.
Reynolds, G. (2008). *Presentation Zen design*. Berkeley, CA: New Riders.
Ronis, D. (2007). *Brain-compatible assessments*. Thousand Oaks, CA: Corwin Press.

CHAPTER TEN

The Future of Neuroeducation
Opportunities and Considerations

In the middle of difficulties lies opportunity.
—Albert Einstein

In neuroeducation, context is important. Learning is not approached as an isolated problem in a specific area of content; rather, learning is studied in the context of integrated systems. Fortunately, the brain is highly plastic, and that fundamental fact allows enormous opportunities in learning, but the same plasticity is bound by the constraints of nature. Those, too, must be considered.

In this final chapter I will explore the developing opportunities of neuroeducation and some areas of concern on two different scales. In the first portion of the chapter I look at broader, global issues that are likely to influence neuroeducation in the future, including the role of technology, informing policy, the challenges of educator training, and student health. In the second and final portion of the chapter I turn to more local or classroom-specific problems that are emerging, along with a short discussion of teachers finding their voices in order to collaborate with researchers.

Neuroeducation is in its infancy, but it is also international in scope, with research and efforts to implement the findings that are emerging from around the world. We are learning from each other. However, the secrets of the brain are given up incrementally. We are in a period of fits and starts, trying to find our way. Educational advances are made more difficult when some neuroscience discoveries are oversimplified and embraced with enthusiasm. Neuromyths sometimes result. However, the most significant concern, which has been repeatedly stated, is that most neuroscience discoveries are not directly applicable to education and the classroom. Educators, including those skilled in reading neuroscience findings must be cautious lest they build strategies on neuromyths and misconceptions. New education models are being discussed to address the problem of appropriate application to help both the teacher and the researcher determine what really works and why. It is a time of opportunity and thoughtful consideration. New models testing instructional strategies that may reduce these application errors are presented later in the chapter. Until dependable testing takes place, we still rely on science's sporadic rechecking of claims.

To illustrate the rechecking, recall two examples where neuroscience research does not support the practice claims. These include the Brain Gym method of exercise, and learning styles. Both demonstrated a mismatch between practice and research, which suggests these practices should be discontinued, significantly changed, or, if they create success, should be attributed to some other cause than what was claimed. All of these are a drain on the key resources of teacher talent, time, and money that could be used elsewhere. As of yet, there is no systematic testing of instructional strategies. Neuroeducation is still evolving.

The brain's inherent complexity also affects the neuroeducation community in unanticipated ways. For example, one sector of research may have applications in others, permitting researchers to solve problems that have the potential to affect many instructional practices. Technology is an example.

The Impact of Technology

Technological advances facilitate our creativity in addressing long-standing and difficult problems and the impact of technology will likely increase. One of these tools, mentioned in Chapter 1, is near-infrared optical topography (NIROT). The potential here lies in being able to detect infants who are at high risk for reading-language disorders, and getting real-time information on other frontal lobe processes. Early screening and detection of language problems might have a positive effect on the success of these children. By starting reading and language interventions well before children grow into adolescence, students may be prevented from falling seriously behind and becoming discouraged. In a similar vein, a small portable ultrasound (Doppler sonography) may be able to monitor what students are actually paying attention to, whether they are reading something on a computer screen, sitting in a lecture, watching a demonstration in a classroom, reading, or driving. The technology may permit researchers to go beyond simple eye-tracking to what is simultaneously happening in the brain. Clearly, technology will permit wider and deeper investigations into the mind. Some digital technologies are already having an impact on education.

There is a widening application of electronic learning from the use of laptop computers (the One Laptop, One Child worldwide computer program) to the use of cell phones and classroom clickers. Whether you like them or not, they change the dynamics of education, not just in the United States but in poor rural areas of the world. The connectivity of students and the methods of instruction are shifting. These shifts affect industry, infrastructure, local cultures, politics, and education, to name a few.

Technology also forces us to rethink how lessons are taught and, if we dig deep enough, to more closely examine our beliefs about learning. However, technology is a double-edged sword. It is not at all farfetched to see teachers' roles becoming subservient to the computer, in which the teacher becomes a tech manager of sorts and does little teaching. It has already happened with schools where students who either do not or are unable to interact with other students or teachers. In these classrooms, the instruction is almost entirely done on the computer. As students have complained, "There really isn't someone to explain things to you if you get confused. You either figure it out on your own or fail." The socio-emotional connections seem greatly reduced between student and teacher. The teacher becomes a manager. The other side of the sword is to use the computer or technology as an adjunct to the teacher, not to be the teacher. Used skillfully, it can allow for faster and deeper processing of traditional lessons. However, a machine can do many things, but it does not have empathy and it cannot teach a person to become human. It cannot speak of dreams or worries. Despite the problems humanity creates, I prefer human company to a machine, though I'll still use the machine.

There are also immediate and acute practical problems with digital technology. There are limited resources and digital technologies can potentially impact many. How should we allocate the resources for these valuable, yet expensive tools? What are the most effective ways to improve student performance? What areas of student performance do we want to target? For example, two technologies gaining more use are clickers and computers in the classroom. Computers are becoming more commonplace but eat up resources in both money and time. People go back and forth about whether it is better for everyone in a class to each have a simple computer or for the teacher to use just one computer and a projector with a whiteboard. There are fundamental questions and a profound ethical problem underlying this argument. First, do we understand enough about learning to know which instructional methods using those technologies will yield the most stable learning in the content and in the needed skills? And, more important, what theory of teaching and learning, if any, are the designers basing the instruction on? Computer engineers, software designers, and neuroscientists aren't teachers. They may design the equipment and software to input information, to do it faster and more efficiently, but do they understand how the brain "receives" and processes that information? For example, teachers also teach humanity in the context of their culture, something we can't define and stick in a machine. While we struggle with what it means to be human, we must address this ethical issue at some point if we are really considering having the computers doing the instruction.

Humans can communicate more fully on all levels and teach at all levels, characteristics that distinguish us from all other species and from machines. However, there is potentially a more insidious problem. The brain is plastic: How it wires and fires together is heavily influenced by the environment. The number of synaptic connections is constantly in flux due to the experiences we have. Computers also change our ways of thinking and problem solving. Nicholas Carr (2010) has argued that our thinking and problem solving have become shallower. With computers, we browse much faster, but we rarely pause to completely or thoroughly read the material in depth. For example, I've learned to read abstracts almost as fast as I can scroll. ClickTale, an Israeli software company, found that web surfers spend from 19 seconds to 25 seconds per page before moving on (ClickTale, 2008). Our browser behavior is rewarded by near instantaneous feedback. Neural circuitry for critical skills that are needed for habits of deep thinking are not utilized, and those circuits are replaced, dissolved, or co-opted for other uses. Jeffrey Schwartz of UCLA's medical school called it "survival of the busiest" (Schwartz & Begley, 2002). Carr argued that those circuits that are the busiest for reading and thinking appear to give way to our browsing Internet habits. Our brain defaults to what it uses the most. For educators, that creates a conundrum not just for the future, but right now. How do we get students to think more deeply, especially outside of the relatively controlled learning environment of the classroom when their super-fast and shallow browsing habits are reinforced hundreds if not thousands of times a day? At this point, we simply don't know.

Technology also creates new challenges for administrators. At the beginning of this book, in the introduction, I argued that too often educators and administrators frequently operate without a coherent theory of learning. That often means the school may be moving in some direction but does not have a rudder to really guide where it is going. Without a functional theory, the acquisition of technologies is a quagmire. It can easily result in some technologies being used for a while and then abandoned. The technologies get purchased and are introduced, and teachers can be left scrambling where students are teaching not only each other (which can be a good thing), but helping the teacher to figure it out. For example, in schools where most students have their own laptops, the method of instructional delivery is forced to change. Teachers must move around among the students to monitor, and new problems emerge as students find different ways to connect with each other and the Internet that we did not fully anticipate. Indeed, the most powerful lessons a teacher can learn are to understand the deeper meanings of what the students are really saying and how they are responding. However, it is not all doom and gloom. New ways of learning and keeping students engaged become new opportunities.

New Opportunities With Technology

Technology allows many students to explore lessons in greater depth and to create rapid feedback through discussions. One technology that can facilitate this is the "clicker." These are small cell-phone-sized units where students can click in responses to questions and surveys. The anonymous responses allow the teacher to have on-the-spot formative evaluations of their students, and these provide very rapid feedback to and from the students without embarrassing them (Henderson, 2010). The quality of the questions, in their level of cognitive demand, such as simple recall, recognition, or probing questions that require some reflective thought, is an important determinant of the usefulness of technology. Potentially, clickers may be most useful in rapidly determining where, or when, students are overloading their working memory and missing crucial information. Technologies drive changes, but without at least a working theory of teaching and learning at the classroom, building, local, or higher level that is understood by the teachers the use of the technologies to advance learning will probably be suboptimal. Clickers used with brain breaks would be an example of combining technology with working memory theory. How do we address the problem of how we should teach and now make appropriate use of the neuroscience findings? That argument goes back farther than even the time of Plato and Socrates, to as far as we can trace written history when records show that students were beaten when they did not learn their lessons in early written language called cuneiform well enough (Wolf, 2007).

Learning is a biological process involving the brain, which is impacted by the body housing it and the environment surrounding it. The health of the body affects the mind, and so does the environment around the body. New problems, including ethical and moral issues that affect the health of the mind, are emerging.

Student Health

The learner's health is another foundational issue. Although how diet affects the mind was described briefly in Chapter 2, more pressing concerns have developed. How do obesity, lack of exercise, too much time in front of a digital device, and lack of sleep affect learning? Studies on sleep deprivation demonstrate that it is very difficult for a student who has been up all night and had very little sleep to either learn new information or recall information from previous lessons. Sleep must be in place at the right time and in the right amounts if learning is to occur, let alone achieve optimal levels. We have partial answers to some of these neuro-related health issues, but they are also huge societal problems that affect not only students, but also productivity, the economy (including lowering the competitive ability to generate income and drain by health care costs) to mention just a few things. If the economy is the engine that drives societies, the mind/brain systems behind the economy are the ultimate resources on which it relies.

Another menacing health issue but one that is not well known has emerged in academic performance. Everyone is familiar with the problem of drug-enhanced athletic performances. It has become apparent that academic performances are also becoming more drug-enhanced in students' efforts to get higher grades. Precise levels of abuse in older adolescents, such as in college students, is not known but it is estimated that around 25% of the students have used drugs in efforts to improve their academic performances (Stix, 2009). There are significant ethical, moral, and practical dilemmas with such usage. In the first chapter, I suggested a working definition of learning that included being able to retrieve memories. If information can be retrieved only in a drug-induced state, what does that suggest for the person's daily performance when he or she is not using drugs? Think about an engineer designing a bridge, a chemist evaluating some pollutant, or a doctor trying to recall information about a disease symptom. As time goes by, the effects of different drugs may not create the same cognitive benefits. What happens to their performance then? How do older learners compete? Other issues include the advantages gained over those who don't use or can't afford the drugs. It is a form of cheating, as it were, but with many consequences. It is nightmarish to consider, but it is not fantasy. The problem is real and sizable, but virtually without notice in the media.

Another health-related and neuroeducational issue is whether student cognitive activity—use it or lose it—builds up a cognitive reserve that becomes so important in later life. Can educational practices build up a "brain bank account" that will slow or mitigate cognitive decline? The implications are enormous. Consider a very low cost estimate of $40,000 a year for the health care of an elderly person who must be institutionalized and can no longer make decisions or care for herself. If her cognitive reserve could have been increased, perhaps through more effort when she was younger, allowing mental acuity to be maintained longer, it might help her to continue her independence. Maintaining independence for even 1 year longer could save a society anywhere from *$3 to $60 billion* per year, based on the increasing elderly population. Dialogue about this is not even on the politician's radar. Yet as the baby boom generation now enters retirement the costs related to cognitive inability are already huge and rising. The ultimate resources on which the economic engine of society relies are the mind/brain systems of its citizens. We would do well to cultivate these systems and to determine whether educational efforts can positively affect cognitive reserve.

Training Educators for the Future

Training in the Biology of Learning

The approach to learning and teaching in neuroeducation is interdisciplinary. It requires both a broader and deeper understanding of how students learn and the effect of our teaching on the process. In reviewing the curricula of teacher-training programs, they appear to make very limited use, if any, of the research that is emerging from the neurosciences. This may mean that future educators will be ignorant of the biological processes of learning. In my experience, prospective and student teachers now appear to be improving in their content knowledge and use of standards, but they are almost totally lacking in the understanding of how learning works. The college curriculum contributes to the problems. For example, in higher education prospective teachers can expect to see courses on student behaviors, as well as course work about specific content such as mathematics or middle school science. However, few colleges offer studies about education as a science of learning—for example, studying the development of mathematic reasoning skills

(Haridman & Denckla, 2010). For more effective teaching and educational leadership, training and professional development in neuroeducation is needed.

Global and Local Forces

Educators' needs are framed by the world in which we find ourselves. There is no denying that we function in a global economy, and even the most rural areas are affected by what happens out in the rest of the world. Our students must not only achieve, but they must also be able to think creatively, problem solve, work with others, and understand others. Both veteran educators and those in training must be able to meet the twin demands of student higher achievement; they should have an understanding of how their students learn if they are going to adequately equip them to function in an increasingly competitive world.

However, neuroeducation is more than just about how the mind/brain system works in the individual student. Neuroeducation must also consider how the world outside of the student's body affects the systems inside the brain. Much of what we learn is through society. That means educators must pay close attention to the socio-emotional environment around their students. The environment may include the role of cultures (cultural neuroscience) or the physical environment in immediate proximity to the learner. The teacher and the classroom, the school environment, and local culture are significant elements within neuroeducation. An effective teacher must take into account how the individual student learns, and also how the contexts of the classroom and school affect learning for that student and the rest of his classmates. The daily, real-world problems that teachers face with students will also have to be seriously thought about by neuroeducation researchers if any real progress is to be made. Several universities are beginning to do just that, such as Harvard's master's program in Mind, Brain, and Education; John Hopkins's Mind, Brain, and Teaching program; the Rossier School of Education at University of Southern California; as well as developing programs at the University of Texas, Austin, and a promising assortment of others around the world. What might these schools of neuroeducation look like?

Kurt Fischer of Harvard advocates research schools that are markedly different from the "lab schools" of the education colleges; they would be more similar to a medical school model. When researchers and practitioners working closely together with real-life schools, findings can be used to guide educational training and policy in a manner similar to medical schools (Fischer & Heikkinen, 2010). A major advantage is that medical schools are able to test potential interventions rapidly and get their findings out to physicians. Research schools would not only study and test cognitive aspects of learning and teaching , but they would be integrated with cognitive neuroscience research. What might be incorporated in such an educational program was developed by Tracey Tokuhama-Espinosa (2008), who directs an educational development program in Quito, Ecuador. Some recommendations included having a common vocabulary about neuro-anatomy, having curricular topics of significance, noting what research is sure of or relatively certain of in relation to neuromyths, and conducting rigorous classwork, presentations, and reflective exercises.

Neuroeducation programs must also avoid the pitfalls of becoming too specialized and should expand their research to focus beyond students with impairments to include the typical student as well (Battro, 2010). In order to carry such investigations out, it is necessary to see how students learn in their natural environment. Like a naturalist trying to learn about animals, only limited information can be obtained when the subjects are in a controlled, artificial environment. Too often, seemingly successful practices that worked well in clinically controlled studies have made a resounding thud in the messy world of real classrooms. Teachers obviously play significant roles in the practices that actually work and they need to be partners in the research, including engaging in action research. In the neuroeducation approach they should be equal partners in testing, evaluating, suggesting, piloting, and teaching. The ideas to be reviewed may originate from any group before research and design of practices begins. One possible model to bridge research to practice is represented in Figure 10.1.

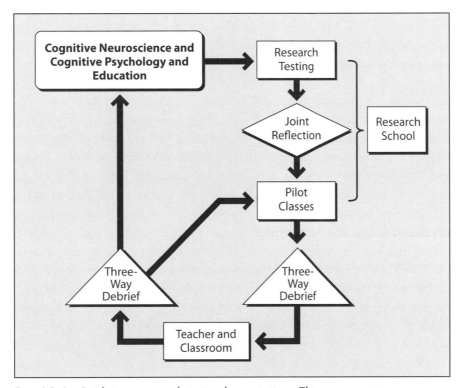

Fig. 10.1. Bridging research to implementation. This represent one possible model of a learning cycle that combines the efforts of cognitive neuroscientists, cognitive psychologists and educators. The cycle allows for systematic testing and re-evaluation of instructional practices before widespread implementation.

The research school, of which teachers are a part, may function like a medical school, testing practices and fine-tuning as best they can before the practitioners in the field give it a really thorough workout. The joint reflection is used in a fractal-like learning cycle by a team made of the classroom teachers and researchers, all carefully evaluating what happened, what worked, what didn't and why, and what changes to make before moving on, or perhaps going back to another pilot before larger-scale implementation. The three-way debrief or reflection is a little different. With that, the student joins as a participant in the lesson evaluation to help give the necessary input on such things as the emotional connections that are essential for building a lasting memory. His or her perceptions are important in understanding the level of involvement.

Problems, Questions, and Possibilities

The final section presents a sampling of specific questions, emerging problems, and topics with significant neuroeducation possibilities as expressed by number of educators and researchers in neuroeducation. Without question there are many other worthy problems not mentioned in this brief compilation.

Partnering With Parents

Many children are at a significant disadvantage before they ever get to school. The lack of exposure to reading and language is difficult to overcome, and they may remain behind their peers throughout school. By exposing infants and toddlers to the joy of reading and storytelling, along with early testing for language or working memory disorders, then some of the problems can be alleviated. A significant number of parents are teens, are in dysfunctional families with poor parenting skills, or have poor role models, if any, to look upon. One challenge is for schools to develop partnerships with parents to help with these problems rather than to put parents into an adversarial role.

Preparing the child to be more successful in learning can start in infancy, such as holding the child and reading to him or her with free books provided by the community. The challenge is how schools can connect, win, and provide support and guidance and do this in an affordable manner while avoiding the impression of being a part of government telling people what they have to do. I have seen first-hand parents rejecting any free support offered by the school because it was secular and from the government. Consequently, the student's problem, which could have been readily reduced, or even corrected, was ignored, leaving the child severely handicapped throughout his or her entire school career and possibly for life. Some people have considerable ignorance and a deep distrust of science and do not want anything to do with government. Part of developing the necessary parenting skills could be done through broad public education aimed at new parents. Often their own parents lacked parenting skills, and critical skills were not passed down.

Public Education

The public's general understanding of how the mind learns is poor at best. Educators still hear, "When I was in school . . ." There is a need for parents, teachers, and professors alike to come up to speed about the mind/brain function. As the field of medicine was over 100 years ago, the field of education is at a place where our collective understanding needs to move up to a more testable, biological standard. For example, many mental disorders are not caused by people being possessed but by disorders in the neural circuitry; this provides a biological basis that can be measured and in some cases located physically in scans (Raichle, 2010). As such, a number of these disorders are potentially treatable because they have real, physical origins in the brain. Students should not be dismissed as being "lazy, incorrigible, or possessed." (I do still run into those claims on an almost weekly basis.) Merely labeling a student potentially avoids confronting the problem, and it is not a solution.

To illustrate the necessity for greater understanding of the mind/brain systems and learning, a few school personnel, parents, and physicians are just beginning to develop an awareness of the damage caused by sports head injuries, such as in football or soccer. The damage is not visible in brain scans. Instead, there are micro-lesions, tears in the neural circuitry that do not show up on MRI scans. Just breaking a few axons in a circuit can have devastating effects (Tang-Schomer, Patel, Baas, & Smith, 2010). The injury often does not show up immediately, but the damage can accumulate. Many youth are seriously injured with brain concussions. The public needs to be more alert about precautions and students need better postinjury care. How do educators and researchers increase public awareness and move toward changing policies?

Policy

How do we get change to occur? The question is as old as politics. Schools and governments have repeatedly attempted "reform" with spectacular failures. Are changes best forced by top-down management, or experienced by those who must work with the students, such as through experiential learning, or some combination? One thought is to have those in charge experience the benefits of neuroeducation, rather than passively read or hear about what it can do. Ideas might be spread by memes, which may have the peculiar potential to be passed along and change, but can memes be intentionally designed to create change? How does the creation of a meme, such as "brain break" or "twitter," become viral and spread on its own across the Internet? To have change must there be a necessary critical mass? Are there necessary preexisting conditions for changing the collective mind? How do individuals change brain responses when in groups (the mob mentality)? Can personality theory be used to sculpt a message to create change? Chaos-complexity theory may also be able to describe change, and if that is so, perhaps we may eventually have the ability to predict when certain types of change will occur or to learn of the conditions necessary for change. Better mathematical models, along with better methods of data collection, are under continual study. Clearly, such questions have enormous implications beyond education, but these are also neuroscience questions in the realm of cultural neuroscience.

Attention Gets More Attention

The more we look, the more attention seems to be involved with working memory, problem solving, intelligence, and academic performance. While there are studies involving driving and viewing computer screens, educational practices where the brain's attention is formally monitored in functioning classrooms could help teachers understand how and what students are really paying attention to. For example, focusing on fundamental issues of attention, investigations could use the Doppler or NORIT technologies to observe how a student's attention system functions under different forms of instruction. Further, long-term memory performance could be followed in conjunction with the student's level of attention to determine correlates. Dopamine effects on attention might also be traced along with actual student performances. From the teacher's perspective, what interventions actually make a difference on the brain's attention as opposed to just what we observe in external student behavior and performance? Which teaching interventions work best, and are there developmental differences? With exercise, how long do the chemical changes or a state change help to maintain attention? How much exercise is optimal and when should it be? Does diet affect student attention and memory? Do all students benefit from an individual analysis with a blood panel? While all of these questions and hundreds more might be investigated piecemeal, they could be also be conducted in coordinated studies in an educational research school.

Effectiveness of the Teaching

The complexity of the mind/brain system, and its interaction with the environment in which students finds themselves, makes it unlikely that strict adherence to a teaching prescription or a particular intervention will work for everyone. We can't script a series of questions or directions that will function universally; our students' brains have too much variation. One size does not fit all.

How effective are specific teaching methods in creating lasting memory? Effective teaching and learning is considerably more difficult to measure than from just test scores despite the myopic nationwide tendency to do this. To reliably raise the level of a student's learning, it would be nice to know in general what a teacher can roughly expect students to retain if certain instructional methods are used. This is not teaching by prescription, but simply learning the effectiveness or potential gain of a particular method. For example, can educators expect approximately X amount will be remembered Y days later? This goes beyond simple retention and considers the stability of that retention. Are there strategies that are more effective in stabilizing the memory? Pashler, Roediger, Karpicke, and others have been pursuing this very practical and rich avenue of research (Carrier & Pashler, 1992; Roediger &

Karpicke, 2006). Suppose we teach with a complex mind map that can be manipulated and find a consistent, predictable fading of the memory. When is the most optimal time to do a short, intensive review? In addition, if the review creates a stable long-term memory that the students can recall, how well does it last *after* the course is over? If an entire lesson appears to be forgotten, will re-teaching the lesson with a particular method allow for faster relearning by building on what remains of existing networks? There is partial information on these questions but it is insufficient to make good decisions. Different forms of instruction may necessitate different optimal times of reinforcement. These are practical instructional questions of consequence to the teacher and public alike. What did the student retain and could still use? How long will it take to relearn a section of history or of math?

There is the research capability to look more closely at the efficacy of a particular teaching method, but researchers do not have the data banks from many learning circumstances on which to make decisions. However, the building of such data banks is possible. Perhaps in the future the Department of Education or a foundation might help create a national data bank that could be used in such a manner.

However, the effectiveness of different teaching methods is an integral part of neuroscience. What happened at the neuronal level so that teaching method A works better than B, and can the influences on method A be used with other methods to produce better, stable, and retrievable results? There are so many variables to consider. Research along those lines is largely beyond our present reach. John Ratey made a passing remark a decade ago in respect to the mind/brain systems: "Everything counts." Indeed, so much of it does; we simply don't know how many variables affect the mind and brain. In addition, some things count more, but which things and when? What the teacher can control and does in the delivery of a lesson counts for much. This sort of fundamental but highly practical problem might fit the research school paradigm rather well.

Teacher Training and Professional Workshops

Are the programs and staff training aligned with the school's theory of teaching and learning? Will such programs be integrated, actively monitored, and used? As more than one teacher has said to me about trainers, "They blow in, blow off, and blow out." There is often excellent training available, and there is much to be learned from professional development trainers, but if it is not fully integrated, the mind's Darwinian selection on neurons follows: "use it or lose it."

Resiliency

Is there anything teachers can consistently do that makes a difference with our students who are hammered by life? What is the role of mirror neurons in resiliency? These are closely aligned with the ever-perplexing, multifaceted issues of motivation. Why are some students better able to withstand terrible homes or bad school environments and possibly even thrive while many students do not?

The Military

The military is the largest single organization with direct responsibility for educating adolescents. They have a huge interest in adolescents being able to learn faster, be smarter, and have learning last longer. They have a number of ongoing research groups investigating human learning, including DARPA, and the Mind Research Network is working on the multilayered puzzle that makes up the mind/brain systems. Astonishing developments in mind/brain research, whether from these research labs or others, may bring high hopes or crushing disillusionment. Consequently, the neuroscience findings must be placed in proper context to avoid overreaching. As the learning cycle in Figure 10.1 implies, any announcement or program being proffered should go through testing, verification, and testing again.

Mathematics

Mathematics is a frustrating area for teaching. There are mountains of research, but getting usable information for teachers that will provide some guidance in reaching more students with greater effectiveness, or knowing when teachers need to try a specific instructional method, is sorely lacking. There may be some answers in the research, but if there are, they are not where teachers can access them. To start with, it would be helpful to know if the students have reached a level of cognitive development where they can even do the math problems. Are they developmentally ready? Perhaps they can memorize how to do a problem, but they still can't comprehend the underlying principles. In regard to the cycles of cognitive skill development, when are students ready for the next level of math? Can evaluation tools help teachers to be more certain? Some of the research tools that can provide answers are in place, but the sheer scale of the problem is daunting.

Math teachers also have a huge toolbox of different ways to do problems, but they need better on-the-spot diagnostics for when to use a particular tool. The comment I've repeatedly heard is, "What do I do when . . . ?" Teachers try different approaches, but those do not reveal why, or necessarily where, the student ran into problems. In addition to learning about how to do math, and various ways to teach it, teachers could use some help in figuring out what underlies the students' problems. Solving that mystery alone would be worth the Field Prize for mathematics.

Arts and the Brain

Should schools cut the arts? After all, one argument goes, they *aren't* academic core programs and schools need more time for test prep. That situation is being played out in school after school. A more important question is, Do the arts help the brain in learning? If so, how much is the effect? Is there a generalization to other areas of learning by the brain's action observation network that utilizes spatial-observational learning, attention skills, passion, and self-regulation (Grafton, 2010; Posner & Patoine, 2010) Exercise, as we observed in earlier chapters, has academic benefits. Cutting the arts to make more time for boosting test scores is dubious at best, harmful at worst. Test scores themselves, the supposed measures of the students' minds, are probably more art than science. Volumes of opinion contending one view or another have been written, but educators must again look at what *should* be guiding their teaching and learning policies. Do the policy makers, and test designers have a working theory of teaching and learning that is *actively* guiding the design of the assessment or the framing of the probes? Are the goals of achieving higher test scores appropriate? Assessments measure more than just learning. Neuroeducation assessments, based on brain function and cognitive skill development, may potentially offer a more insightful look into not only what the students know and can do, but also what needs to be taught next based upon the stability of their knowledge/skill set, why they can or can't do it, as well as the success of the instructional approach. To design such assessments requires current neuroscience knowledge of teaching theory and learning theory. Standardized measures fall a bit short for now.

Final Thoughts

The brain is not a fad that is going to go away, as one college dean bluntly asserted. While it is true there are currently few instructors at the college level who have sufficient background across the wide array of disciplines that are involved, that does not mean the faculty should ignore the massively growing body of data. The problem of too few skilled instructors has been anticipated, and the foundations for a solid, productive start in graduate neuroeducation programs have already been developed. In addition, members of IMBES, the International Mind, Brain, and Education Society, work at many levels, including providing professional development to help educators learn about the brain.

There are a lot of important, practical, yet fascinating problems to solve, and educators play a significant role in finding answers. When you run into a problem in the classroom, and wonder what is going on in the student's mind, or if some strategy would really work, write it down and communicate it to researchers. Research schools and evidence-based communities are developing. To locate these, contact or join IMBES. Give voice not to gripes but to learning problems that you need answers to, whether big or small. Conduct some action research in your school or classroom, and methodically test some ideas, but never do harm. Always consider what might happen if the methods don't work. Will the students be worse off?

Also, never give up on your students. I know it is hard at times, but we don't always know when we've touched someone, made a difference, and created a memory that will help the students. Educators and their students in different learning environments are the scientists who ultimately test what we all have learned. What you do is very important.

A final thought: Never stop learning. Don't stop firing and wiring. For if you do, yor brain starts dying. As for me, I'm still learning.

RESOURCES

International Mind, Brain, and Education Society. http://www.imbes.org

Glycemic Loads of Common Foods

	GLYCEMIC LOADS OF COMMON FOODS		
	FOOD	SERVING SIZE (gms)	GL/serving
1	Soya bean, average	150	1
2	Peanuts, average	150	1
3	French fries	150	2
4	Milk, full fat	250 ml	3
5	Grapefruit	120	3
6	Cashews, salted	50	3
7	Green peas, average	80	3
8	Carrots, average	80	3
9	Tomato juice, canned	250 ml	4
10	Milk, skim	250 ml	4
11	Peach, canned in light syrup	120	4
12	Pear, average	120	4
13	Watermelon	120	4
14	Quick Chocolate, Nestlé)	250 ml	5
15	Apricots, raw	120	5
16	Orange, average	120	5
17	Peach, average	120	5
18	Pear, canned in pear juice	120	5
19	Plums	120	5
20	Lentil, average	150	5
21	Pumpernickle	30	6

22	Sourdough rye	30	6
23	Apple, average	120	6
24	Kiwi, average	120	6
25	M&M's, Peanut	30	6
26	Microwave popcorn, plain, average	20	6
27	Coarse barley bread, 75%–80% kernels, average hamburger bun	30	7
28	Reduced-fat yogurt with fruit, average	200 ml	7
29	Pineapple, average	120	7
30	Baked beans, average	150	7
31	Black Beans	150	7
32	Kidney beans, average	150	7
33	Chicken nuggets, frozen, reheated in microwave 5 minutes	100	7
34	Sucrose, average	10	7
35	Wheat tortilla	50	8
36	Ice cream regular	50	8
37	Grapes, average	120	8
38	Chickpeas, average	150	8
39	Apple pie, made without sugar	60	9
40	Healthy Choice Hearty, 100% whole grain	30	9
41	Whole wheat bread, average	30	9
42	100% Whole grain bread (Natural Ovens)	30	9
43	Hamburger bun	30	9
44	All-Bran, average	30	9
45	chickpeas, canned in brine	150	9
46	Pizza, super supreme (Pizza Hut)	100	9
47	Waffles, Aunt Jemima–Quaker Oats	35	10
48	White Wheat flour bread	30	10
49	Wonder bread, average	30	10
50	Pita bread, white	30	10
51	White flour average	30	10
52	Shortbread	25	10
53	Rye crisps, average	25	10
54	Prunes, pitted	120	10

55	Lima beans, baby, frozen	150	10
56	Honey, average	25	10
57	Grapefruit juice, unsweetened	250 ml	11
58	Pearled Barley, average	150	11
59	Complete Hot Chocolate (Nestlé)	250 ml	11
60	Corn chips, plain, salted (Doritos)	50	11
61	Potato chips,average	50	11
62	Kaiser roll	30	12
63	50% cracked wheat kernel	30	12
64	Corn tortilla	50	12
65	Gatorade	250 ml	12
66	Apple Juice, unsweetened, average	250 ml	12
67	Rasin Bran (Kellogg's)	30	12
68	Buglur, average	150	12
69	soda crackers	25	12
70	Navy beans, average	150	12
71	Parsnips	80	12
72	Apple pie, made with sugar	60	13
73	Orange Juice, average	250ml	13
74	Ice cream, premium	50	13
75	Banana,ripe	120	13
76	Black-eyed peas, avererge	150	13
77	Yam, average	150	13
78	Oatmeal, average	250	14
79	Special K (Kellogg's)	30	14
80	Whole Wheat kernels, average	50	14
81	Graham crackers	25	14
82	Vanilla Wafers	25	14
83	Smoothie, raspberry	250 ml	14
84	spaghetti, wholemeal, boiled, average	180	14
85	Boiled white potato, average	150	14
86	Potato, microwaved	150	14
87	Baguette, white, plain	70	15

88	Banana cake make without sugar	80	16
89	Melba toast	30	16
90	Coca Cola, average	250 ml	16
91	Cranberry juice cocktail (Ocean Spray)	250 ml	16
92	Pineapple juice, unsweetened (Dole)	250 ml	16
93	Puffed wheat, average	30	16
94	Figs, dried	60	16
95	Pretzel, oven baked	30	16
96	Sponge cake, plain	63	17
97	Cream of Wheat (Nabisco)	30	17
98	Muesli, average	30	17
99	Instant oatmeal, average	250	17
100	Shreaded Wheat (Nabisco)	30	17
101	Rice cakes, average	25	17
102	Apricot fruit bar	50	17
103	Instant mashed potato, average	150	17
104	Sweet potato, average	150	17
105	Banana cake make with sugar	80	18
106	Froot Loops (Kellogg's)	30	18
107	Brown rice, average	150	18
108	White rice, converted (Uncle Ben's)	150	18
109	Fettuccini, average	180	18
110	Spaghetti, white, boiled 5 min., average	180	18
111	Ensure	250 ml	19
112	Coco Puffs (Kellogg's)	30	20
113	Sweet corn on the cob, average	150	20
114	Corn Pops (Kellogg's)	30	21
115	Pancakes	77	22
116	Crispix (Kellogg's)	30	22
117	Cream of Wheat, instant (Nabiso)	250	22
118	Quick cooking white basmati rice	150	22
119	Long grained rice, boiled white, average	50	22
120	Spaghetti, white, 20 min., average	180	22

121	Jelly beans, average	30	22
122	Pizza, plain baked dough, served with parmesan chesse and tomato sauce	100	22
123	Fanta, orange soft drink	250 ml	23
124	Rice Chex, (Nabisco)	30	23
125	Couscous, average	150	23
126	Rice, boiled white, average	150	23
127	White rice, average	150	23
128	Linguine, average	180	23
129	Macaroni, average	180	23
130	Vanilla cake made from packet mix with vanilla frosting	111	24
131	Cornflakes, average	30	24
132	Fruit roll-ups	30	24
133	Power Bar, average	65	24
134	Bagel, white, frozen	70	25
135	Pop Tarts, double chocolate (Kellogg's)	50	25
136	Baked russet potato, average	150	26
137	Mars candy bar	60	27
138	Raisins	60	28
139	Corn muffin	57	30
140	Macaroni and chesse (Kraft)	180	32
141	Hummus (chickpea salda dip)	120	39
142	Lucozade, original (sparkling glucose drink)	250 ml	40
143	Dates, dried	60	42

Foster-Powell, K., Holt, S.A., Brand-Miller, J.C. (2000). International Table of glycemic index and glycemic load value: 2002. *The American Journal of Clinical Nutrition*, 76(1), 5–56.

Diagnostic Criteria for Attention-Deficit/Hyperactivity Disorder

A. Either (1) or (2)

(1) six (or more) of the following symptoms of *inattention* have persisted for at least 6 months to a degree that is maladaptive and inconsistent with developmental level:

Inattention
(a) often fails to give close attention to details or makes careless mistakes in schoolwork, work, or other activities
(b) often has difficulty sustaining attention in tasks or play activities
(c) often does not seem to listen when spoken to directly
(d) often does not follow through on instructions and fails to finish schoolwork, chores, or duties in the workplace (not due to oppositional behavior or failure to understand instructions)
(e) often has difficulty organizing tasks and activities
(f) often avoids, dislikes, or is reluctant to engage in tasks that require sustained mental effort (such as schoolwork or homework)
(g) often loses things necessary for tasks or activities (e.g., toys, school assignments, pencils, books, or tools)
(h) is often easily distracted by extraneous stimuli
(i) is often forgetful in daily activities

(2) six (or more) of the following symptoms of *hyperactivity-impulsivity* have persisted for at least 6 months to a degree that is maladaptive and inconsistent with developmental level:

Hyperactivity

(a) often fidgets with hands or feet or squirms in seat

(b) often leaves seat in classroom or in other situations in which remaining seated is expected

(c) often runs about or climbs excessively in situations in which it is inappropriate (in adolescents or adults, may be limited to subjective feeling of restlessness)

(d) often has difficulty playing or engaging in leisure activities quietly

(e) is often "on the go" or often acts as if "driven by a motor"

(f) often talks excessively

Impulsivity

(g) often blurts out answers before questions have been completed

(h) often has difficulty awaiting turn

(i) often interrupts or intrudes on others (e.g., butts into conversations or games)

B. Some hyperactive-impulsive or inattentive symptoms that caused impairment were present before age 7 years.

C. Some impairment from the symptoms is present in two or more settings (e.g., at school [or work] and at home).

D. There must be clear evidence of clinically significant impairment in social, academic, or occupational functioning.

E. The symptoms do not occur exclusively during the course of a Pervasive Developmental Disorder, Schizophrenia, or other Psychotic Disorder and are not better accounted for by another mental disorder (e.g., Mood Disorder, Anxiety Disorder, Dissociative Disorder, or a Personality Disorder).

Reprinted with permission from the *Diagnostic and Statistical Manual of Mental Disorders*, Text Revision, Fourth Edition. Copyright © 2000 by the American Psychiatric Association.

Multiple Intelligences Mind Map

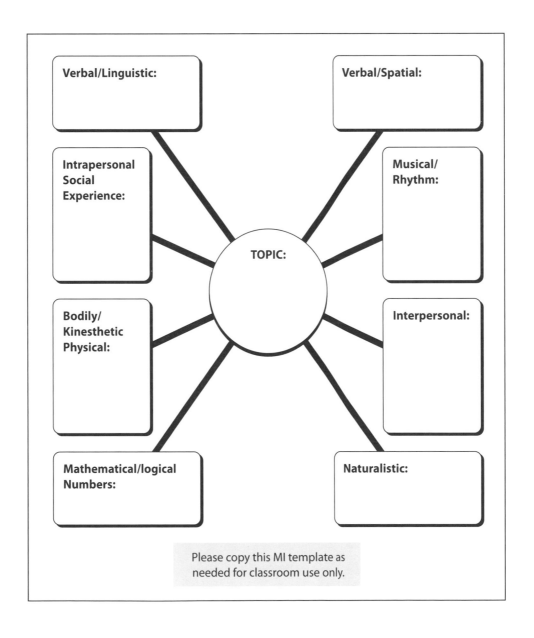

Verbal/Linguistic:

Verbal/Spatial:

Intrapersonal Social Experience:

Musical/ Rhythm:

TOPIC:

Bodily/ Kinesthetic Physical:

Interpersonal:

Mathematical/logical Numbers:

Naturalistic:

Please copy this MI template as needed for classroom use only.

RESOURCES

Abused or Assault Interview Criteria, Interview Protocol
(full version, background is given first, protocol is further down in the document):
http://www.ncbi.nlm.nih.gov/pmc/articles/PMC2180422/

Abused or Assault Interview Criteria, Simpler 10-Step Interview Protocol
http://works.bepress.com/cgi/viewcontent.cgi?article = 1004&context =
thomaslyon

Automated Working Memory Assessment (AWMA)
http://www.psychcorp.co.uk/awma
This computer program helps to identify students who have working memory
problems and are more likely to miss instructions or not quite qualify for special
assistance.

CogMed
This is the only working memory program to date that can be validated through
research for improving student performance.

Developmental Testing Service (DTS)
http://www.devtestservice.com
This site provides testing and assessments based on brain growth. The assessments and ongoing research can be very informative to the educator or administrator.

International Mind, Brain, and Education Society
http://www.imbes.org
This society has an extremely high-quality quarterly journal and it superbly represents the leading work in mind/brain education.

REFERENCES

Aber, J. L., Jones, S. M., Brown, J. L., Chaudry, N., & Samples, F. (1998). Resolving conflict creatively: Evaluating the developmental effects of a school-based violence prevention program in neighborhood and classroom context. *Development and Psychopathology, 10,* 187, 213.

Abikoff, H., Courtney, M. E., Szeibel, P. J., & Koplewicz, H. S. (1996). The effects of auditory stimulation on the arithmetic performance of children with ADHD and nondisabled children. *Journal of Learning Disabilities, 29,* 238–246.

Abrami, P., Leventhal, L., & Perry, R. (1982). Educational seduction. *Review of Educational Research, 52,* 446–464.

Abramowitz, A., & O'Leary, S. (1991). Behavioral interventions for the classroom: Implications for students with ADHD. *School Psychology Review, 20,* 220–234.

Agung, S., & Schwartz, M. S. (2007). Student's understanding of conservation of matter, energy, stoichiometry and balancing equations in Indonesia. *International Journal of Science Education, 29*(13), 1679–1702.

Akerjordet, K., & Severinsson, E. (2009). Emotional intelligence. Part 1: The development of scales and psychometric testing. *Nursing and Health Sciences, 11,* 58–63.

Alexander, J. M., Carr, M., & Schwanenflugel, P. J. (1995). Development of metacognition in gifted children: Directions for future research. *Developmental Review, 15,* 1–37.

Alkire, L., & Westgermna-Alkire, C. (2006). *Periodical title abbreviations: By title* (16th ed., Vol. 2). New York, NY: Thomson Gale.

Allen, T. (1986). Styles of exploration in control attention, attention deficit disorder with hyperactive and learning disabled children. *Journal of Learning Disabilities, 19,* 351–353.

Amen, D. (2001). *Healing ADD: The breakthrough program that allows you to see and heal the 6 types of ADD.* New York, NY: Berkley.

American Academy of Pediatrics. (1968). The Doman-Delacato treatment of neurologically handicapped children. *Neurology, 18,* 1214–1215.

American Academy of Pediatrics. (1998). Learning disabilities, dyslexia, and vision: A subject review. *Pediatrics, 103,* 1217–1219.

Anderson, C., Berkowitz, L., Donnerstein, E., Huesmann, L. R., Johnson, J. D., Linz. D., Malamuth, N. M., & Wartella, E. (2003). The influence of media violence on youth. *Psychological Science in the Public Interest, 4,* 81–110.

Anderson, C., Gentile, D., & Buckley, K. (2007). *Violent video game effect on children and adolescents.* New York, NY: Oxford University Press.

Anderson, C., Sakamoto, A., & Gentile, D. (2008). Longitudinal effects of violent video games on aggression in Japan and the United States. *Pediatrics, 122*(5), 1067–1072.

Andrade, J. (2009). What does doodling do? *Applied Cognitive Psychology, 23*(3), 1–7.

Andreasen, N., O'Leary, D. S., Paradiso, S., Cizadlo, T., Arndt, S., Watkins, G. L., Boles Ponto, L. L., & Hichwa, R. D. (1999). The cerebellum plays a role in conscious episodic memory retrieval. *Human Brain Mapping, 8*(4), 226–234.

Angevaren, M., Aufdemkampe, G., Verhaar, H., Aleman, A., & Vanhees, L. (2008). Physical activity and enhanced fitness to improve cognitive function in older people without known cognitive impairment [Review]. *Cochrane Database of Systemic Reviews*, Issue 2.

Arnold, L. (2001). Alternative treatments for adults with attention-deficit hyperactivity disorder (ADHD). *Adult Attention Deficit Disorder, 931*, 310–341.

Aronson, E. (2000). *Nobody left to hate: Teaching compassion after Columbine.* New York, NY: Worth.

Arter, J., & Jenkins, J. (1979). Differential diagnosis—prescriptive teaching: A critical appraisal. *Review of Educational Research, 49*, 517–555.

Atkinson, J. 1964. *An introduction to motivation.* Princeton, NJ: Van Nostrand.

Atkinson, R. C., & Raugh, M. R. (1975). An application of the mnemonic keywords method to the acquisition of Russian vocabulary. *Journal of Experimental Psychology, Human Learning and Memory, 104*(2), 126–133.

Atkinson, R. C. & Shiffrin, R. M. (1968). Human memory: A proposed system and its control processes. In Spence, K. W. & Spence, J. T.. *The psychology of learning and motivation (Volume 2).* New York: Academic Press. pp. 89 195.

Atkinson, R. C., & Shiffrin, R. M. (1971). The control of short-term memory. *Scientific American, 225*(2), 82–90.

Baars, B. J. (1988). *A cognitive theory of consciousness.* London: Cambridge University Press.

Baddeley, A. D. (1966a). The influence of acoustic and semantic similarity on long-term memory for word sequences. *Quarterly Journal of Experimental Psychology, 18*, 302–309.

Baddeley A.D. (1966b). Short-term memory for word sequences as a function of acoustic, semantic, and formal similarity. *Quarterly Journal of Experimental Psychology, 18*, 362–365.

Baddeley, A. D. (1997). *Human memory: Theory and practice* (Rev. ed.). Hove, United Kingdom: Psychology Press.

Baddeley, A. D. (2007). *Working memory, thought, and action.* Oxford, United Kingdom: Oxford University Press.

Baddeley, A. D. & Hitch, G. (1974). Working memory. In G.H. Bower (Ed.). The psychology of learning and motivation, *8*, 47–90. New York: Academic Press.

Baddeley, A. D., Thomson, N., & Buchanan, M. (1975). Word length and structure of short-term memory storage. *Journal of Memory and Language, 27*, 586–595.

Bailey, R. (2002). The effects of highlighting on long-term memory. Retrieved from http://clearinghouse.missouriwestern.edu/manuscripts/294.asp

Bandura, A. (1969). *Principles of behavior modification.* New York, NY: Holt, Rinehart & Winston.

Bandura, A. (1986). *Social foundations of thought and action: A social cognitive theory.* Englewood Cliffs, NJ: Prentice-Hall.

Banikowski, A. K., & Mehring, T. A. (1999). Strategies to enhance memory based on brain research. *Focus on Exceptional Children, 32,* 1–16.

Barkley, R. (1998). *Attention-deficit hyperactivity disorder: A handbook for diagnosis and treatment* (2nd ed.). New York, NY: Guilford Press.

Barkley, R. A., Guevremont, D. C., Anastopoulos, A. D., DuPaul, G. J., & Shelton, T. L. (1993). Driving-related risks and outcomes of attention deficit hyperactivity disorder in adolescents and young adults. A 3–5 year follow-up survey. *Pedicatrics, 92,* 212–218.

Barnes, M.A., Faulkner, H., Wilkinson, M., & Dennis, M. (2004). Meaning construction and integration in children with hydrocephalus. *Brain and Language, 89,* 47–56.

Baroff, G. A. (1999). General learning disorder: A new designation for mental retardation. *Mental Retardation, 3*(71), 68–70.

Bar-On, R. (1997). *The Bar-On emotional quotient inventory (EQ-i): A test of emotional intelligence.* Toronto, Canada: Multi-Health Systems.

Baron-Cohen, S. (2003). *The essential difference: Male and female brains and the truth about autism.* New York, NY: Basic Books.

Barr, J. J., & Higgins-D'Alessandro, A. (2009). How do adolescent empathy and prosocial behavior change in the context of school culture: A two-year longitudinal study. *Adolescence, 44*(176), 751–772.

Barrington, E. (2004). Teaching to student diversity in higher education: How multiple intelligence theory can help. *Teaching in Higher Education, 9*(4), 421–434.

Barrouillet, P., Gavens, N., Vergauwe, E., Gaillard, V., & Camos, V. (2009). Working memory span development: A time-based resource-sharing model account. *Developmental Psychology, 45*(2), 477–490.

Battro, A. (2010). The teaching brain. *Mind, Brain, and Education, 4*(1), 28–32.

Benedetti, F., Amanzio, M., Baldi, S., Casadio, C., & Cavallo, A (2003). Conscious expectation and unconscious condition in agalgesic motor and hormonal placebo/nocebo response. *Journal of Neuroscience, 23*(10), 4315–4323.

Bennett, D., Zentall, S., Giorgetti, K., & French, B. (2006). *Computer-administered choice and modality of math instructions for students with and without attention deficit hyperactivity disorder.* Manuscript submitted for publication.

Berlyne, D. (1960). *Conflict, arousal, and curiosity.* New York, NY: McGraw-Hill.

Beyerstein, B. L. (1999). Whence cometh the myth that we use only 10% of our brains? In S. D. Salla (Ed.), *Mind myths.* Chichester, United Kingdom: John Wiley & Sons.

Bhatia, M., Nigam, V. R., Bohra, N., & Malik, S. C. (1991). Attention deficit disorder with hyperactivity among paediatric outpatients. *Journal of Child Psychology and Psychiatry, 32,* 297–306.

Biedman, J., Faraone, S., Mick, E., Williamson, S. Wilens, T., Spencer, T., Weber, W., Jetton, J., Kraus, I., Pert, J., & Zallen, B. (1999). Clinical correlates of AD/HD in females: Findings from a large group of girls ascertained from pediatric and psychiatric referral services. *Journal of the American Academy of Child and Adolescent Psychiatry, 38,* 966–975.

Biemiller, A. (1999). *Language and reading success*. Cambridge, MA: Brookline.

Binder, L., Dixon, M., & Ghezzi, P. (2000). A procedure to teach self-control to children with attention deficit hyperactivity disorder. *Journal of Applied Behavior Analysis, 33,* 233–237.

Binet, A., & Simon, T. (1905). Methodes nouvelles pour le diagnostic duy niveau intellectual des anormaux [A new method for the diagnosis of intellectual level of abnormal persons]. *L'annee Psychologique, 11,* 191–244.

Bliss, T., & Lømo, T. (1973). Long-lasting potentiation of synaptic transmission in the dentate area of the anaesthetized rabbit following stimulation of the perforant pathway. *Journal of Physiology, 232,* 331–356.

Blos, P. (1979). *The adolescent passage*. New York, NY: International Universities Press.

Boch, F., & Piolat, A. (2004). Note taking and learning: A summary of research. (Summarized from Pilot & Boch, Apprendes en nutant et apprendre á noter. Retrieved from WAC.colostate.edu/journal/vol16/boch)

Bookheimer, S., Zeffiro, T. A., Blaxton, T., Gaillard, W. D., Malow, B., & Theodore, W. H. (1998). Regional blood flow during auditory response naming: Evidence for cross-modality neural activation. *Neuroreport, 9*(10), 225–240.

Boorstin, D. J. (1983). *The discoverers*. New York, NY: Random House.

Bouchard, T. J. (2004). Genetic influence on human psychological traits: A survey. *Current Directions in Psychological Science, 13,* 148–151.

Bower, G. H., & Clark, M. C. (1969). Narrative stories as mediators for serial learning. *Psychonomic Science, 14,* 181–182.

Bowers, J. S., & Schacter, D. (1990). Implicit memory and test awareness. *Journal of Experimental Psychology: Learning, Memory, and Cognition, 16,* 404–416.

Brand-Miller, J., Wolever, T. M. S., & Colagiuri, S., (1999). The glucose revolution: the authoritative guide to the glycemic index. New York, NY: Marlow & Co.

Braumeister, R. F., Campbell, J. D., Krueger, J. I., & Vohs, K. D. (2005). Exploding the self-esteem myth. *Scientific American, 284*(4), 96–101.

Brody, N. (2004). What cognitive intelligence is and what emotional intelligence is not. *Psychological Inquiry, 15,* 234–238.

Brophy, J. (1983). Fostering student learning and motivation in the elementary school classroom. In S. Paris, G. Olson, and H. Stevenson (Eds.), *Learning and motivation in the classroom* (pp. 283–305). Hillsdale, NJ: Lawrence Erlbaum.

Brophy, J., Rohrkemper, M., Rashid, H., & Goldberger, M. (1983). Relationships between teachers' presentations of classroom tasks and students' engagements in those tasks. *Journal of Educational Psychology, 75,* 544–552.

Brown, A. L., & Palincsar, A. S. (1989). Guided cooperative learning and individual knowledge acquisitions. In L. G. Resnick (Ed.), *Knowing and learning: Essays in honor of Robert Glaser* (pp. 393–451). Hillsdale, NJ: Lawrence Erlbaum.

Brown, T., & Summerbell, C. (2008). Systematic review of school-based interventions that focus on changing dietary intake and physical activity levels to prevent childhood obesity: An update to the obesity guidance produced by the National Institute for Health and Clinical Excellence. *Obesity Reviews, 10,* 110–141.

Bryan, J., & Walbek, N. (1970). Preaching and practicing generosity: Children's actions and reactions. *Child Development, 41,* 329–353.

Brynes, J., & Fox, N. (1998). The educational relevance of research in cognitive neuroscience. *Educational Psychology Review, 10*(3), 297–342.

Budd, G., & Volpe, S. (2006). School-based obesity prevention: Research, challenges, and recommendations. *Journal of School Health, 76*(10), 485–495. doi: 10.1111/j.1746-1561.2006.00149.x

Bus, A., & Van Ijzendoorn, M. (1999). Phonological awareness and early reading: A meta-analysis of experimental training studies. *Journal of Educational Psychology, 218*, 163–186.

Cahill, L., & McGaugh, J. L. (1995). A novel demonstration of enhanced memory associated with emotional arousal. *Consciousness and Cognition, 4*, 410–421.

Callender, A. A., & McDaniel, M. A. (2008). The limited benefits of rereading educational texts. *Contemporary Educational Psychology, 34*, 30–41.

Carr, N. (2010). *The shallows: What the internet is doing to our brains*. New York, NY: W. W. Norton.

Carrier, M., & Pashler, H. (1992). The influence of retrieval on retention. *Memory and Cognition, 20*, 632–642.

Carroll, J. (1993). *Human cognitive abilities: A survey of factor-analytic studies*. Cambridge, United Kingdom: Cambridge University Press.

Centers for Disease Control and Prevention. (2004). Participation in high school physical education—United States, 1991–2003. *Morbidity and Mortality Weekly Report, 53*(36), 844–847.

Cherry, E. (1953). Some experiments on the recognition of speech, with one and two ears. *Journal of the Acoustical Society of America, 25*, 975–979.

ChinaCulture.org. (2009). Retrieved October 4, 2010, from http://www.chinaculture. org/gb/en_artqa/2003-09/24/content_41869.htm

Chomitz, V. R., Suning, M. M., McGowan, R. J., Mitchell, S. E., Dawson, G. F., & Hacker, K. A. (2009). Is there a relationship between physical fitness and academic achievement? Positive results from public school children in the Northeastern United States. *Journal of School Health, 79*(1), 30–37.

Clancy, S. A., Schacter, D. L., McNally, R. J., & Pitman, R. K. (2000). False recognition in women reporting recovered memories of sexual abuse. *Psychological Science, 11*, 26–31.

ClickTale. (2008, July 31). Puzzling web habits across the globe. Retrieved from http://www.clicktale.com/2008/07/31/puzzling-web-habits-across-the-globe-part-1/

Coe, D. P., Pivarnik, J. M., Womack, C. J., Reeves, M. J., & Malina, R. M. (2006). Effect of physical education and activity levels on academic achievement in children. *Medicine & Science in Sports & Exercise, 38*(8), 1515–1519.

Cohen, A. (2005, April 6). U.S. kids get new therapies to aid in learning. *Wall Street Journal Europe,* p. A.8.

Cohen, Y. (2003). The transmission and reception of Mesopotamian scholarly texts at the City of Emar, Harvard University, unpublished dissertation. In M. Wolf (2007), *Proust and the squid: The story and science of the reading brain* (pp. 37). New York, NY: Harper Perennial.

Colcombe, S., & Kramer, A. (2003). Fitness effects on the cognitive function of older adults: A meta-analysis study. *Psychological Science, 14*(2), 125–130.

Commons, M. L., Trudeau, E. J., Stein, S. A., Richards, F. A., & Krause, S. R. (1998). Hierarchical complexity of tasks shows the existence of developmental stages. *Developmental Review, 18*, 237–278.

Connell, J. (1985). A new multidimensional measure of children's perceptions of control. *Child Development, 56*, 1018–1041.

Conners, C. (1997). *Conner's teacher rating scale—Revised (L)*. North Tonawanda, NY: Multi-Health Systems.

Cooper, J. O., Heron,, T. E., & Heward, W. L. (2007). *Applied Behavior Analysis (2nd Edition)*. Upper Saddle River, NJ: Merrill Prentice Hall.

Cotugno, A. (1987). Cognitive control functioning in hyperactive and nonhyperactive learning disabled children. *Journal of Learning Disabilities, 20*, 563–567.

Covington, M. (1992). *The will to learn: A guide for motivating young people*. New York, NY: Cambridge University Press.

Covington, M. (2002). Rewards and intrinsic motivation, a needs-based, developmental perspective. In F. Pajares and T. Urdan (Eds.), *Academic motivation of adolescents* (pp. 169–192). Greenwich, CT: Information Age Publishing.

Cowan, N. (2001). The magical number 4 in short-term memory: A reconsideration of mental storage capacity. *Behavioral and Brain Sciences, 24*, 87–185.

Cowan, N. (2005). *Working memory capacity*. New York, NY: Psychological Press.

Craik, F. (1982). Selective changes in encoding as a function of reduced processing capacity. In J. Hoffman & E. Van der Meer (Eds.), *Cognitive research in psychology* (pp. 152–161). Berlin, Germany: Deutscher Verlag der Wissenschaaffen..

Craik, F., Govoni, R., & Naveh-Benjamin, M. (1996). The effects of divided attention on encoding and retrieval processes in human memory. *Journal of Experimental Psychology: General, 125*, 159–180.

Craik, F. I. M., & Lockhart, R. S. (1972). Levels of processing: A framework for memory research. *Journal of Verbal Learning and Verbal Behavior, 11*, 671–684.

Crandall, V., Katkovsky, W., & Crandall, V. (1965). Children's beliefs in their own control of reinforcement in intellectual-academic achievement situations. *Child Development, 36*, 91–109.

Cross, D. R., & Paris, S. G. (1988). Developmental and instructional analysis of children's metacognition and reading comprehension. *Journal of Educational Psychology, 80*, 131–142.

Cruickshank, J. (2009). Personal communication regarding Solid Rock Outdoor Ministries, Laramie, WY, http://www.SROM.org

Cryer, P. E. (2001). Hypoglycemia. In L. Jefferson, A. Cherrington, & H. Goodman (Eds.), *Handbook of physiology; Section 7, The endocrine system. II. The endocrine pancreas and regulation of metabolism* (pp. 1057–1092). New York, NY: Oxford University Press.

Dahl, R. (2004). Adolescent brain development: A period of vulnerabilities and opportunities. In R. Dahl & L. Patia Spear, *Adolescent brain development, vulnerabilities and opportunities, Annals of the New York Academy of Sciences* (pp. 1–22). New York, NY: New York Academy of Sciences.

Damasio. A. (1989). Time-locked multiregional retroactivation: A systems-level proposal for the neural substrates of recall and recognition. *Cognition, 33*, 25–62.

Damasio, A. (1999). *The feeling of what happens: Body, emotion and the making of consciousness*. London: Heinemann.

Dapretto, M., Davies, M., & Pfeifer, J. (2006). Understanding emotions in others: Mirror neurons dysfunction in children with autism spectrum disorder. *Nature Neuroscience, 9,* 28–30.

Davies, M., Stankov, L., & Roberts, R. (1998). Emotional intelligence: In search of an elusive construct. *Journal of Personality and Social Psychology, 75,* 989–1015.

Dawson, T. (2009a). Developmental testing service data. Retrieved from http://testingsurvey.us/survey/2009/results.php

Dawson, T. (2009b). Welcome to DTS. Retrieved from http://www.devtestservice.com

Dawson, T., Fischer, K., & Stein, Z. (2006). Reconsidering qualitative and quantitative research approaches: A cognitive developmental perspective. *New Ideas in Psychology, 24,* 229–239.

De Beni, R., & Palladino. P. (2000). Intrusion errors in working memory tasks: Are they related to reading comprehension ability. *Learning and Individual Differences, 12,* 131–143.

Deci, E. L., Schwartz, A. J., Sheinman, L., & Ryan, R. M. (1981). An instrument to assess adults' orientations toward control versus autonomy with children: reflections on intrinsic motivation and perceived competence. *Journal of Educational Psychology, 73,* 642–650.

Dehaene, S., Changeux, J.-P., Naccache, L., Sackur, J., & Sergent, C. (2006). Conscious, preconscious, and subliminal processing: A testable taxonomy. *Trends in Cognitive Sciences, 10,* 204–211.

Dehn, M. (2008). *Working memory and academic learning, assessment and intervention.* New York, NY: John Wiley & Sons.

DeKosky, S., Williamson, J. D., Fitzpatrick, A. L., Kronmal, R. A., Ives, D. G., Saxton, J. A., Lopez, O. L., Burke, G., . . . & Furberg, C. D. (2008). *Ginkgo biloba* for prevention of dementia, a randomized controlled trial. *Journal of the American Medical Association, 300*(19), 2253–2262.

Demetrious, A., & Papadopoulos, T. (2003). Human intelligence, from local models to universal theory. In R. J. Sternberg, *International handbook of intelligence* (pp. 445–474). New York, NY: Cambridge University Press.

Denckla, M. (1972). Color naming defects in dyslexic boys, *Cortex, 8,* 164–178.

Denckla, M., & Rudle, G. (1976). Rapid automatized naming (RAN): Dyslexia differentiated from other learning disabilities, *Neuroypsychologia, 14*(4), 471–479.

DeNoon, D. (2005). Boy dies after controversial treatment for autism. Retrieved October 5, 2010, from http://www.webmd.com/brain/news/20050826/boy-dies-after-controversial-treatment-for-autism

Deshler, D. D., & Schumaker, J. B. (1993). Strategy mastery by at-risk students: Not a simple matter. *The Elementary School Journal, 94,* 153–167.

De Volder, M., & Lens, W. (1982). Academic achievement and future time perspectives as a cognitive motivational concept. *Journal of Personality and Social Psychology, 42,* 566–571.

Dodge, H., Zitzelberger, T., Oken, B. S., Howieson, D., & Kaye, J. (2008). A randomized placebo-controlled trial of ginkgo biloba for the prevention of cognitive decline. *Neurology, 19*(Pt. 2), 1809–1817.

Driskell, J. E., Willis, R. P., & Copper, C. (1992). Effect of overlearning on retention. *Journal of Applied Psychology, 77,* 615–622.

Driver, J., & Baylis, G. (1998). Attention and visual object segmentation. In R. Parasuraman (Ed.), *The attentive brain* (pp. 299–325). Cambridge, MA: MIT Press.

Duit, R., & Treagust, D. (1998). Learning in science—from behaviorism towards social constructivism and beyond. In: B. Fraser & K. Tobin (Eds.), *International handbook of science education* (pp. 3–26). Dordrecht, The Netherlands: Kluwer Academic.

Duit, R., & Treagust, D. (2003). Conceptual change: A powerful framework for improving science teaching and learning. *International Journal of Science Education*, *25*(6), 671–688.

Ebbinghaus, H. (1913). *Memory: A contribution to experimental psychology* (H. A. Ruger & C. E. Bussenues, Trans.). New York, NY: Teacher College, Columbia University. (Original work published 1885.)

Eccles, J., Adler, T. F,, Futterman, R., Goff, S. B, Kaczala, C. M, Meece, J. L., & Midgley, C. (1983). Expectancies, values, and academic behavior. In J. T. Spence (Ed.), *Achievement and achievement motives: Psychological and sociological approaches* (pp. 75–146). San Francisco, CA: Freeman.

Edwards, B. (1979). *Drawing on the right side of your brain*. New York, NY: Penguin Putnam.

Eisenberg, D., Campbell, B., Gray, P. B., & Sorenson M. D. (2008). Dopamine receptor genetic polymorphisms and body composition in undernourished pastoralists: An exploration of nutrition indices among nomadic and recently settled Ariaal men of northern Kenya. *BMC Evolutionary Biology*. *8*, 173. doi: 10.1186/1471-2148-8-173.

Ekman, P., & Friesen, W. (1976). *Pictures of facial affects*. Palo Alto, CA: Consulting Psychologists Press.

Ekman, P., Friesen, W., & Ellsworth, P. (1972). *Emotions in the human face: Guidelines for research and integration of findings.* New York, NY: Pergamon.

Elias, M. J., & Clabby, J. (1992). Building social problem solving skills: Guidelines from a school-based program. San Francisco, CA: Jossey-Bass.

Elias, M. J., Gara, M., Ubriaco, M., Rothbaum, P. A., Clabby, J. F., & Schuyler, T. (1986). Impact of a preventive social problem solving intervention on children copying with middle-school stress. *American Journal of Community Psychology*, *14*, 259–275.

Encyclopedia of China. (1985). *Encyclopedia of China* (pp. 202–206). Bejing: Publishing House of Encyclopedia of China.

Etnier, J., Salazar, W., Landers, D. M., Petruzzello, S. J., Han, M., & Nowell, P. (1997). The influence of physical fitness and exercise upon cognitive functioning: A meta-analysis. *Journal of Sport and Exercise Psychology*, *19*(3), 249–277.

Eysenck, M. W., & Eysenck, M. C. (1979). Processing depth, elaboration of encoding, memory stores and expended processing capacity. *Journal of Experimental Psychology: Human Learning and Memory*, *5*, 472–484.

Fantuzzo, J., & Atkins, M. (1992). Applied behavior analysis for educators—Teacher centered and classroom based. *Journal of Applied Behavior Analysis*, *25*, 37–42.

Fawcett, A., & Nicolson, R. (2001). Speed and temporal processing in dyslexia. In M. Wolf (Ed.), *Dyslexia, fluency and the brain* (pp. 24–40). Timonium, MD: York Press.

Feifer, S., & De Fina, P. (2000). The neuropsychology of reading disorders: Diagnosis and intervention workbook. Middletown, MD: School Neuropsych Press.

Fenn, K., Gallo, D. A., Margoliash, D., Roediger, H. L. & Nusbaum, H. C. (2009). Reduced false memory after sleep. *Learning and Memory, 16*, 509–513. doi:10.1101/lm.1500808

Fenske, E., Krantz, P. J., & McClannahan, L.E. (2001). Incidental teaching: A non-discrete trial teaching procedure. In C. Maurice, B. Green & R. Foxx (Eds.), *Making a difference: Behavioral intervention for autism* (pp. 75–82). Austin, TX: Pro-Ed.

Ferna dez-Ballesteros, R., & Colom, R., (2004). The psychology of human intelligence in Spain. In R. J. Sternberg (Ed.), *International handbook of intelligence* (pp. 79–103). New York, NY: Cambridge University Press.

Fine, C. & Blair, R. (2000). A minireview: The cognitive and emotional effects of amygdale damage. *Neurocase, 6*, 435–450.

Fischer, F., Radosevic-Vidacek, B., Koscec, A., Teixeira, L. R., Moreno, C. R. C., & Lowden, A. (2008). Internal and external time conflicts in adolescents: Sleep characteristics and interventions. *Mind, Brain, and Education, 2*(1), 17–23.

Fischer, K. W. (1980). A theory of cognitive development: The control and construction of hierarchies of skills. *Psychological Review, 87*(6), 477–531.

Fischer, K. W., & Bidell, T. (2006). Dynamic development of action, thought, and emotion. In W. Damon. & R. M. Lerner (Eds.), *Theoretical models of human development: Handbook of child psychology* (6th ed., Vol. 1, pp. 313–399). New York, NY: Wiley.

Fischer, K., & Daley, S. (2007). Connecting cognitive science and neuroscience to education, potentials and pitfalls in inferring executive processes. In. L. Meltzer (Ed.), *Executive function in education, from theory to practice* (pp. 55–75). New York, NY: Guilford Press.

Fischer, K. W., Daniel, D. B., Immordino-Yang, M. H., Stern, E., Battro, A., & Koizumi, H. (2007). Why mind, brain, and education. Why now? *Mind, Brain, and Education, 1*(1), 1–2.

Fischer, K. W., & Heikkinen, K. (2010). The future of educational neuroscience. In *Mind, brain, and education: Neuroscience implications for the classroom* (David Sousa, Ed.). Bloomington, IN: Solution Tree Press. pp. 249–269.

Fischer, K. W., & Immordino-Yang, M. H. (2008). *The Jossey-Bass reader on the brain and learning* (pp. xvii–xxi). San Francisco, CA: Jossey-Bass.

Fischer, K. W., Yan, Z., & Stewart, J. (2003). Adult cognitive development: Dynamics in the developmental web. In J. Valsiner and K. Connolly (Eds.), *Handbook of developmental psychology* (pp. 491–516). Thousand Oaks, CA: Sage.

Fledge, J., & Fletcher, K. (1992). Talker and listener effects on degree of perceived foreign accent. *Journal of Acoustical Society of America, 91*, 370–389.

Flynn, J. (2007). *What is intelligence?* Cambridge, United Kingdom: Cambridge University Press.

Funk, J. B., Flores, G., Buchman, D. B., & Germann, J. N. (1999). Rating electronic games: Violence is in the eye of the beholder. *Youth & Society, 30*, 283–312.

Gadow, K., & Sprafkin, J. (1997). *Child symptom inventory 4: Norms manual*. Stony Brook, NY: Checkmate Plus.

Gannon, N., & Ranzijn, R., (2005). Does emotional intelligence predict unique variance in life satisfaction beyond IQ and personality? *Personality and Individual Differences, 38*, 1353–1364.

Gardner, H. (1983). *Frames of mind: The theory of multiple intelligences.* New York, NY: Basic Books.

Gardner, H. (1999). *Intelligence reframed: Multiple intelligences for the 21st century.* New York, NY: Basic Books.

Gathercole, S., and Alloway, T. (2008). *Working memory and learning: A practical guide for teachers.* New York, NY: Sage.

Gathercole, S. E., & Baddeley, A. (1993). *Working memory and language.* East Sussex, United Kingdom: Lawrence Erlbaum.

Gathercole, S., Lamont, E., & Alloway, T. (2006). Working memory in the classroom. In S. Pickering (Ed)., *Working memory and education.* New York, NY: Academic Press.

Gathercole, S., Pickering, S. J., Ambridge, B., & Wearing, H. (2004). The structure of working memory from 4 to 15 years of age. *Developmental Psychology, 40*(2), 177–190.

Gaub, J., & Carlson, C. (1997). Gender differences in ADHD: A meta-analysis and critical review. *Journal of the American Academy of Child and Adolescent Psychiatry, 36,* 1036–1045.

Gazzaniga, M., Ivry, R., & Mangun, G. (2009). *Cognitive neuroscience* (3rd ed.). New York, NY: W. W. Norton.

Geary, D. C., Hoard, M. K., & Byrd-Craven, J. (2004). Strategy choices in simple and complex addition: Contributions of working memory and counting knowledge for children with mathematical disability. *Journal of Experimental Child Psychology, 88,* 121–151.

Gentile D. (2003). *Media violence and children.* Westport, CT: Praeger.

Gentile, D., & Gentile, J. R. (2008). Violent video games as exemplary teachers: A conceptual analysis. *Journal of Youth and Adolescence, 37*(2), 127–141.

Gentile, D., Lynch, P. J., Linder, J. R., & Walsh, D. A. (2004). The effects of violent video game habits on adolescent hostility, aggressive behaviors, and school performance. *Journal of Adolescence, 27,* 5–22.

Gibson, E. L. (2007). Carbohydrates and mental function: Feeding or impeding the brain? *Nutrition Bulletin, 32,* S71–S83.

Giedd, J. (2008). The teen brain, insights from neuroimaging, *Journal of Adolescent Health, 42*(4), 335–343.

Gillberg, C., Johansson, M., Steffenburg, S., & Berlin, O. (1997). Auditory integration training in children with autism: A case study. *Journal of Research in Childhood Education, 18*(20), 125–140.

Gladwell, M. (2008). *Outliers: The story of success.* New York, NY: Little, Brown.

Goleman, D. (1995). *Emotional intelligence.* New York, NY: Bantam.

Gonzales, L. (2003). *Deep survival, who lives, who dies, and why.* New York, NY: W. W. Norton.

Gopnik, A., Meltzoff, A., & Kuhl, P. (1999). *The scientist in the crib: What early learning tells us about the mind.* New York, NY: Harper Collins.

Gordon, A., Crepinsek, M. K., Briefel, R. R., Clark, M. A. & Fox, M. K. (2009). The third school nutrition dietary assessment study: Summary and implications. *Journal of the American Dietetic Association,* s129–s135. doi: 10.1016/j.jada.2008.10.066

Goulandris, N., & Snolwing, M. (2003). Dyslexia in adolescence: A five year follow-up study. In M. Hunter-Carsch & M. Herrington, (Eds.), *Dyslexia and effective learning* (pp. 12–32). London: Whurr Publications.

Gould, S. (1981). *The mismeasure of man*. New York, NY: W. W. Norton.

Grafton, S. (2010). What can dance teach us about learning? *Cerebrum*, 23–33.

Green, C. S., & Bavelier, D. (2003). Action video games modify visual selective attention. *Nature, 423*, 534–537.

Greenberg, M.T., Kusche, C. A., Cook, E. T., & Quamma, J. P. (1995). Promoting emotional competence in school-aged children: The effects of PATHS curriculum. *Development and Psychopathology, 7*, 117–136.

Greenblat, A. (1994). Gender and ethnicity bias in assessment of attention deficit disorder. *Social Work in Education, 16*, 89–95.

Greenleaf, R. (2008). *Formative assessment micro-feedback loops: Using the student centered accountability for learning process*. Newfield, ME: Greenleaf & Papanek.

Gregg, N. (2009). *Adolescents and adults with learning disabilities and ADHD, assessment and accommodation*. New York, NY: Guilford Press.

Grigorenko, E. L., Meier, E., Lipka, J., Mohatt, G., Yanez, E., & Sternberg, R. J. (2004). Academic and practical intelligence: A case study of the Yup'ik in Alaska. *Learning & Individual Differences, 14*(4), 183–207.

Grskovic, J., & Zentall, S. (2007). *The behavioral, social, and emotional characteristics and self-concepts of a school base sample of girls with symptoms of ADHD*. Manuscript in preparation.

Guilford, J. P. (1967). *The nature of human intelligence*. New York, NY: McGraw-Hill.

Hall, J. (1978). Gender effects in decoding nonverbal cues. *Psychological Bulletin, 85*, 845–857.

Hall, J. (1984). *Nonverbal sex differences: Communication accuracy and expressive style*. Baltimore, MD: Johns Hopkins University Press.

Hall, J., Carter, J., & Horgan, T. (2000). Gender differences in the nonverbal communication of emotion. In A. H. Fischer (Ed.), *Gender and emotion: Social psychological perspectives* (pp. 97–117). Paris: Cambridge University Press.

Hall, J., & Matsumoto, D. (2004). Gender differences in judgments of multiple emotions from facial expressions. *Emotion, 4*(2), 201–206.

Hallam, S., & Price, J. (1998). Can the use of background music improve the behavior and academic performance of children with emotional and behavioral difficulties? *British Journal of Special Education, 25*, 88–91.

Hampson, E. (2006). A female advantage in the recognition of emotional facial expressions: Test of an evolutionary hypothesis. *Evolution and Human Behavior, 27*(6), 401–416.

Hanson, E., Kalish, L. A., Bunce, E., Curtis, C., McDaniel, S., Ware, J., & Petry, J. (2006). Use of complementary and alternative medicine among children diagnosed with autism spectrum disorder. *Journal of Autism and Development Disorders*.

Haridman, M., & Denckla, M., (2010). *The science of education. Cerebrum, emerging ideas 2010*. New York, NY: Dana Press.

Harris, K. R., & Graham, S. (1992). Self-regulated strategy development: A part of the writing process. In K. E. Pressley Harris, & J. G. Guthrie (Eds.), *Promoting academic competence and literacy in schools* (pp. 277–309). New York, NY: Academic Press.

Harrison, Y., & Horne, J. A. (2000). Sleep loss and temporal memory. *Quarterly Journal of Experimental Psychology, 53*, 271–279.

Hart, B., & Risely, T. (1968). Establishing use of descriptive adjectives in the spontaneous speech of disadvantaged preschool children. *Journal of Applied Behavioral Analysis, 1,* 109–120.

Hart, B., & Risley, T. (2003). The early catastrophe: The 30 million word gap. *American Educator, 27*(1), 4–9.

Harter, S. (1974). Pleasure derived by children from cognitive challenge and mastery. *Child Development, 45,* 661–669.

Hartmann, T. (1997). *Attention Deficit Disorder: A different perception* (Rev. ed.). Grass Valley, CA: Underwood Books.

Hattie, J. (1992). Measuring the effects of schooling. *Australian Journal of Education, 36i*(1), 5–13.

Hebb, D. (1949). *The organization of behavior: A neurophysiological theory.* New York, NY: Wiley.

Hedley, A.A., Ogden, C. L., Johnson, C. L., Carroll, M. D., Curtin, L. R., & Flegal, K. M. (2004). Prevalence of overweight and obesity among U.S. children, adolescents, and adults, 1999–2002. *Journal of the American Medical Association, 291*(23), 2847–2850.

Henderson, J. (2010). Education update. *ASCD, Learn, Teach, Lead, 52*(2), 3–5.

Henry, L. A., & Millar, S. (1993). Why does memory span improve with age? A review of the evidence for two current hypotheses. *European Journal of Cognitive Psychology, 5,* 241–287.

Herrenstein, R., & Murray, C. (1994). *The bell curve: Intelligence and class structure in American life.* New York, NY: Free Press.

Hibbeln, J. R., Davis, J. M., Steer, C., Emmett, P., Rogers, I., Williams, C., & Golding, J. (2007). Maternal seafood consumption in pregnancy and neurodevelopmental outcome in childhood (ALSPAC study): An observational cohort study. *Lancet, 369,* 578–585.

Hobson, R., & Lee, A. (1999). Imitation and identification in autism. *Journal of Child Psychology and Psychiatry, 40,* 649–659.

Hofer, S. B., Mrsic-Flogel, T. D., Bonhoeffer, T., & Hübener, M. (2008). Experience leaves a lasting structural trace in cortical circuits. *Nature, 457,* 313–317.

Holmes, J., Gathercole, S. E., & Dunning, D. L. (2009). Adaptive training leads to sustained enhancement of poor working memory in children. *Developmental Science.* doi: 10.1111/j.1467-7687.2009.00848.x

Holmes, J., Gathercole, S., Place, M., Dunning, D., Hilyon, K., & Elliot, J. (2009). Working memory deficits can be overcome: Impacts of training and medication on working memory in children with ADHD. *Applied Cognitive Science, 23*(9). doi: 10.1002/acp.1589

Hopkins, K., Stanley, J., & Hopkins, B. (1990). *Educational and psychological measurement and evaluation* (7th ed.). Needham Heights, MA: Allyn & Bacon.

Horn, J., & Cattell, R. (1966). Refinement and test of the theory of fluid and crystallized ability intelligences. *Journal of Educational Psychology, 57*(5), 253–270.

Horn, J., & Noll, J. (1997) Human cognitive capabilities: Gf-Gc theory. In D. Flanagan, J. Genshaft, & P. Harrison (Eds.), *Contemporary intellectual assessment: Theories, tests, and issues* (pp. 53–91). New York, NY: Guilford Press.

Huarte de San Juan, J. (1575/1969). The examination of men's wits. New York : Da Capo Press. (Original edition: Examen de los ingenious par alas ciencias [1594]. London: Baeza.)

Hull, C. (1943). *Principles of behavior*. New York, NY: Appleton-Century-Crofts.

Hull, C. (1951). *Essentials of behaviors*. New Haven, CT: Yale University Press.

Hunter-Carsch, M., & Herrington, M. (2001). Dyslexia and effective learning in secondary and tertiary education. London: Whurr Publications.

Hurford, D., Johnston, M., Nepote, P., Hampton, S., Moore, S., Neal, J., Mueller, A., McGeorge, K., . . . & Huffman, D. (1994). Early identification and remediation of phonological-processing deficits in first-grade children at risk for reading disabilities. *Journal of Learning Disabilities, 27*, 647–659.

Huttenlocher, R., & Dabholkar, A. (1997). Regional differences in synaptogenesis in the human cerebral cortex. *Journal of Comparative Neurology, 387*, 167–178.

Hyatt, K. (2007). Brain Gym: Building stronger brains or wishful thinking? *Remedial and Special Education, 28*(2), 117–124.

Iacoboni, M. (2008). *Mirroring people*: *The new science of how we connect with others*. New York, NY: Farrar, Straus and Giroux.

Ikonomidou, C., Bittigau, P., Koch, C., Genz, K., Hoerster, F., Felderhoff-Mueser, U., Tenkova, T., Dikranian, K., & Olney, J. W. (2001). Neurotransmitters and apoptosis in the developing brain. *Biochemical Pharmacology, 62*(4), 401–405.

Immordino-Yang, M. H. (2008).The smoke around the mirror neurons: Goals as sociocultural and emotional organizers of perception and action in learning. *Mind, Brain, and Education, 2*(2), 67–73.

Immordino-Yang, M. H., & Damasio, A. (2008). We feel, therefore we learn. In K. Fischer and M. H. Immordino-Yang (Eds.), *Jossey-Bass reader on the brain and learning.* San Francisco, CA: Jossey-Bass.

Ingersoll, B., Lewis, E., & Kroman, E. (2007). Teaching the imitation and spontaneous use of descriptive gestures to young children with autism using a naturalistic behavioral intervention. *Journal of Autism and Developmental Disorders, 37*, 1446–1456.

Ingersoll, B., & Gregans, S. (2007). The effect of a parent-implemented naturalistic imitation intervention on spontaneous imitation skills in young children with autism. *Research in Developmental Disabilities, 28*, 163–175.

Ingwersen, J., Defeyter, M. A., Kennedy, D., Wesnes, K. A., & Scholey, A. (2007). A low-glycemic index breakfast cereal preferentially prevents children's cognitive performance form declining throughout the morning. *Appetite, 49*, 240–244.

Institute of Medicine of the National Academies. (2002). IOM Dietary Reference Intakes for energy, carbohydrate, fiber, fat, fatty acids, cholesterol, protein, and amino acids. Released September 5, 2002.

Ivrin, D.S. (2006). Using analog assessment procedures for determining the effects of gluten-free and casein-free diet on rate of problem behaviors for an adolescent with autism. *Behavioral Interventions, 21*. 281–286.

Izard, C. (2001). Emotional intelligence or adaptive emotions? *Emotion, 1*, 249–257.

Jackson, L. A., von Eye, A., Fitzgerald, H. E., Zhao, Y., & Witt, E. A. (in press). IT use and academic performance: A longitudinal study of the impact of gender, race, income and IT use on 12 year olds' grades in school, GPAs and standardized test scores in reading, mathematics, and spatial skills. *Developmental Psychology*.

Jaeggi, S., Buschkuehl, M., Jonides, J., & Perrig, W. J. (2008). Improving fluid intelligence with training on working memory, *Proceedings of the National Academy of Sciences, 105*(15), 6829–6833.

Johnson, D. W., & Johnson, R. T. (1999). Learning together and alone: Cooperative, competitive, and individual learning. Boston, MA: Allyn & Bacon.

Jonassen, D. H., Beissner, K., & Yacci, M. (1993). *Structural knowledge: Techniques for representing, conveying, and acquiring structural knowledge.* London: Lawrence Erlbaum.

Jung, R., & Haier, R. J. (2007). The Pareto-Frontal integration theory (P-FIT) of intelligence: Converging neuroimaging evidence. *Behavioral and Brain Sciences, 30,* 135–187.

Kamin, L. (1995). The pioneers of IQ testing. In R. Jacoby and N. Glaubermann (Eds.), *The bell curve debate* (pp. 476–509). New York, NY: Times Books.

Kane, A., Luiselli, J., Dearborn, S., & Young, N. (2004). Wearing a weighted vest as intervention for children with autism/pervasive development disorder. *The Scientific Review of Mental Health Practice, 3*(2), 19–24.

Kane, M., & Engle, R. (2000). Working-memory capacity, proactive interference, and divided attention: limit\s on long-term memory retrieval. *Journal of Experimental Psychology: Learning, Memory, and Cognition, 26*(2), 336–358.

Kanner, L. (1943). Autistic disturbances of affective contact. *Nervous Child, 2,* 217–250.

Karpicke, J., Butler, A. C., & Roediger, H. L. (2009). Metacognitive strategies in student learning: Do students practice retrieval when they study on their own? *Memory, 17*(4), 471–479.

Karpicke, J. D., & Roediger, H. L. (2006). Repeated retrieval during learning is the key to long-term retention. *Journal of Memory and Language, 57,* 151–162.

Karpicke, J. D., & Roediger, H. L. (2007). Expanding retrieval practice promotes short-term retention, but equally spaced retrieval enhances long-term retention. *Journal of Experimental Psychology, 33*(4), 704–719.

Kasser, T., Ryan, R. M., Zax, M., & Sameroff, A. J. (1995). The relations of maternal and social environments to late adolescents' materialistic and prosocial values. *Developmental Psychology, 31,* 907–914.

Kavale, K., & Forness, S. (1987). Substance over style: Assessing the efficacy of modality testing and teaching. *Exceptional Children, 54,* 228–239.

Kavale, K., & Mattson, P. (1983). "One jumped off the balance beam": Meta-analysis of perceptual-motor training. *Journal of Learning Disabilities, 16,* 165–173.

Kay, S. & Vyse, S. (2005). Helping parents separate the wheat from the chaff: Putting austim treatments to the test. *In controversial therapies for developmental disabilities: Fad, fashion and science in professional practice* (J. W. Jacobson, R. M. Foxx, & J. Mulick, eds.). Mahwah, NJ: Lawerence Erlbaum Associates, pp. 265–277.

Keenan, P. A., Jacobson, M. W., Soleymani, R. M., Mayes, M. D., Stress, M. E., & Yaldoo, D. T. (1996). The effect on memory of chronic prednisone treatments in patients with systemic disease, *Neurology, 47,* 1396–1403.

Kensinger E. A., & Corkin, S. (2003). Memory enhancement for emotional words: Are emotional words more vividly remembered than neutral words? *Memory and Cognition, 31,* 1169–1180.

Kezar, A. (2001). Theory of multiple intelligences: Implications for higher education. *Innovative Higher Education, 26*(2), 141–154.

Kiewra, K. A. (1985a). Learning from a lecture: An investigation of note taking, review and attention at a lecture. *Human Learning, 4,* 73–77.

Kiewra, K. A. (1985b). Students' note taking behaviors and the efficiency of providing the instructor's notes for review. *Contemporary Educational Psychology, 10*(4), 378–386.

King, A. (1991). Effects of training in strategic questioning on children's problem-solving performance. *Journal of Educational Psychology, 83,* 307–317.

Kirsch, S. (2006). *Children, adolescents and media violence: A critical look at the research.* Thousand Oaks, CA: Sage.

Klauer, K. C., & Zhao, Z. (2004). Double dissociations in visual and spatial short-term memory. *Journal of Experimental Psychology: General, 133,* 355–381.

Klein, C. (2001). Staff development in further education. In M. Hunter-Carsch & M. Herrington (Eds.), *Dyslexia and effective learning in secondary and tertiary education* (pp. 143–154). London: Whurr Publications.

Klin, A.,,Lin, D., Gorrindo, P., Ramsay, G. & Jones, W. (2009). Two-year-olds with autism fail to orient toward human biological motion but attend instead to non-social physical contingencies. *Nature, 459*(7244), 257–261,

Koegel, L. K., Carter, C. M., & Koegel, R. I. (2003). Teaching children with autism self-initiations as a pivotal response. *Topics in Language Disorders, 23,* 134–145.

Kohlberg, L. (1984). Moral stages and moralization: The cognitive developmental approach. In L. Kohlberg (Ed.). *The psychology of moral development: The nature and validity of moral stages moral development* (pp. 170–205). San Francisco, CA: Harper & Row.

Koizumi, H. (2007). *Understanding the brain: The brain of a learning science.* Paris: OECD.

Konrath, S. H. (2010). Empathy is declining over time in American college students. Paper presented at the Association for Psychological Science Annual Convention, Boston, May 27–30.

Koretz, D. (2008). *Measuring up: What educational testing really tells us.* Cambridge, MA: Harvard University Press.

Kosslyn, S., Michael, S., Alpert, N. M., Thompson, W. L., Maljkovic, V., Weise, S. B., Chabris, C. F., Hamilton, S. E., . . . & Buonanno, F. S. (1993.) Visual mental imagery activates topographically organized visual cortex: PET investigations. *Journal of Cognitive Neuroscience, 5*(3), 263–287.

Kretchmer, N., & Zimmermann, M. (1997). *Developmental nutrition.* Boston, Allyn & Bacon.

Kulhavy, R. W., Schwartz, N. H., & Peterson, S. (1986). Working memory: The encoding process. In G. D. Phye & T. Andre (Eds.), *Cognitive classroom learning* (pp. 115–140). New York, NY: Academic Press.

LaBar, K. S., & Phelps, E. A. (1998). Arousal-mediated memory consolidation: Role of the medial temporal lobe in humans. *Psychological Science, 9,* 490–493.

La Guardia, J., & Ryan, R. (2002). What adolescents need, a self-determination theory perspective or development within families, school and society. In F. Parajes and T. Urdan (Eds.), *Academic motivation of adolescents.* Greenwich, CT: Information Age Publishing.

Lande, R., & Nadel, L. (2000). *Cognitive neuroscience of emotions.* Oxford, United Kingdom: Oxford University Press.

Larson, R. (2009). Enhancing the recall of presented material. *Computers and Education, 53,* 1278–1284.

LeDoux, J. (1996). *The emotional brain*. New York, NY: Simon and Schuster.

Lens, W., Simon, J., and Dewitte, S. (2002). From duty to desire, the role of students' future time perspective and instrumentality perception for study motivation and self-regulation. In F. Pajares and T. Urdan (Eds.), *Academic motivation of adolescents* (pp. 221–245). Greenwich, CT: Information Age Publishing.

Lepper, M. (1973). Dissonance, self-perception, and honesty in children. *Journal of Personality and Social Psychology, 25*, 65–74.

Levin, D. T., Simons, D. J., Angelone, B. L., & Chabris, C. F. (2002). Memory for centrally attended changing objects in an incidental real-world change detection paradigm. *British Journal of Psychology, 93*, 289–302.

Levine, M. (2003). *The myth of laziness*. New York, NY: Simon and Schuster.

Leyse-Wallace, R. (2008). A scientific exploration: Linking nutrition to mental health. New York, NY: iUniverse.

Lin, C. T. (1980). A sketch of the methods of mental testing in ancient China. *Acta Psychologicia Sinica, 1*, 75–80.

Lindquist, E. L. (1951). Preliminary considerations in objective test construction. In E. F. Lindquist (Ed.), *Educational measurement*. Washington, DC: American Council on Education.

Locke, E., & Latham, G. (1990). *A theory of goal setting and task performance*. Englewood Cliffs, NJ: Prentice-Hall.

Loftus. E. F., & Ketcham, K. (1994). *The myth of repressed memory: False memories and allegations of sexual abuse*. New York, NY: St. Martin's Press.

Loftus. E. F., & Palmer, J. C. (1974). Reconstruction of automation destruction: An example of the interaction between language and memory. *Journal of Verbal Learning and Verbal Behavior, 13*, 585–589.

Lord, C., & McGee, J. (Eds.). (2001). *The committee on educational interventions for children with autism*. Washington, DC: National Academy Press.

Lou, H., Henriksen, L., & Bruhn, P. (1984). Focal cerebral hypoperfusion in children with dysphasia and/or attention deficit disorder. *Archives of Neurology, 41*, 825–829.

Luaria, A. (1973). *The working brain: An introduction to neuropsychology*. New York, NY: Basic Books.

Lufi, D., Tzischinsky, O., & Hadar, S. (2011–in press). Delaying school start time by one hour: Effects on attention levels in adolescents. *Journal of Clinical Sleep Medicine*.

Lupien, S. L., King, S., Meaney, M. J., & McEwen, B. S. (2000). Child's stress hormone levels correlate with mother's socioeconomic status and depressive state. *Biological Psychiatry, 48*(10), 976–980.

Lyman, R., Kwan, S., & Chao. W. (1938). Left occipito-parietal brain tumor with observations on alexia and agraphia in Chinese and English. *Chinese Medical Journal, 54*, 491–515.

Lyon, R., Shaywitz, S., & Shaywitz, B. (2003). A definition of dyslexia. *Annals of Dyslexia, 53*, 1–14.

Lyons, J. B., & Schneider, T. R. (2005). The influence of emotional intelligence on performance. *Personality and Individual Differences, 39*, 693–703.

MacLeod, C. M. (1988). Forgotten but not gone: Savings for pictures and words in long-term memory. *Journal of Experimental Psychology: Learning, Memory, and Cognition, 14*, 195–212.

Magariños, A., & McEwen, B. (1995). Stress-induced atrophy of apical dendrites of hippocampal tCA3c neurons: Involvement of gluccortiocoid secretion and excitatory amino acid receptors. *Neuroscience, 69*, 88–98.

Magariños, A. M., McEwen, B. S., Flügge, G., & Fuchs, E. (1996). Chronic psychosocial stress causes apical dendritic atrophy of hippocampal CA3 pyramidal neurons in subordinate tree shrews. *Journal of Neuroscience, 16*, 3534–3540.

Makany, T., Kemp, J., & Dror, I. (2009). Optimizing the use of note-taking as an external cognitive aid for increasing learning. *British Journal of Educational Technology, 40*(4), 619–635.

Marcus, G. (2004). *The birth of the mind: How a tiny number of genes creates the complexities of human thought*. New York, NY: Basic Books.

Marzano, R. M., Norford, J. S., Paynter, D. E., Pickering, D. J., & Gaddy, B. B. (2001). *A handbook for classroom instruction that works*. Alexandria, VA: Association for Supervision and Curriculum Development.

Mastropieri, M. A., & Scruggs, T. E. (1998). Constructing more meaningful relationships in the classroom: Mnemonic research into practice. *Learning Disabilities Research and Practice, 13*(3), 138–145.

Matousek, M., & Petersen, I. (1973). Frequency analysis of the EEG in normal children and adolescents. In, P. Kellaqway & I. Petersen (Eds.), *Automation of clinical electroencephalography* (pp. 75–102). New York, NY: Raven Press.

Mayer, J. D., Caruso, D., & Salovey, P. (2000). Emotional intelligence meets traditional standards for an intelligence. *Intelligence, 27*(4), 267–298.

Mayer, J. D., DiPaolo, M., & Salovey, P. (1990). Perceiving affective content in ambiguous visual stimuli: A component of emotional intelligence. *Journal of Personality Assessment, 54*, 772–781.

Mayer, J. D., & Salovey, P. (1997). What is emotional intelligences? In P. Salovey & D. J. Sluyter (Eds.), *Emotional development and emotional intelligence: Educational implications* (pp. 3–31). New York, NY: Basic Books.

Mayringer, H., & Wimmer, H. (2002). No deficits at the point of hemispheric indecision. *Neuropsychologia, 40*, 701–704.

McArdle, J., & Prescott, C. (1997). Contemporary models for the biometric genetic analysis of intellectual abilities. In D. Flanagan, J. Genshaft, & P. Harrison (Eds.), *Contemporary intellectual assessment: theories, tests, and issues* (pp. 403–436). New York, NY: Guilford Press.

McClelland, J., Fiez, J., & McCandliss, B. (2002). Teaching the /r/-/l/ discrimination to Japanese adults: Behavioral and neural aspects. *Physiology and Behavior, 77*, 657–662.

McDaniel, M. A., Howard, D. C., & Einstein, G. O. (2009). The read-recite-review study strategy, effective and portable. *Psychological Science, 20*(4), 516–522.

McGuiness, D. (1997). Introduction. *Why our children can't read and what we can do about it* (p. ix). New York, NY: Simon & Schuster.

McLeod, J., & Kessler, R. (1990). Socioeconomic status differences in vulnerability to undesirable life events. *Journal of Health, Society and Behavior, 31*, 162–172.

Merten, J. (2005). Culture, gender and the recognition of the basic emotions. *Psychologia, 48*(4). 306–316.

Mestre, J. M., Lopes, P. N., Salovey, P., & Olarte, P. G. (2006). Emotional intelligence and social and academic adaptation to school. *Psicothema, 18*, 112–117.

Metz, B., Mulick, J., & Butter, E. (2005). Autism: A late 20th century fad magnet. In J. W. Jacobson, R. M. Foxx, & J. A. Mulick (Eds.), *Controversial therapies for developmental disabilities: Fad, fashion, and science in professional practice* (pp. 237–263). Mahwah, NJ: Lawrence Erlbaum.

Midgley, C., Anderman, E., & Hicks, L. (1995). Differences between elementary and middle school teachers and students: A goal theory approach. *Journal of Early Adolescence, 15,* 90–113.

Miller, G. A. (1956). The magical number seven, plus or minus two: Some limits on our capacity for processing information. *Psychological Review, 63,* 81–97.

Miller, J., Rosenbloom, A., & Silverstein, J. (2004). Childhood obesity. *Journal for Clinical Endrocrinology and Metabolism, 89*(9), 4211–4218.

Mills, D., Coffey-Corina, S., & Neville, H. (1997). Language comprehension and cerebral specialization from 13–20 months. *Developmental Neuropsychology, 13*(3), 397–445.

Mohan, A., Singh, A., & Mandal, M. (2001). Transfer and interference of motor skills in people with intellectual disability. *Journal of Intellectual Disability Research, 45,* 361–369.

Morgan, H. (1992). An analysis of Gardner's theory of multiple intelligences. Paper presented at the meeting of Eastern Educational Research Association, Atlanta, GA.

Moya-Albiol, L., Herrero, N., & Bernal, M. C. Bases neuronales de la empatía. *Revista de Neurología, 50*(2), 89–100.

Mrug, S., Hoza, B., & Gerdes, A. C. (2001). Children with attention-deficit/hyperactivity disorder: Peer relationships and peer-oriented environments. *New Directions for Child and Adolescent Development, 91,* 51–76.

Nadeau, K., Littman, E., & Quinn, P. (1999). *Understanding girls with AD/HD.* Washington, DC: Advantage Books.

Nakayama, K., & Joseph, J. (1998). Attention, pattern recognition, and pop-out in visual search, In R. Parasuraman (Ed.), *The attentive brain* (pp. 279–298). Cambridge, MA: MIT Press.

National Academy of Sciences. (1989). *Food and nutrition board of the National Research Council, recommended dietary allowances* (10th ed.). Washington DC: National Academy Press, 1989.

National Commission on Excellence in Education. (April 1983). A nation at risk: The imperative for educational reform. Retrieved October 7, 2010, from http://www2. ed.gov/pubs/NatAtRisk/index.html

Naveh-Benjamin, M., & Jorides, J. (1984). Maintenance rehearsal: A two-component analysis. *Journal of Experimental Psychology: Learning, Memory, and Cognition, 10,* 369–385.

Naveh-Benjamin, M., Guez, M., & Sorek, S. (2007). The effects of divided attention on encoding processes in memory: Mapping the locus of interference. *Canadian Journal of Experimental Psychology, 61*(1), 1–12.

Nelson, D. L., & Schreiber, T.A. (1992). Word concreteness and word structure as independent determinants of recall. *Journal of Memory and Language, 31,* 237–260.

Neumark-Sztainer, D., French, S. A., Hannan, P. J., Story, M., & Fulkerson, J. A. (2005). School lunch and snacking patterns among high school students: Associations with school food environment and policies. *International Journal of Behavioral Nutrition and Physical Activity.* doi: 10.1186/1479-5868-2-14

Neville, H., & Bruer, J. (2001). Language processing: How experience affects brain organization. In D. B. Bailey, Jr., J. T. Bruer, F. J. U. Symons, and H. J. W. Litchman (Eds.), *Critical thinking about critical thinking periods* (pp. 151–172). Baltimore, MD. Paul H. Brookes.

Newell, A., & Rosenbloom, P. S. (1981). Mechanisms of skill acquisition and the law of practice. In J. R. Anderson (Ed.), *Cognitive skills and their acquisition*. Hillsdale, NJ: Prentice-Hall.

Newton, I. (1675). Letter to Robert Hooke Principia by I. Newton, and Stephen Hawking (Ed.). (2002). Philadelphia, PA: Running Press Book Publishers.

New York State Department of Health, Early Intervention Program (1999). Clinical practice guideline: The guideline technical report. Autism/pervasive development disorders: Assessment and intervention for young children (age 0–3 years). Publication No. 4217, Albany, NY: Author.

Notbohm, E., & Zysk, V. (2004). *1001 Great ideas for teaching and raising children with autism spectrum disorders.* Arlington, TX: Future Horizons.

Oberauer, K. (2002). Access to information in working memory: Exploring the focus of attention. *Journal of Experimental Psychology: Learning, Memory, and Cognition, 28*, 411–421.

Oberman, L., & Ramachandran, V. S. (2007). The simulating social mind: The role of mirror neuron system and simulation in the social and communicative deficits of autism spectrum disorders. *Psychological Bulletin, 133*(2), 310–327.

Ochsner, K. N. (2000). Are affective events richly recollected or simply familiar? The experience and process of recognizing feelings past. *Journal of Experimental Psychology: General, 129*, 242–261.

O'Conner, R., & Jenkins, J. (1993). Cooperative learning as an inclusion strategy: The experience of children with disabilities. Paper presented at the annual meeting of the American Educational Research Association, Atlanta, GA. ERIC Document Reproduction Service # ED360778.

Organisation for Economic Co-operation and Development (OECD). (2007). *Understanding the brain: The birth of a learning science.* Paris: Author.

Osgood, C., Suci, G., & Tannengaum, P. (1957). *The measurement of meaning.* Urbana: University of Illinois Press.

Pacheco-López, G., Engler, H., Niemi, M.-B., & Schedlowski, M. (2006). Expectations and associations that heal: Immunomodulatory placebo effects and its neurobiology. *Brain, Behavior, and Immunity, 20*(5), 430–446.

Padilla-Walker, L. M., Nelson, L. J., Carroll, J. S., & Jensen, A. C. (2009). More than just a game: Video game and internet use during emerging adulthood. *Journal of Youth and Adolescence.* doi: 10.1007/s10964-008-9390-8

Paivio, A. (1969). Mental imagery in associative learning and memory. *Psychological Review, 76*, 241–262.

Palfreman-Kay, J. (2001). Students' view of learning support. In M. Hunter-Carsch & M. Herrington, (Eds.), *Dyslexia and effective learning in secondary and tertiary education* (pp. 206–221). London: Whurr Publications.

Parajes, F. (1996). Self-efficacy beliefs in achievement settings. *Review of Educational Research, 66*, 543–578.

Parasuraman, R. (1998). The attentive brain: Issues and prospects. In R. Parasuraman (Ed.), *The attentive brain.* Cambridge, MA: MIT Press.

Pashler, H., McDaniel, M., Rohrer, D., & Bjork, R. (2008). Learning styles: Concepts and evidence. *Psychological Science in the Public Interest, 9*(3), 105–119.

PE4life. (2007). PE4LIFE: *Developing and promoting quality physical education*. Champaign, IL: Human Kinetics.

Pelham, W. E., Gnagy, E. M., Greenslade, K. E., & Milich, R. (1992). Teacher ratings of DSM-III-R symptoms for the disruptive behavior disorders. *Journal of the American Academy of Child and Adolescent Psychiatry, 31*, 210–218.

Pelham, W. E., Carlson, C., Sams, S. E., Vallano, G., Dixon, M. J., & Hoza, B. (1993). Separate and combined effects of metahylphenidate and behavior modification on boys with attention deficit-hyperactivity disorder in the classroom. *Journal of Consulting and clinical Psychology; 61*, 506–515.

Perez, J. C., Petrides, K. V., & Furnham, A. (2005). Measuring trait emotional intelligence. In R. Schulze, and R. D. Roberts (Eds.), *International handbook of emotional intelligence* (pp. 123–143). Cambridge, MA: Hogrefe & Huber.

Perry, R. (1985). Instructor expressiveness: Implications for improving teaching. In J. G. Donald & A. M. Sullivan (Eds.), *Using research to improve teaching* (pp. 35–49). San Francisco, CA: Jossey-Bass.

Pessiglione, M., Petrovic, P., Daunizeau, J., Palminteri, S., Dolan, R. J., & Frith, C. D. (2008). Subliminal instrumental conditioning demonstrated in the human brain. *Neuron, 59*, 561–567.

Pettito, L. A., & Dunbar, K. (2004). New findings from educational neuroscience on bilingual brains, scientific brains and the educated mind. Presentation at Usable Knowledge in Mind, Brain, and Education, Harvard Graduate School, October 6–8, Cambridge, MA.

Phillips, M., Young, A. W., Senior, C., Brammer, M., Andrew, C., Calder, A. J., Bullmore, E. T., Perrett, D. I., . . . & David, A. S. (1997). A specific neural substrate for perceiving facial expressions of disgust. *Nature, 389*, 495–498.

Piaget, J. (1983). Piaget's theory. In W. Kessen (Ed.), *History, theory and methods* (Vol. 1, pp. 103–126). New York, NY: Wiley.

Pickering, S. (2006). *Working memory and education*. New York, NY: Academic Press.

Pickering, S. & Gathercole, S.E. (2001). *Working memory test battery for children*. London: Pearson Assessment.

Pinker, S. (1997). *How the mind works*. New York, NY: W. W. Norton.

Pintrick, P., & Schunk, D. (2002). *Motivation in education, theory, research, and applications*. (2nd ed.). Upper Saddle River, NJ: Pearson Education.

Piolat, A., Olive, T., & Kellogg, T. (2005). Cognitive effort during note-taking. *Applied Cognitive Psychology, 19*, 291–312.

Plato. (2000). *Socrates*. In G. R. F. Ferrari (Ed.), *The republic*. (Book 7, pp. 220–251).

Plomin, R., & Rende, R. (1990). Human behavioral genetics. *Annual Review of Psychology, 42*, 161–190.

Poole, D. A., & Lindsay, D. S. (1995). Interviewing preschoolers: Effects of nonsuggestive techniques, parental coaching, and learning questions on reports on non-experienced events. *Journal of Experimental Child Psychology, 60*, 129–154.

Posner, G. J., Strike, K. A., Hewson, P. W., & Gertzog, W. A. (1982). Accommodation of a scientific conception: Towards a theory of conceptual change. *Science Education, 66*(2), 211–227.

Posner, M., & Patoine, B. (2010). How arts training improves attention and cognition. *Cerebrum*, 2010, 12–22.

Posner, M., & Raichel, M., 1994, *Images of mind*. New York, NY: Scientific American Library.

Pressely, M., & Dennis-Rounds, J. (1980). Transfer of a mnemonic keywords strategy at two age levels. *Journal of Educational Psychology, 72*, 575–582.

Pressley, M. J., & Woloshyn, V. (1995). *Cognitive strategy instruction that really improves children's academic performance* (2nd ed.). New York, NY: Brookline Books.

Przybylski, A. K., Ryan, R. M., & Rigby, C. S. (2009). The motivating role of violence in video games. *Personality and Social Psychology Bulletin, 35*(2), 243–259.

Qualter, P., Gardner, K. J., & Whiteley, H. E (2007). Emotional intelligence: Review of research and educational implications. *Pastoral Care in Education, 25*(1), 11–20.

Qualter, P., Whiteley, H. E., Hutchinson, J. M., & Pope, D. (2007). Supporting the development of emotional intelligence competencies to ease the transition from primary to high school. *Educational Psychology in Practice: Theory, Research and Practice in Educational Psychology, 23*(1), 79–95.

Radvansky, G. A., & Copland, D. E. (2006). Walking through doorways causes forgetting: Situation models and experienced space. *Memory and Cognition, 34*, 1150–1156.

Raichle, M. (2010). The brain's dark energy. *Scientific American, 301*(4), 44–49.

Ramirez, P., Desantis, D., & Opler, L., (2001). EEG biofeedback treatment of ADD, a viable alternative to traditional medical intervention? *Adult Attention Deficit Disorder, 931*, 342–358.

Rasch, B., & Born, J. (2008). Reactivation and consolidation of memory during sleep. *Current Directions in Psychological Science, 17*(8), 188–192.

Ratey, J. (2008). *Spark: The revolutionary new science of exercise and the brain*. New York. NY: Little, Brown.

Ratey, J. (2009), November 21, keynote address, the Learning and Brain Conference, Cambridge, MA.

Ratey, N. (2008). *The disorganized mind: Coaching your ADHD brain to take control of your time, tasks, and talents*. New York, NY: St. Martin's Press.

Rawson, V. A., & Kintsch, W. (2005). Rereading effects depend upon time of test. *Journal of Educational Psychology, 97*, 70–80.

Reid, R., & Harris, K. R. (1993). Self-monitoring of attention versus self-monitoring performance: Effects on attention and academic performance. *Exceptional Children, 60*, 29–40.

Reul, J., & deKloet, E. (1985). Two receptor systems for corticosterone in rate brain: Microdistribution and differential occupation. *Endrocrinology, 117*, 2505–2511.

Richdale, A., & Schreck, K. (2008). In J. Matson (Ed.), *Clinical assessment and intervention for autism spectrum disorder*. New York, NY: Academic Press.

Riding, R. J., Grimley, M., Dahraei, H., & Banner, G. (2003). Cognitive style, working memory and learning behaviour and attainment in school subjects. *British Journal of Educational Psychology, 73*, 149–169.

Roberts, J. M. & Prior, M. R. (2006). A review of the research to identify the most effective models of practice, in early intervention of children with autism spectrum disorders. Canberra, Australia: Australian Government Department of Health and Ageing.

Robins, A. (1998). *ADHD in adolescents, diagnosis and treatment.* New York, NY: Guilford Press.

Rode, J. C., Mooney, C. H., Arthaud-Day, M. L., Near, J. P., Baldwin, T. T., Rubin, R. S., & Bommer, W. H. (2007). Emotional intelligence and individual performance: Evidence of direct and moderated effects. *Journal of Organizational Behavior, 28,* 399–421.

Rode, J. C., Mooney, C. H., Arthaud-Day, M. L., Near, J. P., Rubin, R. S., Baldwin, T. T., & Bommer, W. H. (2008). An examination of the structural, discriminant, nomological, and incremental predictive validity of the MESDEIT V2.0. *Intelligence, 36,* 350–366.

Roediger, H. L., & Karpicke, J. D. (2006). Test enhanced learning: Taking memory tests improves long term retention. *Psychological Science, 17*(3), 249–255.

Rogers, S., Ludington, J., & Graham, S. (1999). *Motivation and learning: A teacher's guide to building excitement for learning and igniting the drive for quality.* Evergreen, CO: Peak Learning Systems.

Rogers, T., Kuiper, N. A., & Kirker, W. S. (1977). Self-reference and the encoding of personal information. *Journal of Personality and Social Psychology, 35,* 677–688.

Rohrer, D., & Pashler, H. (2007). Increasing retention without increasing study time. *Current Directions in Psychological Science, 16*(1), 183–186.

Ronis, D. (2007). *Brain-compatible assessments* (2nd ed.). Thousand Oaks, CA: Corwin Press.

Rosenthal, T., & Zimmerman, B. (1978). *Social learning and cognition.* New York, NY: Academic Press.

Rossen, E., & Kranzler, J. H. (2009). Incremental validity of Mayer-Salovey-Caruso intelligence test version 2.0 (MSCEIT) after controlling for personality and intelligence, *Journal of Research in Personality, 43,* 60–65.

Rossiter, T., & LaVaque, T., (1995). A comparison of EEG biofeedback and psychostimulants in treating Attention Deficit/Hyperactivity disorders. *Journal of Neurotherapy* 48–59.

Rotter, J. (1966). Generalized expectancies for internal versus external control of reinforcement. *Psychological Monographs,* 80 (1, whole # 609).

Rubin, E. (1915). *Visuell wahrgenommene.* Copenhagen: Glydendalske.

Russell, J. (1979). Affective space is bipolar. *Journal of Personality and Social Psychology, 37,* 345–356.

Ryan, R., & Grolnick, W. (1986). Origins and pawns in the classroom: Self-report and projective assessments of individual differences in children's perceptions. *Journal of Personal and Social Psychology, 50,* 550–558.

Ryan, R., & Kuczkowski, R. (1994). Egocentrism and heteronomy: A study of imaginary audience, self-consciousness, and public individualities in adolescence. *Journal of Personality, 62,* 219–238.

Ryan, R., & La Guardia, J. (1999). Achievement motivation within a pressured society: Intrinsic and extrinsic motivations to learn and the politics of school reform. In J. Urdan (Ed.) *Advances in motivation and achievement* (Vol. II, pp. 45–85). Greenwich, CT. JAI Press.

Ryan, R., & Lynch, J. (1989). Emotional autonomy versus detachment: Revisiting the viscissitudes of adolescence and young adulthood. *Child Development, 60,* 340–356.

Sadler, P. M. (2000). The relevance of multiple choice tests in assessing science understanding. In J. J. Mintzes, J. H. Wandersee & J. D. Novak (Eds.), *Assessing science understanding: A human constructivist view* (pp. 249–278). San Diego, CA: Academic Press.

Saklofske, D. H., Austin, E. J., & Minski, P. (2003). Factor structure and validity of a trait emotional intelligence measure. *Personality and Individual Differences, 334,* 707–721.

Salovey, P., & Sluyter, D. (1997). *Emotional development and emotional intelligence: Educational implications.* New York, NY: Basic Books.

Salvia, J., & Ysseldyke, J. (2004*). Assessment in special and inclusive education* (9th ed.). New York, NY: Houghton Mifflin.

Sapolsky, R. (2008). Selections from *Why Zebras don't get ulcers.* In K.Fischer and M. H. Immordino-Yang (Eds.), *Jossey-Bass reader on the brain and learning* (p. 210). San Francisco, CA: Jossey-Bass.

Sapolsky, R., Krey, L., & McEwen, B. (1985). Prolonged glucocortiocoid exposure reduces hippocampal neuron number: Implications for aging. *Journal of Neuroscience, 5*(5), 1222–1227.

Saunders, B., & Chambers, S. (1996). A review of the literature on attention-deficit hyperactivity disorder children: Peer interactions and collaborative learning. *Psychology in Schools, 33,* 333–340.

Schacter, D. (1995). *Memory distortion.* Cambridge, MA: Harvard University Press.

Schacter, D. (2001a). *How the mind forgets and remembers.* New York, NY: Houghton Mifflin.

Schacter, D. (2001b). *The seven sins of memory: How the mind forgets and remembers.* New York, NY: Houghton Mifflin.

Schenck, J. (1989–1999). Teaching and the brain: Confronting student misconceptions. *NISDC Insider, 4*(1), 3–5.

Schenck, J. (2003). *Learning, teaching, and the brain, a practical guide for teachers.* Thermopolis, WY: Knowa Publishing.

Schmidt, M. (2007). Brain-building nutrition (3rd ed.). Berkeley, CA: Frog Books.

Schmitz, B., & Skinner, E. (1993). Perceived control, effort, and academic performance: Inter-individual, introindividual, and multivariate time-series analyses. *Journal of Personality and Social Psychology, 64,* 1010–1028.

Schoenfeld, A. (Ed.). (2007). *Assessing mathematical proficiency* (Vol. 53). New York, NY: Cambridge University Press.

Schooler, J. W., Ryan, R. S., & Reder, L. (1996). The costs and benefits of verbally rehearsing memory for faces. In D. Herrmann, C. McEvoy, C. Hertzog, P. Hertel., & M. K. Johns (Eds.), *Basic and applied memory research* (Vol 2., pp. 51–65). Mahwah, NJ: Lawrence Erlbaum.

Schraw, G. (1994). The effect of metacognitive knowledge on local and global monitoring. *Contemporary Educational Psychology, 19,* 143–154.

Schraw, G. (1998). Promoting general metacognitive awareness. *Instructional Science, 26,* 113–125.

Schunk, D. (1987). Peer models and children's behavioral change. *Review of Educational Research, 57,* 149–174.

Schwartz, J., & Begley, S. (2002). *Mind and the brain: Neuroplasticity and the power of mental force.* New York, NY: Regan Books.

Scott, T. 1970. The use of music to reduce hyperactivity in children. *American Jour-*

nal of Orthopsychiatry, 36, 671–686.

Semin, G., & Manstead, A. (1982). The social implications of embarrassment displays and restitution behaviour. *European Journal of Social Psychology, 12,* 367–377.

Shallice, T. (2002). Fractionation of the supervisory system. In D. T. Stuss & R. T. Knight (Eds.), *Principles of frontal lobe function* (pp. 261–277). New York, NY: Oxford University Press.

Shaw, P., Eckstrand, K., Sharp, W., Blumenthal, J., Lerch, J. P., Greenstein, D., Clasen, L., Evans, A., . . . & Rapoport, J. L. (2007, November). Attention-deficit/hyperactivity disorder is characterized by a delay in cortical maturation. *Proceedings of the National Academy of Science, 104*(49), 19649–19654, doi: 10.1073/pnas.0707741104

Shaywitz, B. A., & Shaywitz S. E. (1991). Comorbidity: A critical issue in attention deficit disorder. *Journal of Child Neurology 6*(Suppl.), S13–S22.

Shaywitz, S. (2003). *Overcoming dyslexia: A new and complete science-based program for reading problems at any level.* New York, NY: Knopf.

Sibely, B., & Etnier, J. 2003. The relationship between physical activity and cognition in children: A meta-analysis. *Pediatric Exercise Science, 15*(3), 243–256.

Simons, D., & Chabris, C. (1999). Gorillas in our midst: Sustained inattentional blindness for dynamic events. *Perception, 28,* 1059–1074.

Singer, T., Seymour, B., O'Doherty, J., Kaube, H., Dolan, R. J., & Frith, C. D. (2004). Empathy for pain involves the affective but not sensory components of pain. *Science, 303,* 1157–1162.

Skinner, B. F. (1974). *About behaviorism.* New York, NY: Knopf.

Skinner, E., Zimmer-Gembeck, M., & Connell, J. (1998). Individual differences and the development of perceived control. *Monographs of the Society in Child Development, 63*(2–3), 1–220.

Skottun. B. C., & Skoyles, J. (2002). Yellow filters, magnocellular responses, reading. *International Journal of Neuroscience, 77,* 437–445.

Slotte, V., & Lonka, K. (2000). Spontaneous concept maps aiding the understanding of scientific concepts. *International Journal of Science and Education, 21,* 515–531.

Slutsky, I., Abumaria, N., Wu, L., Huang, C., Zhang, L., Li, B., Zhao, X., Govindarajan, A., . . . & Liu, G. (2010). Enhancement of learning and memory by elevating brain magnesium. *Neuron, 65*(2), 178–190.

Small, G. (2002). *The memory bible.* New York, NY: Hyperion.

Smith, C., & Constantino, R. (1997). Library differences in print environment. *Emergency Librarian, 24*(4), 81.

Smith, M., McEvoy, L., & Gevins, A. (1999). Neurophysiological indices of strategy development and skill acquisition. *Cognitive Brain Research, 7,* 389–404.

Smith, T., Mruzek, D. W., & Mozingo, D. (2005). Sensory integration therapy. In *Controversial therapies for developmental disabilities: Fad, fashion and science in professional practice.* (J. W. Jacobson, R. M. Foxx, & J. Mulick, eds.).Mahwah, NJ: Lawerence Erlbaum Associates, pp. 341–350.

Spearman, C. (1904). "General intelligence" objectively determined and measured. *American Journal of Psychology, 15*(2), 201–293.

Spence, J. D. (1984). *The memory palace of Matteo Ricci.* New York, NY: Viking.

Sperry, R., Gazzaniga, M., & Bogen, J. (1969). Interhemispheric relationships: The neocortical commissures; syndromes of hemisphere disconnection. In P. Vinken and G. Bruyn (Eds.), *Handbook of clinical neurology* (Vol. 4, pp. 273–290). New York, NY: John Wiley and Sons.

Stage, F., Mullen, P., Kinzie, J., & Simmons, A.. (1998). *Creating learning centered classrooms: What does learning theory have to say?* Washington, DC: ASHE-ERIC Higher Education Report Series.

Standing, L. (1973). Learning 10,000 pictures. *Quarterly Journal of Experimental Psychology, 25*, 207–222.

Standing, L., Conezio, J., & Haber, R. N. (1970). Perception and memory for pictures: Single trial learning of 2,560 visual stimuli. *Psychonomic Science, 19*, 73–74.

Stanovich, K. (2009). *What intelligence tests miss: The psychology of rational thought.* New Haven, CT: Yale University Press.

Starkman, M. N., Gebarski, S. S., Berent, S., & Schteingart, D. E. (1992). Hippocampal formation volume, memory dysfunction, and cortisol levels in patients with Cushing's syndrome. *Biological Psychiatry, 32*, 756–765.

Stein, Z., Dawson T., Schwarz, M., & Fischer, K. (2009, May 28). Educational testing for the 21st century: Challenges, models, and solutions. Presentation at IMBES, Philadelphia.

Steinberg, L., & Silverberg, S. (1986). The vicissitudes of autonomy in adolescents. *Child Development, 57*, 841–851.

Stepans, J. I, Saigo, B. W., & Ebert, C. (1999). *Changing the classroom from within.* Montgomery, AL: Saiwood.

Sterman, M., LoPresti, R., & Fairchild, M. (1969). *Electroencephalographic and behavioral studies of monomethyl hydrazine toxicity in the cats* [Technical report AMRL-TR-69–3]. Air Systems Command, Wright-Patterson Air Force Base, Ohio.

Sterman, M., MacDonald, L., & Stone, R. (1974). Biofeedback training of the sensorimoto electroencephalogram rhythm in man: Effects on epilepsy. *Epilepsia, 15*, 395–416.

Sternberg. R. (1997a). *Successful intelligence.* New York, NY: Plenum.

Sternberg, R. (1997b). *Thinking styles.* New York, NY: Oxford University Press.

Sternberg, R. (1999). A propulsion model of types of creative contributions. *Review of General Psychology, 3*, 83–100.

Sternberg, R. (Retrieved 2010). Teaching and assessing for successful intelligence. Retrieved October 4, 2010, from http://www.cdl.org/resources-library/articles/teaching_assessing.php

Sternberg, R. (2004). North American approaches to intelligence. In R. J. Sternberg (Ed.), *International handbook of intelligence* (pp. 411–444). Cambridge, United Kingdom: Cambridge University Press.

Sternberg, R., Ferrari, M., Clinkenbeard, P., & Grigorenko, E. (1996). Identification, instruction, and assessment of gifted children: A construct validation of a triarchic model. *Gifted Child Quarterly, 40*(3), 129–137.

Sternberg, R. J., Torff, B., & Grigorenko, E. L. (1998). Teaching triarchically improves school achievement. *Journal of Educational Psychology, 90*, 1–11.

Stipek, D. (2002). *Motivation to learn: Integrating theory and practice* (4th ed.). New York, NY: Allyn & Bacon.

Stipek, D., & Seal, K. (2001). *Motivated minds: Raising children to love learning*. New York, NY: Henry Holt.

Stix, G. (2009). Turobcharging the brain. *Scientific American, 302*(3), 46–55.

Squeglia, L. M., Spadoni, A. D., Infante, M. A., Myers, M. G., & Tapert, S. F. (2009). Initiating moderate to heavy alcohol use predicts changes in neuropsychological functioning for adolescent girls and boys. *Psychology of Addictive Behaviors, 23*(4), 715–722. doi: 10.1096/fj.09-142844

Swanson, H. L. (1990). Influence of mutative knowledge and aptitude on problem solving. *Journal of Educational Psychology, 82*, 306–314.

Swanson, H. L., & Siegel, L. (2001). Mathematical problem solving and working memory in children with learning disabilities: Both executive and phonological processes are important. *Journal of Experimental Child Psychology, 7*, 1–48.

Szatmari, P., Offord, D., & Boyle, M. (1989). Correlates, associated impairments, and patterns of service utilization of children with attention deficit disorders: Findings from the Ontario Child Health Study. *Journal of Child Psychology and Psychiatry, 30*, 205–217.

Tan, L., Spinks, J., Feng, J., Siok, W., Perfetti, C. A., Xiong, J., Fox, P. T., & Gao, J. (2003). Neural systems of second language reading are shaped by native language. *Human Brain Mapping, 18*, 158–166.

Tang-Schomer, M. D., Patel, A. R., Baas, P. W., & Smith, D. H. (2010). Mechanical breaking of microtubules in axons during dynamic stretch injury underlies delayed elasticity, microtubule disassembly and axon degeneration. Federation of American Society For Experimental Biology, doi: 10.1096/fj.09-142844

Tanner, K., & Allen, D. (2005). Approaches to biology teaching and learning: Understanding the wrong answers—teaching toward conceptual change. *Cell Biology Education, 4*(2), 112–117. doi: 10.1187/cbe.05-02-0068

Tarnopolsky, M. (1988). Influence of protein intake and training status on nitrogen balance and lean body mass. *Journal of Applied Physiology, 64*, 187–193.

Terman, L. M. (1919). The IQ as a basis for prediction. In *The intelligence of school children: How children differ in ability, the use of mental tests in school grading, and the proper education of exceptional children* (pp. 135–164). Boston, MA: Houghton Mifflin.

Terman, L. M. (1921). Mental growth and the IQ. *Journal of Educational Psychology, 12*(7), 401–407.

Terry, S. (2009). *Learning and memory, basic principles, processes and procedures* (4th ed.). New York, NY: Allyn & Bacon.

Thatcher, P. V. (2008). University students and the "all nighter": Correlates and patterns of students' engagement in a single night of total sleep deprivation. *Behavioral Sleep Medicine, 6*(1), 16–31.

Thayer, J. F. (2000). Sex differences in judgment of facial affect: A multivariate analysis of recognition errors. *Scandinavian Journal of Psychology, 41*(3), 243–246.

Thomas, W. (1995). Black intellectuals on IQ tests. In R. Jacoby and N. Glaubermann, (Eds.), *The bell curve debate* (pp. 510–541), New York, NY: Times Books.

Thompson, R. (2000). *The brain: A neuroscience primer*. New York, NY: Worth.

Thompson-Schill, S., Aguirre, G., Desposito, M, & Farah, M. (1999). A neural basis for category and modality specifics of semantic knowledge. *Neuropsychologia, 37*, 671–676.

Thorndike, E. (1898). Animal intelligence: An experimental study of the associative processes in animals. *Psychological Review Monograph, 2*(4).

Thorndike, E. (1920, May). The reliability and significance of tests of intelligence. *Journal of Educational Psychology, 11*(5), 284–287.

Thorndike, R. (1997). The early history of intelligence testing, In D. Flanagan, J. Genshaft, and P. Harrison (Eds.), *Contemporary intellectual assessment, theories, tests, and issues* (pp. 3–31). New York, NY: Guilford Press.

Titsworth, B. S., & Kiewra, K. A. (2004). Spoken organizational lecture cues and student notes taken as facilitations of student learning. *Contemporary Educational Psychology, 29*(4), 447–461.

Tokuhama-Espinosa, T. (2008). The scientifically substantiated art of teaching: A study in the development of standards in the new academic field of neuroeducation (mind, brain, and education science). PhD Dissertation, Capella University, Minnesota. AAT 3310716.

Toleman, E. (1949). There is more than one kind of learning. *Psychological Review, 56*, 144–155.

Tomlinson, D., Wilkinson, H., & Wilkinson, P. (2009). Diet and mental health in children. *Child and Adolescent Mental Health, 14*(3), 148–155.

Tulving, E. (2002). Does memory encoding exist? In M. Naveh-Benjamin, M. Moscovitch, & H. Roediger III, (Eds.), *Perspectives on human memory and cognitive aging: Essays in honor of Fergus Craik*. Philadelphia, PA: Psychology.

Ungerleider, L., & Miskin, M. (1982). Two cortical visual systems. In D. J. Engle, M.A. Goodale, & R. J. Mansfield (Eds.), *Analysis of visual behavior* (pp. 549–586). Cambridge, MA: MIT Press.

Urdan, M., and Anderman, (1998). *The role of classroom goal structure in student's use of self-handicapping strategies.*

USDA. (2007). Oxygen radical absorbance cap (ORAC) of selected foods. Retrieved from http://www.aars.usda.gov/sp2userfiles/place/1234500/data/orac/oraco7.pef

Van Der Sluis, S., VanDer Leij, A., & De Jon, P. F. (2005). Working memory in Dutch children with reading and arithmetic related LD. *Journal of Learning Disabilities, 38*, 207–221.

Van Dijk, T. A., & Kintsch, W. (1983). *Strategies of discourse comprehension*. New York, NY: Academic Press.

Verhaegben, P., Cerella, J., & Basak, C. (2004). A work-memory workout: How to expand the focus of serial attention from one to four items in ten hours or less. *Journal of Experimental Psychology: Learning, Memory, and Cognition, 30*, 1322–1337.

Vitamin String Quartet. (2009, March 27). Retrieved from http://www.vitaminrecords.com

Voelker, S., Carter, R. A., Sprague, D. J., Gdowski, C. L., & Lachar, D. (1989). Developmental trends in memory and metamemory in children with attention deficit disorder. *Journal of Pediatric Psychology, 14*, 75–88.

von Bergmann, H., Dalrymple, K. R., Wong, S. & Shuler, C. F. (2007). Investigating the relationship between PBL process grades and content acquisition performance in a PBL dental program. *Journal of Dental Education, 71*, 1160–1170.

Vygotsky, L. S. (1962). *Thought and language* (E. Hanfmann & G. Vakar, Eds. & Trans.). Cambridge, MA: MIT Press.

Vygotsky, L. (1978). *Mind in society: The development of higher psychological processes* (M. Cole, V. John-Steiner, S. Scribner, & E. Souberman, Trans.). Cambridge, MA: Harvard University Press.

Walberg, H. J. (1999). Productive teaching. In H. C. Waxman & H. J. Walberg (Eds.), *New directions for teaching practice and research* (pp. 75–104). Berkeley, CA: Mc-Cutchen.

Walker, M. P. (2008). Sleep-dependent memory processing. *Harvard Review of Psychiatry, 16*(5), 287–298. doi: 10.1080/10673220802432517

Walker, M. P., et al. (2003). Dissociable stages of human memory consolidation and reconsolidation. *Nature, 425*, 616–620.

Walsh, D. (2000). *Fifth annual video and computer game report card*. Minneapolis, MN: National Institute on Media and the Family.

Walsh, D., Gentile, D., Gieske, J., Walsh, M., & Chasco, E. (2003). *Eighth annual mediawise videogame report card*. Minneapolis, MN: National Institute on Media and the Family.

Ward, J. (2006). *Student's guide to cognitive neuroscience*. New York, NY: Psychological Press.

Warwick, J., & Nettlebeck, T. (2004). Emotional intelligence vs. . . . ? *Personality and Individual Differences, 37*, 1091–1100.

Waterhouse, L. (2006). Inadequate evidence for multiple intelligences, Mozart effect, and emotional intelligence theories. *Educational Psychologist, 41*(4), 247–255.

Watson, J. M., & Strayer, D. L. (2010). Supertaskers: Profiles in extraordinary multitasking ability. *Psychonomic Bulletin and Review, 17* (4), 479–485. doi: 10.3758/PBR.17.4.479

Weiner, B. (1985). An attributional theory of achievement motivation and emotion. *Psychological Review, 92*, 548–573.

Weiner, B. (1986). *An attributional theory of motivation and emotion*. New York, NY: Springer-Verlag.

Weiner, B. (1992). *Human motivation: Metaphors, theories, and research*. Newbury Park, CA: Sage.

Weiss, M. J., Fiske, K., & Ferraioli, S. (2008). Evidence-based practice for autism spectrum disorders. In J. Matson (Ed.), *Clinical assessment and interventions for autism spectrum disorders* (pp. 33–63). New York, NY: Academic Press.

Wetheimer, M. (1923). Untersuchen zu lehre von der Gestalt. *Psychologische Forschung, 1*, 47–48.

Whalen, C. (1989). Attention deficit and hyperactivity disorders. In *Handbook of Child Psychology* (2nd ed., pp. 131–160). New York, NY: Plenum.

Wigfield, A., Eccles, J. S., MacIver, D., Reuman, D. A., & Midgley, C. (1991). Transitions during early adolescence: Changes in children's domain-specific self-perceptions and general self-esteem across the transition to junior high school. *Developmental Psychology, 27*, 552–565.

Willcutt, E., Pennington, B., & Defries, J. (2000). Etiology of inattention and hyperactivity/impulsivity in a community sample of twins with learning disabilities. *Journal of Abnormal Child Psychology, 28*, 149–159.

Willerman, L. (1973). Activity level and hyperactivity in twins. *Child Development, 44*, 288–293.

Williams, D., & Skoric, M. (2005). Internet fantasy violence: A test of aggression in an online game. *Communication Monograph, 72*(2), 217–233.

Willis, J. (2006). *Research-based strategies to ignite student learning*. Alexandria, VA: ASCD.

Winograd, E. (1988). Some observations on prospective remembering. In M. M. Gruneberg, P. E. Morris, & R. N. Sykes (Eds.), *Practical aspects of memory: Current research and issues* (Vol. 1, pp. 348–353). New York, NY: Cambridge University Press.

Wlodkowski, R. (2008). *Enhancing adult motivation to learn: A comprehensive guide for teaching all adults* (3rd ed.). San Francisco, CA: Jossey-Bass.

Wolf, M. (2007). *Proust and the squid: The story and science of the reading brain*. New York, NY: HarperCollins.

Wood, J. (2007). Visual working memory for observed actions. *Journal of Experimental Psychology: General, 136*(4), 639–652.

Wood, W. B. (2004). Clickers: A teaching gimmick that works. *Developmental Cell, 7,* 796–798.

Wright, J. D., Wang, C. Y, Kennedy-Stevenson. J., & Ervin. R. B. (2003). Dietary intake of ten key nutrients for public health, United States: 1999–2000. Advance data from vital and health statistics, no. 334. Hyattsville, MD: National Center for Health Statistics.

Yerkes, R., Bridges, J., & Hardwick R. (1915). *A point scale for measuring ability*. Baltimore, MD: Warwick & York.

Yeung, J. S., Jin, P., & Sweller, J. (1997). Cognitive load and learner expertise: Split attention and redundancy effects in reading with explanatory notes. *Contemporary Educational Psychology, 23,* 1–21.

Yoo, S.-S., Hu, P. T., Gujar, N., Jolesz, F. A., & Walker, M. P. (2007). A deficit in the ability to form new human memories without sleep. *Nature Neuroscience, 10*(3), 385–391.

Yuill, N. M., Oakhill, J. V., & Parkin, A. J. (1989). Working memory, comprehension ability and the resolution of text anomaly. *British Journal of Psychology, 80,* 351–361.

Zametkin, A., & Rapoport, J. (1986). The pathophysiology of attention deficit disorder with hyperactivity: A review. In B. Lahey & A. Kazdin (Eds.), *Advances in clinical child psychology* (pp. 177–216). New York, NY: Plenum.

Zeidner, M., Roberts, R., & Matthews, G. (2002). Can emotional intelligence be schooled? A critical review. *Educational Psychologist, 37*(4), 215–231.

Zeki, S. (1993). *A vision of the brain*. Oxford, England: Blackwell.

Zentall, S. (2006). *ADHD and education: Foundations, characteristics, methods, and collaboration*. New York, NY: Prentice Hall.

Zentall, S., & Dwyer, A. (1988). Color effects on the impulsivity and activity of hyperactive children. *Journal of School Psychology, 27,* 165–174.

Zentall, S., Moon, S. M., Hall, A. M., & Grskovic, J. A. (2001). Learning and motivational characteristics of boys with giftedness and/or attention deficit/hyperactivity disorder. *Exceptional Children, 67,* 499–519.

Zentall, S., & Smith, Y. (1993). Mathematical performance and behavior of children with hyperactivity with and without coexisting aggression. *Behavior Research and Therapy, 31,* 701–710.

Zentall, S., & Zentall T. (1976). Activities and task performance of hyperactive children as a function of environmental stimulation. *Journal of Consulting and Clinical Psychology, 44,* 693–697.

Zimmerman, B., Bandura, A., & Martinze-Pons, M. (1992). Self-motivation for academic attainment: The role of self-efficacy beliefs and personal goal setting. *American Educational Research Journal, 29,* 663–676.

INDEX